African Encounters with Domesticity

African Encounters with Domesticity

Edited by Karen Tranberg Hansen

Rutgers University Press
New Brunswick, New Jersey

Library of Congress Cataloging-in-Publication Data

African encounters with domesticity / Karen Tranberg Hansen, editor.
    p.   cm.
    Includes bibliographical references and index.
    ISBN 0-8135-1803-2 (cloth)—ISBN 0-8135-1804-0 (pbk.)
    1. Sex role—Africa.   2. Sexual division of labor—Africa.
3. Home economics—Africa.   4. Home—Africa.   5. Women—Africa—
Social conditions.   6. Africa—Social life and customs.
I. Hansen, Karen Tranberg.
HQ1787.A34 1992
305.42′096—dc20   91-32144
                                                                    CIP

British Cataloging-in-Publication information available

HQ
1787
·A34
1992

10/52

Contents

Part 1: Varieties of African Domesticity

Part 2: Domestic Encounters

Part 3: Race, Class, Gender, and Domestic Work

Tables

Preface

This book examines how ideologies of domesticity have been constructed and transformed in the meeting between a variety of African notions of domesticity and European selective interpretations of Western domestic forms. The essays collected here depart from existing scholarship on the division of labor and gender ideology in African studies by questioning the unexplored status of domesticity. The contributors investigate how actors, activities, and boundaries of domesticity have been defined and changed in encounters between Africans and others, and how race, gender, and class are involved in these processes. Representing several disciplines and different theoretical orientations, the book demonstrates the important role ideologies of domesticity have played in the cultural ordering of African history by shaping notions of labor and time, architecture and space, consumption and accumulation, body and clothing, and sexuality and gender. By using domesticity as a focus of research the contributors cast unprecedented light both on the changing relationship between work, space, and gender, and on broader politico-economic processes in different parts of twentieth-century Africa.

Many people, graduate students and colleagues alike, have influenced our thinking about the research potential entailed in ideologies of domesticity in Africa, and helped to tease out constructively their complex meanings from seemingly trivial activities. Among them are Margaret Strobel, whose historical insights into gender and imperialism have enriched this particular project, and Jane Guyer, whose reminders about the material underpinnings of ideological expressions have helped to ground it. But above all, I would like to thank the contributing authors for delivering thought-provoking chapters and for doing so while being temporarily or permanently scattered across much of the world encompassed by this book: LaRay Denzer in Nigeria; Nancy Hunt in Zaire and Belgium; Elizabeth Schmidt in Guinea; Janet Bujra in Britain; Nakanyike Musisi in Canada; as well as the authors in the United States. I am particularly grateful to Jean Comaroff for stimulating the thoughts that led to this effort and for her persistent encouragement in its development. Mette Shayne of the Africana Library at Northwestern University offered prompt and helpful bibliographical assistance, and Andrea Dubnick of the Department of Anthropology provided all kinds of clerical support. I thank them for their readiness and cheerfulness. I hope that they, the contributors, and the readers of this book will help to promote an understanding of domesticity that is less restrictive for women than that which surrounds us in late twentieth-century western society.

Karen Tranberg Hansen
Evanston, Illinois

Contributors

JANET M. BUJRA is Lecturer in Sociology at the University of Bradford in Great Britain. She is joint editor with Patricia Caplan of *Women United, Women Divided* (1978), and a variety of articles concerning gender and class in the Third World. She is currently completing a book about domestic service in Tanzania.

JEAN and JOHN L. COMAROFF are Professors of Anthropology at the University of Chicago. Their most recent book, *Of Revelation and Revolution* (1991), will shortly be followed by *Ethnography and the Historical Imagination*. They have published widely on the culture and history of the Tswana peoples of Southern Africa and on general issues concerning colonialism, power, and meaning.

LARAY DENZER is Senior Lecturer in History at the University of Ibadan in Nigeria. She has published a variety of articles on West African responses to colonial rule, as well as women's history and biography. Currently she is completing a study on the changing patterns of work among Yoruba women in colonial Nigeria.

KAREN TRANBERG HANSEN is Associate Professor of Anthropology at Northwestern University. She has published *Distant Companions: Servants and Employers in Zambia, 1900–1985* (1989) and is writing a book on urban life in Zambia. Her published articles are concerned with urbanization, housing, gender, wage labor, the informal sector, and development questions in Southern Africa.

NANCY ROSE HUNT recently received her doctorate in history at the University of Wisconsin at Madison. She is preparing a book about childbirth and the negotiation of colonial meaning in a British Baptist mission context in the Belgian Congo. She has published articles on domesticity, marriage, and gender in Africa.

BEVERLY B. MACK teaches African literature and Hausa cultural studies at George Mason University. Her research interests concern African literature, Hausa poetry, and Muslim women in West Africa. She has published on these topics and is coeditor, with Catherine Coles, of *Hausa Women in the Twentieth Century* (1991).

MARY H. MORAN is Associate Professor of Anthropology at Colgate University. Her research interests and publications pertain to West Africa (Liberia) and focus on gender, power, and prestige. She is the author of *Civilized Women: Gender and Prestige in Southeastern Liberia* (1990).

NAKANYIKE B. MUSISI is Assistant Professor of History at the University of Toronto. She has conducted research in Uganda. Her interests include education, marriage, religion, and politics as they relate to women.

SITA RANCHOD-NILSSON recently received her doctorate in political science at Northwestern University based on research into women's participation in the liberation war in Zimbabwe. She is writing about African politics, gender relations, and nationalist movements.

ELIZABETH SCHMIDT is Assistant Professor of History at Loyola College in Baltimore. Her research examines the effects of colonial land and labor policies and gender ideology on women in Zimbabwe. She has published several articles based on this work as well as a book, *Peasants, Traders, and Wives: Shona Women in the History of Zimbabwe, 1870–1939*. More recently, she has conducted research in Guinea.

KATHLEEN SHELDON did her doctorate in African History at the University of California, Los Angeles. She is currently an Affiliated Scholar with UCLA's Center for the Study of Women, where she is continuing her work on issues concerning Mozambican women's history. Her published articles focus on different occupational groups and women's organizations.

African Encounters with Domesticity

Introduction: Domesticity in Africa

Karen Tranberg Hansen

*domes`t|ic, a. & n. 1. Of the home, household, or family affairs\ ~science, study of household management\; of one's own country, not foreign\ or international (*domestic *TRADE)\; native, homemade; (of animals) kept by or living with man; home-keeping, fond of home; hence ~ICALLY adv. 2. n. Household servant, [f. F* domestique *f. L* domesticus *(*domus *home)]*

domes`tic|ate, v.t. Naturalize (colonists, animals) \plant\; make fond of home \life\(esp. in p.p.); bring (animals) under human control, tame; civilize (savages)\omitted in 1982 edition\; so ~ABLE a., ~ATION n. [f. med. L domesticare *(prec., -ATE)]*

domesti`cit|y (or do-), n. Domestic character; home life or privacy; homeliness; the ~ies, domestic affairs, domesticated state [-ITY]~n. being domestic; home life or privacy\(The Concise Oxford Dictionary of Current English, fifth edition, 1964, 363\ seventh edition 1982, 285\)

Domesticity: Empirical and Historical Issues

Domesticity has many meanings. To define it is to describe a set of ideas that over the course of nineteenth-century Western history have associated women with family, domestic values, and home, and took for granted a hierarchical distribution of power favoring men. Today women's growing involvement in wage labor may have helped diminish the importance of the home as woman's place, but it has not changed substantially cultural ideas of domesticity. Such ideas are expressed through the routines and rituals of everyday life and may be teased out of studies of family and sexuality; diet, hygiene and health; body and clothing; fashion, consumption, and accumulation;

architecture and space; and labor, leisure, and time. Domesticity is thus concerned with gender, space, work, and power.

Throughout Europe's colonial experience, the colonizers tried to bring their notions of domesticity along to new locations. In her epistolary novel written for a fictitious young friend about to join her husband in Africa, Emily Bradley, the wife of a colonial civil servant in Northern Rhodesia, described a particular form of domesticity by giving advice on household management and servants, children and health, entertainment, and male/female relations. She also appended a list of thirty-one things to bring to the colony, including a smart day dress for official occasions and lunch parties, and several evening dresses; a sewing kit, patterns and needlework, and engraved calling cards (1950, 238–239). Outfitted in this way, young Priscilla was to assume her place in a man's world as "the silent partner," adept as housekeeper and charming hostess, at a time when growing numbers of women in Europe and North America were working away from home (111). Priscilla was also to set an example to her African sisters, teaching them how to make a pleasant home "on the European model" (190).

When Africans were confronted with this European model, Western-derived ideas about domesticity were often culturally redefined and put to different uses as the Africans selected some aspects of the model and discarded others. For instance, while living quarters were often changed from a round hut to a square house and the interior furnished in the European style, such reordering of space did not necessarily change the existing structure of gender relations (Moore 1986, 147–152). The ways in which the idea of home was realized, lived in, and experienced were mediated by African notions of space, work, gender, and power.

The title *African Encounters with Domesticity* reflects the dual focus of this collection. The contributors examine how African notions of domesticity and selective interpretations of Western-derived forms combine to change relationships between gender, race, and class. This book is about such encounters, about the struggles they have inspired over the contents and meanings of domesticity, and about the kinds of personal troubles and public issues they have provoked. The contributors take the readers inside African and colonial homes; invite them to teas and dinners; show them different kinds of kitchens; dazzle them with changing fashion and styles; accompany them to schools, training centers, and clubs; bring them to markets, shops, and factories; and bother them with problems of child care. In effect, these essays draw the reader's attention to African constructions of domesticity that differ in many respects from their Western time-bound and gender-restrictive counterparts.

Domesticity: Historical and Cultural Logics

Domesticity is a historically constructed notion with many layers of meaning. Except for the feminine gender of the French noun *domestique,* the English dictionary definitions in this book's epigraph of matters associated with the "domestic" are gender-neutral. The denotations of the term domestic that are most important for our analysis involve: a space, or physical setting (home); a type of activity, work (home-keeping) or preoccupation (domestic affairs); a relationship implying power (controlling, taming, civilizing) or organization (household management); and an occupational title (household servant).

Ideas associated with domesticity in a particular society may not be accepted by all segments of that society. Such ideas are not static in their meaning and usage but have evolved in a dialogue with social and economic changes of society. For example, between 1964 and 1982 the *Oxford Concise Dictionary* omits the verb "to civilize" as one of the meanings of domestication, an omission that graphically highlights the socially devalued status of domesticity in the contemporary West. As for the former colonial world, the omission of the verb "to civilize" with reference to populations termed savage in all likelihood indicates a growing sensitivity to its implicit discriminatory meanings. The attribution of civilizing functions to domestic activities was a product of the colonial encounter, the economics and ideology of which we discuss below. In the West, as in Africa, the different ideas that constitute domesticity suggest changing and potentially contradictory meanings about actors and agency, dependency and power, and about the home as both an enclosed space and a political economy. There is nothing simple about this interplay, taking place as it did against the changing backdrop of history, influenced both by broad economic shifts and by social and cultural practices.

Over the course of the nineteenth century in Europe and North America the domestic domain took on changing meanings of privacy, emotions, and moral authority that accorded domesticity a civilizing function reaching far beyond the threshold of the home. Much of this positive evaluation of domesticity was undercut by the gradual development of modern scientific thought that culminated in Darwinism and helped to celebrate the white male as the epitome of the evolution of Western civilization (Jordanova 1989; Poovey 1989; Russett 1989). This period redefined women in scientific terms that made them biologically and intellectually inferior to men and denied them any role in the progress of society. At the same time, economic changes contributed to the spatial reorganization of productive and reproductive activities in bourgeois and middle-class households into two gender-associated domains of distinctly different value (Frykman and Löfgren 1987; Davidoff and Hall 1987). Beyond those circles, the changing meanings of domesticity created different dilemmas for the women who toiled downstairs and often came from different class, regional, ethnic, and (in North America) racial backgrounds from their employers (Gillis 1979; Stanley 1984). Domesticity must also have had different meanings for women who contributed to tight household budgets by laboring in factories, taking in lodgers, or selling in the streets (Boydston 1986).

In the early twentieth century, the moral power of domesticity in unifying society eroded further when middle-class women were taught to manage their homes along lines of the public world of work through the intervention of the home economist. The combination of subsequent technological innovations and advertising increasingly reduced the potential of domesticity to function as a moral force beyond the home. In the modern world the home has been turned into a site of consumption, generating demands for the wider economy that—ironically enough—are considered so important as to be almost invaluable in conventional economic terms (Folbre 1991).

Empire, Africa, and Domesticity

Transferred to the African context, ideas associated with domesticity conjure up an encounter that is part of the process through which the spread of capitalism is reshaping the world's political economy. Of particular interest to us in this book is the notion of empire and the struggles colonialism provoked between preindustrial African societies and the ideologies of space, gender, and work that characterised industrial, bourgeois Western society during the nineteenth and early twentieth centuries. As a prop in the politics of colonial domination, the conceptual construction of domesticity was at the forefront of change, as were those who gave it institutional efficacy. Thus ideas of domesticity constitute a central dimension of this encounter and offer startling insights not only into the development of empire and the colonial experience, but also into the everyday world of the postcolonial era. By shaping notions of labor and time, architecture and space, consumption and accumulation, body and clothing, diet and hygiene, and sexuality and gender, the ideologies associated with domesticity played a crucial and as yet insufficiently acknowledged role in influencing the cultural ordering of African history.

Many scholars have discussed colonialism from a variety of perspectives, but we are only beginning to recognize the extent to which gender had a central effect on the reactions of both the European and the African ends of this encounter (Das 1986; Davin 1978; Mohanty 1984; Strobel 1987). "Colonization," observe Knibiehler and Goutalier, "is an essentially male act, meaning to conquer, penetrate, possess, fertilize" (1985, 17, my translation). It is an act that turned the organization of household activity and sexuality into political matters (Alloula 1986; Ballhatchet 1980; Stoler 1989a). Consolidating colonial rule required the colonizers to contain African women and men on terms unfamiliar to them, imposing Western notions of household organization and gender on local conceptualizations, and to instill new regimens of wage labor and housewifery, as well as notions of pride, property, and responsibility.

Colonialism was a transforming encounter in which African women and men played active but different parts in shaping new spatial boundaries and experimenting with the many meanings of domesticity, in the process constructing and apportioning on their own terms boundaries between home and work, male and female, labor and leisure. First-generation urbanites setting up new households could rarely call on members of organized kin groups or extended families for advice, but had to rely on their own resources. Conflicts in outlook over old and new ways between the generations exacerbated tensions that already too easily arose between women and men because of the different terms on which they were incorporated into wage labor. Throughout much of colonial Africa, state and private industry initially recruited mainly men for wage labor, although women at times were drafted for public works like road construction and porterage. Exceptions aside, the stage was set for a new spatial division of labor according to gender, with African women largely in charge of household production in either rural or urban areas (Chauncey 1981).

While the civilizing function of domesticity was aimed particularly at African women, both men and women experienced the contradictions between the new domestic ideologies and the material realities of African life. The poverty of many urban households prompted African women to perform income-generating work and made the Western domestic ideal of housewifery and responsible motherhood difficult to realize (Gaitskell 1983). Men as much as women were troubled and puzzled by the socioeconomic changes that were invading their households, reshaping spatial arrangements and the division of labor and authority (Epstein 1981). As they confronted the ideologies behind these changes in their everyday lives, they suspended or reinterpreted them in the face of economic imperatives. Thus, their everyday domestic world became a context for action and reaction, intimately tied up with the larger political economy.

These processes as they relate to gender and domesticity cannot be explained by social Darwinist accounts. Gender is not a biological cause but a product, a cultural construct invoking sexuality and power. It cannot be understood apart from the social, economic, and political relations in which women and men live their lives. Gender is a relationship rather than a role, status, or position (Moore 1988), and gender construction results from the meanings women's and men's activities acquire through actual social interaction (Rosaldo 1980, 399–400). Throughout Africa, women have historically defined themselves as individuals whose self-validation was associated in important ways with their sex, as wives, mothers, and nurturers of children. But in African social life the construction of gender rarely turned domesticity into a notion that singly defined women's identity. In many parts of the continent, women were also key workers in agricultural production while their children, or others' children, at times did even more domestic work than the biological mother of the household. In some regions, women were autonomous actors in the market, sometimes employing young female apprentices whom they socialized for nondomestic work. In the twentieth century, many joint production and consumption functions of rural households were torn apart by urbanization and incipient industrialization, which introduced new distinctions between home and work. In the process, women and men struggled with each other, their seniors, and agents of the state about their place in the evolving division of labor.

Such gender redefinitions did not mirror old constructs or subsume new ones without meeting with questions and opposition. On the contrary, this book's chapters illustrate a number of available and competing gender scripts and interpretations, which themselves were the outcomes of complex historical interactions: rural African versions that stressed the complementary productive role of women and men; West African urban models in which women operated in the market without much deference to men; Western designs that separated men's and women's roles between work and home, stressing women's importance as wife, housekeeper, and mother. Swahili culture on the East African coast contended with an Arab, Muslim-influenced gender script, as did many West African societies. In some West African societies, Afro-Americans and liberated slaves introduced additional elements into gender construction. Across most of Africa, a variety of mission Christianity offered potentially new gender conventions. Such competing gender interpretations were negotiated among a variety of social and historical relationships: growing economic disparities between rural and urban populations, widening stratification by class, and rigid stratification by race—a factor in some places during the colonial period and still today in the Republic of South Africa.

In the postcolonial era, the African terms on which Western-derived notions of domesticity were previously appropriated have at times had to bend to the economic imperatives of shrinking economies. Today in Africa domesticity has less to do with the technology of household production and standards of housekeeping than with ideologies of gender. Save among a tiny segment of wealthy households with the means to install the props of the Western suburban home, basic amenities such as running water, electricity, and labor-saving devices remain beyond reach. So does *haute cuisine,* owing to the recurrent scarcities in many countries of basic consumer goods like flour, sugar, salt, cooking oil, and rice, not to mention spices and condiments. Household technology is held at bay by the ready availability of domestic servants, their widespread employment, and the keeping of young relatives as child-nurses among both people of means and those less well situated. Taken together, these factors allow some African women householders an identity distinct from domesticity as we have come to know it in the West, and others to utilize their domestic skills for commercial purposes, thus strengthening their identity as autonomous actors in the public arena.

While the material realities of economic life have not fostered domesticity in the Western mode, tensions exist between the ideologies associated with the concept and the actualities of African economic life. Thus domesticity may serve as both a prop and an index of class in the politics of domination and resistance. Since their independence, most African st⁻tes h?ve sought to incorporate class-divided, ethnically diverse populations into a society based on capitalist relations of production. Defining conceptions of women is part of this process, and at the governing heights of many African states the notion often persists that women ought to be wives and mothers, that the home rather than the market is their proper place. Views to that effect are voiced even in countries such as Mozambique and Zimbabwe, where independence was won recently after lengthy liberation struggles that included gender on their revolutionary agendas. But class differentiation fueled by postcolonial economic developments is jeopardizing the construction of a national culture and vexing the discussion of what sorts of members of society women should be.

At the level of public policy in many African countries today, the official discourse is slowly abandoning its long-standing evocation of women as mothers and turning to a consideration of gender as a relational concept. The 1985 international meeting in Nairobi, Kenya, marking the close of the United Nations Women's Decade, may have helped strengthen gender awareness, as no doubt have the foreign aid and development institutions that target gender-specific projects. But program policy aside, local and foreign development intervention in many cases have recreated domesticity through projects that increase rather than lessen women's work burden and dependence in the household (Rogers 1980). African women in many countries still face an uphill battle to shape these discourses so as to reduce entrenched gender inequities in many aspects of life. The slowness with which discriminatory laws concerning marriage, inheritance, employment, and housing have been reformed bear dramatic evidence of the blurred line between the domestic and the public, turning the household into a political arena. Uncertainties about how to define space and gender are accentuated in today's declining economies, and they prompt an ongoing struggle between women, men, and the state over the boundaries of domesticity, its contents, and its participants.

Domesticity as it has emerged in Africa thus remains a force to be reckoned with for both its material and its ideological ramifications. The changing and contested nature of the Western concept itself demands caution in our thinking about its export to Africa. Recent research on the missionary project of transformation in Africa, including that by Jean and John Comaroff and Nancy Hunt in this book, reveals the introduction of very particular constructs of domesticity (Comaroff and Comaroff 1991; White 1987). Missionary teaching and pedagogy in Africa were bound up with metropolitan notions of class practice and with the missionaries' own class and gender backgrounds (Comaroff 1989; Prodolliet 1987). The colonial civil service, largely of middle-class background (Furse 1962; Gann and Duignan 1978; Kucklick 1979), helped shape domesticity through its policies on labor, wages, housing, education, and the law either in conflict or in collusion with local white residents and rural African authorities. The discussion of Southern Rhodesia by Elizabeth Schmidt and Sita Ranchod-Nilsson in this book demonstrates some of these policies, which affected gender relations, conjugality and sexuality, consumption and accumulation. They contributed not only to the construction of an ideology of African man- and womanhood, but also to the creation of the commoditized domesticity of prostitutes (White 1990).

Both missionary and civil-service notions of domesticity altered in the face of a combination of processes involving shifting metropolitan discourses on empire, ongoing changes within the colonies, and tensions inherent in their very enterprises. The universal challenge of transforming Africa often conflicted with the particular challenge of reckoning with Africans as social and cultural beings (Cooper 1989), whose conceptual schemes bore varied or partial resemblance to the introduced notions of domesticity. The selective appropriations, redefinitions, and innovations that African women and men made of such Western gender-marked phenomena as labor, space, sexuality, child care, food, and hygiene perhaps reflect the very different connections they drew between such ideas, invoking differently constructed hierarchies of gender and power (Comaroff 1985; Moore 1986).

The cultural redefinitions of particular elements of Western-derived domesticity and the different uses to which African women and men put them raise questions that this book's contributors are only beginning to explore. Thus far it seems that practices of sexuality and conjugality were affected far less than regimes of labor (Clark 1989); that rather than taking over the entire organization of (for example) standard English meals, some culinary practices were incorporated or shifted to new settings without altering meal consumption patterns by age and sex (Wilson 1972); that social relations and inter-personal networks were slow to yield to contemplative individualism (Berry 1985); and that consumption and accumulation for the purpose of asserting status and rank did not easily give way to frugality and savings (McCaskie 1983; 1986). The ways such selectivity work have something to do both with the cultural context of African experiences and the material and political structures that condition livelihoods. I return to this and other issues for future research at the end of my introduction.

Colonial Cultural Studies and Postcolonial Africa

Africa represented a major arena of European colonialism from the middle of the nineteenth century until the late 1950s. Pre-ceded by trading companies and missionary societies, the major European powers formally partitioned the continent between 1885 and 1889. They set out to legitimate colonial rule at the metropolitan end and to establish administrations overseas. In the process, they sought to assert technological, racial, and cultural dominance. Aside from three chapters—Mary Moran's on Liberia, settled by emanci-pated American slaves of African descent, Nancy Hunt's on the former Belgian Congo, and Kathleen Sheldon's on the formerly Por-tuguese colony of Mozambique—the research in this book has been undertaken in former British colonies. For this reason much of our colonial focus is on British imperialism.

Of the major European powers Great Britain controlled the larg-est colonial Empire (including India) for over seventy-five years, in a domain that contained a great diversity of imperialist practices and enormous regional and cultural variations. The administrative model of direct rule in many parts of India contrasted with the model of indirect rule in much of British-controlled Africa. There, so-called traditional political institutions were the vehicles for colo-nial objectives delegated through descending levels of white civil servants. In countries where Great Britain encouraged white settle-ment, such as Kenya, Northern and Southern Rhodesia, and South Africa, the administrative situation differed somewhat. Most Brit-ish colonies in Africa gained their independence between 1957 and 1965, with the exception of the settler colonies in Southern Africa, where after protracted liberation struggles Southern Rhodesia be-came independent as Zimbabwe in 1980 and South West Africa as Namibia in 1990. The Republic of South Africa forms as yet an unfinished agenda. It received self-government from Great Britain in 1910, was expelled from the British Commonwealth in 1961, and is at the moment in the throes of major political upheavals.

Our concerns in this book have benefited from the new light that recent scholarship in anthropology, history, and literary criticism has shed on the study of colonialism (e.g., Cooper and Stoler 1989; Jolly and Macintyre 1989; Stocking 1991). This work is recasting a previous era's imperial history of great men and public events into an interdisciplinary study of colonial cultures that draws attention to the objects, routines, and rituals of everyday life. Scholars from former colonies and metropoles are examining how both colonizer and colonized, at each end of the imperial divide, responded to and experienced colonialism (Callaway 1987; Chauduri and Strobel 1992; Sangari and Vaid 1990; Stoler 1989b; Strobel 1991). Many of these works draw on explanatory frameworks in which colonizer and colonized engage with each other in conflict or accommodation over a whole range of issues, including domesticity. In the process, they define and redefine both one another and what they view as important in their own culture and society.

The hallmark of the new scholarship on colonial culture is historical analyses of the changing intersections between race, gender, and class relations. For example, studies of the relationship between European missionaries and their African subjects or of colonial white employers and their African servants demonstrate the complexities of these intersections. They also reveal some of the contradictions inherent in the particular set of ideas about domesticity that were introduced. For instance, class- and time-bound European notions of sexuality confronted but did not always subjugate African attitudes that differed from the monogamous ideal and gendered notions of sexual permissiveness (Hansen 1990a). Such studies illustrate some of the dilemmas Africans experienced when faced with new ideas that they did not entirely accept or that the political and economic structures of the colonial situation prevented them from fully adopting. White missionaries and colonists encouraged Africans to don European dress, to attempt spotless hygiene, and to behave impeccably. The race, gender, and class lines that circumscribed African activity were made explicit by uniforms for different types of servants, clerks, and messengers; shoes and boots to be worn in some places but not others; modest dresses for African women; and subordinate behavior in relation to whites regardless of age, gender, and class. Europeans viewed a bra on top of a blouse, a dinner jacket on top of khaki shorts, and unsolicited questions as inappropriate imitations that signaled the Africans' ignorance of civilized manners and mores. This new scholarship questions such accounts because they conceal the ability of Africans to define sexuality, dress, and behavior themselves, and thus to have some influence on their relationship to the colonizers. In effect, the new scholarship helps us to identify African agency and struggle in everyday life. Much of the work on colonial cultures concerns domination and power without invoking these terms as explanations or conclusions, but recognizing that such terms imply relationships whose changing configurations help constitute the very subject of study (Bourdieu 1977; Foucault 1990; Giddens 1983).

But while the flourishing field of colonial culture studies has accentuated our historical sensibilities, several contributors to this book develop these insights further in analyses of postcolonial situations. The new scholarship on colonialism has been accompanied by a proliferation of nostalgic depictions of colonial culture in film, on television, and in best-selling books. This popular depiction of famous, infamous, and eccentric white women and men in idealized colonial settings must leave feminist scholarship unsatisfied with the portrayal of lives lived far away and long ago. As Third World countries have replaced most of the former Empire, nationals and expatriates have moved into the bungalows of yesteryear's *bwanas* and *donas*. Class, race, gender, and sexual relations are being renegotiated daily by women and men from many backgrounds (Enloe 1990). Their experiences and relations with persons less well-off in and out of homes, at work, and during leisure time, constitute an unfolding history of global cultures whose recreated notions of domesticity and gender are a central part of our research endeavor.

Contributing to the literature on colonial and postcolonial cultures elsewhere, this book focuses on Africa for several reasons. In spite of long-term involvements with different forms of capitalism (i.e., mercantile, colonial, industrial), the social and cultural practices of Africa's diverse societies never became marginalized to the extent experienced by such populations as indigenous Americans and Australians. Local structures had an important effect on the way in which African societies engaged with these capitalisms. A major challenge to African studies in general and to our research on African encounters with domesticity in particular lies in describing and conceptualizing such engagements in process-oriented terms, with careful attention to shifts in power relations.

The research potential of domesticity in Africa has been far from exhausted. From among the multiple and shifting meanings of domesticity in the West, those pertaining to space, activity, power, and gender are relevant to the general goals of this book and are discussed in diverse ways by all contributors. Individual chapters in turn provide different degrees of emphasis on one or several aspects of domesticity such as notions of labor and time, architecture and space, consumption and accumulation, body and clothing, diet and hygiene, and sexuality and gender. Beyond this, we all ask questions about the ways in which certain activities rather than others become construed as domestic; explore a variety of diverse forms and contents of African domesticity; examine the processes by which such activities become inscribed in gender term; and seek to unravel how gender, race, and class interact in particular encounters with domesticity.

Domains and Gender: Conceptual Issues

The domestic domain still puzzles its actors and observers, both of whom have trouble defining its boundaries, activities, and participants. The problems stem in part from conflating the domestic as an analytical domain of study with cultural meanings that vary cross-culturally and historically. Although Africanists certainly have studied the domestic domain, household work, and its leading performers, women, they have barely begun to explore the importance of domesticity as an ideological construct. Other than in studies of the ambiguous gender legacy of mission-sponsored education, colonial training initiatives (Cock 1979; Gaitskell 1979; Hunt 1990; Marks 1987; Morrow 1986), and domestic service (Cock 1980; Hansen 1989), questions pertaining to the construction of domesticity in Africa have been little explored.

In their lack of attention to the cultural dimensions of domesticity, African studies differ from both American- and European-focused scholarship, where domesticity has been the subject of several studies exploring its shifting cultural meanings against the backdrop of economic and political changes in the West (e.g., Davidoff 1973; Hall 1979; Ryan 1982; Smith-Rosenberg 1985). Research on changing practices and standards of domesticity has seen a sudden upswing (e.g., Berk 1985; Cowan, 1983; Hayden, 1981; Strasser 1982), as has scholarship on the construction of ideologies about domesticity and the home (Matthews, 1987; Parker 1989; Rowbotham 1989; Rybczynski 1986; Wright 1980). Throughout the 1980s the literature on paid domestic service and its transformations both in the West (e.g., Dudden 1983; Glenn 1986; Maza 1983; Rollins 1985; Sutherland 1981; van Raaphorst 1988) and the Third World (e.g., Bunster and Chaney 1985; Chaney and Castro 1989; Graham 1988) has also grown.

Reasons for the lack of exploration of domesticity in African studies are not hard to identify and I briefly discuss them in turn below. Firstly, the emphasis that research on the gender division of labor in Africa has placed on economic questions easily contributed to the overlooking of domesticity. Secondly, the socially devalued status of domesticity in the twentieth-century West may have made Africanist researchers reluctant to turn to domesticity as a legitimate area of study. And last but not least, the scholarly preoccupation with dichotomies that for so long has characterized research on gender has hampered our understanding of the ideological dimensions of domesticity.

Since African women's work in fields and markets was so obviously economic it is perhaps not surprising that researchers rarely raised questions about domesticity (cf. Robertson 1987), and that what they recognized as domesticity in Africa initially looked to them like fragments of Western-style idealizations. Scholars have neglected both African reformulations and appropriations of elements of Western-derived domesticity, and their variously constituted indigenous counterparts, perhaps due to the denigration of domesticity and its association with women in the West (Strathern 1984). Finally, the entrenched dichotomies in much gender research such as those between biology and culture, nature and culture, and the domestic and the public have contributed to deter questions from being raised concerning the gender association between women and domesticity (Kerber 1988; Strathern 1987).

While it may be dull, domesticity comprises more than a particular type of work, for it has powerful ideological functions. The preoccupation with conceptual dichotomies has helped obscure the ideological dimensions of domesticity and their broader ramifications. This becomes evident from an examination of two sets of literatures that, although they have separate histories, coalesce in equating the domestic with women. The first, inspired by Meyer Fortes's notion of the division into domestic and politico-jural domains, was elaborated and revised for its relevance to explanations of gender inequality by feminist scholarship of the 1970s and 1980s. The second, inspired by Friederich Engels's concern with private property, the family, and the state when explaining women's subordination, prompted a rethinking of the relationship between women, class, and the family. Since both these literatures have been discussed extensively elsewhere, my comments concern their specific relevance to the goals of this book.

The domestic domain, as a field of family, kinship, affinal, and gender relations, has claimed the attention of anthropologists and historians, particularly in African studies, since Fortes's influential writing (1958). Claiming that kinship had a jural, political dimension, he separated a politico-jural domain from the rest of the aspects of social interaction involved in kinship and left the domestic domain to sexuality and childrearing, associating the sphere of rules and authority with men and that of affect and morality with women. During the 1980s, the importance that previous scholars attributed to the distinction between the domestic or private, and the politico-jural or public domains when explaining women's and men's different societal involvement has been subjected to much criticism (Collier and Yanagisako 1987; Comaroff 1987). So in turn has the reformulation of the distinction between domestic and public into a symbolic divide between nature and culture (Strathern 1980). Taken together, these criticisms have highlighted the historical and cross-cultural variability of the distinction into two domains, and have noted the diverse meanings different societies attribute to differently structured spheres (Strathern 1987).

As a field of family relations, the domestic domain held center stage in Engels's evolutionary scheme (1972). He linked the existence of surplus and the beginning privatization of property to the emergence of the family and the oppression of women. Private property, which he considered responsible for class domination, was thus also connected with the domination of women: from changes in the organization of the economy would follow changes of both the state and the family. The domestic domain, as the sphere of home and family, would thus wither away as a result of the steady advancement of capitalism and the establishment of socialism. One body of feminist criticism has blamed this analysis for giving priority to the economic sphere, thus dismissing the domestic sphere as having no practical and theoretical importance. Such criticism then expended much effort on examining domestic labor or reproduction from a variety of theoretical angles for the purpose of exploring its role in capitalist production (e.g., Himmelweit and Mohun 1977). These viewpoints were extended by subsequent analyses of the domestic domain that elaborated the functionality of women's reproductive labor for capitalism and emphasized the interdependence of the two spheres (Harris and Young 1981; Mackintosh 1979).

But other scholars who found Engels's analysis ahistorical observed that inequality between women and men predates capitalism. Patriarchy, they argued, existed prior to capitalism, and household, family, and kinship structures were its carriers. In Heidi Hartman's dual-systems formulation, patriarchy and class were seen as two independent relations that have become mutually supportive under capitalism (1981). Yet precisely how the two sets of relations articulate remains problematic if not unclear in this analysis. Some of the work inspired by dual-systems thinking reduced patriarchy to questions about marriage, domestic life, and sexuality, and reduced questions of capitalism to work. Hartman saw capitalism as producing the places in which work was performed, and gender (and race) as constructing the persons who performed it. Such an analysis does not explain women's oppression, but takes it for granted (Bozzoli 1983). By allocating workers to different activities without explaining why gender structures the division of labor, this analysis, like that of domestic labor and reproduction, too readily conflates gender with biological sex.

Contesting Domains

What insights may we draw from the conceptual scholarship on the domestic that are relevant to our examinations of the construction and meanings of domesticity in Africa? Although they are different, the literatures on the domestic/public divide, the domestic labor debate, and dual-systems approaches share a number of characteristics that are crucial to this book.

First, these literatures confuse two distinct sets of relations, those concerned with the domestic and those concerned with gender, both of which they associate with women. As two sets of distinct relations, gender and the domestic may at times overlap in some of their dimensions and intersect in others. The domestic is not everywhere nor exclusively organized by gender, but also by class and race relations, and gender relations are not only or even primarily negotiated across a politico-jural/domestic divide. Both women and men live in households and society. So, rather than assuming that gender and the domestic encompass each other, we should ask questions about their changing interrelationship.

Secondly, if arguments about the domestic and public domains tend to omit culture and ideology from the analysis of historical change, debates about domestic labor and dual systems relegate them to an epiphenomenal status. Thus they lack, for different theoretical reasons, an analysis of the dynamic relationship between changes in the material aspect of the social relations of production and the sociocultural resources with which people construct their world, giving meaning to their activities and place in it. In effect, the social actor drops from sight and the problematic relationship between history and culture remains unexplored.

The fact that domestic service is one of the earliest labor forms through which African men were incorporated into wage labor challenges the assumption that the domestic sphere is gender-bound to women. The development and persistence in several countries today of male domestic service cannot be understood without reference to the ideological, cultural, and historical contexts in which this takes place. African men servants were obviously not domestic "by nature." They were taught skills that both they and their employers considered to be not "female," but marketable. Their story unfolded within at least three intersecting axes of differentiation: the racial structure of the colony that at a very general level restricted labor, mobility, and political participation; developments in relations between classes; and changes in relations between the sexes.

Class accounts of the historical development of wage labor in Africa as male have been written many times. In this book, Janet Bujra offers her version, emphasizing how women's agricultural work benefited the emerging capitalist economy. But capitalist developments alone do not explain why and how men rather than women were made into a particular kind of worker whose domesticity "did not follow" from being female. I have suggested elsewhere that African women by their very absence from domestic service were central to the structuring of this labor process in male terms (Hansen 1989, 84–153). Both Nancy Hunt and I argue in our respective chapters on mission homes in the Congo and civil service households in Northern Rhodesia that the dominant ideology of white over black rested on assumptions about Africans that did not consistently oppose Western-derived notions of male and female, skills and emotions, and the economic and the domestic. In colonial domestic service, ideas about African women's and men's capabilities clashed dramatically with Western notions of gender, construing men rather than women as better suited for paid household work.

The construction of gender in male as much as female terms belongs to our inquiry into domesticity and its uneasy relationships to sometimes very differently constituted and evaluated aspects of life in African societies. The shifts in such constructions hinged on women's and men's experiences as members of households and as workers, as well as, in racially structured societies, on their color. How the gender division of labor in race- and class-divided colonial settings received ideological expression and how it responded to the passage of time must be studied with reference to culturally constructed notions of gender. This observation is particularly pertinent to qualify Ester Boserup's notions of female and male sex roles and their mechanistic changes as a result of the meeting of tradition and imported cultural patterns (1970, 70). Partial or ongoing "Westernization" has not replaced men servants with women everywhere in Africa. Although sluggish economic development has something to do with this, so do cultural ideas about women's and men's places.

As suggested earlier, the construction of domesticity in Africa today depends less on household technology than on ideologies about gender. The labor-intensive form of male domestic service, which both Janet Bujra and I describe in this book, reveals an interesting angle on the connection drawn in some feminist scholarship between changes in skills and technology, and definitions and redefinitions of women's work in the West (e.g., Cockburn 1983; McGaw 1987; Tobias and Milkman 1987). The devaluation of their domestic work that Western women experienced as their homes became increasingly mechanized (Matthews 1987) is not experienced to any large degree in African households because economic stringencies and unemployment, which make labor readily forthcoming and cheap, are holding the mechanization of household work at bay. When African men servants contested their jobs with their employers and in relationship to African women, they did not struggle over control of tools and technology. Rather, they battled over a task-oriented specialization of labor between kitchen, house, and grounds (Hansen 1990b). In this instance, tools and technology have little direct bearing on the gender construction of work and its evaluation, yet the work of the male servant is emphatically differently valued than that of the woman.

Finally, the scholarship on the domestic/public divide, domestic labor, and dual systems teaches us to be wary of both single- and dual-systems explanations. An analysis that encompasses the interaction of the domestic and the public, and production and reproduction presents the most useful challenge to these unsatisfactory approaches (Collier and Yanagisako 1987). While the Western devaluation of domesticity and the conceptual preoccupation with dichotomies have provided inspiration for the questions raised in this book, they also give rise to assumptions that we find problematic. We specifically question the taken-for-granted status of domesticity by asking questions about the construction of its actors, activities, and boundaries. Our book seeks to transcend two common approaches: overly economistic analyses of the division of labor that discount agency and assign a passive role to culture and ideology; and cultural analyses that pay little attention to the social, economic, and political context in which symbolic constructs emerge. Viewing society as materially constituted and both gender and the domestic as contestable, we are advocating a research approach that is open to historical contingency, to diversity of cultural practices, and to women and men as social actors who with the resources at hand confront and at times transform the circumstances of their own lives.

The Chapters: Themes and Interpretations

Representing several disciplines and different theoretical orientations, the contributors to this book examine the construction of domesticity in Africa, exploring the complex and changing meanings Africans and others attributed to it in different cultural and economic regions. At a very general level, the chapters reveal at least two broad regional differences concerning the outcomes of domesticity in the confrontation between colonial capitalism and various forms of African social organization: West Africa versus East and Southern Africa. These contrasts are the products of historical processes and may reflect the impacts of different modes of imperialist intervention: indirect rule in West Africa versus different forms of settler colonialism in much of East and Southern Africa. Themes of European domination and ideological hegemony tend to be less strong in the chapters on West Africa, where African cultural constructs are brought to bear with different emphasis than in the chapters on Southern Africa.

Because of our distinct backgrounds and particular interests, we examine the significance of domesticity with regard to key issues like space, activity, power, and gender from several angles, thus adding to the richness of our collective endeavor. Some authors apply the notion of the domestic in an analytical sense to refer to the domestic domain; others use it literally with reference, for example, to domestic science training; some use it pragmatically to indicate a locus of activity; and most of us mobilize it ideologically in analyses of particular cultural constructs that produce tensions between a variety of African and Western conceptualizations.

The book is divided into three parts, each of which suggests several contexts for exploring the changing meanings of domesticity and the ways in which women and men have grappled with these meanings in different parts of twentieth-century Africa. Part I, "Varieties of African Domesticity," deliberately juxtaposes very diverse constructions of domesticity in order to indicate the broad scope of this terrain of study and some of the many issues involved. Several of these issues are dealt with in detail throughout the remainder of the book. The chapters in the first section focus on the actual process of constructing domesticity, implicating Christian, Islamic, and indigenous concepts in the outcomes. Anthropologists Jean and John L. Comaroff's "Home-Made Hegemony: Modernity, Domesticity, and Colonialism in South Africa" discusses the way nonconformist evangelism in South Africa attempted to transform African lives at the same time as social reformers in England sought to upgrade the lives of the English working poor. Drawing connections between these processes, they suggest that each came to mirror the other, with Africa representing everything that bourgeois refinement was not. They explore the very particular cultural and social project entailed in the construction of the domestic world by singling out the Tswana house as a symbol of several other aspects of life: social boundaries, property, sexuality, body, and clothing. The multiple referents that shaped the selective appropriation of architectural innovations introduced by missionaries illustrate the ideological battle between missionary and African intensions.

Local ideologies about domestic space receive further attention in the next chapter, which reveals the way in which cultural assumptions colored by Islam and indigenous notions informed and confronted externally introduced ideas. In "Harem Domesticity in Kano, Nigeria" Beverly Mack, a specialist in the literature and culture of the Hausa region of Nigeria, looks at the Hausa interpretation of Islamic doctrine concerning housing and space. Describing the historical evolution of the influence of Islam as an ideological focus in the area, she views the royal community as the prototype of the Hausa household, and as a central influence on Hausa notions of domesticity that cuts across all socioeconomic levels. Based on her exceptional research locus within the ruler's palace, she discusses how secluded women successfully mediate Islamic obligations regarding the cultural and spatial ordering of their movements and activities within a changing world.

In her chapter "Civilized Servants: Child Fostering and Training for Status among the Glebo in Liberia," anthropologist Mary Moran pushes the examination of the cultural construction of space in a different direction by reckoning with the notions of civilization introduced by Afro-American settlers. Her concerns are with status, habitus, and the making of cultural standards, and with the ways in which these get reproduced in housekeeping practices like etiquette, hygiene, and dress. Conceptualizing such processes as class embodiment, she examines their reproduction in the relationship between foster children and householders who are responsible for their training in civilization.

The chapter "Domestic Science Training in Colonial Yorubaland, Nigeria," by historian LaRay Denzer, introduces a different angle. In examining those aspects of domesticity that Yoruba women developed in ways neither indigenous nor Western, she traces the unexpected outcome of the two-fold purpose of domestic science training in the women's education curriculum. The training aimed to transmit new knowledge about health care and domesticity and to use domestic subjects to break down deep-seated parental objections against women's education. But the women who underwent this training employed their skills in new contexts and for different purposes than those intended by their instructors, opening bakeries, restaurants, and tailoring shops.

The diverse domesticities introduced in Part 1 contrast with those described in Part 2, "Domestic Encounters," which focuses more directly on African responses to outright policy formulations involving missionaries, colonial educators, welfare workers, philanthropic volunteers, and community developers. Historian Nancy

Hunt's "Colonial Fairy Tales and the Knife and Fork Doctrine in the Heart of Africa" examines the construction of domesticity in the efforts of British Baptist missionaries to create civilized African homes in the wilderness on the upper Congo river in Colonial Zaire. Where the Comaroffs singled out the Tswana house, she focuses on the mission home as both a symbol of domesticity and a training site for the transfer of knowledge about hygiene. Examining missionary school manuals, she observes how hygiene became a colony-wide but gender-specific project to restructure, sanitize, legislate, and regulate African spaces, homes, gender relations, and eating and eliminating practices. Her chapter illustrates vividly how domesticity may be explored productively through its representation not only in archival texts, but also in a variety of events such as royal visits, teas, dinners, and marriage stories.

The next chapter, also by a historian, highlights some of the tensions inherent in missionary and colonial efforts aimed at the training of women for domesticity, looking particularly at some of the reactions women had to the contradictions between the ostensible goals of those efforts and their own material realities and social and cultural aspirations. Nakanyike Musisi's "Colonial and Missionary Education: Women and Domesticity in Uganda, 1900–1945," examines the effects and outcomes of training in homecrafts and household work in schools for Ugandan women during the colonial period. In doing so she reveals striking disagreements between Ugandan women and men on the one hand, and white educators—male and female—on the other, as well as between African elites and commoners, over what girls' education should be. Her discussion offers rich insights into how debates over girls' education were generated, who participated, and which curricular issues caused divisions and changes of opinion.

Sita Ranchod-Nilsson, a political scientist, applies the theme of unanticipated consequences from women's training for domesticity, which LaRay Denzer introduced in regard to colonial Yorubaland, to Zimbabwe in " 'Educating Eve': The Women's Club Movement and Political Consciousness among Rural African Women in Southern Rhodesia, 1950–1980." She focuses on domestic skills taught to rural Shona women by the wives of white civil servants who did volunteer work from the early 1940s on. This is a rather special case, since most scholarship on clubs and homecrafts has concerned the training of urban rather than rural African women. Her discussion concentrates on the period during which African nationalists increasingly questioned the racial underpinnings of the settler economy and polity. She shows how the provision of domestic skills had rather different meanings of domesticity for African and European members of the Federation of African Women's Clubs, given the different material circumstances of their lives. Rather than adopting such skills to improve the management of their own households, African women in these homecraft clubs were able to change the agenda of club activities to meet their own needs. In the process, they developed a gendered political consciousness, which they raised during the rural mobilization for the liberation war.

The four chapters in the book's last part, "Race, Class, Gender, and Domestic Work," bring up questions concerning paid and unpaid domestic work, skills, sexuality, and gender. The first three chapters focus specifically on domestic service rather than on domestic skills viewed more broadly, as in some of the previous chapters. These last four chapters all draw on research in former colonies with varying degrees of settler influence, and are concerned with the debates and vexations of colonial officials and white householders over the definition of a particular form of wage labor, the construction of gender in specific jobs, and the acquisition and transfer of specific skills and styles from the employing households to the very differently structured sociocultural space of African households. Historian Elizabeth Schmidt's "Race, Sex, and Domestic Labor: The Question of African Female Servants in Southern Rhodesia, 1900–1939," singles out the debate about the possibility of employing African women, rather than men, in domestic service. The period she covers precedes that considered by Sita Ranchod-Nilsson; and she in fact analyzes an altogether different process of gender and societal incorporation. The participants in the debate—European colonial wives, missionaries, male civil servants, African women and men—did not agree about the desirability of the proposal to utilize women in domestic service. Despite the conflicts of opinion, they all, although for different reasons, contributed to maintain the male employment convention. She is particularly concerned with unraveling the economic interests, racial stereotypes, and gender prejudices in the double standard of the European moral code that helped hold back the employment of African women in white colonial homes.

The contrast between the two chapters on Southern Rhodesia draws attention to broader labor issues and the way that racially segmented labor markets use gender for inclusion or exclusion. Sociologist Janet Bujra picks up this theme in her "Men at Work in the Tanzanian Home: How did They Ever Learn?" With a theoretical discussion about class and skill and their political mediation in the workplace rather than in the cultural context of women's and men's lives, she explains how domestic service is reproduced as a male labor form. Providing detailed information, she describes how servants learn, how they consider their knowledge, and how their skills are transferred to the labor force.

In "Cookstoves and Charcoal Braziers: Culinary Practics, Gender, and Class in Zambia" I provide an anthropological analysis of the acquisition and transfer of domestic service skills by African male servants, in this case from the employer's household to the servant's. Actively implicating gender ideology and sexuality in the expression of cultural assumptions about women's and men's work, I consider the acquisition of skills and styles of cooking and their gendered and class-specific meanings. I examine these practices and their continuities and changes, from white colonial cuisine to styles of cooking in present day Zambian households where men work as cooks, nannies feed children, and wives take special care to prepare their husband's Zambian meals. Describing how culturally preferred consumption styles in Zambia's depressed economy are being affected by International Monetary Fund (IMF) priorities and foreign food aid policies, I suggest that the work of class and gender in the kitchen cannot escape being reshaped in such new encounters.

The last chapter in our book, by historian Kathleen Sheldon, focuses on child care, the stubbornly resistant bedrock in so many discussions about women's place in society. In "*Creches, Titias,* and Mothers: Women and Child Care in Mozambique," she addresses issues of state policies toward women's household duties, including child care. Women's liberation was an important component of the postcolonial government's policies, informed by an orthodox Marxist position that called for women to join the wage labor force. Yet her chapter demonstrates clearly that while women's child-care options have expanded, gender inequality in the domestic domain has not been questioned.

Collectively, these chapters illustrate the significance of domesticity in the changing constructions of space, activity, power, and gender in Africa, and prompt us to raise questions about the political and economic ramifications of spatiotemporally organized activities and their cultural evaluations. The door to the domestic domain opens up in two directions. Our close-range observations add history and agency to a domain of interaction that has long been taken for granted. Above all, our findings challenge us not to confuse our Western construction and denigration of domesticity with its actors' own intentions.

Emerging Issues

Our book carves out a domain of inquiry, encouraging research into ongoing encounters that continually reshape the meanings of domesticity as African political and household economies battle over access to scarce economic and cultural resources in a shrinking global economy. Although their languages differ, the powers that be—management and technology experts, development specialists, and medical interventionists—raise questions about entitlements to labor and skills, housing space, consumption, property, and medical hygiene that continue to invoke gendered notions of domesticity, power, and sexuality, male domination and female subordination. Although trying to understand domesticity differently as we have done here is important to African women's and men's transformative projects and to us as academics, our comprehension of the problems African women and men face in their struggles with domesticity must develop beyond this book.

A major research issue concerns the evolution of changing ideas of domesticity in a changing dialogue between the West and the rest of the world, including Africa. Future work must specify in more detail the historically and socially variable meanings of domesticity in areas of Africa and the West not considered in this book for lack of space. Our present research demonstrates that broader processes of ideological reconstruction are at work at both ends of the former imperial divide, producing very particular outcomes in the private and public recesses of African societies. The influence of changing indigenous conceptual schemes on these processes remain an area wide open to inquiry. So does the question of which aspects of culturally constituted notions of domesticity get accepted, reworked, or changed, in which domains of life, and why. It is a challenging order for anthropologists, historians, and other social scientists to fill in the gaps in the trajectories of these interactive processes and to chart their unfolding reformulations in Africa today without losing track of the African voice.

Together with Africans, the enterprise we have staked out comprises missionaries, colonial officials, educators, and social reformers of all kinds. Future research might add new agents to this list. For example, today's experts in local and foreign policy, management, and development do not always see eye to eye with African governments on what constitutes human capital and how to improve it. Like their colonial predecessors, these new actors must contend with popular reactions that often differ in gender terms. Struggles over the meanings of domesticity thus continue to be fought on the household front and at the level of the state, and they require unrelenting attention.

Future work on domesticity and its reformulations might develop some of these issues in several directions. In the contemporary encounter between Africa and the West, the tensions between universalism and particularism persist, but with a new twist. At a very general level, western-derived technology, consumption style, and popular culture are homogenizing formerly distinct practices. The West's cultural industries export new scripts for household management, marriage practices, childrearing, and food preparations, as well as for gender relations and sexuality, providing filtered-down models for or against local African domestic arrangements. These ongoing processes cannot be satisfactorily explained as involving unidirectional transfers from the West to Africa. How African culture, class, and ethnic/religious distinctions shape today's appropriations and reworkings of notions associated with domesticity remains as challenging to explore for the present as for the past. So too does the way in which conventional concerns with the domestic get translated into gender terms that shape aspects of both private and public space arrangements and city planning, including access to and location of such gender-inflected services as maternity clinics, markets, and recreational facilities. There is tourism to consider, as well as foreign military establishments and the sex trade that often accompany them, no doubt affecting African household arrangements in many ways by turning aspects of domesticity into commerce. Questions about how race and class relate to all of this belong to inquiries of both colonial and postcolonial cultures.

New research is called for to examine how domesticity gets reinvented or changed in the process of local and foreign development planning, and how project implementation affects the attempts of women and men of different backgrounds to bridge or widen the gulf between their personal lives and public activities. How variously constituted feminisms in Africa react to and incorporate ideological elements of domesticity is a question of critical concern for social movements aimed at transforming gender, race, and class inequalities in many societies. Western feminist scholars cannot be complacent about these processes but must join their African colleagues in intellectual efforts to comprehend why notions of motherhood are recreated even against backdrops of revolutionary change. Understanding the ideological and material forces that prompt such outcomes has implications for both theory and practice.

Methodological considerations also demand further examination, especially strategies aimed at unpacking the unspoken meanings of domestic ideologies that are lodged so uneasily in domains of life concerned with space, work, power, and gender and expressed in a miscellany of practices. The contributions to this book demonstrate the fine analyses that can be derived from using conventional and nonconventional archives, formal statistics, interviews and life histories, and they draw additional insights from household manuals and recipe books, newspapers and popular magazines, and didactic and creative literatures. Increased understanding can also be gained from texts that are not written but performed in the broadest sense of the word: interactive encounters, social events, parties, rituals, and theater. The study of the gendered, sexualized, and classed meanings that are produced by recreations of the body through diet, adornment, cosmetics, hygiene, clothing, and comportment can shed additional light on the cultural construction of domesticity. In conclusion, imaginative approaches and thinking regarding seemingly trivial aspects of everyday lives and their representations, their traces, their written and unwritten records, are part of the methodological and interpretive challenge through which we as scholars may publically reveal some of the significant facets of domesticity. Africa is a particularly challenging setting for a materially based and culturally sensitive investigation of domesticity that offers rich insights into what interdisciplinary Africanist research can bring to studies of our contemporary world.

Acknowledgments

Several collegues have commented on different versions of this introduction. I wish particularly to thank Jean Comaroff for prodding my understanding of domesticity, Jane Guyer for challenging me to develop this understanding more substantively, and Margaret Strobel for keeping my tendency to ramble within bounds. I am also grateful to the participants in the South African reading group at Northwestern University for their comments, criticisms, and constructive suggestions.

Bibliography

Alloula, Malek. 1986. *The Colonial Harem.* Vol. 21, *Theory and History of Literature.* Manchester, England: Manchester University Press.

Ballhatchet, Kenneth. 1980. *Race, Sex, and Class under the Raj: Imperial Attitudes and Policies and their Critics, 1793–1905.* New York: St. Martin's Press.

Berk, Sarah F. 1985. *The Gender Factory: The Apportionment of Work In American Households.* New York: Plenum.

Berry, Sara. 1985. *Fathers Work for Their Sons: Accumulation, Mobility and Class Formation in an Extended Yoruba Community.* Berkeley: University of California Press.

Boserup, Ester. 1970. *Woman's Role in Economic Development.* New York: St. Martin's Press.

Bourdieu, Pierre. 1977. *Outline of a Theory of Practice.* Cambridge, England: Cambridge University Press.

Boydston, Jeanne. 1986. To Earn Her Daily Bread: Housework and Antebellum Working-Class Subsistence. *Radical History Review* 35:7–25.

Bozzoli, Belinda. 1983. Marxism, Feminism and South African Studies. *Journal of Southern African Studies* 9:139–171.

Bradley, Emily. 1950. *Dearest Priscilla: Letters to the Wife of a Colonial Civil Servant.* London: Max Parrish.

Bunster, Ximena, and Elsa M. Chaney, eds. 1985. *Sellers and Servants: Working Women in Lima, Peru.* New York: Praeger.

Callaway, Helen. 1987. *Gender, Culture and Empire: European Women in Colonial Nigeria.* Urbana: University of Illinois Press.

Chaney, Elsa M., and Mary Garcia Castro, eds. 1989. *Muchacas No More: Household Workers in Latin America and the Caribbean.* Philadelphia: Temple University Press.

Chauduri, Nupur, and Margaret Strobel, eds. 1992. *Complicity and Resistance: Western Women and Imperialism.* Bloomington: Indiana University Press.

Chauncey, George, Jr. 1981. The Locus of Reproduction: Women's Labour in the Zambian Copperbelt, 1927–1953. *Journal of Southern African Studies* 7:135–164.

Clark, Gracia. 1989. Money, Sex and Cooking: Manipulation of the Paid/Unpaid Boundary by Asante Market Women. In *The Social Economy of Consumption,* ed. H. Rutz and B. Orlove, 323–348. *Society for Economic Anthropology Monographs* no. 6. Washington, D.C.: University Press of America.

Cock, Jacklyn. 1979. Domesticity and Domestication: A Note on the Articulation of Sexual Ideology and the Initial Incorporation of Black Women into Wage Labour. *Africa Perspective* 13:16–26.

————. 1980. *Maids and Madams. A Study of the Politics of Exploitation.* Johannesburg: Ravan Press.

Cockburn, Cynthia. 1983. *Brothers: Male Dominance and Technological Change.* London: Pluto Press.

Collier, Jane F., and Sylvia J. Yanagisako, eds. 1987. *Gender and Kinship: Essays Toward a Unified Analysis.* Stanford: Stanford University Press.

Comaroff, Jean. 1985. *Body of Power, Spirit of Resistance.* Chicago: University of Chicago Press.

Comaroff, Jean, and John L. Comaroff. 1991. *Of Revelation and Revolution.* Vol. 1, *Christianity, Colonialism and Consciousness in South Africa.* Chicago: University of Chicago Press.

Comaroff, John L. 1987. *Sui Genderis:* Feminism, Kinship Theory, and Structural Domains. In *Gender and Kinship: Essays Toward a Unified Analysis,* J. ed. J. Collier and S. Yanagisako, 53–85. Stanford: Stanford University Press.

————. 1989. Images of Empire, Contests of Conscience: Models of Colonial Domination in South Africa. *American Ethnologist* 16 (4):661–685.

Concise Oxford Dictionary of Current English. 1964 (5th ed.). 1982 (7th ed.). Oxford: Clarendon Press.

Cooper, Frederick. 1989. From Free Labor to Family Allowances: Labor and African Society in Colonial Discourse. *American Ethnologist* 16 (4):745–765.

Cooper, Frederick, and Ann L. Stoler, eds. 1989. Tensions of Empire. *American Ethnologist* 16 (4): special issue.

Cowan, Ruth S. 1983. *More Work for Mother: The Ironies of Household Technology from the Open Hearth to the Microwave.* New York: Basic Books.

Das, Veena. 1986. Gender Studies, Cross-Cultural Comparison and the Colonial Organization of Knowledge. *Berkshire Review* 26:58–76.

Davidoff, Leonore. 1973. *The Best Circles: Society, Etiquette and the Season.* London: Croom Helm.

Davidoff, Leonore, and Catherine Hall. 1987. *Family Fortunes: Men and Women of the English Middle Class, 1780–1850.* Chicago: University of Chicago Press.

Davin, Anna. 1978. Imperialism and Motherhood. *History Workshop* 5:9–65.

Dudden, Faye E. 1983. *Serving Women: Household Service in Nineteenth-Century America.* Middletown, Conn.: Wesleyan University Press.

Engels, Friederich. [1884] 1972. *The Origin of the Family, Private Property and the State,* ed. Eleanor Burke Leacock. New York: International Publishers.

Enloe, Cynthia. 1990. *Bananas, Beaches & Bases: Making Feminist Sense of International Politics.* Berkeley: University of California Press.

Epstein, Arnold L. 1981. *Urbanization and Kinship: The Domestic Domain on the Copperbelt of Zambia 1950–1965.* New York: Academic Press.

Folbre, Nancy. 1991. The Unproductive Housewife: Her Evolution in Nineteenth-Century Economic Thought. *Signs* 16 (3):463–484.

Fortes, Meyer. 1958. Introduction. In *The Developmental Cycle in Domestic Groups,* ed. J. Goody, 1–14. Cambridge, England: Cambridge University Press.

Foucault, Michel. 1990. *The History of Sexuality.* Vol. 1, *An Introduction.* New York: Vintage Books.

Frykman, Jonas, and Orvar Löfgren. 1987. *Culture Builders: A Historical Anthropology of Middle Class Life.* New Brunswick, N.J.: Rutgers University Press.

Furse, Ralph. 1962. *Aucuparius: Recollections of a Recruiting Officer.* London: Oxford University Press.

Gaitskell, Deborah. 1979. "Christian Compounds for Girls": Church Hostels for African Women in Johannesburg, 1907–1970. *Journal of Southern African Studies* 6:44–69.

————. 1983. Housewives, Maids or Mothers: Some Contradictions of Domesticity for Christian Women in Johannesburg, 1903–39. *Journal of African History* 24:241–256.

Gann, Lewis H., and Peter Duignan. 1978. *The Rulers of British Africa, 1870–1914.* Stanford: Stanford University Press.

Giddens, Anthony. 1983. *Central Problems in Social Theory: Action, Structure and Contradiction in Social Analysis.* Berkeley: University of California Press.

Gillis, John R. 1979. Servants, Sexual Relations and the Risks of Illegitimacy in London, 1801–1900. *Feminist Studies* 5 (1):142–173.

Glenn, Evelyn Nakano. 1986. *Issei, Nisei, War Bride: Three Generations of Japanese American Women in Domestic Service.* Philadelphia: Temple University Press.

Graham, Sandra L. 1988. *House and Street: The Domestic World of Servants and Masters in Nineteenth-Century Rio de Janeiro.* New York: Cambridge University Press.

Hall, Catherine. 1979. The Early Formation of Victorian Domestic Ideology. In *Fit Work for Women,* ed. S. Burman, 14–32. New York: St. Martin's Press.

Hansen, Karen Tranberg. 1989. *Distant Companions: Servants and Employers in Zambia. 1900–1985.* Ithaca, N.Y.: Cornell University Press.

————. 1990a. Body Politics: Sexuality, Gender, and Domestic Service in Zambia. *Journal of Women's History* 2 (1):745–765.

————. 1990b. Domestic Trials: Power and Autonomy in Domestic Service in Zambia. *American Ethnologist* 17 (2):360–375.

Harris, Olivia, and Kate Young. 1981. Engendered Structures: Some Problems in the Analysis of Reproduction. In *The Anthropology of Pre-Capitalist Societies,* ed. J. Kahn and J. Llobera, 109–147. London: Macmillan.

Hartman, Heidi. 1981. The Unhappy Marriage of Marxism and Feminism: Toward a More Progressive Union. In *Women and Revolution: A Discus-*

sion of the Unhappy Marriage of Marxism and Feminism, ed. L. Sargent, 1–41. Boston: South End Press.

Hayden, Dolores. 1981. *The Grand Domestic Revolution: A History of Feminist Designs for American Homes, Neighborhoods, and Cities.* Cambridge, Mass.: MIT Press.

Himmelweit, Susan, and Simon Mohun. 1977. Domestic Labour and Capital. *Cambridge Journal of Economics* 1:15–31.

Hunt, Nancy Rose. 1990. Domesticity and Colonialism in Belgian Africa: Usumbura's *Foyer Social*, 1946–60. *Signs* 15 (3):447–474.

Jolly, Margaret, and Martha Macintyre, eds. 1989. *Family and Gender in the Pacific: Domestic Contradictions and the Colonial Impact.* Cambridge: Cambridge University Press.

Jordanova, Ludmilla. 1989. *Sexual Visions: Images of Gender in Science and Medicine between the Eighteenth and Twentieth Centuries.* Madison: University of Wisconsin Press.

Kerber, Linda. 1988. Separate Spheres, Female Worlds, Woman's Place: The Rhetoric of Women's History. *Journal of American History* 9 (1):9–39.

Knibiehler, Yvonne, and Goutalier, Regine. 1985. *La femme au temps des colonies.* Paris: Editions Stock.

Kucklick, Henrietta. 1979. *The Imperial Bureaucrat: The Colonial Administrative Service in the Gold Coast, 1920–1939.* Stanford: Stanford University Press.

McCaskie, Thomas C. 1983. Accumulation, Wealth and Belief in Asante History. I: To the Close of the Nineteenth Century. *Africa* 53:23–43.

———. 1986. Accumulation, Wealth and Belief in Asante History. II: The Twentieth Century. *Africa* 56:3–23.

McGaw, Judith A. 1987. *Most Wonderful Machine: Mechanization and Social Change in Berkshire Paper Making, 1801–1885.* Princeton: Princeton University Press.

Mackintosh, Maureen. 1979. Domestic Labour and the Household. In *Fit Work for Women*, ed. S. Burman, 173–191. New York: St. Martin's Press.

Marks, Shula. 1987. *Not Either an Experimental Doll: The Separate Worlds of Three South African Women.* London: The Women's Press Ltd.

Matthews, Glenna. 1987. *"Just a Housewife": The Rise & Fall of Domesticity in America.* New York: Oxford University Press.

Maza, Sarah C. 1983. *Servants and Masters in Eighteenth-Century France: The Uses of Loyalty.* Princeton, N.J.: Princeton University Press.

Mohanty, Chandra Talpade. 1984. Under Western Eyes: Feminist Scholarship and Colonial Discourses. *Boundary* 2:338–358.

Moore, Henrietta L. 1986. *Space, Text and Gender: An Anthropological Study of the Marakwet of Kenya.* Cambridge: Cambridge University Press.

———. 1988. *Feminism and Anthropology.* Minneapolis: University of Minnesota Press.

Morrow, Sean. 1986. "No Girl Leaves the School Unmarried": Mabel Shaw and the Education of Girls at Mbereshi, Northern Rhodesia, 1915–1940. *International Journal of African Historical Studies* 19:602–636.

Murray, Colin. 1981. *Families Divided: The Impact of Migrant Labour in Lesotho*. Cambridge: Cambridge University Press.

Parker, Rozsika. 1989. *The Subversive Stitch: Embroidery and the Making of the Feminine*. New York: Routledge & Kegan Paul.

Poovey, Mary. 1989. *Uneven Development: The Ideological Work of Gender in Mid-Victorian England*. Chicago: University of Chicago Press.

Prodolliet, Simone. 1987. *Wider die Schamlosigkeit und das Elend der Heidnischen Weiber: Die Basler Mission und der Export des Europäischen Frauenideals in die Kolonien*. Zurich: Limmat Verlag.

Robertson, Claire. 1987. Developing Economic Awareness; Changing Perspectives in Studies of African Women, 1976–1985. *Feminist Studies* 13:97–135.

Rogers, Barbara. 1980. *The Domestication of Women: Discrimination in Developing Societies*. London: Tavistock.

Rollins, Judith. 1985. *Between Women: Domestics and Their Employers*. Philadelphia: Temple University Press.

Rosaldo, Michelle Z. 1980. The Use and Abuse of Anthropology: Reflections on Feminism and Cross-Cultural Understanding. *Signs* 5:389–417.

Rowbotham, Judith. 1989. *Good Girls Make Good Wives: Guidance for Girls in Victorian Fiction*. London: Basil Blackwell.

Russett, Cynthia E. 1989. *Sexual Science: The Victorian Construction of Womanhood*. New York: Columbia University Press.

Ryan, Mary P. 1982. *The Empire of the Mother: American Writing about Domesticity 1830–1860*. New York: Harrington Park Press.

Rybczynski, Witold. 1986. *Home: A Short History of an Idea*. New York: Penguin.

Sangari, Kumkum, and Sudesh Vaid, eds. 1990. *Recasting Women: Essays in Indian Colonial History*. New Brunswick, N.J.: Rutgers University Press.

Smith-Rosenberg, Carroll. 1985. *Disorderly Conduct: Visions of Gender in Victorian America*. New York: Alfred A. Knopf.

Stanley, Liz., ed. 1984. *The Diaries of Hannah Cullwick, Victorian Maidservant*. London: Virago Press.

Stocking, George W., Jr., ed. 1991. *Colonial Situations: Essays on the Contextualization of Ethnographic Knowledge*. History of Anthropology, vol. 7. Madison: University of Wisconsin Press.

Stoler, Ann. 1989a. Making Empire Respectable: The Politics of Race and Sexual Morality in 20th-century Colonial Cultures. *American Ethnologist* 16 (4):634–660.

———. 1989b. Rethinking Colonial Catgories: European Communities and the Boundaries of Rule. *Comparative Studies in Society and History* 31:134–161.

Strasser, Susan. 1982. *Never Done: A History of American Housework*. New York: Pantheon.

Strathern, Marilyn. 1980. No Gender:No Culture. In *Nature, Culture and Gender*, ed. C. MacCormack and M. Strathern, 174–222. Cambridge: Cambridge University Press.

————. 1984. Domesticity and the Denigration of Women. In *Rethinking Women's Roles: Perspectives from the Pacific,* ed. D. O'Brien and S. W. Tiffany, 13–31. Berkeley: University of California Press.

————. 1987. Introduction. In *Dealing with Inequality: Analysing Gender Relations in Melanesia and Beyond,* ed. M. Strathern, 1–32. Cambridge: Cambridge University Press.

Strobel, Margaret. 1987. Gender and Race in the Nineteenth- and Twentieth-Century British Empire. In *Becoming Visible: Women in European History,* ed. R. Bridenthal, C. Koonz, and S. Stuard, 2d ed., 375–396. Boston: Houghton Mifflin.

————. 1991. *European Women and the Second British Empire.* Bloomington: Indiana University Press.

Sutherland, Daniel E. 1981. *Americans and Their Servants: Domestic Service in the United States from 1800 to 1920.* Baton Rouge: Louisiana University Press.

Tobias, Sheila, and Ruth Milkman. 1987. *Gender at Work: The Dynamics of Job Segregtion by Sex during World War II.* Urbana: University of Illinois Press.

van Raaphorst, Donna L. 1988. *Union Maids Not Wanted: Organizing Domestic Workers 1870–1940.* New York: Praeger.

White, Landeg. 1987. *Magomero: Portrait of an African Village.* Cambridge: Cambridge University Press.

White, Luise. 1990. *The Comforts of Home: Prostitution in Colonial Nairobi.* Chicago: University of Chicago Press.

Wilson, Monica. 1972. The Wedding Cakes: A Study of Ritual Change. In *The Interpretation of Ritual: Essays in Honour of Audrey I. Richards,* ed. J. S. la Fontaine, 187–201. London: Tavistock.

Wright, Gwendolyn. 1980. *Moralism and the Model Home: Domestic Architecture and Cultural Conflict in Chicago 1873–1913.* Chicago: University of Chicago Press.

Part I

Varieties of African Domesticity

1 Home-Made Hegemony: Modernity, Domesticity, and Colonialism in South Africa

Jean and John L. Comaroff

It is not so much the reality of the home that is my subject as the idea of the home. . . .

Rybczynski (1986, viii)

Prologue

Witness a curious parallel between two turn-of-the-century pieces of social commentary. One, by the Nonconformist missionary Rev. W. C. Willoughby (1911, 70), describes the peoples of Bechuanaland. In it, he laments the impossibility of a "beautiful, healthy home-life" for "people who live in one-roomed mud-huts," and goes on to speak of the need to teach the natives how to build proper, civilized homes. The other, by Henry Jephson (1907, 31), sometime chief sanitary engineer of London, bemoans the condition of the urban poor in England:

> Physically, mentally and morally, the overcrowded people suffered . . . [and it] was usually at its worst in one-roomed tenements. . . . In one room they were born, and lived, and slept and died amidst the other inmates. . . . The consequences to the individual living in an overcrowded . . . dwelling were always disastrous.

Could the similarity in subject and tone have been mere coincidence, or did these texts have some historical link? Was there any connection between the aspirations of African missions and the exertions of London's sanitary supervisor? Between the effort to "improve" those who live[d] "in one-roomed mud-huts" on the imperial frontier and those who lived "in one-roomed tenements" at its core, within walking distance of the palace gates? Was the making of modern "home-life" in black South Africa—which is what Willoughby sought to justify—somehow implicated in the making of modern English society? Linking all these questions are three historical motifs: domesticity, modernity, and colonialism. Together they weave a compelling tale, a nineteenth-century narrative about the establishment of bourgeois hegemony in Europe and its overseas "possessions."

Precepts, Programs, and Problems

Several studies have argued recently that "the home"—as place or precept—has long been a crucial focus of European efforts to colonize Africa (e.g., Hansen 1989; Gaitskell 1983; Cock 1980), in particular, to instill "Western family ideology" (Hunt 1990, 449). But these studies have left a number of problems unresolved. Precisely *which* Western models of domesticity, for instance, were exported to the colonies? How stable and consensual were they in their own societies? Were they merely the vehicles of European "family ideology," or did they implicate more thoroughgoing social and cultural forces? And did the transformations wrought on the imperial fringe—which were distinctly variable—have any reciprocal impact on the colonizing world whence they came?

If we are to analyze the connection between domesticity and colonialism, then, we have first to situate the phenomenon of "domesticity" itself. This construct, Rybczynski (1986) reminds us, had its roots in the seventeenth century: it was with the demise of "the public, feudal household" that "the private family home" (49) began to seed itself as a generic European social and cultural form. Social historians now observe as commonplaces (1) that the emergence of a developed "domestic domain"—associated with women, unwaged housework, child raising, and the "private"—was a corollary of industrial capitalism (e.g., Davidoff and Hall 1987; Hall 1985; Morgan 1985; Hausen 1981; Darrow 1979); (2) that "domesticity" was integral to the cult of "modernity" at the core of bourgeois ideology; and (3) that, far from being a natural or universal social institution, it grew to maturity with the rise of the factory system, which entailed the reconstruction of relations of production, of personhood and value, of class and gender. Oakley (1974, 42f.) points out, however, that the "doctrine of (female) domesticity" had not spread far beyond the bourgeoisie before the 1840s. Only after 1841, with the call for the gradual withdrawal of women from industry (43), did this doctrine begin "to permeate downwards to the working classes" (50).

Of course, there remained great variation in actual patterns of family organization within and across the social strata of Europe (e.g., Pawley 1971, 6; cf. Stedman Jones 1971), a variation that persists today. But that is sociology. The ideological struggle to naturalize the doctrine of domesticity was, from the first, part of the middle-class endeavor to secure its cultural hegemony. As Gallagher (1985:passim) observes, it was a struggle that reverberated through the literary discourses of the age. We use the term "naturalize" advisedly here. The effort to disseminate the idea of domesticity was saturated with natural imagery, as Oakley (Ibid.:43–46) goes on to show: the report of the Royal Commission on the Mines (1842), for example, spoke of women workers as "disgusting and unnatural"; Engels ([1844] 1968, 160–161) added that factory toil deformed their bodies, making mothers liable to miscarry. In another genre, Charlotte Tonna's *The Wrongs of Woman* (1844) decried female employment for having "reversed the order of nature." If the likes of Foucault are correct, this process of naturalization was an element in the making of a total moral order, a silent edifice in which family and home served as internalized mechanisms of discipline and social control. The general argument states that vested in dispersed regimes of surveillance and in the texture of everyday habit, the doctrine of domesticity facilitated new forms of production, new structures of inequality. Nevertheless, we repeat, it did not prevail immediately or without resistance.

All this underscores the danger of assuming that a full-grown, stable model of "home life" was taken from Europe to the colonies. Nor can we safely assume, *pace* Fortes (e.g., 1978, 14f.), that "the domestic" may be conceptually freed from its historical context, presumed, that is, to be universal and thus to have existed in some form in precolonial Africa. In its precise English sense, "domesticity" connotes a particular order of values and dispositions. It cannot be used, without distortion, for *any* form of cohabitation, residence, and/or reproduction. In Africa and Europe alike the construction of the domestic world was a highly specific cultural and social project, invariably shaped by—and, in turn, itself influenced—the political worlds in which it occurred (J. L. Comaroff 1987).

But there is more to the matter than this. Carefully disinterred and read anew, the evidence suggests that colonialism itself, and especially colonial evangelism, played a vital part in the formation of modern domesticity *both* in Britain and overseas; that each became a model for, a mirror image of, the other; that historians have underplayed the encounter with non-Europeans in the development of Western ideas of modernity in general, and of "home" in particular. The imperial fringe, as Achebe (1978) points out, was an imaginative frontier on which Europe retooled its self-awareness, its metaphysical reflections on its own "nature." Scenes of distant battles with savagery, we shall see, became the cautionary currency of an urgent moral offensive in the urban "jungles" of Victorian Britain (Hebdige 1988, 20f.), where the poor were seen to be as uncivilized as the most beastly blacks in the bush.[1] Here lay the basis of a *dialectic* of domesticity, a simultaneous, mutually sustaining process of cultural reconstruction at home and abroad.

Unnatural Africa

In the late eighteenth century, Britain was caught up in a vigorous debate about humanity, reason, and civilization. It was a debate in which Africa occupied a singular symbolic place (Curtin 1964). In the varied discourses of modernity, themselves fuelled by the upheavals of the Age of Capitalism, the "dark continent" loomed as a negative trope, an inversion of all that had evolved toward enlightenment (Brantlinger 1985). Europe came to stand in relation to Africa as does the refined to the raw, light to dark, the knower to his object. In due course, this relationship took on an historical imperative: the blank spaces of the continent were to be mapped, the wild cultivated, the suffering saved.

The Nonconformist mission to South Africa was a product of this historical moment. Spawned by the great British revival of the period, the London and Wesleyan Methodist Missionary Societies (LMS and WMMS) sent agents into the interior in the early nineteenth century, and built permanent stations among the Southern Tswana in the 1820s. After the long sea voyage to the Cape, the churchmen trekked deep into the uncharted hinterland (cf. Beidelman 1982, 63), their tales of epic journeys coming to hold a special place in contemporary popular literature. For these writings added moral authority to the titillating images of otherness that framed the Victorian imagination—and ethical virtue to cultural imperialism.

The evangelical gaze perceived Africa as a "desert." This was due less to its climate than to the fact that it was preconceived as a moral wasteland. Its inhabitants, peoples of the wild, shared its qualities: unable to master their environment, they lacked all culture and history (cf. Ranger 1987). The popular accounts of early missionaries and travelers fostered this view: the "Bechuana" were incapable of proper cultivation, merely "scratching the surface" of the earth (Broadbent 1865, 105; Pratt 1985, 124). They covered themselves in "filthy animal fat and skins" rather than wearing clothes (Hughes 1841, 523) and "moped" in mud huts rather than living in houses (Moffat 1842, 507). In telling of "dreadful heathenism," the evangelists reserved special opprobrium for native domestic life—or, rather, its absence. Broadbent (1865, 204) wrote that they

> *had no marriage,* nor any proper domestic order, nor acknowledged any moral obligation to the duties arising out of that relation. Females were exchanged for others, bartered for cattle, given away as presents, and often discarded by the mere caprice of men.
>
> The misery arising out of this state of society cannot be easily described. . . . [Nor can the] absence of the proper domestic affections, and unnatural treatment of children.

One might well ask, "Whose misery? Whose happiness?" But such questions went unanswered: by this time, the image of "diseased, suffering Africa" was taken for granted in Europe (J. Comaroff n.d.). Indeed, the "dark continent" was more than just sick; it was considered downright unnatural. Satan had succeeded here in setting up his riotous realm, wiping clean the savage mind and corrupting the laws of nature.

During the 1820s the Tswana world was changing from both within and outside; the latter, in part, a result of the rise of the Zulu state and of long-distance trade with the Colony. For present purposes, however, its internal dynamics may be summarily described in terms of a few general principles.[2] Each chiefdom comprised a hierarchy of social and administrative units (households, family groups, wards, sections). All of these units were founded ultimately on the model of the polygamous family—itself made up of uterine houses[3]—and were ranked according to (often contested) agnatic rules of seniority. And all were bound to the chiefship by a complex set of connections at once substantial and symbolic. At the same time, the Tswana had a marked preference for marrying close kin, which limited the emergence of large descent corporations and bred a field of ambiguous, individuated social ties. Great onus was placed on families to forge social and material relations on their own account and to keep as free as possible from bonds of dependency. As a result, the forces of political centralization and hierarchy were countered by tendencies toward the dispersal and autonomy of households. This ensured that, anywhere and at any time, a variety of social forms existed on the landscape. Broadly speaking, the more centralized and hierarchical a chiefdom, the less independent were households, the more gender roles were marked, and the greater was male control; conversely, the less the degree of centralization, the more autonomous were households, the less marked was the sexual division of labor, and the more attenuated was male authority (J. L. Comaroff 1987).

Such variations notwithstanding, agriculture centered on the household: uterine houses were the primary units of cultivation, just as they were the primary units in the social and imaginative production of the political community. Women did most of the work—which, again, struck the evangelists as profoundly unnatural—and often cooperated with their own kin in the process. Given an uncertain ecology, farming had to be supplemented with gathering, both activities drawing mothers and their children away from the densely populated town for long periods. Rather than the bounded British "home," then, it was a matricentric group, with a radiating network of ties through females, that was the focus of material subsistence, reproduction, and nurture among contemporary Tswana.

The male world, by contrast, centered on the chiefly court. Here men participated in political and legal processes; here, too, they performed the communal rites on which depended the triumph of the state over the social and natural forces that threatened it. Their role in the division of labor was nothing less than the construction of the body social itself. It was a role that made little sense to the missionaries, however. In their eyes, Tswana men appeared distressingly indolent, lacking all ambition. The Europeans failed to see that the Africans engaged energetically in social management, mainly through the currency of cattle, the chief units of wealth, signs of status, and media of relationship.

Pastoralism, in fact, was male activity *par excellence:* it denoted forceful control over the wild. Agriculture, on the other hand, like female procreation, was fragile and perpetually endangered. No wonder the Christian idea of a civilized division of labor was greeted with astonishment; or that, in the early 1820s, some local women offered to plant fields for the benighted whites. Among Tswana, the objective of adult men was to own beasts and to transact the value embodied in them (Comaroff and Comaroff 1990), though day-to-day herding was done by their dependents, their "bushman" serfs, or their sons. By means of these beasts, they produced and reproduced the bonds that wove together the social fabric: through bridewealth they made marital ties, exchanging rights in women's labor and offspring; through the loan of stock they forged loyalties and relations of clientship; through sacrifice they communed with ancestors. In addition to accumulating allies and dependents, such exchanges transformed the yield of female fertility—grain to feed retainers, sons to tend herds, daughters to marry off—into social resources and value. Predictably, it was marginal men, those who lacked bovine capital, who were the first to be attracted by the mission.

It is clear why the evangelists, themselves drawn from the lower fringes of the rising British middle-class, saw African life as moral and social chaos (cf. Vilakazi 1962, 121). In violation of the bourgeois ideal of domesticity, Tswana houses were enmeshed in dense kinship networks and social units; marriages were bonds between groups; polygyny was no more than undignified promiscuity. Furthermore, the labyrinthine architecture of "native" homes and towns was palpable proof of the lack of clear boundaries in this strange society: boundaries between persons, their property, and their productive practices. Before all else, then, the missionaries would have to liberate would-be converts from the enchanted webs of their world, to domesticate the breeding grounds of savagery. In their restored Kingdom of God, marriage was to be a sacralized union between consenting, loving, and faithful individuals; the nuclear household was to be the basis of the family estate; male and female were to be associated, complementarily, with the public and the private, production and reproduction. After all, domestic order was meant to be a microcosm of both the church and the world. Wesleyans had long preached that, as the "husband is head of the wife," so "Christ is head of the Church" (Whitefield 1772, 185); and nineteenth-century social paternalism taught that "society could be regenerated by duplicating the family's benevolent hierarchy" (Gallagher 1985, 117). Moreover, proper domestic arrangements were held to be vested in specific forms of property. Flora Tristan, a remarkable nineteenth-century French feminist, noted in her *London Dairy* ([1840] 1980, 192) that this image of family life was a "far remove from reality." A "pretence" even among the wealthy, it had little purchase on the British working population. But such things did not stand in the way of its enthusiastic export to Africa.

Capturing Hearths and Minds: The Domestication of Satan's Kingdom

"The elevation of a people from a state of barbarism to a high pitch of civilization," wrote the Reverend John Philip (1828, 2:355), "supposes a revolution in [their] habits." Among the Tswana—who, complained Moffat (1842, 243), had not idols to shatter, no altars to seize, no fetishes to smash—this revolution had to be won on the diffuse terrain of everyday life.[4] If colonial evangelism was going "to turn the [heathen] world upside down" (Moffat 1842, 235–236), it would have to do so by reforming the minutiae of practical existence. And so the churchmen set about staging a matter-of-fact theater of Protestant industry in which they set forth the mode of rural production through which they hoped to remake Tswana society. Thus, soon after he arrived among the Tlhaping, James Read erected a house, making sure that he was widely observed: "Had great numbers of people flocking to see [the spectacle]," he reported, "which was as a wonder to all."[5] When he finished, he set up a forge and began to fashion ploughshares, the biblically valued tools of peasant agriculture with which Tswana families might one day make a "proper" livelihood.[6]

It is no coincidence that this early performance featured the building of a house. According to Nonconformist ideology, all self-conscious improvement was rooted in the elementary forms of life: the habits of hearth and home. These, said the churchmen repeatedly, were the key to the epic task of bringing Africa into the modern world—and, not incidentally, into the British Empire. No usage was too unimportant, no activity too insignificant to escape the stern gaze of the civilizing mission. Charity, for the English middle classes, might begin at home. For colonial evangelists, it began by giving heathens the idea of home. The basis of universal civility was bourgeois domesticity.

The missionary effort to create domesticity from degeneracy took many forms. And it had many consequences, some of them unforeseen. Here we consider two related aspects of the enterprise: the attempt to remake the realm of production and the effort to recast the tangible shape of the "home." Our focus is not arbitrary: the rise of domesticity—however much contested (Gallagher 1985, 113–146)—involved the convergence of two conceptual planes, one socioeconomic and the other architectural. For "the domestic" (1) connoted a social group (the family) whose interrelated roles composed the division of labor at the core of "civilized" economy and society; and

(2) presupposed a physical space (the "private" household) that was, in principle, clearly marked and bounded.

It thus made perfect sense that, in building their kingdom on a firm domestic foundation, the evangelists would work to institute the practices and forms that were its icons and instruments. As John Philip (1828, 2:72–73) put it, the sacred task of the civilizing mission was to "[get Africans] to build houses, inclose gardens, cultivate corn land, accumulate property, and . . . [increase] their artificial wants." As this suggests, the Nonconformists had a clear appreciation of the vital role of production in forging persons and relations; from their theological standpoint, self, society, and salvation were a laborious human construction. However, being at the vanguard of colonialism, they had little with which to realize their vision save the tools of persuasion.

As a result, the churchmen had no choice but to build from the bottom up—on humble, homely ground. But this ground was already host to the architectural forms of Tswana production and procreation. For the Africans, too, the "house" (*ntlo*) was an elemental structure; a sign in concrete (or, rather, clay) of the relations within it and the ties that radiated outward from it. Although very different from its British counterpart, it also condensed the values inscribed in a particular cultural context. Thus, as both a social and a physical entity, the "house" was destined to be a major site of challenge and contest, of the complex encounter between Africa and Europe. The dialectic of domesticity was to play itself out in various ways within Tswana communities. Some would emulate white ways, others would appropriate them piecemeal, and a few would refuse them outright. The patterns were complex: mission converts were not beyond reproducing "traditional" forms, while self-conscious "traditionalists" often conjured with those forms in creative ways. Nonetheless, although unanticipated, these patterns were far from random: the manner in which Tswana engaged with European signs and practices turned out to be closely connected to emerging lines of social difference in this part of South Africa.

Moral Economics, Material Signs

To the missionary eye, at home in the bounded and enclosed English countryside, the Tswana landscape appeared uncontained and unfixed. Biblical Hebrews might have been nomadic pastoralists, but modern civilization was built on a solid foundation of immovable wealth. "Shifting" peoples were "shifty," inherently incapable of sustaining a lawful society based on individual rights and stable families (Muldoon 1975). The relative mobility of the Tswana, their complex territorial arrangements, and the transhumance of women during the agricultural cycle thwarted the evangelists from the beginning and offended their sense of order. As Dr. Philip told his colleagues in 1830, "When men have no settled homes . . . it is easy for them to desert the means of instruction on any provocation" (Macmillan 1929, 76). The civilizing mission thus encouraged its subjects to take possession of the land by investing themselves in it, anchoring themselves through their labor and the weight of domestic possessions.

For the churchmen, cultivation was almost synonymous with salvation. The belief in the civilizing role of horticulture was as old as English colonialism itself: in the seventeenth century, Spenser had advocated a settled agrarian existence for the "wild Irish"; their "barbarous and warlike" state, he said, was due to their seminomadic pastoralism (Muldoon 1975, 275). Similar notions were carried to the peoples of Africa, whose devotion to cattle keeping was taken as proof of their primitiveness: agriculture would cultivate the worker as he cultivated the land—and then sold his produce to the market. Tswana were to be encouraged to grow sufficient surpluses to link them through trade with Christian Europe (cf. Bundy 1979, 39); this, believed the evangelists, would put them on the universal path to progress, albeit many paces behind white Britons. The model here was the much-romanticized English yeomanry, sturdy independent peasants who had been devastated during the Age of Revolution.

Significantly, when the mission tried to place plows in the hands of Tswana males, and to consign females to "indoor" housework and childraising, it was the women who first resisted. Their anxieties were well-founded: largely through the actions of the Christians, they were to lose control over agrarian production and its harvest. This change in the division of labor was meant to replicate the ideal of gentility that had enclosed bourgeois European women in idle domestic seclusion while their poorer sisters remained in the "male" labor market as devalued beings. The Africa of which the churchmen dreamed might have evoked a vanishing yeomanry at home, a rural peasant idyll. But Nonconformist ideology grew out of the industrial revolution. It presupposed a social order that divided sharply between production and reproduction, public and private, maximization and moral nurture, male and female.

The evangelists' determination to "buy" the land that they cultivated reflected their origins in a caplitalist culture. The Tswana made it quite clear that, in the circumstances, this was a meaningless gesture. But the Europeans wished to ensure that their venture was legitimately founded on the laws of private property.[7] Once they had acquired the land, they set about enclosing and planting it: the irrigated garden was held up as an example to the Africans, and came to stand as an icon of the civilizing mission at large. Within its fenced confines were enacted the principles of "proper" production, rooted in material individualism: the creation of value by means of self-possessed *male* labor, the forceful domination of nature, and the accumulation of surplus through a rational expenditure of effort. Recalled Broadbent (1865, 104–105):

> I and my colleague had each enclosed a plot of ground, which we had . . . cleared of weeds, and then sown with Kaffir corn, which we had obtained from the natives, and with sweet cane and various kinds of beans, also melons and pumpkins. . . . These vegetables grew much more luxuriantly, and were more productive, in our grounds than theirs. One day a number of respectable natives came to ask the reason of this difference. . . .
>
> My first answer was, "Your idleness. . . . [W]e have dug the ground ourselves; you leave it to your women. We dig deep into the soil; they only scratch the surface. . . . Our seed is protected from the sun and nourished by the moisture in the ground; yours is parched with the heat of the sun, and, therefore, not so productive as ours." I added "Work yourselves, as you see we do, and dig the ground properly, and your seed will flourish as well as ours."

The mission garden, in short, was not just a lesson in the contrast of labor and idleness. It also taught the difference between male and female work. The Nonconformists continued to insist that African production was "topsy-turvy" (Crisp 1896, 16). To them, as we have said, Tswana men appeared to be lazy "lords of creation" (Moffat 1842, 505); women, on the other hand, "scratched" desultorily on the face of the earth, much like uncomprehending "beasts of burden" (Kinsman 1983), since they did what was properly masculine labor. Rather than till fields neatly tied to a family home, they took themselves to lands well beyond the settlement for days on end, where their efforts were unregulated by their menfolk.[8] There was no sign here of the "healthy, individualistic competition," the self-possession, and the conservation of time and effort that the churchmen saw as righteous industry. To the contrary, "communistic relations" were everywhere in evidence (Mackenzie; in Dachs 1972, 652).

Determined to instruct by example, the evangelist and his wife made themselves into metonyms of the European division of labor. Livingstone (1857, 22) talks of "the accomplishments of a missionary in Central Africa, namely, the husband to be a jack-of-all-trades without doors, and the wife a maid-of-all-work within." Here lay the key both to civilizing reform and to the problem of the displaced, uncontained black female: many Tswana women were to be confined to home and family, and many were indeed to be maids in modern South Africa. The missions stressed that female nature was designed for the backstage work of nurture, caring for the bodies and souls of those whose destiny lay in the rough-and-tumble public world. For his part, the Tswana male was exhorted to pursue his rightful occupation in his field over which, as "yeoman" and "breadwinner," he was called upon to assert his mastery.

The first reaction of the Tswana to the mission garden was to steal its fruit. In the early days at least, its bounty was seen to flow from the innate powers of the evangelists themselves. Among the Rolong, for instance, men vied to have their wives cultivate fields next to the fertile WMMS plots.[9] But the Christians persisted in offering new agricultural techniques and, in time, the Tswana began to differentiate these forces of production from the personal potency of their owners. First came the well and irrigation ditch, next the plow, each being as vital to the Protestant moral order as it was to the material basis of the civilizing mission. Both were used to draw the "fitful and disorderly heathen" into settled communities founded on private property and a new, domestically ordered division of labor (Shillington 1985, 17).

Central to this process of transformation was the perceived need to recast indigenous concepts of time. The evangelists began at once to break into the cycle of seasons and communal rites, and tried to disrupt the so-called cattle clock, the reckoning of diurnal rhythms with reference to practical tasks. (For example, the Tswana term for "evening" was *maitseboa*, "when they [the cattle] returned home.") To churchmen, any notion of temporality tied to mundane routines was unable to accomodate transcendant visions of history and salvation. It was also unsusceptible to mission control. For the Europeans, time was primarily an abstract thing in itself. An objective medium capable of reducing all mankind to a common measure of fate, it had the power to order or subsume events, was a commodity to be "spent" in the cause of self-improvement, and served as a standard of value that allowed labor to be sold in the market. Africans, said the churchmen, were intrinsically indolent, tardy, and irrational in its use, as were the premodern producers and the neophyte proletarians of Europe (Thompson 1967; Weber 1958, 63; cf. Alatas 1977). The civilizing mission hoped to make them march to the grand imperial clock, and synchronize their domestic schedules to serve the fixed agendas of public domain: the workplace, the school, and the church.

All this presupposed a world of commodities and wage labor; bourgeois family ideology, after all, was both an effect and a cause of the consolidation of capitalism in Europe. It did not take long for the missions to introduce market forces to the Tswana or to teach them the meaning of "real" work. Not only were the LMS and WMMS the earliest employers in the region, making much use of black toil in the building of their stations; they were also conduits of the first sustained commerce (LMS 1830, 86; Tilby 1914, 192). By 1830, their reports noted that many "natives" were "becoming industrious," and that more sought work than could be hired (Livingstone 1857, 46). For all their talk of creating a God-fearing peasantry, the churchmen were laying the basis for the alienation of Tswana men from the local economy by, among other things, making them receptive to wage work. In due course, the family "home" here took on features familiar in proletarian Europe, serving as a female-serviced dormitory for males who labored elsewhere. It also became a workplace for those women tempted or pressed to commodify their new domestic skills. As soon as English dress became a requirement for converts, for instance, seamstresses began to sew for pay (Moffat 1967, 17).

In the short run, the civilizing mission and its material innovations were bound to run into difficulties. Given their division of labor, with its rigid separation of pastoralism from cultivation, Tswana were unlikely to show enthusiasm for hitching the beast to the plow, which was demanded by the new technology. Indeed, since women were debarred from managing stock, this technology called for a thorough reorganization of relations of production. In the event, most men only turned serious attention to mission agriculture after *difaqane*—the upheavals in the wake of the rise of the

Zulu state—had disrupted the local economy, and the viability of hunting and foraging had begun to decline (Tilby 1914, 193; Broadbent 1865, 105; also Shillington 1985, 17). Of course, only those with sufficient cattle could even consider using plows; and only they could profit from transporting surpluses and trade goods to distant markets. Among the Southern Tswana, it was thus junior royals who became the first members of the Christian peasant elite.

In the longer term, the plow overtook the hoe in all Tswana communities (Parsons 1977, 123); its capacity to increase the productivity of agriculture, especially in this ecology, was not liable to go unnoticed by a people with a keen interest in the accumulation of practical knowledge. In addition, the evangelists soon induced traders to settle on their stations and to supply British commodities—farming equipment, wagons, and clothing in particular (Northcott 1961, 148). The impact on cultivation, among those willing and able to use the new technology, was striking. So greatly did arable outputs rise that, by 1844, Dutch farmers were leaving "the colony . . . to purchase [Tswana] wheat" (Broadbent 1865, 106). But there was another side to this: as drought and disease threatened the cattle economy, and as an ever-increasing amount of pasturage was brought under cultivation, emerging elites gained control of a disproportionate amount of land, including the best acreages around water sources (Shillington 1985, 62). The material bases of inequality were being dramatically and irrevocably recast in the image of commodity production.

Mission agriculture did more than force a distinction between a class of commercial farmers and a growing mass of dispossessed families. In reconstructing relations of production, it also altered the role of females and their kin in the social division of labor. As the evangelists had hoped, "the work of the gardens cease[d] to belong to the women" (Mackenzie 1871, 70), who were reduced to doing the menial tasks of tending and reaping. Men seized control over the harvest, cut it loose from family consumption, and sold it (Kinsman 1983). Freed from communal obligation and tempted by new commodities, most marketed as much grain as possible. In so doing, they greatly depleted household resources—to the extent that, fearing famine, some chiefs tried to limit sales (Schapera 1943, 203). Commercially oriented farmers grew reluctant to share with dependents or to invest in domestic brewing and hospitality; their status was now vested in other sorts of transactions and in private property. The families of the wealthy became ever more bounded, ever more nuclear. Simultaneously, accounts of destitution, especially among older women and children, became more common.

The Benthamite goal of advancement through commodity production and trade, then, was achieved by reducing a growing number of Tswana to economic dependency (Kinsman 1983, 39f.). Overtaken by an increasingly dominant class of farmers, who continued to enhance their royal privilege by applying agrarian techniques learned from the mission (Mackenzie 1871, 70),[10] many were never able to own plows, could not irrigate, and gradually lost access to adequate land. Others were caught in between: while they struggled to acquire the wherewithall for commercial agriculture, they found it hard to produce even small surpluses. By the late 1870s, the destruction of natural resources was driving more and more of them into the labor market. The process was yet further accelerated by the predations of settlers on their land and stock (Shillington 1985, 99f.).

Among the Tshidi-Rolong, another Southern Tswana people, it was the industrious Christian community at Mafikeng that made most use of irrigation and the plow. White visitors found the town a "pleasing" sight, with recognizable "enclosures" and "farmsteads." By 1877, although constantly harassed by Boers, it supported considerable plow agriculture and its wealthier citizens, some of the royals, were thoroughly familiar with money and western commodities (Holub 1881, 2:13). Their houses, built in colonial style, reflected not merely the growing importance of "Christian family life" (see 52). They also signaled a standard of living far above that of the general population: despite its overall "progress," the community was undergoing rapid internal differentiation. This process was to be exacerbated by bitter regional conflict and, in the 1890s, by rinderpest and drought, which seriously eroded local agriculture. While the economy did not collapse altogether, the turn of the twentieth century saw most families dependant on the labor market for survival. Only the wealthiest survived with fortunes intact. This small elite stood in stark contrast to the impoverished majority and to the shrinking proportion of those trapped somewhere in between.

As a result, while the technological innovations of the mission gave rise to a class of commercial farmers, the plow brought most Tswana a harvest of hunger. It also ushered in an era in which *all* Tswana would have to turn toward the market, orienting themselves to the culture and material conditions of commodity production. But an ever greater number would have to do so as laborers.

Having come, many years before, to recreate the lost British yeomanry, the Christians had laid the ground for an army of peasant
proletarians caught in a promiscuous web of economic dependency.

The impact of colonial evangelism on the Southern Tswana division of labor, in sum, varied along the emerging axes of social class.
Only the affluent could sustain domestic arrangements that, according to mission ideology, were "civilized." As migrant labor fractured
the households of the rank and file, relict wives and daughters
reassumed responsibility for what survived of local agriculture.
Those who remained at home had much to gain from cooperative
practices; as we shall see, their life-styles continued to express the
salience of agnatic and matrilateral relations. But new principles of
domestic collaboration arose as well, such as those of small, tightly
knit Zionist churches, whose female-headed households clustered
around the headquarters of male charismatic leaders (J. Comaroff
1985, 199). As this implies, while Nonconformist family ideology was
to influence those outside the small elite, it was also to be widely
contested. Even in the 1960s, residents of old Mafikeng, with its circular homes and wards, spoke disparagingly of people who rented
square, fenced houses in the nearby "Government" township and
worked in the wage economy. Their satirical jibes—that these people
were "naked" like "plucked birds," lacking "the shelter of a homestead wall"—offered a lively critique of the discrete, self-reliant domestic unit of bourgeois orthodoxy.

The terms of this subversive rhetoric suggest a close association, in
Tswana consciousness, between the forms of housing and the force of
habit, between architecture and the socioeconomic arrangements of
domestic life. Whatever their precolonial legacy, the Africans were
powerfully affected by the churchmen's assumption that bounded
dwellings begat bourgeois domesticity and all that it entailed. In
order to explore the role of built form in the colonial encounter, let us
return to the early moments of the civilizing mission.

The Architecture of Modernity

The design of Tswana towns and villages was an immediate
obstacle to the evangelists' goal of establishing a stable, European-
like peasantry. Indigenous settlements, some of them as large as
Cape Town (Barrow 1806, 404), seemed a "bewildering maze" (Moffat 1842, 274) of circuitous pathways and courtyards. "Bechuanas,"
noted Philip (1828, 2:126), "are very partial to the figure of the

circle. Their houses are all of a circular form; [towns are] composed of a series of concentric lines." Like cultural imperialists elsewhere (cf. Levi-Strauss 1972, 204), the churchmen sought from the first to impose the square on the "primitive" arc. They were determined to rationalize the undifferentiated chaos of "native" society by laying upon it the rectangular grid of civilization (Comaroff and Comaroff 1986, 13). Observed Livingstone (1857, 26):

> Bakwains [Kwena] have a curious inability to make or put things square: like all Bechuanas, their dwellings are made round. In the case of three large houses, erected by myself at different times, every brick had to be put square by my own right hand.

The right hand of civilization would try unceasingly to reorder the Tswana sense of space and line; to wit, evangelists came to judge the march of progress by the rectilinear extension of fence and furrow, hedge and homestead, across African soil. Cameron records the first impact of the town of Thaba 'Nchu on the missionary gaze (Broadbent 1865, 189):

> Here he sees a vast assemblage of houses teeming with inhabitants. This [is] widely different from a European town. No splendid fanes, or spires, no public buildings to serve the ends of either justice or benevolence, greet the heavens; a heap of Bechuana huts jostled together without any apparent order, and their indispensable appendages, cattle-folds, make up the scene.

This scape, a jumble of human and animal life, lacked the contrasts on which rested true refinement: the heights of spirituality and justice, the separation of private and public, the marks of individuated property. Neat four-sided cottages were urgently needed to close off nuclear families and their possessions in indoor privacy; only there would they be safe from the indecent flux of heathen life (cf. Krige and Krige 1943, 318 on the Lovedu). To the Christians, Tswana living arrangements were not only unaesthetic; they were unhealthy. Wrote Mackenzie (1833, 222–223):

> viewed from the adjoining mountain, the town . . . is really beautiful. But however charming in the distance, it is not at all pleasant to thread those narrow, winding, and gourd-shaded lanes . . . I found the atmosphere of the town to be quite oppressive, and constantly wondered that cases of fever were not even more numerous.

In the rhetoric of nineteenth-century reformers, social disorder was associated with disease, the latter being not merely an issue of dirt but also of the improper distribution of bodies in space (Foucault 1973). The absence of well-bounded and visibly distinct persons, families, and habitations—or the presence of "winding paths" rather than rational roads—was often dubbed "unhygienic," even, despite all the evidence to the contrary, "unhealthy" (J. Comaroff n.d.).

In this regard, the missionaries saw building and clothing as two sides of a single coin. They set about reforming Tswana dress along with their dwellings; seeking at once to contain the "greasy" black body in "clean, decent" habits and habitations (Moffat 1842, 287). Cleanliness was taken to be a sociomoral condition: Africa was unbounded rather than merely unwashed (cf. Burke n.d.). Together, European architecture and attire would enclose it and embrace it in an enlightened order of production and reproduction. Thus freed from entropic entanglements, Africans might build civilized relations through the circulation of modern media: commodities, money, and printed words. Recall that Read's first act, on arrival among the Tlhaping, was to build a home, a "wonder for all to see"; he then offered to erect an identical one for the chief's wife. The mission garden might have introduced Tlhaping to Christian ideas of productive toil. But it was in the "home" that they would learn to dispose of its yield through responsible habits.

From the outset, the mission, with its church, house, and garden, was the irreducible atom of Christian society. When they arrived, remembers Edwards (1886, 101), evangelists had to "rough it," living in wagons and then in rudimentary residences. Yet the architecture of even the most simple station already laid out the basic design of a world conceived in the image of modern Europe. This design was built on a fundamental principle of space and time: that order and refinement inheres in functional separation and specificity. Thus the domestic should be set off from the public, the religious from the secular; similarly, sleeping and "sitting," cooking and dining, each required a discrete place. Even the missionary's wagon—with its private interior, its communal exterior, and its black staff of guides and laborers—anticipated this principle. On it rested the bourgeois notion of advancement, both within and outside the home. Hence the distressing implications of families living primitively "all in one room" (see 37f.).

Would-be converts were told repeatedly that minimal Christian living standards had to be signaled in their dwellings and dress; the internal transformations assumed to be taking place inside them and their families had to be played out on socially legible surfaces, for all to read. But there was more at issue than just the expression of change. Anticipating Bourdieu (1977) by more than a century, the evangelists believed that "houses" literally constructed their inhabitants, that their functionally specific spaces laid out the geometry of cleanliness and godliness. By contrast, "huts" and "hovels," undifferentiated within and made of all but raw materials, were brutish and transient—like filthy nests in the bush (cf. Ranger 1987). Most Tswana, it turned out, were not enamored of European architecture. Their round houses, like their cloaks, would remain undivided in form and function for a long time to come.

The churchmen persisted nonetheless, and tried actively to assist the Tswana with the practical adoption of "modern" built forms. Before traders arrived with commercial materials, they advocated reshaping local substances—clay, oxhide, and powdered anthills—into square houses on enclosed lots. They stressed the value of doors that locked, ensuring the security of possessions, and windows that let in light (Tilby 1914, 192; Broadbent 1865, 61). The latter were especially important. Glass, as we have written (Comaroff and Comaroff 1991, chap. 5), was the portal of civilization for post-Enlightenment Europeans. The mission sought to use its illuminating influence, thereby to penetrate the dark interiors of Africa and encourage the "domesticating" pursuits of reading and sewing. Behind secure walls, the inward-looking Protestant person would be cultivated in private, albeit under the all-seeing eye of God.

Tswana women had formerly been responsible for most building and men for sewing and shoemaking. But those who fell within the orbit of the evangelists were pressed to reverse this "unnatural" arrangement. While mission wives set about teaching local females to stitch and cook, males learned the basic crafts of "civilized" housebuilding, notably carpentry and iron-working.[11] All this of course implied a new relationship to goods and commodities: once merchants set up shop in the mid 1830s, they catered to a range of wants fostered in families with an altered perception of domestic space and time—and with an awakened sense of private property. Wrote Moffat (1842, 507) approvingly of the early converts:

> Formerly a chest, a chair, a candle, or a table, were things unknown, and supposed to be only the superfluous accompaniments of beings of another order. . . . [W]hen they had milked their cows, they retired to their houses and yards, to sit moping over a few

embers; . . . at night, spreading the dry hide of some animal on the
floor. . . . They soon found to read in the evening or by night required a more steady light. . . . Candle moulds and rags for wicks
were now in requisition, and tallow carefully preserved, . . . an indi-
cation of the superior light which had entered their abodes.

European goods had opened a space in which the habits of the bourgeois home might take root. New furnishings, like new architecture,
would lift the Tswana out of their dirty, unreflective existence. Or so
said the missionaries, who had sensed that commodities had the
power to socialize. Indeed, the logic of the market, and the infinitely
growing wants that drive it, played an integral role in colonial evangelism. A steadily expanding range of clothes and household objects
was made available to Tswana in the late nineteenth century, both by
rural merchants and by urban retailers catering to the black migrant
trade (Schapera 1947, 228f.). Although they later became wary of the
dangers of "vanity," at first the churchmen blatantly encouraged com-
petitive consumption (Mary Moffat 1967, 19). Certain key items—
among them, candles, iron bedsteads, and soap—carried great
weight as signs and instruments of Christian domesticity (Schapera
1936, 247; Burke n.d.). But other goods such as apparel, hand mirrors,
umbrellas, and toiletries were also seen as "tools" for remaking body
and self in the Protestant image (cf. Hannerz 1983).

The bourgeois home was only one element, albeit the most fundamental, in the order of institutions that made up civilized society. As
we have already intimated, early mission stations, the coordinates
on a European map slowly unfurling across the interior, were built
to be microcosms of that society. At mid-century an observer described Kuruman, the first LMS outpost, as a "village," with superior stone houses "thatched in the Devonshire style"; a wagon house,
a smith, and carpenter's shop; a school and printing office; a mer-
chant establishment and fenced gardens; "all lined up on either side
of a dead straight street" (Burrow [ed Kirby] 1971, 33f.). Slowly the
mission was gaining in complexity, its scale dwarfing the surrounding settlements with the shapes and routines of a colonial frontier
town.

Such towns proclaimed the emerging division of labor in their
spatial arrangements. Places of worship were set off from those of
secular pursuits, sites of work from those of leisure, the public from
the private. All, however, were integrated into rational bourgeois
routines and a universal calendar. Time was literally built into the

LMS and WMMS churches from the start: their chiming clocks and school bells punctuated the daily round, coordinating household with communal rhythms (cf. Wilson 1971, 73; Oliver 1952, 52). Thus the secular schedules of the British schoolroom complemented the religious order of Sunday services, weekly classes, quarterly communions, and annual feasts; together they imposed a temporal grid upon domestic life (J. Comaroff 1985, 141). In his first letters from the field, Broadbent (1865, 86f.) expressed concern that, for heathens, "every day was alike." In less than a year he noted with pride that Sunday had become "as quiet and still as in England."

For all the exertions of the evangelists, the transformation of the Tswana world was not a straightforward affair; nor was it pliantly accepted. In fact, the battle over built form became implicated in a highly complex historical process. By the 1850s, colonial penetration had ensured that many Southern Tswana were living within the shadow of the mission, which had interpolated itself between black and white on the frontier. Given that the power of the Protestants was seen to inhere in *sekgoa* ("European ways"), it is not surprising that some local men learned the craft of European construction, or that a growing number of "traditional" dwellings began to include windows, doors, and fences—features that altered received relations between inner and outer, private and communal space. In Kuruman, wealthy Christians had put up "good houses of stone, stone-walled gardens and cornfields" (Read 1850, 446)—which connoted stability and domestic containment, and bespoke the strength of their owners. On the other hand, Anthony Trollope (1878, 2:279f.), who visited the capital of the Seleka at Thaba 'Nchu in the late 1870s, reported that, although "dressed like whitemen," royals lived in homesteads constituted of round mud huts, smeared courtyards, and circular brush fences. For the most part, however, the designs of *sekgoa* were appropriated selectively, as if to deploy their power to local ends. Even in 1970, one-roomed mudbrick "huts," intricate earthen homesteads, and semicircular wards still dominated most Tswana towns. They overshadowed the weather-beaten colonial houses dotted over the landscape, themselves an epitaph to the mission dream of a prosperous black peasantry.

Indeed, vernacular architecture remained the most durable abode of *setswana* ("Tswana ways"). Given the political ecology of local chiefdoms, missions had no option but to situate themselves in large towns and villages; as a result, their followers lived at home, not in communities set apart. By contrast, stations among the more scattered Nguni were built on open terrain between hamlets. Here "conversion" entailed a tangible movement, Christians leaving their extended family compounds; hence a wedge was driven between converts and conservatives (Etherington 1978, 117). In the case of the Tswana, other than for those who lived alongside the mission, the path to church and school traced out a journey between two worlds: between *setswana,* itself linked ever more to a marked "domestic" domain (*mo gae,* translated as "at home"), and *sekgoa,* increasingly the culture of the white public realm. While colonial evangelism certainly reached deep into domestic life, the churchmen were correct in their perception that Tswana architecture served to perpetuate an order of values and routines that flourished in spaces beyond their influence.

Thus, although features of Western architecture and domestic styles were assimilated during the nineteenth century, the process was very uneven—if not, as we shall see, historically random. Perhaps the best evidence, at least for the late nineteenth century, comes from a photographic essay by Rev. Willoughby (n.d.). Intended to popularize the work of the LMS, its pictures do not focus intentionally on buildings; nevertheless, they provide revealing images of "Native Life on the Transvaal Border." These show that, by 1899, a tripartite scheme of architectural forms had emerged, each associated with a distinct type of domestic group. At one extreme were "traditional" dwellings, which lacked windows, doors, or other Western features, and were always part of larger compounds; in the households of wealthy Christian families, such structures, where they were still found, were used as "outhouses" for storage or sleeping accommodation for young children. In this century they have become the architectural counterpart of "heathen dress," embodiments of devalued "custom." At the other extreme were the residences of the rich, which were barely distinguishable from those of the burghers of white towns in the interior; they centered on a nuclear family with its few dependents and servants. Between the two were the synthetic structures of the majority, whose homesteads, with their mazes of courtyards and hearths, proclaimed the continuing relevance in daily life of agnatic and matrilateral ties. Still single-roomed, these mudbrick houses were now square and had flat roofs, windows, and other European fixtures bought with the wages of migrant labor.

In short, most habitations, like family arrangements, gave expression to the simultaneous incorporation and yet marginalization of the Tswana within the Kingdom of God and Great Britain. They spoke of the status of their owners as peasant proletarians, of the creation, on the colonial fringe, of a new bricolage out of older forms of production and reproduction, "public" and "home" life. The architecture dominant among rural Tswana today still bears some imprint of Nonconformist ideas of property and privacy, domestic space and time. Yet, as with other cultural items, these have been fashioned by the rank and file into new ensembles of aesthetic and material practices, ensembles neither bourgeois nor "traditional."

Reflections: Domesticating the Tribes of London and Liverpool

As we noted in the introduction to this chapter, the campaign of the African mission to instill a particular idea of home was only one side of the way the dialectic of European domesticity played itself out. The other was the effort by the bourgeoisie and the evangelists who essayed its ideology to mobilize Africa in the cause of remaking the British underclasses, to hold up the "dark continent" as a negative image with which to damn its own peasants and proletarians. This presumed a likeness, even a structural equivalence, between the benighted back home and the aborigines abroad. The presumption was often put into words, both on the colonial frontier and in the metropolis. Missionaries and travelers in early nineteenth-century South Africa were quick to associate indigenous communities with peripheral peoples in Britain. Said John Philip (1828, 2:70): in "intelligence and morals," Griqua "bear a comparison with . . . the peasantry of England." Clearly both groups remained far from the pinnacle of progress. Both, thought Philip, could do with the ministrations of the civilizing mission. He went on (316–317):

> We are all born savages, whether we are brought into the world in the populous city or in the lonely desert. It is the discipline of education, and the circumstances under which we are placed, which create the difference between the rude barbarian and the polished citizen—the listless savage and the man of commercial enterprise. . . . [In South Africa] we see, *as in a mirror*, the features of our own progenitors. . . . [our italics]

As this implies, it was within the exploding nineteenth-century city that the bourgeoisie met with its most immediate experience of alien unreason. The poor of London and Liverpool, went the common lament, were indeed closer to rude barbarians than to refined burghers. Their foetid, fitful presence threatened to contaminate the citadels of the middle class, to pollute all that was sane and sanitary (Jephson 1907). Hebdige (1988, 20) notes that the scourge of polite society were youthful "street urchins" and "nomads" who were often compared to African savages. We are reminded, in particular, of Mayhew's (1851) classic account of costermongers (poor street traders). Younger costers wore beaver-skin hats and moleskin collars—just as, it was said, Tswana wore greasy animal hides.[12] Both shunned civilized clothing of "cotton and woollen manufacture." Furthermore, "eyewitness" reports (e.g., Garwood 1853; Hollingshead 1861) suggest that the lack of a settled home life among these destitute youths made them seem like the "wandering tribes" of "unknown continents" (Hebdige 1988, 21); their plight justified "the growing moral impetus towards the education, reform and civilisation of the working-class masses." Echoes of colonial evangelism could not be more audible. Interestingly, James Greenwood's popular travels in *The Wilds of London* (1874) were guided by a missionary, from whose house in the dark innards of the city beamed the light of Christianity. The pastor's effort to "improve" the slum people—especially their domestic lives—surfaces as a subtext in the narrative. Nor was Greenwood unusual. The figure of the civilizing missionary appears in many tales of urban Britain, voyeuristic adventures and philanthropic manifestos alike. We shall return to him.

Significantly, writers like Mayhew (1851) and Greenwood (1874) portrayed themselves as "social explorers";[13] the former, in fact, introduced himself (p.iii) as a "traveller in the undiscovered country of the poor." In so doing, they evoked a parallel with the geographical mission abroad, the exploratory project in which Europeans visited remote parts of the world, "discovered" them, and brought them within the compass of intellectual and material control. This recalls Stedman Jones's (1971, 14) comment about the poverty-stricken districts of London: "a *terra incognita* periodically mapped out by intrepid missionaries and explorers who catered to an insatiable middle-class demand for travellers' tales." Note that the goal of *The Association for Promoting the Discovery of the Interior Parts of Africa,* formed in the late eighteenth century, had been to "penetrate the *terra incognita* of the globe" (*The Monthly Review,* 1790 (2): 60–68). Note also that the products of its expeditions, most famously

Mungo Park's *Travels* (1799), fed the same appetite for adventure, exoticism, and the pornography of others' suffering. These were precursors of mass-circulation abolitionist and evangelical writings,[14] part of the popular literary fare of bourgeois Britain.

The connections between accounts of Africa and those of the poor in England varied in their explicitness and elaboration. Often the mere use of metaphors in otherwise unconnected descriptions conjured up potent parallels: talk of urban "jungles"—in which the poor lived, like "wandering tribes," in "nests" and "human warrens"— brought the dark contintent disconcertingly close to home (see, e.g., Hollingshead 1861, 8, 165). Sometimes, however, the parallelism was less a matter of lexicon than genre. A striking instance is to be found in another text by Greenwood, published before *The Wilds*. In his *Seven Curses of London* (1869), he describes a "strange observance" in the vicinity of the Cow Cross Mission (20). The evangelist there had seen many "instances of this strange custom; but even he, who is as learned in the habits and customs of all number of outcasts of civilization as any man living, was unable to explain its origin." The "strange observance" was the display by many a couple of their marriage certificate on the livingroom wall, under a clock if they had one. Given the low rate of matrimony among the poor, the centrality of the conjugal family in bourgeois morality, and the role of the clock in marking work-time, the symbolism of the practice is hardly mysterious. To be sure, the joining of these tokens of respectability gives graphic evidence of the impact of philanthropic efforts to reform domestic values, to place legitimate marriage under the regime of responsible self-regulation. But even more salient here is the fact that this passage might easily have come from Moffat (1842) or Livingstone (1857), or other missionary accounts. Its distancing, objectifying style, its synthesis of the tropes of ethnography (habits, customs) and evangelism (civilization), of science (learning, explanation) and moralism (outcasts), conveyed a cogent message: the poor of Britain were as "strange," as much "other" as any African aborigine, and as urgently in need of improvement. The bourgeois burden in Britain, it followed, was no less pressing than the white man's burden abroad. The point was argued by many literati of the period, including Charles Dickens, though his objectives were somewhat unusual.[15] Dickens said many times (e.g. 1908a; 1908b) that the call for overseas evangelism, and for grand imperial schemes, distracted attention from England's own dire social problems.

The drawing of imaginative parallels between the "dangerous classes" at home (Stedman Jones 1971, 11) and savages abroad thus took place first and foremost at the level of unmarked imagery, of more-or-less direct intertextual and lexical references that forged a link across the genre of travel and missionary literature, fusing evangelical zeal with exotic didacticism. A notable example, with particular reference to the theme of domesticity itself, is Thomas Archer's *The Pauper, the Thief, and the Convict* (1865). Archer begins by insisting that "there is little of the picturesque in poverty" (1); and then, like an African explorer evangelist (Comaroff and Comaroff 1991, chap. 5), he takes us with him to the *terra incognita* of Bethnal Green. He refers to the inhabitants' houses as "dens" and assures us that, while "the main thoroughfares [are] ruinous and dirty," they give no idea of how awful are the "teeming and filthy rooms," how awful are the "ragged, dirty children, and gaunt women, from whose faces almost all traces of womanliness have faded" (10).

But we have not yet reached the depths of Archer's Africa in London. "Let the traveller penetrate further," he urges (11):

> he will enter upon a maze of streets, each of which is a social crime, and each of which contains tributary hovels many degrees worse than itself. They are not always easy to find, since, if they ever had any names, the names have been obliterated.

In London, as in Africa, the wilderness is unnamed, unmarked, and uncharted. Archer assures us (10) that this is "as foul a neighborhood as can be discovered in the civilized world." The verb, in ironic juxtaposition to its object, discloses the essential spirit of the voyage. So does the parenthetic comment that follows immediately: "(savage life has nothing to compare to it)."

The moral spirit, the ideological project, in the writings of this tradition[16] is most articulately—and, perhaps, intriguingly—laid out in Hollingshead's *Ragged London* (1861, v–vi): "With all our electro-plated sentiment about home and the domestic virtues, we ought to wince a good deal at the houses of the poor." The qualifier here is itself revealing: electroplating, the coating of domestic tableware with silver by electrolysis, was a brilliant symbol of the newly acquired, skin-deep sensibilities of the bourgeoisie. Those sensibilities were offended by misery. The poor might themselves have been to blame; as Hollingshead said, "less drunken indulgence in matrimony and child-breeding would at once better their condition," but the point was to do something about it.

This is where the analogy with Africa took on practical salience: what was needed was an army of missionaries who would reform the needy from the core of their very beings: "In no part of the world— not even in the remotest dens of the savage wilderness—is there such a field for labour as in our London courts and alleys" (221). Shades, once more, of Dickens.

The circle is closed. The wilderness of London and Africa, teeming habitats of the benighted, were little different from one another. The primitive and the pauper were equally "other," equally undomesticated. The sacred task of the colonizing mission was thus to reconstruct the home lives of both in the cause of universal civilization. Philip (1828, 2:316–317; see above) was correct: the "dark continent" *was* a metaphorical mirror held up between savagery and civility, past and present, bourgeois ideology and its reflections at home and abroad.

In this respect, the encounter with savagery was deployed in the dialectic of domesticity in two distinct, if interrelated, ways, in two discourses—one negative, one positive—that followed upon each other conceptually and, broadly speaking, chronologically. The first has permeated everything we have said so far, namely, the invocation of Africa as a negative inversion of the ideal of bourgeois refinement. Hence the flood of popular descriptions, distinctly didactic in tone, of the "indescribable" uncleanliness of Africans: their "filth" and "promiscuity" became a measure against which (1) to evaluate conditions back home and (2) to frame appropriate social and evangelical policy.

If writings in this genre made Africans out to lead fitful lives on intimate terms with animal nature—and, as unregenerate polygynists, to wallow in sexual depravity—it remained only to show how similarly disreputable were the English poor. Jephson (1907, 56) quotes an authoritative report written in London at mid-century:

> It is no uncommon thing, in a room twelve feet square or less, to find three or four families *styed* together . . . filling the same space night and day—men, women, and children, in the promiscuous intercourse of cattle. . . . [I]n all offices of nature they are gregarious and public; . . . every instinct of personal or sexual decency is stifled; . . . every nakedness of life is uncovered there.

If this account had humans, promiscuous as cattle, living in styes, another had them yet further down on the scale of nature. Thomas

Beames, in his extraordinary *Rookeries of London* (1852), likens "pauper colonies" to the nests of rooks (2), the "lowest" of birds. That the term "colony" is used to describe poor city districts is itself telling, but even more noteworthy is his description of these "colonies." In perhaps the most pejorative text of the age, he asserts that (2–4):

> [paupers] belong to the . . . section of the social body . . . descended to the lowest scale which is compatible with human life. Other birds are broken up into separate families—occupy separate nests; rooks seem to know no such distinction. So it is with the class whose dwellings we describe. [These colonies house] the pariahs, so to speak, of the body social, a distinct social caste.

How similar this sounds to the missionary sense that Tswana lacked properly bounded families, that they were caught up in unhealthy "communistic relations," and that they showed no signs of true individuality.

The practical conclusions were clear. Both social policy and the civilizing mission had urgently to transform the domestic life of the poor: (1) to create the conditions for—and an attitude of—"cleanliness," thereby to achieve a world in which all matter, beings, and bodies were in their proper place; (2) to reform sexuality by encouraging legal, Christian marriage and the creation of nuclear households, thus putting an end to "drunken indulgence" in "child-breeding"; (3) to spread the ideal of private property, beginning with the family home; and (4) to reconstruct gender relations and the social division of labor. These, of course, were also the objectives of Nonconformist evangelism in Africa; it followed that, insofar as the English underclass fell short of them, Britain's right to its own refined self-image, its claim to stand at the pinnacle of modernity and civilization, was called into question. All such sentiment made it the common duty of the middle classes to "improve" the habits and habitats of the "less fortunate."

Africa, then, was as a *camera obscura* of British civilization, a virtual portrait of all that bourgeois refinement was not. To the degree that anything in England could be likened to life on the dark continent, it failed the test of enlightenment, and stood condemned in terms of the lexicon of domestication itself: *nomadic* costermongers, *wandering* paupers, the *teeming, filthy* poor *styed, promiscuously,* in their *haunts* and *hovels, dens* and *nests.* No better than savages, any of them.

Nor was the inference left unstated. On the first page of his *mag-*

num opus, Mayhew (1851, 1) quotes the ethnographic explorations of Andrew Smith in South Africa as a model. In every society, he says, wanderers are distinct from settlers, vagabonds from citizens, nomads from civilized people; in every society, elements of each "race" are to be found. According to this Africa-derived scheme, London laborers have a "savage and wandering mode of life" (2)— much like "bushmen" living beside more settled ("Hottentot") peoples. Similarly, Perkin (1969, 149–150) cites a widely read contemporary text by Gaskell (1836, 89):

> a [poor] household . . . in which all the decencies . . . of domestic life are constantly violated, reduces its inmates to a condition little elevated above that of the savage. Recklessness, improvidence, and unnecessary poverty, starvation, drunkenness, parental cruelty and carelessness, filial disobedience, neglect of conjugal rights, absence of maternal love . . . are too often its constituents, and the result of such a combination are moral degradation . . . and social misery.

Recall, lastly, the term "misery." As noted above (52), Broadbent (1865, 204) used it when he claimed that Tswana "had no marriage, nor any proper domestic order." It was the word used most often by the churchmen to describe African "home" life before the advent of colonial evangelism. In making the other a passive sufferer, the term evoked the conceit of heroic salvation, and simultaneously established an alibi for intervention. The metaphors of misery thus reverberated through the literature of outcast London, coupling the pauper and the primitive in a common destiny.

The other way in which the "dark continent" was deployed in the dialectic of domesticity, especially toward the end of the century, expressed itself in the positive voice: Africa also became a model for the possibilities of constructive transformation. The rhetorical basis of this model, and its presentation in the popular media, lay in a simple, blatantly racist claim. Under the impact of the civilizing mission, some savages could be shown to have bettered themselves, to have established decent homes, and to have enjoyed just moral and material rewards; if these blacks, with their inherent limitations, could have climbed the ladder of refinement, so might the most destitute of Englishmen.

Several texts framed in the positive voice have already been mentioned. Read's (1850, 446) description of Kuruman in the 1850s (above, 57) was an unusually early one of its kind. In it we are told that wealthy Christians had erected "good houses of stone"—conspicuously different from "rude" mud huts—and had laid the basis for modern family living; all around, in fact, were to be seen signs of "improvement" in building. But most revealing of all, as we suggested earlier, is Willoughby's chapter on "homes" in his *Native Live on the Transvaal Border* (n.d. [1899]). Here we see, in a (photo)-graphic series, the entire gamut of Tswana dwellings, from the most "primitive" to the most "advanced," from simple "traditional" structures to colonial-style Victorian residences. The evolutionary message is clear, as is its moral subtext: the development of domestic life, expressed in architectural form, was an index of Christian (self-)improvement, successful inculcation of bourgeois values, and civilized self-realization. That is why the evangelists took such triumphant delight in telling of Africans who had demonstrated their personal cultivation in bricks and mortar. These "sable brethren" stood out as a shining light, a humiliating example to (white) people back home who lived still in the rookeries and recesses of the urban wasteland.

We should like to end by making a few observations of general significance, some about colonialism, others about domesticity. None of them is entirely new, but all are worth reiterating.

Colonialism, it goes without saying, was an epochal movement, a world historical process. Until recently, its dominant narratives were written as global economic epics, expansive political sagas, dramas of international conflict and center–periphery relations. Its active agents were Europeans, its objects, the "natives" of "other" lands. Colonial agency, as this suggests, was presumed to go in only one direction. Our analysis makes two points in this respect. First, the *experience* of colonization on the part of peoples like the Tswana occurred in a quite different, much more quotidian key. The European embrace presented itself less in the form of portentous stately action than in the apparently utilitarian signs, practices, knowledge, and techniques introduced by the frontiersmen of empire—missionaries and merchants, settlers and smallholders. Of these, for obvious reasons, evangelists were often the most heavily implicated, at least in the first instance. They set about the task deliberately and comprehensively, as part of their calling and not as a by-product of their interests. Nor was the colonial process a highly methodical, linear affair. It proceeded amidst arguments among colonizers, some of them bitter and violent (J. L. Comaroff 1989), and against resistance on the part of the colonized, albeit intermittent and often unpredictable in form (J. Comaroff 1985). Still, to the degree that it was effective, the colonization of the Tswana entailed the reconstruction of the ordinary, of things at once material, meaningful, and mundane. This is not to say, as we have noted many times, that global economics or regional politics did not have a significant impact on the predicament of black South Africans. It clearly did. But it was from the bottom up, through the remaking of the inhabited environment, that the vehicles of European modernity first seeded themselves on the African landscape.

Second, we have sought to show that colonization was not a one-sided affair. Nor was it two-sided only to the extent that the colonized may be shown to have had some influence on the way in which colonizers acted upon them. It was a more complex business all-round: in seeking to cultivate the "savage"—with, as we said, variable success—British imperialists were actively engaged in transforming their own society as well; most explicitly, in domesticating that part of the metropolis that had previously eluded bourgeois control. Cultural colonialism, in short, was also a reflexive process whereby "others" abroad were put to the purposes of reconstructing the "other" back home. The two sites, the two impulses, went hand-in-hand. Not incidentally, both contributed to the triumph of the bourgeoisie in the European "age of revolution" (Hobsbawm 1962). If anything is to be learned from this, it is that colonialism is as much about making the center as it is about making the periphery. The colony was not a mere extension of the modern world, but was part of what made that world modern in the first place. And the dialectic of domesticity was a vital element in the process.

This returns us to the question of domesticity itself. Given that the seeds of cultural imperialism *were* most effectively sown along the contours of everyday life, it is no surprise that the process emphasized the physical and social architecture of the household. As this implies, conversely, the inculcation of modern domesticity was (and always is) much more than a matter of spreading the "Western ideology of family" (above, 38). Most missionaries understood that the construction of the "private" domain was fundamental to the anatomy of their social world. Within it were contained the elemental relations of gender and generation on which social reproduction depended; in its routines and conventions were vested the signs and practices on which was based the social order *tout court*. At the dawn of modernity in Europe, moreover, the nuclear family was becoming the point of articulation between civil society and the (ostensibly) free individual, the ideological atom upon which bourgeois economy and society depended.

In seeking to recast Africa domesticity in the same mold, then, colonial evangelists hoped to bring about a New Society, a New Civility. Ironically, as creatures of their time, they took for granted what it was to take social scientists many decades to learn: that existing forms of domesticity and the dominant social order in which they are embedded depend, for their construction and reproduction, on one another. Hegemony is indeed homemade.

Acknowledgments

We should like to thank the Spencer Foundation, the American Bar Foundation, and the Lichtstern Fund of the University of Chicago for their generous support of our research and writing. Note that all primary materials used here are annotated in footnotes; references to secondary writings are cited by author and year in the text, and annotated fully in the bibliography. Archival documents are cited by author, place of writing, date, and storage classification. CWM is the Council of World Mission, whose papers (including the records of the London Missionary Society [LMS]) are housed at the School of Oriental and African Studies, London. WMMS refers to the (Wesleyan) Methodist Missionary Society. A longer and slightly amended version of this essay is to be found in J. and J. L. Comaroff, *Ethnography and the Historical Imagination: Selected Essays* (Boulder, Colo. Westview Press, 1992).

Notes

1. See Gallagher (1985:122–123) for examples.

2. We have published several accounts of these systems in the nineteenth century: see, e.g., J. Comaroff (1985), J. L. Comaroff (1982; 1987), Comaroff and Comaroff (1991). Since pressures of space do not allow us to detail our sources here, we rely on those writings—which are very fully annotated—as colateral evidence.

3. A "house," in standard anthropological usage, consists of a married woman and her own children (as the latter are indigenously defined).

4. Some passages of this section are drawn, in amended form, from our *Of Revelation and Revolution,* Vol. 2 (n.d.); see also Comaroff and Comaroff (1989).

5. J. Read, Lattakoo, 14 March 1817 (CWM, LMS South African Journals, 3). Note that the Tlhaping were the southernmost Tswana people.

6. This is not an isolated case; mission archives are filled with similar accounts. See, for just one further example, R. Hamilton, Lattakoo, 15 May 1817 (CWM, LMS Incoming Letters [South Africa], 7-1-C).

7. J. Archbell, Platberg, 2 September 1833 (WMMS, South Africa Correspondence [Albany], 303); Livingstone (1857,21).

8. J. Archbell, Cradock, 23 May 1831 (WMMS, South Africa Correspondence [Albany], 303).

9. T. Hodgson, Matlwassie, 12 January 1824 (WMMS, South Africa Correspondence, 300).

10. See also A. Wookey, Kuruman, 23 May, 1884 (CWM, LMS Incoming Letters [South Africa], 42-3-C). J. Mackenzie, Kuruman, 17 February 1882 (CWM, LMS South Africa Reports, 2–1) details how farmers unable to irrigate were being displaced by the "wealthy" who could.

11. J. Hughes, Lattakoo, 17 December 1824 (CWM Archives, LMS South Africa Journals, 4).

12. See, e.g., Lichtenstein ([1807] 1973,67); Campbell (1822,2:219); Hughes (1841:523); Mackenzie (1883); Moffat (1842,502f.).

13. Hebdige (1988,21) makes a similar point, but does not annotate it.

14. The circulation of some missionary texts was very substantial indeed; for example, Brantlinger (1985,176) notes that Livingstone's *Missionary Travels* (1857) sold 70,000 copies in just a few months.

15. Dickens's object was *not* to draw an unflattering parallel between the English poor and savage Africans. He sought to call attention to the dreadful conditions under which the former were forced to live.

16. A point is in order here. As Stedman Jones (1971,part III) correctly points out, late nineteenth-century writings on the predicament of the casual poor in London underwent several transformations—largely as a product of rapidly changing social and economic conditions. For present purposes, however, these transformations are not directly significant. The bourgeois ideology of domesticity did not change much over the period; nor did the efforts of middle-class reformers and missionaries to reconstruct the home life of the poor.

Bibliography

Achebe, Chinua. 1978. An Image of Africa. *Research in African Literatures* 9:1–15.

Alatas, Hussein S. 1977. *The Myth of the Lazy Native: A Study of the Image of the Malays, Filipinos and Javanese. . . .* London: F. Cass.

Archer, Thomas. 1865. *The Pauper, the Thief, and the Convict; Sketches of Some of their Homes, Haunts, and Habits.* London: Groombridge.

Barrow, John. 1801–1804. *An Account of Travels into the Interior of Southern Africa in the Years 1797 and 1798.* 2 vols. London: Cadell & Davies.

———. 1806. *A Voyage to Cochinchina.* London: Cadell & Davies.

Beames, Thomas. 1852. *The Rookeries of London: Past, Present, Prospective.* London: Thomas Bosworth.

Beidelman, Thomas O. 1982. *Colonial Evangelism: A Socio-historical Study of an East African Mission at the Grass Roots.* Bloomington: Indiana University Press.

Bourdieu, Pierre. 1977. *Outline of a Theory of Practice,* trans. R. Nice. Cambridge: Cambridge University Press.

Brantlinger, Patrick. 1985. Victorians and Africans: The Genealogy of the Myth of the Dark Continent. *Critical Enquiry* 12:166–203.

Broadbent, Samuel. 1865. *A Narrative of the First Introduction of Christianity amongst the Barolong Tribe of Bechuanas, South Africa.* London: Wesleyan Mission House.

Bundy, Colin. 1979. *The Rise and Fall of the South African Peasantry.* London: Heinemann.

Burke, Timothy. n.d. "Nyamarira That I Love": Commoditization, Consumption, and the Social History of Soap in Zimbabwe. Paper read to the African Studies Seminar, Northwestern University, 9 May 1990.

Burrow, John. 1971. *Travels in the Wilds of Africa. . . .* ed. P. R. Kirby. Cape Town: A. A. Balkema.

Campbell, John. 1822. *Travels in South Africa . . . Being a Narrative of a Second Journey. . . .* 2 vols. London: Westley.

Cock, Jacklyn. 1980. *Maids and Madams: A Study of the Politics of Exploitation.* Johannesburg: Ravan Press.

Comaroff, Jean. 1985. *Body of Power, Spirit of Resistance: The Culture and History of a South African People.* Chicago: University of Chicago Press.

———. n.d. The Diseased Heart of Africa: Medicine, Colonialism, and the Black Body. In *Analysis in Medical Anthropology,* ed. Margaret Lock and Shirley Lindenbaum. Dordrecht and Boston: Kluwer.

Comaroff, Jean and John L. Comaroff. 1986. Christianity and Colonialism in South Africa. *American Ethnologist* 13:1–20.

———. 1989. The Colonization of Consciousness in South Africa. *Economy and Society* 18:267–295.

———. 1990. Goodly Beasts, Beastly Goods: Cattle and Commodities in a South African Context. *American Ethnologist* 17:195–216.

———. 1991. *Of Revelation and Revolution: Christianity, Colonialism, and Consciousness in South Africa.* Vol. 1. Chicago: University of Chicago Press.

Comaroff, John L. 1982. Dialectical Systems, History and Anthropology: Units of Study and Questions of Theory. *Journal of Southern African Studies* 8:143–172.

———. 1987. *Sui Genderis:* Feminism, Kinship Theory, and Structural Domains. In *Gender and Kinship,* ed. Jane F. Collier and Sylvia J. Yanagisako. Stanford: Stanford University Press.

———. 1989. Images of Empire, Contests of Conscience: Models of Colonial Domination in South Africa. *American Ethnologist* 16:661–685.

Crisp, William. 1896. *The Bechuana of South Africa.* London: SPCK.

Curtin, Philip D. 1964. *The Image of Africa: British Ideas and Action, 1780–1850.* Madison: University of Wisconsin Press.

Dachs, Anthony J. 1972. Missionary Imperialism: The Case of Bechuanaland. *Journal of African History* 13:647–658.

Darrow, Margaret H. 1979. French Noblewomen and the New Domesticity 1750–1850. *Feminist Studies* 5:41–65.

Davidoff, Leonore, and Catherine Hall. 1987. *Family Fortunes: Men and Women of the English Middle Class, 1780–1850.* Chicago: University of Chicago Press.

Dickens, Charles. 1908a. The Niger Expedition. In *The Works of Charles Dickens* (National ed.), Vol. 35, *Miscellaneous Papers, Plays and Poems* (vol. 1). London: Chapman and Hall. (First published in *The Examiner*, 19 August 1848.)

———. 1908b. The Noble Savage. In *The Works of Charles Dickens* (National ed.). Vol. 34, *Reprinted Pieces.* London: Chapman and Hall. (First published in *Household Words*, 11 June 1853.)

Edwards, John. 1886. *Reminiscences of the Early Life and Missionary Labours of the Rev. John Edwards*, ed. W. C. Holden. Grahamstown: T. H. Grocott.

Engels, Friedrich. [1844] 1968. *The Condition of the Working Class in England*, trans. and ed. W. O. Henderson and W. H. Chaloner. Stanford: Stanford University Press.

Etherington, Norman. 1978. *Preachers, Peasants, and Politics in Southeast Africa, 1835–1880: African Christian Communities in Natal, Pondoland, and Zululand.* London: Royal Historical Society.

Fortes, Meyer. 1969. *Kinship and the Social Order.* London: Routledge & Kegan Paul.

———. 1978. An Anthropologist's Apprenticeship. *Annual Review of Anthropology* 7:1–30.

Foucault, Michel. 1973. *The Birth of the Clinic*, trans. A. M. Sheridan Smith. New York: Pantheon Books.

Gaitskell, Deborah. 1983. Housewives, Maids or Mothers: Some Contradictions of Domesticity for Christian Women in Johannesburg, 1903–1939. *Journal of African History* 24:241–256.

Gallagher, Catherine. 1985. *The Industrial Reformation of English Fiction: Social Discourse and Narrative Form 1832–1867.* Chicago: University of Chicago Press.

Garwood, John. 1853. *The Million-Peopled City: The Rise of Urban Britain.* London: Wertheim and Macintosh.

Gaskell, P. 1836. *Artisans and Machinery: The Moral and Physical Condition of the Manufacturing Population.* London: J. W. Parker.

Greenwood, James. 1869. *The Seven Curses of London.* London: S. Rivers.

———. 1874. *The Wilds of London.* London: Chatto and Windus.

Hall, Catherine. 1985. Private Persons versus Public Someones: Class, Gender and Politics in England, 1780–1850. In *Language, Gender and Childhood*, ed. Carolyn Steedman, Cathy Urwin, and Valerie Walkerdine. London: Routledge & Kegan Paul.

Hannerz, Ulf. 1983. Tools of Identity and Imagination. In *Identity: Personal and Socio-Cultural: A Symposium,* ed. Anita Jacobson-Widding. Atlantic Highlands, N.J.: Humanities Press.

Hansen, Karen Tranberg. 1989. *Distant Companions: Servants and Employers in Zambia, 1900–1985.* Ithaca, N.Y.: Cornell University Press.

Hattersley, Alan F. 1952. The Missionary in South African History. *Theoria* 4:86–88.

Hausen, K. 1981. Family and Role-division: the Polarisation of Sexual Stereotypes in the Nineteenth Century. In *The German Family,* ed. Richard J. Evans and W. R. Lee. London: Croom Helm; Totowa: Barnes and Noble.

Hebdige, Dick. 1988. *Hiding in the Light: On Images and Things.* London and New York: Routledge & Kegan Paul.

Hobsbawm, Eric J. 1962. *The Age of Revolution, 1789–1848.* New York: New American Library.

Hollingshead, John. 1861. *Ragged London in 1861.* London: Smith, Elder.

Holub, Emil. 1881. *Seven Years in South Africa: Travels, Researches, and Hunting Adventures, between the Diamond Fields and the Zambesi* (1872–79), trans. E. Frewer. 2 vols. Boston: Houghton Mifflin.

Hughes, Isaac. 1841. Missionary Labours among the Batlapi. *Evangelical Magazine and Missionary Chronicle* 19:522–523.

Hunt, Nancy Rose. 1990. Domesticity and Colonialism in Belgian Africa: Usumbura's *Foyer Social,* 1946–1960. *Signs* 15:447–474.

Hutchinson, Bertram. 1957. Some Social Consequences of Nineteenth Century Mission Activity among the South African Bantu. *Africa* 27:160–177.

Jephson, Henry. 1907. *The Sanitary Evolution of London.* New York: A. Wessels.

Kinsman, Margaret. 1983. "Beasts of Burden": The Subordination of Southern Tswana Women, ca. 1800–1840. *Journal of Southern African Studies* 10:39–54.

Krige, Eileen J. and Jacob D. Krige. 1943. *The Realm of a Rain-Queen: A Study of the Pattern of Lovedu Society.* London: Oxford University Press for the International African Institute.

Levi-Strauss, Claude. 1972. *Tristes Tropiques,* trans. John Russell. New York: Atheneum.

Lichtenstein, W. H. C. [1807] 1973. *About the Bechuanas,* trans. and ed. O. H. Spohr. Cape Town: A. A. Balkema.

———. [1811] 1973. *Foundation of the Cape,* trans. and ed. O. H. Spohr. Cape Town: A. A. Balkema.

Livingstone, David. 1843. State and Progress of the Kuruman Mission. *Evangelical Magazine and Missionary Chronicle (Missionary Magazine and Chronicle)* 8 (94):57–58.

———. 1857. *Missionary Travels and Researches in South Africa. . . .* London: Murray.

London Missionary Society. 1830. *Report of the Directors of the London Missionary Society, May 1830.* London: Westly & Davis.

Mackenzie, John. 1871. *Ten Years North of the Orange River: A Story of*

Everyday Life and Work among the South African Tribes. Edinburgh: Edmonston & Douglas.

———. 1883. *Day Dawn in Dark Places: A Story of Wanderings and Work in Bechwanaland*. London: Cassell.

Macmillan, William M. 1929. *Bantu, Boer, and Briton: The Making of the South African Native Problem*. London: Faber & Gwyer.

Mayhew, Henry. 1851. *London Labour and the London Poor: a cyclopaedia of the condition of those that will work, those that cannot work, and those that will not work*. Vol. 1. London: G. Woodfall.

Moffat, Mary. 1967. Letter to a Well-Wisher. *Quarterly Bulletin of the South African Library* 22:16–19.

Moffat, Robert. 1842. *Missionary Labours and Scenes in Southern Africa*. London: Snow.

Monthly Review. 1790. Review of *Proceedings of the Association for Promoting the Discovery of the Interior Parts of Africa* 2:60–68.

Morgan, David H.J. 1985. *The Family, Politics and Social Theory*. London and Boston: Routledge & Kegan Paul.

Muldoon, James. 1975. The Indian as Irishman. *Essex Institute Historical Collections* 3:267–289.

Northcott, William Cecil. 1961. *Robert Moffat: Pioneer in Africa, 1817–1870*. London: Lutterworth Press.

Oakley, Ann. 1974. *Woman's Work: The Housewife, Past and Present*. New York: Pantheon Books.

Oliver, Roland A. 1952. *The Missionary Factor in East Africa*. London: Longmans.

Park, Mungo. 1799. *Travels in the Interior Districts of Africa, Performed under the Direction and Patronage of the African Association, in the Years 1795, 1796, and 1797*. London: W. Bulmer.

Parsons, Neil Q. 1977. The Economic History of Khama's Country in Botswana, 1844–1930. In *The Roots of Rural Poverty in Central and Southern Africa*, ed. Robin Palmer and Neil Q. Parsons. London: Heinemann.

Pawley, Martin. 1971. *Architecture versus Housing*. New York: Praeger.

Perkin, Harold. 1969. *The Origins of Modern English Society 1780–1880*. London: Routledge & Kegan Paul; Toronto: University of Toronto Press.

Philip, John. 1825. Report from Kuruman. *MS Quarterly Chronicle* 3:223–224.

———. 1828. *Researches in South Africa; Illustrating the Civil, Moral, and Religious Condition of the Native Tribes*. 2 vols. London: James Duncan.

Pratt, Mary L. 1985. Scratches on the Face of the Country; or, What Mr. Barrow Saw in the Land of the Bushmen. *Critical Inquiry* 12:119–143.

Ranger, Terence O. 1987. Taking Hold of the Land: Holy Places and Pilgrimages in Twentieth-Century Zimbabwe. *Past and Present* 117:158–194.

Read, James. 1850. Report on the Bechuana Mission. *Evangelical Magazine and Missionary Chronicle* 28:445–447.

Rybczynski, Witold. 1986. *Home: A Short History of an Idea*. New York: Viking Penguin.

Schapera, Isaac. 1936. The Contributions of Western Civilisation to Modern

Kxatla Culture. *Transactions of the Royal Society of South Africa* 24:221–252.

———. 1943. *Native Land Tenure in the Bechuanaland Protectorate.* Alice: Lovedale Press.

———. 1947. *Migrant Labour and Tribal Life: A Study of Conditions in the Bechuanaland Protectorate.* London and New York: Oxford University Press.

———, ed. 1974. *David Livingstone: South Africa Papers, 1849–1853.* Cape Town: Van Riebeeck Society.

Shillington, Kevin. 1985. *The Colonisation of the Southern Tswana, 1870–1900.* Johannesburg: Ravan Press.

Stallybrass, Peter and Allon White. 1986. *The Politics and Poetics of Transgression.* London: Methuen.

Stedman Jones, Gareth. 1971. *Outcast London: A Study in the Relationship between Classes in Victorian Society.* Oxford: Clarendon Press.

Thompson, Edward P. 1967. Time, Work-Discipline, and Industrial Capitalism. *Past and Present* 38:56–97.

Tilby, A. Wyatt. 1914. Some Missionary Pioneers in South Africa. *United Empire: The Royal Colonial Institute Journal* 4 (New Series, 1913):190–195. London: Sir Isaac Pitman & Sons.

Tonna, Charlotte. 1844. *The Wrongs of Woman.* New York: J. S. Taylor.

Tristan, Flora. 1980. *London Journal,* trans. D. Palmer and G. Pincetl. Charlestown: Charles River. (Originally published as *Promenades Dans Londres,* 1840.)

Trollope, Anthony. 1878. *South Africa.* 2 vols. London: Chapman & Hall.

Vilakazi, Absolom. 1962. *Zulu Transformations.* Pietermaritzburg: University of Natal Press.

Weber, Max. 1958. *The Protestant Ethic and the Spirit of Capitalism,* trans. T. Parsons. New York: Scribner's.

Whitefield, George. 1772. *The Works of the Reverend George Whitefield, M.A..* Vol. 5. London: printed for Edward & Charles Dilly.

Willoughby, William C. 1899. Our People: What They are Like and How They Live. *News From Afar: LMS Magazine for Young People* 15, no. 6 (n.s.):84–86.

———. 1911. A Paper Read before the South African Council of the London Missionary Society at their Meetings held at Tiger Kloof, March, 1911. (Pamphlet.) Tiger Kloof, Cape Province: Tiger Kloof Native Institution.

———. n.d. [1899] *Native Life on the Transvaal Border.* London: Simpkin, Marshall, Hamilton, Kent.

Wilson, Monica. 1971. The Growth of Peasant Communities. In *The Oxford History of South Africa,* ed. Monica Wilson and Leonard Thompson, vol. 2. New York and Oxford: Oxford University Press.

2   Harem Domesticity in Kano, Nigeria

Beverly B. Mack

It may seem redundant to speak of "harem domesticity." Since the fourteenth century the term "domestic" has referred to the household (Oxford English Dictionary 1971, 594), while the term "harem" itself (Arabic, *harim*) describes a part of the household that is both a sanctuary for women and an area that is forbidden to men outside the family. The harem is the heart of the household, its domestic seat and most private area, where the family's women preside. Women generally are restricted to this part of the household, leaving it only on special occasions, and with the consent of their husbands.[1] Thus the domesticity of the harem may be distinguished both from that of the rest of the household and from that of households without harems.

In Muslim northern Nigeria the Hausa tradition of restricting women to the home is known as wife seclusion (H. *kulle*). Originally a· local custom, it is logically connected to Islamic philosophy by virtue of the Muslim woman's religious obligation to act as guardian of the domestic sphere. As a secluded wife she is restricted to the physical space in which activities relevant to her role are carried out. Furthermore, Islam—which is commonly understood to pervade every aspect of a Muslim's daily life—has as a main focus the unity of the family, in which both men and women hold religiously mandated social roles. Thus the importance of the domestic realm is magnified in Muslim households by the family-oriented nature of Islam, and a woman's domestic role is an integral part of the religious philosophy that directs Muslims' lives. This ideological framework is the central influence on the form domesticity takes among the urban Hausa, and must thus be a central consideration in the study of harem domesticity in Kano.

Among the Hausa of Kano, Nigeria, the Emir is the traditional political and religious leader whose behavior is said to exemplify Hausa Muslim ideals; by extension, his wives and concubines are also expected to uphold traditional and religious ideals. This study explains why the royal harem community in Kano may be considered the archetypical Muslim Hausa household and examines the extent to which domestic practices in the harem relate to those of nonroyal households. It then examines the idea of the domestic spatially, as an arena of influence and a setting allowing for response to changing social situations. Thus the discussion focuses on: (1) domestic space in the royal harem's physical setting; (2) the harem as the domain of women's domestic influence and their responsibilities and authority therein; and (3) the way in which the royal harem responds to external influences—especially with regard to gender relations—constantly revising the nature of the domestic environment. An understanding of the nature of domesticity in the Kano palace can contribute to a better understanding of Hausa domesticity in general and the religions and social relations that determine it.

The material discussed here is culled from research I conducted during two eighteen-month periods of residence in Kano, Nigeria, in 1979–1980 and 1981–1982. On a visit to Kano in 1977 I met the women of the Emir's palace in Kano.[2] When I arrived to stay in 1979 I was welcomed with the hospitality that is so often characteristic of the Hausa. Through the generosity of the Emir of Kano, Alhaji Ado Bayero, and especially that of his four wives (into whose lives I intruded significantly and daily), I was given much leeway in visiting the palace, eventually becoming accepted as a member of the palace community, coming and going with great liberty. As a Hausa speaker and a student of Hausa women's oral poetry (the topic of my initial research) I was prepared to converse directly with women in Kano and learn about their domestic situations firsthand. Through months of daily visits and long conversations—some tape-recorded, others informal—I began to see how royal Hausa women viewed their own situation, meeting the demands of tradition and Islam, fulfilling responsibilities inherent in the context of palace residence, and finding time to pursue their own interests. This study focuses on the idea of the domestic as manifested in Kano's royal harem community, emphasizing the reasons and extent to which this harem is exemplary of domesticity among the Hausa.

The Historical Background

The Emir's palace in Kano, Nigeria, has for centuries been the center of sociopolitical and socioreligious power in the region. It was established around the fourteenth century, as the Hausa developed extensive trade contacts with Arab cultures to the north. Islam was introduced into the area along with trade, the Arabic language, and literacy necessary to both commerce and religious practice. Trade contacts grew, and the influence of Arab culture on the Hausa increased proportionately, but for centuries Islam was observed alongside traditional animist practices, and only by the elite, rather than practiced strictly and throughout all strata of Hausa society. By the fifteenth century, Kano was a major terminus for trans-Saharan trade routes, along which Arabic social customs, scholarly influences, and commodities were conveyed. Together with these, Islam's importance in the area grew. Over the next few centuries the Fulani filtered into Hausaland from the West, carrying with them more orthodox Islamic practices. By the nineteenth century some Fulani had established themselves as influential advisors to Hausa kings (still known at that time by the Hausa term *sarki*), and began to express their dissatisfaction with the unorthodox religious practices around them by participating in campaigns of reform, *jihads,* throughout West Africa. The largest and most effective *jihad,* promoted by Shehu ("learned and pious"[3]) Usman dan Fodio, swept across Hausaland in the early nineteenth century, replacing Hausa kings with Muslim Fulani emirs presiding over theocratic states of Hausa populations.

Although Islam had been an influential factor in Hausa culture for centuries, it took this *jihad* to establish Islam as a pervasive belief system at all levels of society. The Shehu's *jihad* had profound consequences both for Hausa society as a whole, and for women's positions in it. Prior to that time, women appear to have occupied an active, public position in society. Legends of warrior queens date to the pre-Islamic period, and women's names in early king lists suggest that women's power and authority were significant in early historical periods (Coles and Mack 1991; Last 1983, 85). European travelers in Hausaland in the seventeenth and eighteenth centuries reported having seen women in the market, on the streets, and mingling freely in public (Mack 1991). Just prior to the *jihad,* in the late eighteenth and early nineteenth centuries, women scholars commonly were found throughout West Africa. The Shehu's own daughter, Nana Asma'u, was herself renowned in her own time as a poet, teacher, and scholar (Boyd 1989).

The revitalization of Islam that resulted from the Shehu's *jihad,* however, may well have had more to do with the narrowing of women's roles to those connected with domestic life than any other single influence since then. Interpreting Islam more narrowly than he did, the Shehu's proponents advocated a nonpublic role for women, in which their religious responsibility was to be fulfilled through a life focused on domestic responsibilities: attending to their children's upbringing as proper Muslims, maintaining the household, and guaranteeing concord in it (Sanday 1981, 35–36). The question as to the extent to which the Shehu intended this to be so is moot, considering his daughter Nana Asma'u's own more publicly active example (Boyd 1989; Hiskett 1973). Nevertheless, women's roles as educators and scholars were overshadowed in the years following the *jihad,* and their opportunities were increasingly prescribed around the home and its dependents, especially children.[4] Thus since the early nineteenth century Hausa women's domestic roles came to fulfill an ideological function expressed in the religious philosophy that now drives their society. A Hausa Muslim woman takes responsibility for certain domestic tasks in the fulfillment of her religious obligation, complementing a man's responsibility for the family's financial well-being.

A century after the *jihad,* British colonizers viewed Hausa women through their own post-Victorian lens, finding it appropriate that women were secluded in the house, without concern for the role that Islam played in such an arrangement. During the colonial period, the British policy of indirect rule in the Muslim north was due in part to the strength of Islam and an effective Muslim theocratic hierarchy there. Although Islam's presence in the north prevented the establishment of Christian mission schools there, eventually western schools were established first for men's and then for women's secular education in Hausaland.

Royal women had some opportunities prohibited to other women during the colonial period; their access to Nigerian and British decision-makers meant that their interest in women's education was heard. In response to such expressions of need, women's schools were established, but the schools were much fewer in number than those for boys, available only to girls of privileged backgrounds; and the curriculum was heavily weighted toward western concepts of the domestic realm, rather than toward leadership skills (Mack 1988). By the twentieth century in northern Nigeria, the public roles women had played in other historical periods had disappeared completely as both British colonizers and the men they sought to colonize agreed—albeit implicitly and perhaps for different reasons—to restrict women to the household.[5] Thus, in contemporary northern Nigeria, the perception of women in society has evolved from an interplay of conservative Muslim male attitudes and western ethnocentric chauvinism.

The Royal Harem as the Prototype of Hausa Domesticity

While it is distinct from other households by virtue of its size and affluence, the Emir's palace is considered to be a prototype of Hausa households because it is the most traditional and conservative. The palace community, whose establishment is contemporaneous with the rise of Hausa culture, has come to symbolize and stand as representative of Hausa tradition. When Fulani emirs replaced Hausa kings after the *jihad,* emirs continued to use the Hausa language, and perpetuated many Hausa royal customs to facilitate control of the Hausa majority. Thus the palace has always been a bastion of Hausa custom. Continuously inhabited since the fourteenth century, the palace until recently was nearly self-sufficient, with fields for crops and grazing, as well as water sources, stables, burial grounds, and its own mosques and schools. Its customs have been preserved in the face of numerous assaults from local threats, western colonizers, and more recently the influence of post-independence political machinations. Ancient symbolic modes of attire and ritual are still followed for the installation of new emirs, honorary titles of at least several centuries' duration are still bestowed, and legends are told about former inhabitants of both genders.

Traditionally the Emir held all land, dispensing residence rights in the city at his discretion, as well as arbitrating certain legal disputes and granting political favors. As the symbolic and actual religious, political, and social leader of the Kano emirate, the Emir was the ultimate authority, representing conservative, customary values. The Emir of Kano is thus considered to embody cultural ideals; he symbolizes traditional culture, and by extension his wives and children are expected to fulfill roles as exemplary family members.

Women of the royal harem in Kano are at once distinct from and typical of their nonroyal urban counterparts; their socioeconomic privilege distinguishes them from less well-off women in town, yet in many respects they live in much the same way as other women in Kano. Women of the palace are atypical in having greater than usual access to utilities (such as running water and electricity) and servants (for household tasks and child care). Nevertheless, the roles they play, the constraints on their activities, and the social and economic obligations they incur often are comparable to those of women dwelling outside the palace.[6] Furthermore, because the palace is, like any other household, dependent on city services, it is subject to the same power cuts, water interruptions, and low market supply that affect the rest of the area. Therefore, their high social status and assistance from servants are the only privileges women of the palace are guaranteed; their daily lives often involve many of the same difficulties faced by other Kano women.

Regardless of status, women in Kano find their roles defined by Islam, which in theory does not distinguish among individuals on grounds of socioeconomic status. A woman's religious obligation to her role as domestic guardian is mandated in the same way for all women. However, the ease with which such obligations can be fulfilled depends a great deal on the economic level of the household—that is, on the husband's income. Therefore a family's affluence, which will facilitate the fulfillment of a Kano woman's domestic obligations, necessarily shapes both her self-image as a Muslim and her sense of accomplishment.[7]

Socioeconomic status also determines whether a woman is a co-wife or not, for poor men cannot afford to have more than one wife. Many Kano men have two wives living together in one household, but only the affluent are likely to have more than two (Mack 1980). Prior to the *jihad* Hausa kings often had many wives; Islam restricts the number to four but allows for the continuation of the practice of concubinage. Thus, like many other Kano women, royal wives are co-wives; but unlike the average woman, a royal wife shares her husband with three co-wives and numerous concubines. This larger number of co-wives and concubines is balanced in the palace by the wives' residence in separate spacious quarters, a situation that mitigates potential conflict among women by providing each with private living space and the implication of exclusivity. Thus while co-wives inhabit formally the harem of a household, among the wealthy, women may avoid the interpersonal conflict that often stems from close daily proximity to one another. Indeed, in the royal harem, under normal circumstances a co-wife does not see her co-wives. Instead other women—concubines—play the roles of co-wives, sharing the same compound with royal wives. Thus, in one of several variations, the arrangement of any Hausa household consists of several women living and working together in fulfillment of their role as guardians of the domestic realm.

Housing and Domestic Space

Early on, local warfare and competition among kingdoms in Hausaland gave rise to fortified cities like Kano. Until the mid twentieth century, when it was allowed to fall into disrepair, a protective wall preserved the security of Kano's inhabitants; when the British attacked the city in 1903 the city wall they faced was fifty feet high and twenty-five feet wide, big enough to function as a roadway for the car they drove atop it, surveying the city. In the center of Kano's Old City, a less grandiose version of this wall still surrounds the several-acre estate of Kano's Emir and its thousands of palace residents. Just as Kano city is divided into wards, the palace itself is organized around comparable quadrants for administrative offices and slave/servant residences. At the heart of this complex is the harem where the Emir's four wives, numerous concubines, servants, and life-long female residents (e.g., widows of previous emirs) reside. The palace itself is a microcosm of the fortified city of Kano and the heart of the palace, the harem, is as representative of traditional Hausa domesticity as the palace is a sanctuary of Hausa traditions.

The royal harem is defined by both its inhabitants and its physical space. The average nonroyal household often has a central courtyard, but in the palace the vast harem courtyard is several hundred yards long and fifty feet wide. It is an arena of constant activity.[8] The living quarters of the four royal wives, current concubines, and all their respective children surround this courtyard roughly at its four corners, just as in other households co-wives' rooms open onto the house's courtyard. In Kano only affluent households have second-story levels; some royal wives' compounds have second-story windows onto the courtyard, providing a clear view of courtyard daily and celebratory activities. In this way strictly secluded royal wives can participate vicariously in the freer movement of lower-status women in the common courtyard. In an average urban Hausa household, a wife has one or two rooms as her private quarters, but each royal wife has her own suite of rooms and courtyards that is itself a fortressed area like the city, surrounded by high walls for privacy, with courtyards open to the sky and a generous arrangement of rooms for receiving guests, cooking, and sleeping. One of the Kano royal wives, Hajiya, explained that each new bride is brought to the palace prior to the marriage to inspect her quarters and recommend changes: "The apartments cannot be the same [for each wife]. . . . An emir has to build a special place for each wife, so that it suits her. . . . We were [each] asked to go and see our apartments before the wedding [so they could be decorated] to our particular tastes" (Interview, 26 May 1982). In Hajiya's case the walls were repainted with bright colors and enamelled decorated plates were embedded in the ceilings.

Each quadrant is known by a name that identifies it with the wife who lives there.[9] Because the Emir establishes sociopolitical bonds through marriage, the fact that each quadrant is known by the resident wife's nickname (which sometimes is her town of origin) serves as a constant reminder of Kano's political ties to other emirates. "Abba's place, Sokoto's place, Takuba's place . . . they are nicknames. Each place is identified with the wife there" (Interview with Hajiya Abba, 26 May 1982). The senior wife's residence is located closest to the Emir's private quarters, and his fourth (newest) wife's compound is the farthest from his, at the other end of the central courtyard. The second and third wives of the present Emir, who are friends and have comparable educations and interests, have adjoining quarters midway between the other two wives. The wives' physical proximity to one another and to the Emir himself thus results from a combination of factors like rank and compatibility.

A larger version of the average household, the royal wife's compound has a common cooking area and bathing and laundry facilities. Depending on the wife's interests, there may also be a kitchen garden with fruits and vegetables grown for consumption or sale.[10] Each royal wife presides over her own area, in which several concubines also have their own small apartments. The Emir and his female advisors try to establish compatibility in assigning concubines to royal wives. These concubines function as a wife's helpmates, and, in the hierarchy of Hausa social order, they themselves can command the women of slave status who work for them all. Thus while her legal co-wives do not share a royal wife's space, concubines do, functioning as informal co-wives. These concubines and their children do not have their own separate quarters within the royal wife's compound, but stay in rooms to which the Emir has access: "they stay in a place where the Emir can pass to any of them without being seen. They don't have actual [private] rooms, only the place where they can birth the babies" and a curtained portion of space for privacy (Interview with Hajiya Abba, 26 May 1982).

While the women of highest status—royal wives and current concubines—live at the center of the palace, the next larger circle of residences in the domestic arena is inhabited by other women of the palace. In this larger ring of compounds circumscribing the central ring, individual living units are considerably smaller and less formal than those of the central harem.[11] Among those who reside there are older concubines who have acquired positions of prominence in the harem. They hold titles bestowed by the Emir that reflect their status, command the respect of both men and women in the palace, and guarantee their security in terms of shelter and income for the duration of their residence there. Others who live there are very old women—concubines of former emirs and royal widows—and female relatives who might have taken up residence with them.[12] This too is the site of the palace women's clinic, and what was once the central kitchen, feeding the thousands of permanent palace residents. Now there are kitchen gardens and smaller cooking units in these areas.

Beyond the harem, the palace slave quarters are located just inside the widest circle of palace walls, at the back of the palace near the stables. Slave quarters are not part of the harem, but the servants are. Royal slaves have been attached to the palace and have lived in the slave quarters for generations; those I interviewed readily identified themselves as slaves to the Emir, regardless of the fact that slavery has been illegal since 1900. Speaking of a very old concubine to a former Emir, Hajiya explained: "She is proud to say she was a slave, and even now wants to die with the name. It means that she served her master properly and honestly" (Interview, 26 May 1982). Women and children of slave status regularly pass through the royal harem on daily business and pleasure, as do eunuchs, guards, and, on special occasions, royal musicians, all of whom may also be of slave status. Often the central courtyard is the scene of dusty soccer games and clapping songs as royal and slave children play together every day.

The harem constitutes the heart of the palace to the same extent that the palace is at the heart of the city: just as the palace is the symbolic center of the city, located at its physical center, so too the harem is both the physical and symbolic focus of the palace community. It is at once the most private set of compounds in Kano, and also the busiest, enjoying a constant flow of traffic from one end of the palace to the other, functioning as a stage for celebration, and an arena for work and leisure activities of women and children. It is the private residence of royal wives, who are restricted by the Hausa tradition of wife seclusion to their own compounds. Royal wives do not move freely about the vast harem, but they may watch harem activities without themselves being seen, and important public festivals such as the annual *salla* parade are brought to the harem courtyard so wives may watch from their compound windows. These conditions testify to the symbolic as well as physical centrality of royal wives in the palace community.[13] The harem, the arena of royal domesticity, is the liveliest portion of the palace estate, and its inhabitants are active participants in a complex network of productive women.

Harem Responsibilities and Authority

Like other Hausa wives outside the palace, royal wives are responsible for the smooth operation of their households. Meals must be prepared, laundry washed, clothes ordered for special occasions, and children's homework supervised. Whenever these tasks are carried out by a royal wife's servants, she is ultimately responsible for directing their completion; sometimes a royal wife will choose to perform these tasks herself, particularly for special occasions and celebrations. For naming or wedding festivities and the annual *salla* parade that follows the month of Ramadan fasting, a royal wife is responsible for feeding large numbers of visitors in addition to the daily complement of residents in her part of the palace. Adequate provision of meals and snacks requires long hours of cooperative activity between wives, concubines, and servants. Celebratory clothing also constitutes a drain on the royal wife's energies and budget. She buys expensive cloth from itinerant women traders who bring it into the harem for her inspection and selection. The cloth is then sent to a tailor outside the palace for appropriate outfits for all children under her jurisdiction, from their infancy until adulthood.[14]

In addition to supervising daily meal preparation, laundry, and adjudicating children's squabbles, Hausa wives are often consulted regarding marriage arrangements, which the Emir makes with the parents of suitable partners. Matches are established according to status, family, and political affiliations, but it is becoming quite common to consider issues of compatibility and the children's own preferences of partners. It is not unusual for royal wives to veto matches that they know, through better familiarity with sons and daughters, to be undesirable, and to assist in making new choices.

Once the marriage is arranged to everyone's satisfaction, wives are responsible for providing their daughters' dowries. Often a royal wife will provide a dowry for foster daughters, or even for the daughters of concubines who live in her compound and serve her.[15] A dowry in Hausa society is essentially a trousseau on a grand scale. A royal wife explained to me in 1983 that the female guardian is expected to provide a new bride's wardrobe and cooking utensils; in addition, a new bride is expected to bring with her all the food staples she needs to set up housekeeping (Interview with Hajiya Abba, 2 May 1983). Among the necessities for a new bride are many costly items that constitute the bride's economic security (e.g., an iron four-poster bed, many dozens of brass or ceramic bowls, cooking pots, gold leaf animal statuettes, lengths of lace and damask, and new ready-made clothes). In the case of divorce this wealth remains with the woman. Years later, a woman may use these items for her own daughters' dowries, either by selling them to get cash for other items or by passing these items on to her daughters.

In 1983 Hajiya, a royal wife in Kano, was preparing a dowry for her foster daughter, Binta, a woman who came to the palace when her parents were unable to provide for her as a child. The prospective husband provided the wardrobe for his bride, which freed Hajiya to use money she had saved over the past few years ("since Binta first told me she had someone she was going to marry") in anticipation of the wedding. In addition, Hajiya had received money from friends and relatives when they heard of Binta's impending marriage. Hajiya explained that the system of mutual assistance allows mothers or guardians to meet the high cost of dowry:

> For instance I will send [another] Hajiya 20 naira [in 1980 one naira was approximately equivalent to $1.61] when I hear about the daughter's wedding, and then when she hears about one of my daughters, she will send me 30. Then the next time when her daughter gets married, I will send her 40. People keep track, they write it down, and then they can send the right thing. But for me, I don't write it down, I just send what I think is right, and I am glad for whatever they send me. This time all my sisters and my mother sent me money when they heard, because they know I will need it; there are so many things to buy. But most people spend all the money they get on these pots that they just stack up and look at. It

[i.e., this practice] is difficult for the bride. Then she has to go out and get money for food. So with me, I just divide the money. I have to get food too; that will make it better for Binta, and I know she will appreciate it. So I get one fifty or one hundred pound sack of rice, one of millet, two garwa [four gallons each] of [cooking] oil, one palm, one groundnut, these big Murtala enamel pans (they are N10 each) full of alkali and other sweets, and cincin [doughnuts], and so on. When I have all that, then I use the rest of the money to buy pots. I don't buy any clothes because Binta says her husband has bought [some], and they are enough for her. (Interview, 2 May 1983)

As this example indicates, a woman relies on a system of reciprocity with her friends and family. In Muslim Hausaland, anyone can rely especially heavily on relatives in times of economic need. Knowing this provides an extra measure of both psychological and economic security for women who are physically removed from their natal families, and theoretically subject only to the support of their husbands.

The extent to which women's financial responsibilities are solely their own concern—even among royalty—became clear when Hajiya explained that her husband, the Emir of Kano, was unaware of both the degree of expense she incurred, and her capacity to cover it:

When the Emir comes—I send for him to show him what I have bought for her—he is shocked, he is surprised. He says, "But where did you get the money to pay for all this?" You see, I have a bed for her that I bought five years ago, very cheap, because I knew I would need it. And Hajiya Amina asked me what I wanted for Binta; I told her a mattress, since I know she can get it. So that's what she gave me. And then the sheets that you [i.e., the author] gave me and six of these matching pillowslips, because you know they have to put pillows on the bed. And I had a cupboard for her things—one of those covered in formica, with the mirrors. And the Emir, he is very surprised, very impressed. He says, "Where did you get all this?" You see, it is because I planned. And we are very pleased, the Emir, Binta and I. That is how we do it. The family and your relatives help you because they know you will need the money. And you must do it. (Interview, 2 May 1983)

As this indicates, women's financial responsibilities are their own in the sense that they are women's concerns, not men's. It is rare that a woman will not offer a gift appropriate to the circumstances, or fail to reciprocate when another voices a need. If the giver has too little money to provide what is appropriate or requested, she might offer something smaller with profuse apology. It is more likely, however, that she will borrow enough from another woman to meet her immediate gift-giving needs. It is very rare to find a woman who does not participate in this system of mutual assistance, for it is itself a form of the alms-giving that is one of the five obligations required of Muslims.[16]

If the investment for an adopted daughter seems large, that which is expected for a royal daughter is even greater. Hajiya continued:

> But now when [my eldest daughter] gets married, she will expect a lot more because she is an emir's daughter, and she thinks he is the richest man in the world. She will expect everything—expensive cloth, food, pans, furniture, everything. And the Emir must provide it. You know, she doesn't get much from him now, but for the wedding she must. She knows she only has to wait until then. (Interview, 2 May 1983)

A daughter's dowry is a major investment for any Hausa woman. In the case of royal wives it might amount to hundreds of dollars.

While a royal wife does receive economic assistance from her husband, it is rarely sufficient to maintain the household and provide the necessary dowries as well. Whether Hajiya relies on her ingenuity in amassing such funds out of choice or necessity is not clear, but such financial independence is not unusual among both royal and nonroyal Hausa women (Schildkrout 1983; 1979). Therefore, royal wives, like their nonroyal counterparts, often engage in petty trade, selling snacks or crafts from inside their compounds or sending their own children, usually daughters, around the palace to hawk items on their behalf. The money thus earned can be used freely for any private needs, such as dowries and clothing. However, for more public concerns or those involving larger expenditures of money—such as sending a daughter to school or on pilgrimage to Mecca—a wife must confer with her husband. To use a wife's money for these expenses would be a public affront to the husband's ability to provide for his family, so it is unlikely that he would agree. Thus a woman's income, however great, can only be dispersed in nonpublic ways.

The fact that a royal wife has servants to fulfill some of her tasks affords her more free time for the production of foods and handicrafts than women at lower socioeconomic levels have. However, her means of producing items, including her use of technology that can save production time, is familiar to affluent nonroyal women as well. Not all Hausa women have cotton candy machines or refrigerators for making popsicles, but such advantages are tied to economic, not royal status. Although she may begin her married life with greater dowry wealth than the average woman, a royal wife is likely to have greater financial and personal responsibilities than even her affluent counterparts by virtue of her royal position.

Not only must she provide dowry for many more young women than usual, but a royal wife also provides services to the many women who come to visit her from both inside and outside the palace. Female visitors from other parts of the palace and from the city make social calls to discuss issues of common concern (whether focused on the domestic scene or current sociopolitical events), request advice or direct arbitration in disputes, or enlist the assistance of the Emir through the wife's intervention. Other women might visit regularly for tutoring by educated royal wives in literacy, numeracy, or handicrafts. Sometimes, women will ask for loans or gifts of money, and to the extent that the wife is able, she will assist them. Thus as hostesses and mentors, royal wives have far greater demands on their time and energy than most Hausa women. Such roles are indications of the extent to which royal wives wield authority among women within and without the palace. In a society built on patron–client relationships, royal wives play the role of patron to many women clients, who consider them to be models of propriety and sources of educational assistance. Royal wives endure significantly greater social pressure than others to perform their roles in a superlative manner.[17]

The four royal wives wield greatest control in the community of women in the harem, and their status is respected by others. Among them, ranking by seniority determines their relative authority over one another. Technically, the senior wife holds greatest control over the others, with the other three wives following in order. Nevertheless, an individual's own personality may distinguish her from others in terms of commanding respect and exerting influence. For instance, two of the wives were trained at Kano's Teacher Training College prior to their marriages to the Emir. These women have at various times held tutorials and larger daily classes in their compounds for adult women from inside and outside of the palace. Thus, while the senior wife is accorded greatest respect, she may choose not to exercise the authority her position carries; conversely, other wives might enhance their positions by involvement in certain activities such as teaching that merit respect and the high regard of the women around them. A royal wife's authority within the community of women is less influenced by her natal family ties than by the reputation she establishes for herself through good works and goodwill. Such a situation reflects the nature of changing bases of power and prestige among women in Hausa society.

Certainly royal wives hold authority on the strength of the level of importance of their natal connections. Each of the four wives is from another important Hausa political region—she might be the daughter of a high official, or the daughter of an important Muslim authority—whose marriage to the Emir of Kano constitutes a political bond. A royal wife is prohibited from receiving male guests, even her father, after being installed in the harem of her marriage home, so she cannot function as a direct mediator between the Emir and men in her own family. Visits with her female relatives are rare because most of them are secluded in their own marriage homes. Nevertheless, her presence in the Kano royal harem symbolizes a continued connection and implications of goodwill among political entities.

Traditionally women of slave heritage were given to the Emir by lesser chiefs trying to curry favor. In such cases the political bond established was less significant than that created through marriage. When a woman becomes a concubine at her own or her parents request, her slave heritage must be proved in order for her to be eligible. In either case, concubinage benefits the woman more than her guardian or the Emir. As a royal concubine, her children are free and enjoy royal status. Since the kingship is not hereditary, but determined by a council of kingmakers who select from a pool of eligible candidates, the Emir can increase his representatives in that pool by having more children by concubines, but he has no guarantee that a son of his will succeed him. The marriages of his concubine's daughters may provide him an opportunity to establish political ties, but this has not seemed to be a major concern in recent times (Mack 1988).

With the Emir himself, a wife's credibility depends more on their personal relationship than on her family background; her education, intellect, and personal character are qualities most important in imbuing her opinion with authority. This is not a new development in interpersonal relations; evidence exists that certain royal wives and mothers advised their husbands and sons long before Western colonial influence developed in the area (Hull 1968; Mack 1988).

Further examination of the extent to which this is the case is important for a more complete image of Hausa social and gender relations.

While women's credibility is indicated by the willingness of decision-makers to accept advice from royal wives and mothers, other women in the Emir's harem are given titles that attest to their credibility and the respect they command. The situation varies in palaces throughout northern Nigeria, but in Kano several concubines hold honorary titles given by the Emir that carry with them responsibility for significant aspects of the operation of the palace, such as the overseeing of harem activities, and coordinating residents' and nonresidents' audiences with the Emir. These women's titles indicate that each holds a particular social status, with attendant responsibilities (Mack 1990). Together these women constitute the managers of nearly all the palace and its daily social and political operations, playing active roles and being recognized as significant officiators there.

Women of all social statuses are overwhelmingly responsible for the management of the royal harem, the household of the palace. A parallel can be drawn with nonroyal households, where women are in charge of maintenance of the home and hold responsibility for individuals within it. This observation can only have significance, however, if the household is understood as a locus of sociopolitical activities, rather than a domestic domain separate from men's spheres of influence (Coles and Mack 1991). Indeed men's decisions are often affected by the opinions of the women in their families. Although rarely documented in historical accounts, examples of women's influence on decisions about warfare and politics do exist (Boyd 1989; Hull 1968; Mack 1988), underlining the pervasive nature of domestic influence in Hausa culture.[18]

Gender Relations and Changing Conditions in the Harem

The harem is by definition a women's sanctuary, forbidden to adult men outside the family (Penzer 1937), but it is not uncommon to see men in the harem area. Depending on their status and reason for being there, men may sometimes converse with the women of the harem. When workers—male inmates at the nearby prison—are brought in to repair a wall or gate, for instance, women are warned so that they may retreat to a spot secluded from view. On the other hand, palace eunuchs have a supervisory role in the harem and thus roam freely there, conversing openly with the harem women. Since eunuchs are of ambiguous sexuality, their resulting social liminality permits them to frequent both male and female domains. From among the royal slaves it is usually women, girls, and prepubescent boys who move in and out of the harem, the latter often carrying out tasks or seeking the camaraderie of adolescent sons of wives and concubines.[19] Thus, all slaves except adult males have regular access to the harem. During the annual *salla* processions, a representative portion of the procession escorts the Emir to his harem reception room; his attendants include royal sons on their mounts, men who are royal musicians, and titled attendants, often themselves royal slaves (Mack 1990).

Young men regularly visit the harem, spending a great deal of time with the women there, visiting a royal wife especially if she is the mother of a woman the young man wishes to marry. Since marriages are still arranged by parents, a wife will take particular note of the qualities she observes in certain young men. Those who are astute enough to realize it, know that their chances of winning a certain girl depend largely on being in good favor with her mother or guardian, who has a great deal of influence in the choice of marriage partners for her children. The young unmarried royal sons of wives or concubines who live in the harem until they go away to secondary school (as do most sons of wives or concubines), live in two worlds, free to attend school and work outside the palace, but always drawn back to the place where they were raised, and where their mothers still live. It is here in the harem that boys are socialized and play together until they reach puberty. At that point they are eager to explore the wider world, but the harem always remains home to them. The young men who visit their fiancees in the palace spend many long hours talking with the women and children, a process that allows them to become one of the family. In such circumstances debates concerning women's role in public affairs, education, and Islam are common. At such times women are not shy to express their disagreement with these young men on matters relating to women's roles in Hausa society. While young men's presence in the harem is in theory not acceptable, that prescription is belied in practice.[20] Thus the Hausa domestic arena is not exclusively women's space, although they hold the authority there.

A further complication in the study of Hausa domesticity outside the palace is the contemporary proliferation of households influenced by western models. Many young couples have been exposed to nontraditional lifestyles, either in the course of living abroad, or through contact with non-Hausas living in increasingly cosmopolitan urban communities. As a result, new patterns of behavior between spouses and family organization are emerging in Hausaland that reflect the integration of useful extradomestic influences. It is important that further research consider these new household patterns on their own terms, rather than simply assuming a wholesale westernization of Hausa domesticity.

Hausa women's domestic roles influence society in ways that transcend the functions of reproducing and socializing new generations. Therefore a better understanding of Hausa culture requires further investigation into the nature of the domestic realm as an integral part of and pervasive presence in Hausa Muslim life. Indeed, the complex linkages between those aspects of the household that are not oriented toward provision or reproduction and wider social and political aspects of society have been little considered in existing studies of Hausa culture. Palace domesticity is considered a model for Hausa society, because the Emir is the social and religious figurehead for his people; he is the traditional "final authority" for his people, and his family—as is often the case with royalty—is expected to be exemplary. The royal harem is like nonroyal domestic realms to the extent that it constitutes an arena for the daily cooperative exchange of intellectual, spiritual, and social "goods," as well as material items in the fulfillment of particular social responsibilities. Both men and women participate in such exchange, fulfilling responsibilities mandated equitably and complementarily for each gender by Islam.

Unlike royal women, nonroyal Kano women are not restricted to their domestic roles. Many hold important positions outside the home in professions like medicine, agricultural development, communications, and education (Coles and Mack 1991; Imam 1991; Yusuf 1991). But whatever else a woman may do professionally or as paid work, it must not conflict with the fulfillment of her domestic role. For the affluent nonroyal woman, there may appear to be more potential to pursue a career while servants help with child care and household tasks. Nevertheless, her high status may involve a more conservative interpretation of the domestic role and the practice of wife seclusion, which could prohibit her public activity. This dilemma, like the question of the appropriate number of wives in an era of "modernity," drives debate among public leaders who are less constrained by tradition than the Emir. In addition to lack of consensus among both men and women about issues such as the appropriate numbers of wives and women in the work force, a rising fundamentalist Muslim women's movement is increasingly vocal in Kano. Significantly, conservative and liberal perspectives appear to cut across political, socioeconomic, educational, and age boundaries. There appears to be no clear cut profile for members of either camp at this time.

Regardless of how conditions change for women, a western domestic pattern cannot be presumed to be in effect in a Hausa context because it does not account for the pervasive social influence of Islam. Whatever new patterns of domesticity might evolve, they will be uniquely suited to Hausa Muslim socioreligious mores. The increasingly cosmopolitan nature of Hausa society will inevitably result in changes that alter both the popularity and viability of the traditional harem. Nevertheless Islamic influence is likely to keep Hausa socioeconomic concerns focused on the family, resulting in new definitions of the domestic and relations within it.

Notes

1. In Middle-Eastern societies women may leave their sanctuary anonymously, hidden by the veil; in Muslim West Africa a woman's veil is her home, the compound walls protecting her from public view.

2. From the Arabic *amir*, an emir is a theocratic leader of a Muslim state. The Emir of Kano is a traditional Hausa ruler presiding over an area often considered to be the seat of Hausaland.

3. "Shehu" is the term for a brotherhood leader and religious teacher in Islam.

4. Boyd (1989) explains that Nana Asma'u was by no means the first of Muslim women scholars in the area, commenting that the Shehu's

> mother, Hauwa and his maternal grandmother Rukayya were also learned and were among the teachers of the community. Two thousand kilometers away in Futa Toro there was at least one Mauritanian woman teacher; so women scholars were not unheard of, and there is evidence of notable scholarly women in Timbuktu who had the title "Nana." (4)

Furthermore, the Emir of Kano, Alhaji Ado Bayero, explained to me in 1983 that "Islamic law under the *jihad* abolished [Hausa] women's role in public offices," including that it had long been the custom for women to hold public office among the Hausa. (This quote is from an interview with Alhaji Ado Bayero, Emir of Kano, in the palace, 9 March 1983.)

5. This was true not only in the North, among the Hausa, but also in the South. A classic example is that of the Aba women's riots of 1929, documented in Ifeka-Moller, "Female Militancy and Colonial Revolt: The Women's War of 1929, Eastern Nigeria" (1975), and Van Allen, "Sitting on a Man" (1972). In this example the female *de facto* control of palm products was eschewed by the British in favor of the male *de jure* authority over them, a situation that was not tolerated by the women involved.

6. As Catherine Coles has noted in commenting on this manuscript in draft, such an observation applies only to women who are economically secure. In times of severe economic constraints, such as those experienced during the late 1980s and the early 1990s, the number of women who are in economically stable households is likely to be far lower than in the period of research for this study, a decade ago. This would render the situation of royal Hausa women far less common than it was perceived to be at that time.

7. The influence of economic resources on the quality of the domestic environment and a woman's self-esteem is an issue that might fruitfully be examined from a cross-cultural perspective.

8. Such activities range from the ordinary (congregating at the end of the day for conversation and pursuing handicrafts) to the celebratory, as a portion of the annual post-Ramadan *salla* procession wends its way into the harem so that those who are secluded there will not miss seeing its pageantry; musicians and dancers perform there for naming and wedding celebrations.

9. Each of the four wives has an area of the harem named after her or her town of origin. Such naming symbolizes her "ownership" of and authority over the area. Area names change with a wife's change of residence.

10. These activities are examples of the "hidden trade" pursued by nonroyal Hausa women, and described by Hill (1969) and Schildkrout (1983).

11. The space involved may be as large and open as that of a royal wife's compound, but it may house greater numbers of women.

12. It is incumbent upon an emir to give shelter to those who request it, especially those attached by blood, service, or marriage to the palace. Once a woman's residence is established, it is understood that she has the right to remain there for the duration of her life (barring exceptionally unacceptable circumstances or behavior), under the protection of the sovereignty of the palace, regardless of changes in emirship.

13. Eleanor Gerber pointed out this symbolic significance of wives' privileged seclusion, for which I am grateful.

14. The implication here is that subordinate women relinquish jurisdiction over their children, who spend sufficient amounts of their youth in other women's compounds to constitute such a situation of fostering. To the extent that the advice, discipline, and financial support of a foster mother

with a higher socioeconomic status is respected and gratefully accepted, this is true, because it is assumed to be the responsibility of the more affluent to provide for the less well-off in Hausa society. Ultimately, however, a mother is responsible for the behavior of her own children.

15. In an interview with one of the Emir's wives (2 May 1983), she explained that somewhat less is spent to provide the dowry for foster daughters than for Emir's daughters; it is still, however, a significant amount of money, as is made clear in her itemization of costs in the text here.

16. Such mutual assistance schemes are common among women and are mentioned in work by Saunders (1979) and Simmons (1975, 1976).

17. A case also can be made for the power wielded by royal wives as they influenced the decisions of emirs and other powerful men throughout recent history. For a discussion of this, see Mack 1988, particularly 65–66.

18. "Female agency . . . [is] not the recounting of great deeds performed by women, but the exposure of the often silent and hidden operations of gender, which are nonetheless present and defining forces of politics and political life" (Joan Wallach Scott, "Women's History and the Rewriting of History," in *The Impact of Feminist Research in the Academy*, ed. Christie Farnham, 44–45. [Bloomington: Indiana University Press, 1987]).

19. Occasionally the royal guards will stroll through the open courtyard area of the harem, chatting with the women there.

20. "[In male-centered structures of hierarchy and segregation] there is a need to view women (and other subdominant segments) not merely as passive participants, but as vital protagonists interacting with the structures of their domination, necessarily exercising some degree of autonomy, not only in defining and interpreting but in redefining and reinterpreting how the dominant structures define and interpret them" (Kaveh Safa-Isfahani, "Female Centered World Views in Iranian Culture: Symbolic Representations of Sexuality in Dramatic Games," *Signs: Journal of Women in Culture and Society,* [1980] vol. 6, 1: 34).

Bibliography

Abraham, R. C. 1962. *A Dictionary of the Hausa Language*. London: University of London Press.

Abu-Lughod, Lila. 1985. A Community of Secrets: The Separate World of Bedouin Women. *Signs: Journal of Women in Culture and Society* 10 (4): 637–657.

Boyd, Jean. 1989. *The Caliph's Sister*. London: Frank Cass Press.

Coles, Catherine M., and Beverly B. Mack. 1991. Women in Twentieth Century Hausa Society. In *Hausa Women in the Twentieth Century*, ed. Catherine M. Coles and Beverly B. Mack, 3–26. Madison: University of Wisconsin Press.

The Concise Edition of the Oxford English Dictionary. 1971. London: Oxford University Press.

Dunbar, Roberta Ann. 1970. Damagaram (Zinder, Niger), 1812–1906: The History of a Central Sudanic Kingdom. Ph.D. diss., University of California, Los Angeles.

Hill, Polly. 1969. Hidden Trade in Hausaland. *Man* 4 (3): 392–409.

Hiskett, Mervyn. 1973. *The Sword of Truth: The Life and Times of Shehu Usman Dan Fodio.* New York: Oxford University Press.

Hogben, S. J., and A.H.M. Kirk-Greene. 1966. *The Emirates of Northern Nigeria: A Preliminary Survey of Their Historical Traditions.* London: Oxford University Press.

Hull, Richard Williams. 1968. *The Development of Administration in the Katsina Emirate, Northern Nigeria, 1887–1944.* Ph.D. Diss., Columbia University, New York.

Ifeka-Moller, Caroline. 1975. Female Militancy and Colonial Revolt: The Women's War of 1929. In *Perceiving Women,* ed. Shirley Ardener. London: Malaby Press.

Imam, Ayesha. 1991. Ideology, the Mass Media, and Women: A Study from Radio Kaduna, Nigeria. In *Hausa Women in the Twentieth Century,* ed. Catherine M. Coles and Beverly B. Mack, 244–252. Madison: University of Wisconsin Press.

Last, Murray. 1983. From Sultanate to Caliphate: Kano ca. 1450–1800. In *Studies in the History of Kano,* ed. Bawuro Barkindo, 67–92. Ibadan: Heinemann.

Mack, Beverly B. 1980. A Socio-Economic Profile of Residents in Kano, Nigeria (Old City). Kano Water Supply/Sanitiation Project Urban Poverty Background Study, Final Report. Kano, Nigeria: World Bank.

———. 1988. Hajiya Ma'daki: A Royal Hausa Woman. In *Life Histories of African Women,* ed. Patricia W. Romero, 47–77. Atlantic Highfields, N.J.: Ashfield Press.

———. 1990. Service and Status: Slave and Concubines in Kano, Nigeria. In *At Work in Homes,* ed. Roger Sanjek and Shellee Colen, 14–34. American Ethnological Society Monograph 3. Washington, D.C.: American Anthropological Association.

———. 1991. Royal Wives in Kano. In *Hausa Women in the Twentieth Century,* ed. Catherine M. Coles and Beverly B. Mack, 109–129. Madison: University of Wisconsin Press.

———. Forthcoming. Women and Slavery in Nineteenth Century Hausaland. In *The Human Commodity: Perspectives on the Trans-Saharan Slave Trade,* ed. Elizabeth Savage. London: Frank Cass.

Penzer, Norman M. [1937] 1975. *The Harem: An Account of the Institution as it Existed in the Palace of the Turkish Sultans with a History of the Grand Seraglio from its Foundation to the Present Time.* Reprint. New York: AMS Press, 1975.

Rosaldo, Michelle Z. 1980. The Use and Abuse of Anthropology: Reflections on Feminism and Cross-Cultural Understanding. *Signs: Journal of Women in Culture and Society* 5 (3): 389–417.

Safa-Isfahani, Kaveh. 1980. Female Centered World Views in Iranian Culture: Symbolic Representations of Sexuality in Dramatic Games. *Signs: Journal of Women in Culture and Society* 6 (3): 33–53.

Sanday, Peggy. 1981. *Female Power and Male Dominance: On the Origins of Sexual Inequality.* Cambridge: Cambridge University Press.

Saunders, Margaret Overholt. 1978. Marriage and Divorce in a Muslim Hausa Town (Mirria, Niger Republic). Ph.D. diss., Indiana University, Bloomington.

———. 1979. Hausa Women in Economic Development: The Case of Mirria, Niger Republic. Paper presented to Society for Applied Anthropology, Philadelphia.

———. 1980. Women's Role in a Muslim Hausa Town (Mirria, Republic of Niger). In *A World of Women,* ed. Erika Bourguignon, et al., 57–86. New York: J. F. Bergin.

Schildkrout, Enid. 1979. Women's Work and Children's Work: Variations Among Muslims in Kano. In *Social Anthropology of Work,* ed. Sandra Wallman, 60–85. ASA Monograph 19. London: Academic Press.

———. 1983. Dependency and Autonomy: The Economic Activities of Secluded Hausa Women in Kano. In *Femalen and Male in Africa,* ed. Christine Oppong, 107–126. London: George Allen and Unwin.

Scott, Joan Wallach. 1987. Women's History and the Rewriting of History. In *The Impact of Feminist Research in the Academy,* ed. Christie Farnham, 34–50. Bloomington: Indiana University Press.

Simmons, Emmy B. 1975. The Small Scale Rural Food Processing Industry in Northern Nigeria. In *Overseas Liaison Committee America Council on Education,* no. 10.

———. 1976. Economic Research and Women in Rural Development in Northern Nigeria. In *Overseas Liaison Committee America Council on Education,* no. 10.

Smith, M. G. 1960. *Government in Zazzau, 1800–1958.* Los Angeles: University of California Press.

———. 1978. *The Affairs of Daura: History and Change in a Hausa State 1800–1958.* Berkeley: University of California Press.

Smith, Mary. 1981. *Baba of Karo: A Woman of the Muslim Hausa.* New Haven: Yale University Press.

Van Allen, Judith. 1972. "Sitting on a Man": Colonialism and the Lost Political Institutions of Igbo Women. *Canadian Journal of African Studies* 6 (2): 165–181.

Yeld, Rachel. 1960. Islam and Social Stratification in Northern Nigeria. *British Journal of Sociology* 11:112–128.

Yusuf, Bilkisu. 1991. Hausa-Fulani Women: The State of the Struggle. In *Hausa Women in the Twentieth Century,* ed. Catherine M. Coles and Beverly B. Mack, 90–106. Madison: University of Wisconsin Press.

3 Civilized Servants: Child Fosterage and Training for Status among the Glebo of Liberia

Mary H. Moran

Among the many legacies of Western contact with and domination of Africa has been the introduction of new systems of prestige and value. These go by a variety of names: westernization, modernization, and civilization, are perhaps the most commonly used. While all of these terms imply access to new kinds of knowledge, wealth, and property, they are also marked by changes in life-style that are often reflected in a new domestic order. Where once people slept or sat on mats on the ground, now they have beds and chairs. Eating utensils replace the fingers and a new etiquette of meal-taking replaces the old. Different standards of dress and definitions of cleanliness are acquired, making both the home and the body a visible manifestation of the new order.

That such details of daily domestic practice can serve as centrally important markers of relative prestige among people experiencing broad social change has become evident from a number of studies. Karen Tranberg Hansen, in her introduction to this volume, notes that scholarly work on the history and ideology of domestic practice in the West has seen a sudden upswing in recent years. By "domestic," I mean both the socially defined space associated with a residential group and the meaningful practices that take place there. Clearly, domestic spaces are neither "natural" nor divorced from other domains of human behavior. Early attempts in feminist anthropology to explain gender hierarchy in terms of a presumed universal human distinction between "domestic" and "public" spheres (Rosaldo 1974) have been challenged in a variety of cultural and historical contexts (Rosaldo 1980; for Africa, Sudarkasa 1986).

Recently, a new direction in scholarship has emerged that explores how the domestic, even when ideologically separated from other aspects of human life, is inextricably bound to and mutually constitutive of broader political and economic structures. For example, Pierre Bourdieu, in his analysis of the aesthetics of class and life-style in France, has noted that even minor domestic conventions provide "a sort of social orientation, a 'sense of one's place,' guiding the occupants of a given place in social space towards the social positions adjusted to their properties, and towards the practices or goods which befit the occupants of that position" (1984,466). Bourdieu uses the concept of habitus, or the relationship between structural principles generating behavior and the apprehension and classification of that behavior. "It is in the relationship between the two capacities which define the habitus, the capacity to produce classifiable practices and works, and the capacity to differentiate and appreciate these practices and products (taste) that the represented social world . . . is constituted" (Ibid., 170). Habitus, therefore, consists of a system of shared cultural standards, the practice of actors in relation to those standards, and the evaluation of such practices by others within the same system. Class habitus, "the internalized form of class condition and of the conditioning it entails" (Ibid., 101), includes the aesthetic markers and practices by which actors differentiate and recognize each others' relative position. As Bourdieu has demonstrated, many of these markers concern the domestic realm, especially the care and presentation of food, the body, and the home.

Civilization in the Liberian Context

While non-Western systems of class habitus have received less attention from theorists, it is clear that European-derived models of domestic order are closely tied up with colonialism, missionization, and perceptions of upward mobility within postcolonial African states. In Liberia, where the distinction between "civilized" and "native" people has a long and complex history and is a major organizing principle, informants cite daily domestic practices as indicators of relative prestige more frequently than structural features such as occupation or level of education. Although the word "civilized" is obviously a European import, it has been invested with new meanings in the Liberian context. The complex of standards, values, and behaviors designated as civilized is also denoted in Liberian English by the Kru word "kwi," a term that has been widespread since at least the early 1900s. Of the concept civilized and its opposite, native, Elizabeth Tonkin has noted: "Every commentator on Liberia this century has mentioned these words and thought them salient" (1981:305).

Liberia is the oldest independent republic on the African continent, settled in 1822 by Americans of African descent under the sponsorship of a private, white-directed, benevolent organization, the American Colonization Society. The immigrants self-consciously saw themselves as civilized, part of a divine plan for the salvation of Africa that had included a period of bondage in the New World. Their civilization was at once the basis of their claim to "return" to Africa and of their "right" to subjugate and dominate the indigenous people. Yet, precisely because that claim was grounded on cultural rather than racial criteria, the civilized category was open to the incorporation of others through adoption, wardship, intermarriage and patronage. Those claiming descent from or connection with the original American settlers monopolized both political and economic power in Liberia until 1980, when a military coup ended almost a century of one-party rule. It is this unique and peculiar history that has shaped Liberian national culture and notions of civilized life.[1]

More than simply a statement about class stratification or ethnic conflict between indigenous and repatriate Liberians, the concept of civilization has been notoriously resistant to definition along the usual sociological parameters of education, income, or property ownership (see Brown 1982; Fraenkel 1964, 1966; Tonkin 1978–1979, 1980, 1981). As Fraenkel noted, the seemingly obvious question of how many years of formal, Western schooling are required to make one civilized is rephrased as, "how much education a man [sic] needs to get a job sufficiently well-paid for him to lead a 'civilized' life" (1964, 67–68). It is the style of life, particularly as enacted in dress, household order, presentation of self, and public comportment, that identifies a person as civilized.

The basic criteria that must be met by those claiming civilized status probably vary regionally across Liberia. Minimally, these include nominal Christianity (which is a necessary but not sufficient condition for civilized status, since there are large numbers of native Christians), facility with spoken English, minimal literacy (which implies some contact with the formal educational system), involvement with the cash rather than the subsistence sector of the economy, and having been "trained" in a civilized household. Training includes the inculcation of civilized standards of dress, home decoration, the preparation and presentation of food, and other features of what Weber has described as "status honor":

> above all else a specific style of life [that] can be expected from all those who wish to belong to the circle. . . . As soon as there is not a mere individual and socially irrelevant imitation of another style of life, but an agreed upon communal action of this closing character, the "status" development is underway. (1946,187–188)

Lack of training in these niceties can seriously undermine an individual's claims to civilized status, even where other criteria of education and income have been met.

Civilized Servants

In this paper, I investigate the cultural and moral construction of the term "servant" among the civilized sector of the Glebo community of Cape Palmas in southeastern Liberia.[2] I argue that rather than the occupational category, the condition of being a servant among the Glebo refers to a relationship of fosterage between persons unrelated by kinship (Moran 1990, 101). The category "servant," therefore, results not from the payment of a wage in a market economy, but from the status and prestige requirements of civilized households (and especially those of the female heads of such households), and from the restricted routes of access to civilized status in Liberian society.

Moreover, by focusing on those whose status as civilized is not yet confirmed, I illustrate the "production" of civilized persons and locate the domestic domain as the site of this production. More than schools, churches, or state-level bureaucracies, domestic groups control recruitment to the civilized category. Although membership by birth in a civilized household is one route of access to this status, the civilized group (like the Liberian "repatriate" ethnic category; Dunn and Tarr 1988) is not limited to augmenting its numbers only through biological reproduction. Institutions of fosterage and incorporation allow persons without genealogical ties to civilized households to receive the training necessary for their future roles. At the same time, the labor of both related and unrelated aspirants maintains the standards of domesticity by which civilized households define themselves.

Among the Glebo of Cape Palmas, the civilized/native distinction bisects towns, lineages, and even households. The Glebo acquired their ideas about what constitutes civilization from a variety of sources. During the eighteenth and nineteenth centuries, Glebo men participated in a system of short-term labor migration, working aboard European ships and in colonial ports along the West African coast (Brooks 1972; Martin 1982). They brought home from these voyages, among other things, trade goods, a facility with foreign languages, and new tastes in clothing.[3]

To this already established base came African American colonists from the United States who settled on Cape Palmas in 1834. Close behind followed Christian missionaries from several denominations, the most successful being those of the Protestant Episcopal Church. Interaction with the colonists gave the Glebo a model of civilized life which was reinforced through missionary instruction. As Martin notes, the missionaries were interested in more than simple conversion:

> A good Glebo Christian observed Sunday, pulled down greegrees [indigenous religious objects], and refused to participate in traditional sacrifices, but a good Glebo Christian also wore western clothes, built a western house, married only one wife, and cultivated a garden of flowers (Martin 1968:206).

The emergence of a civilized Glebo community in the 1840s and 1850s was paralleled by the growth of similar "civilized towns" among the Siklipo and Jlao Kru, along the coast to the north of Cape Palmas (Martin 1968, 207–209; Fraenkel 1966; Tonkin 1978–1979). In the early years, according to Fraenkel, "the separation of the new town from the old not only divided followers of the new religion from the old one, but also divided the younger, educated generation eager for change, from the traditionalists" (1966, 164). Originally marked by such residential segregation, the civilized town of Hoffman Station, located about half an hour's walk from the administrative center of Harper City, had, by the time of my fieldwork in 1982–1983, become a thoroughly mixed community of civilized and native Glebo, as well as migrants to the coast from inland Kru- and Grebo-speaking groups. While a community of unambiguously native subsistence farmers nearby provided a clear contrast, it was evident that simple residence in the civilized town did not confer civilized status. According to my census, fully twenty-one percent of Hoffman Station's adult women are engaged in market trading, an occupation that stamps a woman as native (Moran 1990, 80–81).

Neither is involvement in the wage economy alone a decisive factor, as evidenced by the number of men employed as laborers or drivers who are still native in the eyes of the community. Church affiliation and attendance cuts across the civilized/native line, as many Glebo who are traditionalists in every other respect are also devout Episcopalians. What features, then, serve to distinguish civilized from native Glebo?

When asked this question, informants generally responded by citing some aspect of what we would call housekeeping: "In a civilized house, the first thing people do when they get up in the morning is sweep out all the rooms and around the yard." People also mentioned the covering of cooked food to protect it from flies, the laundering and pressing of clothes worn by household members, and the construction of latrines and permanent bathing shelters as examples of civilized behavior. The equation of cleanliness with civilization is not unique to the Glebo. Tonkin reports that among students in the Government High School in the Kru community of Sasstown, civilization or "Kui" [kwi] was identified with "the use of machines, with hygienic habits and rejection of superstition, and above all with wisdom and knowledge" (1981,322). Among fourteen adult Kru representing both civilized and native backgrounds, "All but one of the respondents define Kuiness especially in terms of cleanliness and proper behavior" (Ibid., 323). To use Bourdieu's terminology, these particular features are clearly "distinctive" practices in determining civilized status.

Here we must note that those aspects cited as indicative of civilization (sweeping, the preparation and presentation of food, the care of clothing, etc.) fall among the responsibilities of women. Women's daily practice therefore helps to define the civilized status of the entire household. From a comparative perspective, none of this is very surprising. Social historians have documented the rise of a "cult of domesticity" (Cott 1977; Ryan 1981), which accompanied the increasing growth of the American middle class during the nineteenth century. The elaboration of housekeeping and child care into a peculiarly women's "profession" and its association with household status involved a complex set of ideas about dirt, cleanliness, the body, the distinction between physical and mental labor, and the separation of the home from the workplace. Among the nineteenth-century Swedish middle-class families documented by Frykman and Löfgren (1987),

> The ideal existence of *femina domestica* was defined by men.
> Middle-class women were supposed to be spared heavy and dirty
> chores at home. Real productive work was not for them; they were
> expected to express their womanhood through other activities.
> (1987, 134)

Rising standards of domestic cleanliness coupled with the elevation
of the status of middle-class housewife as one above manual or
strenuous labor created a demand for a whole category of lower-class
domestic workers, or servants. Domestic work therefore became a
crucial site of production for *two* kinds of emerging class habitus.

As was the case in nineteenth-century Europe and the United
States, however, few Glebo women are economically capable of living according to the ideal model of civilized womanhood. There appears to be very little actual difference in the domestic practices of
civilized and native households. While it is certainly true that civilized households begin their day by sweeping, so too do their native
neighbors and kin. Enamel bowls with covers for keeping off flies
are standard equipment in every home, including the seasonal homesteads of subsistence farmers. While women farmers who are busy
with their agricultural work certainly have less time for housekeeping and home decoration, successful market women, who are also
defined as natives, commonly have homes identical to those of the
civilized wives of prominent men. Housework, under conditions of
alternating dry (dust) and rainy (mud) seasons and where piped
water and electricity are unavailable, involves almost as much manual labor and physical contact with dirt as subsistence farming. As
far as personal, bodily cleanliness is concerned, all Glebo, to my
knowledge, bathe scrupulously twice a day. Lack of attention to
personal hygiene is taken as a sign of mental illness, not of lower
social status.

There is variation, however, in who may carry out some of the
heavier and more public tasks required by all households. Civilized
women, in particular, are constrained by a combination of prestige
and gender constructions which hold that they are "not strong
enough" to carry the heavy loads of water and firewood that native
women transport routinely. Such tasks, however, are not considered
to tax the strength of even very small children. In addition, civilized
women should not appear in the public market place in any role
other than that of consumer. Women can lose their civilized status
when, as occasionally happens, economic necessity forces them to

take up marketing; gossip about women who *used to be civilized* is common in Cape Palmas. Civilized women are either to be employed in white collar, Western-defined female jobs such as teacher, nurse, or clerical worker, or supported entirely by their husband's wages. The severe shortage of such jobs in proportion to the number of school leavers, the overall lower rates of education and employment of women compared with men, and the lack of formalized marriages and child support all combine to make the lives of many civilized women both economically and socially tenuous.[4] Many must depend on some kind of small scale trading to support themselves and their children, even when attached to an employed man. To accomplish this and still maintain their status, civilized women use children to mediate between themselves and the public market place. Children sell garden produce, prepared snacks, and commercial items like blocks of soap in the street, in the market, and in school yards. Thus, while all Glebo children work hard and contribute economically from an early age, civilized households often have as great as or greater demand for child labor than those of subsistence farmers.

Aspirants to civilized status are trained by carrying out all those housekeeping chores that feature so prominently in the definition of the status position. Since these young people are not themselves unambiguously civilized, it is not the performance of the work that alters their status. The skills needed to perform such work are acquired fairly easily and do not take many years to learn; neither is the knowledge of how to perform them considered in any way secret. Rather than being trained in civilized practices, it is the internalizing of the value placed on these activities, not the details of carrying them out, that is learned by the aspirants. The entire process is seen as requiring a number of years, and there is a strong feeling that training should begin at an early age and be continuous. Of Tonkin's forty-nine student informants in Sasstown, who were in the top three high school grades, most considered themselves safely in the Kui category but eleven considered themselves "in between" or "both Kui and country" (1981, 322).

These many years of apprenticeship result in the appropriation of the young people's labor by the household in which he or she resides. In addition to being crucial for the operation of the small businesses run by civilized women described above, there are many uses for this additional household help. To return to the issue of cleanliness and clothing as key markers of civilization, it is easy to see how dependent civilized households are on these young workers. The physical structure of a civilized house is usually larger and contains more furniture and decorative objects requiring care than are commonly found in farming households. Adult clothing and children's school uniforms and sneakers must be scrupulously washed and pressed, all of which demand large amounts of water and physical labor. While native households mobilize the labor of children and teenagers for productive work on subsistence or cash-crop farms, civilized households pour their labor resources into reproductive activities designed to enhance and maintain their prestige.

Both civilized and native households, therefore, depend on the labor of young people, but differ in their ability to attract recruits. In the native context, additions to the household labor force are generally made through polygynous marriage and through birth. Civilized households, however, have something more to offer than hard agricultural work on farms distant from schools and towns. Civilized households can provide an aspirant to civilization not only with room and board while attending school, but also with the training that produces a civilized person; in effect, they offer civilization itself (Moran 1990, 105).

For those not born into a civilized family or for children of civilized men by their secondary wives (who, unlike the official or "married wife," are usually native women), the route of access into a civilized household is generally through kinship. Civilized Glebo actively maintain membership in their patri-clan, town, and town cluster of origin, all of which may be activated in the placement of foster children. Membership in kin groups is patrilineal, but widely ramifying bilateral kin networks are used for making claims. Since schooling beyond the primary level is only available on or near the coast, a young person wishing to continue his or her education must often leave home. Frequently, native families will choose one child, usually male, in which to invest an education. If successful in achieving civilized status and establishing a household, he will be called upon to foster the children of his native siblings. Since, as discussed above, civilized households require extra labor due to the constraints on adult women, the fostering arrangement is seen as mutually beneficial. The foster family provides the child with food and shelter, while the natal family is responsible for the cash outlay for school fees, clothing, and school supplies, often provided by the increased marketing of foodstuffs by native women. The fostering household, in addition, receives the labor of the foster child. Native families also frequently send gifts of agricultural produce to the homes in which their children are residing and receive coastal products such as fish in return.

Census data from six Glebo communities in Cape Palmas containing about three thousand people show a clear demographic shift of children in the age group five or six and above from native to civilized towns (Moran 1990, 87–92). In addition, civilized households (defined as those in which either or both the male and female heads are considered civilized) tend to be larger than those of natives, containing an average of nine people as opposed to five for the households of subsistence farmers. Civilized households contain people related bilaterally to either or both of the household heads, in contrast with native families, where the Glebo emphasis on patrilineality is more evident in actual residence patterns. Household members who are related through kinship to their foster families, even though the connection may be distant and the exact genealogical link not well understood by either party, are referred to as "relatives" or "family." Others, who have been placed through friendship or because they meet the age and gender requirements of the fostering household, are described as servants.

In local Glebo usage, "servant" is clearly distinguished from the adult occupational category of wage-earning domestics (generally called "house boys" or "house girls") who work for repatriate, Lebanese, and expatriate families in nearby Harper City. Glebo servants are not always immediately economically useful; I have heard children as young as two years of age referred to as servants. At least according to my observations, servants in civilized Glebo homes do not appear to be treated differently from the family's own children or other foster children related by kinship. All household members use kin terms of address, including "mother" and "father" for the household heads. Stratification by age, a highly valued tenet of indigenous Glebo culture, requires young persons to respectfully serve their elders, so that all children run errands and perform household chores from an early age.

Case Studies

Not all servants work out or adjust well to their new homes, and thus may be returned to their families for a variety of reasons. One woman who needed child care in the afternoons when the teenage niece she was fostering was in school agreed to take as a servant the twelve-year-old son of a friend. Since the boy's mother lived nearby, the foster mother had not anticipated any problems with homesickness. After a few months, however, she determined that he was "too quiet" and "looking sick" and so she "sent him back to his ma" and tried to solve her child-care problems in other ways.

In another case, the child appeared to be not only unhappy with the household but with the civilizing process itself. A seven- or eight-year-old girl who had been born and brought up in the interior was placed in a coastal, civilized household. The little girl was rather distantly related to the female head of the household, so her status as servant or foster child (she was referred to as both on different occasions) was somewhat ambiguous. Her case, however, illustrates the process by which she was introduced to the training process and the in this case unsuccessful production of civilized from native people.

The girl was brought to her foster household by her paternal grandmother who was a first cousin (FBD) of the female head of the house. The grandmother and most of the girl's other close kin including her parents were considered natives. She arrived in early March, speaking very little English and never having been to school, but her foster mother introduced her as "my new daughter" and bought her a school uniform and some little dresses. The girl was thus, at least on the exterior, transformed from a native (wearing the two wrap-around cloths, or *lappas*) to someone associated with a civilized house. Her training commenced with the assignment of household tasks, including emptying the chamber pots of the adult members of the household, and her work was closely supervised by the oldest foster child, a nineteen-year-old niece of the female head of the house. With the other younger children, the new daughter swept the house and grounds and carried water from the community pump. These were basic household chores that, in addition to weeding and other farm-related work, would be expected of a native child of similar age. The little girl's integration into other civilized institutions, however, was more problematic.

Within two months of her arrival, the female head of the house was beginning to express doubts about the girl. In spite of having been provided with a book by her foster mother, "She can't seem to learn ABC." She misbehaved or fell asleep during church services and in school, and she was caught tormenting the youngest child in the family, a baby of two, by putting pepper in her nose and soap in her mouth. Most disturbing of all, she was strangely active at night, getting up and complaining that her head felt warm, opening the back door of the house so that, according to her foster mother, "People can put something bad in the food." Such behavior was certain evidence of witchcraft, and the foster mother was convinced that this was why her relatives had insisted that the girl be taken from the country and sent to school. Rather than responding to the civilizing influence of an ordered domestic sphere, the girl was introducing disorder and danger with her "country ways."

By early May, the girl had lost her primer and stayed home from school for a week, since she had no book to study. The female head of the house was adamant, saying, "We can't keep her home just to work, she has to go to school," but was unwilling to invest in another book. An elderly female relative searched her things and found a very old primer; the girl was sent off to school and the same day came back without her book. She said she had loaned it to a friend, but the family suspected that she had simply thrown it away. Indeed the child said clearly that she did not like school and had been observed by the other children to have "lost" her pencil by throwing it into the bush. Since books and pencils, to say nothing of school tuition, represent a sizeable cash outlay, the girl was not only rejecting the high value placed on education but wasting her family's resources.

By July, the girl was not only refusing to go to school but also to bathe and wash her face. She said that she wanted to go back to the farm. The foster mother was completely willing that she do so, but the male head of the household gave in to the pleas of the girls' relatives that she be given another chance. The foster mother, in frustration, had all but given up on trying to train her and had concluded that the girl was uncivilizable and simply wicked. She noted that such wickedness ran in the girl's mother's side of the family (recall that the foster mother was a patrilateral relative). She said that another girl from this family had been sent for training to another civilized woman nearby and had behaved in the same way. As a result, she said, "Now, she's wearing lappas and that's what will happen to this one [her own foster daughter] too." In other words, the little girl was destined to be a native woman, barred from wearing dresses for life.

By late August, the girl had been taken back to the interior by her father. For the entire previous week, she had refused to wash or go to school. The final decision to send her back was made in consultation with her mother, father's mother, several mother's brothers and other relatives. It was not easy for either the foster family to admit their inability to civilize her or for her relatives to back off from the investment they had made in her tuition. Although it is impossible to know the child's own intentions and motivations, it is clear that the language barrier was a problem in school and that she really preferred life on the farm with her grandmother. By resisting the civilized code of personal hygiene and the civilizing institution of the school, she successfully thwarted the plans of her entire kin group, both civilized and native. Although her difficulties with school might have abated as her facility with English grew, the fact that she threatened the domestic order—did "bad things in the house"—caused the family actually to fear her presence in their household. The disrupting influence of the girl's very nativeness brought about her being sent back within six months of her arrival.

Even those servants and foster children who are firmly committed to acquiring civilized status may find their continuation on the civilized trajectory somewhat tenuous. A crisis of personnel in the subsistence and cash-crop farming activities of a native family may cause them to recall their child in the middle of the school term. Likewise, a child may be withdrawn from school due to the family's inability to pay for school fees, uniforms, shoes, books, and supplies. Some children spend several years moving back and forth between their native families in the interior and foster households on the coast, a process that does little to enhance academic success or the smooth acquisition of the other skills of civilized life. Servants and foster children are not alone in experiencing this instability, however, as parental death or unemployment, shifts in local and national politics, and other personal disasters can threaten the future of any child.

As seen in the above case, however, servants are protected from outright exploitation by the moral construction of civilization as the Glebo understand it. It is assumed that children are not to be taken into civilized homes simply as unpaid workers; they must be enrolled in school and therefore placed on the road to civilized status. The following case further illustrates this point.

A prominent civilized woman suffered the personal tragedy of losing her only daughter, age nineteen, in childbirth. The baby survived and was brought home by her grieving grandmother. The woman was faced not only with the loss of her daughter but with a new infant to care for; her other children and foster children were all boys. The father of the baby, who came from an interior town, provided a servant, a teenage girl from his village to whom he was distantly related. The girl had had some education in the village and her father, a native man, agreed to pay for her continued schooling. As the foster parents later said, however, when they took her on, they "didn't know she had a husband" (i.e., a boyfriend) in the village. He sometimes came for weekend visits, during which the servant would disappear for the evening. The family's concerns were realized two years later when the servant, then about eighteen, became pregnant. School girls were, at the time, not allowed to remain in public- or mission-sponsored day schools when pregnant nor to return to day school after giving birth. The household heads decided that they had no choice but to send the girl back to her village, possibly cutting her off from any chance of achieving civilized status since she had only reached the seventh grade. It was clear that the pregnancy itself was not the problem, but the fact that the servant would no longer be a student. As the woman said to me, "I can't have people saying that I keep this girl home to cook for my children while they go to school."

The case was hardly unique but in fact represents the typical process by which an entire class of women, overeducated for the life of native agriculturalists yet undereducated for the job market and burdened with young children, is generated. As a young man commented to me, "These country girls just come to peep at Harper; they can't stay long." He described the first pregnancy as usually followed quickly by a second and then the women were "too weak" to continue their education in night school. The likely result would be that such women end up wearing lappas and selling in the market.

Ironically in this case, the fact that the girl was a servant, that is, had no kin connection to the foster family, made it impossible to keep her on under the pretext that she was "visiting relatives." Her presence in the household could not be explained as anything but a moral, contractual claim on the family to provide her with training for civilized status. Once the bargain could no longer be fulfilled, to keep her on was simply untenable. The moral imperative for the foster parents was clear: young people may have to "suffer" as they serve out their apprenticeship to civilized life, but they must also have a reasonable chance of attaining civilized status.

Training for civilized status and the domestic practices and standards it inculcates is clearly an aspect of what Bourdieu has called "embodied class," which is, "distinguished (in its effects) from class as objectified at a given moment (in the form of property, titles, etc.) inasmuch as it perpetuates a different state of the material conditions of existence" (1984, 437). The class relationship between native and civilized Glebo is not a simple one between "workers and managers" or "peasants and bourgeoisie." Civilized Glebo school teachers and native Glebo laborers stand in exactly the same class position; that of being dependent upon governmental paychecks, which these days are likely to be several months in arrears. Both kinds of salaried workers may compare their situations unfavorably at times with native Glebo agriculturalists, among whom subsistence is provided by a woman's rice farm and cash by her husband's crop of sugarcane or rubber. For these reasons, I have argued elsewhere that the civilized/native dichotomy does not describe class relations among the Glebo of Cape Palmas (Moran 1990, 7). It is, however, a distinction of prestige, or status honor, and Bourdieu has alerted us to the potentiality of any such "distinction" as an indicator of domination:

> Principles of division, inextricably logical and sociological, function within and for the purposes of the struggle between social groups. . . . What is at stake in the struggles about the meaning of the social world is power over the classificatory schemes and systems that are the basis of the representations of groups and therefore of their mobilization and demobilization, . . . a separative power, a distinction, . . . drawing discrete units out of indivisible continuity, difference out of the undifferentiated. (1984, 479)

Although the civilized/native distinction may not describe objective class and power relations within the Glebo ethnic category, it clearly did so nationally in Liberia, at least until recently. From independence in 1847 until the military coup of 1980, the Liberian state was ruled by the settler or repatriate elite, who defined and exemplified the national ideal of civilization. For this group, the emergence in the nineteenth century of educated, "civilized natives" represented both a political challenge and a dangerous conflation of categories. Liberians of indigenous background were allowed to participate in national government only in a token manner through the

1970s (Liebenow 1987, 155). The military coup, led by young, non-commissioned officers of indigenous background, was widely seen as the triumph of civilized natives over the settler elite. With the withdrawal of the repatriate elite from at least the most visible government positions, access to power in the Liberian state is beginning to reflect ethnic competition rather than distinctions based on the civilized/native contrast.[5] On the local level and within ethnic groups, however, these definitions of personal status remain salient.

The class habitus of civilized Glebo housekeeping, therefore, is a reflection not of real or "objectified" class relations between them and their native neighbors and kin. Rather than a mirror of local social structural order, it preserves the reflection of an older national power distinction that is rapidly giving way to one based on ethnicity. As a classification system, however, its local-level efficacy is in no way diminished by the shift in national political realities. Any "distinction" that can assign full siblings to different prestige categories in what is still primarily a kin-based society remains a power to be reckoned with. Furthermore, the production and reproduction of civilized households as well as of civilized people still falls most heavily on Glebo women, rendering them economically vulnerable in a way unexperienced by their native sisters. It is here, within a single embodied class category, that the real oppression of the system is located.

Servants, in this context, appear to be caught in a curiously ambiguous position. Like other young people, they are suspended in the process of becoming civilized, the outcome of which is by no means clear. Yet they are also "distinguished" from other aspirants to civilized status, seemingly in contradiction with the extension of kinship status to most co-residents in Glebo households. Servants often have fewer resources, in the form of kin connections to established civilized households and family commitment to education and civilized life, with which to advance their aspirations. They are protected in some measure by the moral pressure on their foster families, exerted through community sanctions such as gossip, to offer them a real chance at achieving prestige. Yet, by controlling an essential, noninstitutional gateway to civilization, namely, the training that only takes place within the domestic unit, civilized households are able to meet their labor needs, uphold the public status of their adult women, and reproduce both the objective and embodied conditions of their status group.

Notes

1. Liberia was founded by the American Colonization Society as a refuge for "free people of color" in the United States and became independent in 1847. The descendents of the settlers were long known in the literature as Americo-Liberians. Recently, Dunn and Tarr (1988) have suggested the term repatriate to designate this group. For more on Liberian history, see Staudenraus 1961; Shick 1980; Liebenow 1987; and Dunn and Tarr 1988, among others.

2. The term "Glebo" refers to a population of roughly 10,000 people who belong, patrilineally, to a series of some thirteen coastal communities between Fishtown Point and the Cavalla River. The Glebo speak one of the many dialects of Grebo, a Kwa language shared by a number of southeastern groups. Although "Grebo" is used by the Liberian government as an ethnic category, Grebo speakers do not recognize a common identity or political unity as such. Fieldwork in Cape Palmas for fifteen months in 1982–1983 was supported by a National Science Foundation Graduate Fellowship and a Hannum Warner Alumnae Travel Grant from Mount Holyoke College.

3. "Traditional" male dress for the Glebo consists, today as in the past, of a long-sleeved white shirt, tie, dark suit coat, and bowler hat from the waist up and, from the waist down, a wrap-around cloth or "lappa."

4. See Carter and Mends-Cole, 1982, for education statistics.

5. This new, polarized ethnicity has been manifest most recently in the tragic civil war that has engulfed Liberia since January of 1990.

Bibliography

Bourdieu, Pierre. 1984. *Distinction: A Social Critique of the Judgment of Taste,* trans. Richard Nice. Cambridge: Harvard University Press.

Brooks, George E. 1972. *The Kru Mariner in the Nineteenth Century.* Newark, Del.: Liberian Studies Monograph Series, No. 1.

Brown, David. 1982. On the Category "Civilized" in Liberia and Elsewhere. *Journal of Modern African Studies* 20:287–303.

Carter, Jeanette, and Joyce Mends-Cole. 1982. *Liberian Women: Their Role in Food Production and Their Educational and Legal Status.* Monrovia: USAID/University of Liberia, Profile of Liberian Women in Development Project.

Cott, Nancy. 1977. *The Bonds of Womanhood: "Women's Sphere" in New England, 1780–1835.* New Haven: Yale University Press.

Dunn, D. Elwood, and Bryon S. Tarr. 1988. *Liberia: A National Polity in Transition.* Metuchen, N.J.: Scarecrow Press.

Fraenkel, Merran. 1964. *Tribe and Class in Monrovia.* London: Oxford University Press.

———. 1966. Social Change on the Kru Coast of Liberia. *Africa* 36:154–172.

Frykman, Jonas, and Orvar Löfgren. 1987. *Culture Builders: A Historical Anthropology of Middle Class Life,* trans. Alan Crozier. New Brunswick, N.J.: Rutgers University Press.

Liberty, C. E. Zamba. 1986. Report from Musardu (Letter to an American Friend): Reflections on the Liberian Crisis. *Liberian Studies Journal* 11:42–81.

Liebenow, J. Gus. 1987. *Liberia: The Quest for Democracy.* Bloomington: Indiana University Press.

Martin, Jane. 1968. The Dual Legacy: Government Authority and Mission Influence Among the Glebo of Eastern Liberia, 1834–1910. Ph.D. diss., Boston University.

———. 1982. Krumen "Down the Coast": Liberian Migrants on the West African Coast in the Nineteenth Century. *Boston University African Studies Center Working Papers,* No. 64.

Moran, Mary H. 1990. *Civilized Women: Gender and Prestige in Southeastern Liberia.* Ithaca: Cornell University Press.

Rosaldo, Michelle Zimbalist. 1974. Woman, Culture, and Society: A Theoretical Overview. In *Woman, Culture, and Society,* ed. M. Z. Rosaldo and L. Lamphere, 17–42. Stanford: Stanford University Press.

———. 1980. The Use and Abuse of Anthropology: Reflections on Feminism and Cross-Cultural Understanding. *Signs* 5:389–417.

Ryan, Mary P. 1981. *The Cradle of the Middle Class: The Family in Oneida County, New York.* New York: Cambridge University Press.

Shick, Tom. 1980. *Behold the Promised Land: A History of Afro-American Settler Society in Nineteenth Century Liberia.* Baltimore: Johns Hopkins University Press.

Staudenraus, P. J. 1961. *The African Colonization Movement: 1816–1865.* New York: Columbia University Press.

Sudarkasa, Niara. 1986. The "Status of Women" in African Societies. *Feminist Studies* 12:91–103.

Tonkin, Elizabeth. 1978–1979. Sasstown's Transformation: The Jlao Kru, 1888–1918. *Liberian Studies Journal* 8:1–34.

———. 1980. Jealousy Names, Civilised Names: Anthroponomy of the Jlao Kru of Liberia. *Man* 15:658–664.

———. 1981. Model and Ideology: Dimensions of Being Civilised in Liberia. In *The Structure of Folk Models,* ed. L. Holy and M. Stuchlik, 305–330. London: Academic Press.

Weber, Max. 1946. *From Max Weber.* New York: Oxford University Press.

———. 1947. *The Theory of Social and Economic Organization.* New York: Oxford University Press.

4 Domestic Science Training in Colonial Yorubaland, Nigeria

LaRay Denzer

Wife and mother; home and family: these concepts are as fundamental to African ideologies of domesticity as they are to the European ideology of domesticity imported by the missionaries (both African and European) and colonial administrators in the late nineteenth and early twentieth centuries. Under colonial domination, the state and the Christian missions encouraged the adoption of European concepts of domesticity through the agency of the schools and the churches. Yet neither institution succeeded in imposing its ideology as a whole on African peoples, who had their own concepts of women's roles in society and the home. As Africans converted to Christianity and assimilated new skills and beliefs, they transformed them, developing a syncretic ideology of domesticity rooted in indigenous customs but also responsive to socioeconomic changes.

In southwest Nigeria, the Yoruba provide an excellent example of how an African society transformed the European ideology of domesticity to fit its indigenous cultural assumptions and changing needs. This chapter will examine the interaction between the two ideologies by analyzing the role of domestic science in the schools, the main agency used by the missions and the colonial administration to inculcate European ideas during the colonial era. There were three main phases in the development of domestic subjects in the school curriculum during the colonial era: the introduction of domestic subjects in the mission schools; the evolution of government policy; and the transition from a home orientation to a employment orientation in the course structure. The objective of this study is to show how Yoruba women used the new techniques and knowledge gained in these subjects to create and exploit new economic opportunities.

Little conflict existed between the Yoruba and their British rulers concerning the basic tenets of domesticity: that a wife's domain was the home and her basic duty to care for her family and husband. Thus, Victorian-Edwardian beliefs coincided with important elements in Yoruba cultural concepts about women's roles and status. Like her contemporary British counterpart, the good Yoruba wife spent much time caring for her husband and children, cooking, cleaning, sweeping, washing clothes, polishing, and nursing sick members in her household (Fadipe 1970). Nevertheless, a fundamental difference did exist between alien and indigenous concepts of domesticity. Whereas the ideal British wife did not work outside the home or play a part in public life, the Yoruba expected women to take an active part in household production, in marketing surplus foodstuffs and other commodities, and in family and community decision-making (Fadipe 1970; Awe 1977; Mba 1982). In addition, many also engaged in crafts such as spinning thread, weaving, dyeing, pottery, soap-making, basket-making, and mat weaving. The profits made through these activities belonged solely to the women themselves and could be used in any way they liked.

British and Yoruba ideas also differed concerning a husband's responsibilities within the household. Yoruba women did not expect their husbands to provide the full support of their households. Usually husbands arranged an allocation of farmland, starting capital for trade, yams and other staples, occasional gifts of clothing, and ideally, school fees for the children. Wives supplied the rest of what she and her children needed. In times of economic crisis such as the depression of the 1930s, women's incomes often saved families from severe hardship.

One of the main instruments used by the missions and the government to change the Yoruba ideology of domesticity was Western education. Until 1926 the administration had left education almost completely in the hands of the missions, which in Yorubaland began being active in the 1840s (Ajayi 1965; Ayandele 1966). From the beginning missionaries, themselves the products of the late eighteenth-century evangelical movement that fostered the "angel in the home" ideology of domesticity, promoted girls' education in the new Yoruba missions (Hall 1979). They believed that educated wives ensured the development of strong Christian families and communities. As a result, girls received training in the earliest mission schools side by side with boys. Although children of both sexes received the same instruction in reading, writing, and arithmetic, they were also taught vocational subjects regarded as appropriate to their sex. Boys learned agriculture and the industrial skills and techniques necessary for the new jobs created in the colonial economy, while girls focused on domestic subjects in preparation for their future vocations as wives and mothers.

Domestic Training in Mission Schools

The ealiest references concerning the curricula of mission schools show that needlework played a prominent role in girls' education from the beginning (Ajayi 1965, 138–139). In 1848, the timetable of the school set up in Badagry by the first Methodist missionary, Reverend Thomas Birch Freeman, included an afternoon session from Monday through Thursday during which girls learned sewing and embroidery. Anna Hinderer, who helped her husband found the first Baptist mission in Ibadan in the 1850s, taught her female pupils needlework daily from 12:00 until 2:00 p.m. as well as a weekly class for adult women (Hinderer 1872, 289–290). As Christian mission activity spread throughout Yorubaland, missions of all denominations adopted the same approach to educating girls. Missionaries viewed needlework as part of their strategy in winning female converts. Moreover, the subject provided a medium for imparting other Victorian middle-class virtues, most of which happily coincided with Yoruba virtues: orderliness, neatness, caution, obedience, and concentration. Accustomed to finely detailed tasks in spinning, weaving, basket-making or dyeing, girls and women enjoyed learning a new and useful skill.

Once the missions were firmly established, some set up single-sex boarding schools for the sons and daughters of the growing Christian elite. Like their prototypes in England, these boarding schools provided a total educational environment, designed not only to teach specific subject matter, but also to shape character and instill evangelical Christian attitudes towards work and social values. In 1869 the Church Missionary Society (CMS) founded the Girls' Seminary in Lagos, the first girls' school (Awe 1969, 5–17). Ten years later the Methodists in Lagos followed with the establishment of the Wesleyan Girls' Seminary (Agiri 1979, 7–37). Between 1923 and 1950 the number of girls' schools slowly rose from fourteen to forty-four, twenty-nine of them located in Yoruba areas (Nigeria, Department of Education, Annual Reports 1923–1950).

In the girls' boarding schools the mission authorities developed a more intensive "industrial" side to their curricula. One of the most all-embracing was that of St. Clara's Convent at Topo (near Bad-

Table 1   TIMETABLE FOR THE C.M.S. GIRLS' SCHOOL, IBADAN, 1908

	A.M.			P.M.	
5:00	Prepare food, fetch water from river for baths, house, and kitchen		12:00	Dinner	
6:15–7:00	Quiet time and prayers		1:30	School	
7:00	Domestic work*		3:30	Recreation	
8:00	School		4:00	Domestic work⁺	
			6:00	Supper	
			7:15	Home lessons	
			8:15	Prayers	

Total time devoted to course work (including domestic subjects), 6 hours
Total time devoted to domestic chores, 4 hours, 15 minutes

SOURCE: CMS-Y 2/1/6.
* Tasks varied according to the day. On Mondays, the pupils did housework, laundry, cleaning the schoolrooms, tidying the garden, sweeping the paths, and did pantrywork. On Wednesdays, they ironed, starched, did housework, bought wood from the market, did pantrywork, and prepared food. On Fridays, they also cleaned the bedrooms.
⁺ Afternoon tasks were similar to the morning tasks, except that on Mondays, Tuesdays, and Fridays, the students beat *ogi* and on Fridays, they plaited their hair.

agry), originally founded as an orphanage for girls in 1892 (Nigeria, Department of Education Annual Report 1926). Here pupils not only received instruction in literary subjects, but performed all the necessary tasks for their daily maintenance and that of the convent. They grew their own food, did the marketing, cooked the meals, swept the compound and the buildings, scrubbed, washed clothes, and ironed. In addition, they earned money to run the convent through working on their farm, taking in laundry and mending from the pupils of the nearby boys' school as well as processing *gari* (a foodstuff made from grated cassava), tapioca, and butter for sale.

Neither the parents nor mission authorities desired the pupils in the elite boarding schools to be so self-sufficient, but nevertheless they stressed the importance of domestic chores and subjects. Parents and the school staffs participated in decisions about expanding the vocational component of the curriculum. In 1906 the Executive

Committee of the CMS in Lagos invited the Visiting Committee of the CMS Girls' Seminary and nine influential women in Lagos society to consider ways of improving the school curriculum.[1] After much discussion, the committee recommended the addition of classes in laundry, darning, mending, dressmaking, and needlework (plain and fancy) to the curriculum, specifying that instruction in these subjects be given for two hours each day. The committee also advised that boarders assume responsibility for all the household work in the school, cleaning the dormitories and washing and ironing their own clothes as well as those of their teachers. Other girls' schools, including St. Mary's Convent (Ebute Metta, Lagos), the Baptist Girls' School (Abeokuta), and the Wesleyan Girls' Seminary (Lagos) adopted a similar plan. In some schools such as the Kudeti School for Girls (Ibadan), girls also fetched firewood, did the marketing, and cooked their own food. As table 1 indicates, domestic subjects and chores in the Kudeti school premises took up a considerable part of the school day. The timetables of other boarding schools displayed a similar allocation of time (e.g., the Methodist Girls' Secondary School in 1979).

Not until the early 1930s did the colonial state begin to take a more active role in planning policy for girls' education. According to the prevailing beliefs of the time, the primary goal of girls' education was to inculcate good morals and modest behavior, not to offer training for new jobs or in academic subjects. Colonial administrators, missionaries, and Christian parents agreed that mission schools provided the best agency for such training. In 1923 the Colonial Secretary Donald Cameron clearly articulated this view in his reply to a petition from the Lagos Women's League, an elite women's organization, demanding that the government build more girls' schools. No such need existed, he contended. Already the government gave grants-in-aid to five mission schools for girls in the city, which was a "more desirable" environment for girls, he said.[2]

Besides elite boarding schools, the missions also pioneered a more specialized type of education for less privileged girls: the marriage training home.[3] Such homes were particularly popular in the eastern provinces where until well into the 1930s parents and guardians opposed sending their girls to regular mission schools. By 1937 the Diocese on the Niger (CMS) operated twenty-five homes in the Delta area alone, competing with other mission groups that also operated similar homes. The objective of those homes was to train girls betrothed to young men in the emerging new class of educated Christians—clergymen, teachers, and clerks—in modern techniques of housewifery, hygiene, and child care without alienating them from their local culture: "They must learn to keep a house under native conditions, yet apply hygiene and order."[4] Prospective husbands paid the fees for the training of their fiancees, many of whom had no formal schooling. Courses varied in duration from six months to three years. They centered on practical household work utilizing indigenous materials and houses. Formal instruction, if offered at all, took place in the vernacular. Such instruction emphasized the habits of good behaviour and manners: punctuality, cleanliness, helpfulness, neatness, talking in moderate tones, decent language, regular bathing, and personal hygiene. Most of these values reflected indigenous Nigerian ideals about the correct comportment of women as much as they did those of the British middle-class.

Except for the CMS Training Class in Akure (Ondo Province) and the Methodist Homecraft Centre in Ilesha (Oyo Province), marriage training homes did not find much favor among Yoruba parents or even among some missionaries. Because of the longer tradition of Christianity and Western education in Yorubaland, by the 1930s a significant section of Christian Yoruba society desired that their wives and daughters acquire more polish and sophistication in Western ways. Simultaneously, a growing number of young women in the towns hoped to take up employment in the period between leaving school and getting married (Denzer 1989). Concerned parents quickly realized that the education furnished by the marriage training homes failed to equip their daughters for success in the rapidly changing colonial society.

A conflict that developed between the education officials and the CMS concerning the Akure training home at the end of the 1920s illustrates these changing attitudes. In 1928, Miss A. J. Wait, a determined, progressive principal, aware of employment and marriage trends, instituted a series of reforms by expanding the literary curriculum. She believed that young CMS clergymen and catechists needed brides who spoke English well and possessed good Western manners in order to carry out their work properly. Further, she felt that her pupils should at least have the right to sit the government school leaving examinations, even though the class did not technically qualify for them. Dismayed by this new policy, the education authorities in Ibadan, only one of them a woman, protested Wait's experiment, intent on returning the school to its original domestic focus. Meanwhile the parents of the girls supported the principal, anxious that their daughters get qualifications suitable for making a good marriage, getting a job or allowing them to take advantage of the new opportunities in self-employment. In 1933, after five years of discussion between the education officers and the CMS, the mission agreed to the state's demands not to turn the training home into a proper school. In return, however, they obtained important concessions from the government. Thereafter, pupils could take advanced English classes and those who qualified could take the standard VI examinations.[5]

Even though Yoruba parents realized the desirability of their daughters gaining new skills as a step toward getting modern jobs, educated parents still wanted their daughter's education to consist of a good amount of domestic as well as literary training. If anything, their demands for such training tended to be stronger than those of the missionaries and administrators. Specifically, they did not want their daughters to get unrealistic aspirations concerning their roles and needs. The editor of the conservative *Nigerian Pioneer* (5 March 1926) expressed the view of many Lagosian parents in warning: "Much learning only became a few women. What society needed was practical women." Elite parents worried that inappropriate education might Europeanize girls too much, making them discontented and "useless" in their future husband's homes, with expensive tastes for imported goods, a burden to their husbands and society. This theme often appeared in articles and letters published in the local press on girls' education throughout the 1920s and 1930s (e.g., Murray, 1933; *Lagos Daily News,* 18 April 1928). Editors and contributors, who were almost without exception men, stressed that the "right" type of Western education should produce a Christian woman, articulate in English, capable of applying selective modern ideas concerning hygiene and consumption, but who still remained basically African in her attitudes and behavior towards parents, husband, children, and the home. A woman's life should revolve around the home and family, no matter what her status or level of education.

Such attitudes featured prominently during the discussions leading to the establishment in 1927 of Queen's College, the first government secondary school for girls.[6] The wives of European administrators, led by Lady Clifford (and later Lady Thomson), combined forces with influential Lagosian women, led by Charlotte Obasa, to overcome the opposition of education authorities, who did not believe in the necessity of such a school. Concerned elite parents, worried about the cultural alienation of their daughters, pressed hard for the foundation of a secondary girls' school of quality. They insisted that it duplicate the British finishing schools to which they sent their children. The curriculum they helped to design provided for a considerable amount of domestic science as well as sound literary training.

The Evolution of Government Policy

With the founding of Queen's College, the colonial state assumed a more assertive role in the development of girls' education in Lagos Colony and the Southern Nigerian Protectorate. The college prospectus declared: "[T]he chief aim of the College will be to fit girls to become cultured women, practical housewives, and wise mothers." A qualified British domestic science mistress joined the staff shortly after the school opened. At the official opening of the school, several speakers emphasized the domestic side of the curriculum. The founding principal, Faith Wordsworth (later Mrs. Tolfree), an Oxford graduate in modern history, stressed the importance of education for the country's future mothers.[7] Frank Baddeley, the Acting Governor, echoed her sentiments, stressing that educated women ensured a nation's progress (*Nigerian Daily Times,* 11 October 1927; *Nigerian Spectator,* 8 and 15 October 1927).

In 1931 the appointment of Gladys Plummer, then forty years old, as Lady Superintendent of Education for the southern provinces marked the beginning of a more active government policy in encouraging girls' education and reforming its curriculum. In her nineteen years of service in Nigeria, until her retirement as Deputy Director of Education (Women) in 1950, she did more than any other colonial civil servant to shape the structure of girls' education. Former female colleagues and Yoruba teachers remember her as a determined individual with a very strong character, as "larger than life" (Alexander Manuscripts, 2; Interviews in Ibadan with Mrs. Kemi Morgan, 29 March 1990, and Mrs. Folayegbe, 1990 Akintunde-Ighodalo, 1990). She employed tact, tenacity, and diplomacy with both her chauvinist male colleagues and Nigerian parents in order to win support for more opportunities for girls. Trained in domestic science, she set out to implement the government's decision to develop domestic science as an integral part of the national curriculum. In doing so she dedicated herself to the goal of broadening opportunities for Nigerian women in colonial society. Under Plummer's guidance, domestic science, which today seems so constraining to female ambition and equality, became a means for increasing women's participation in the colonial economy and raising their social status.

In order to carry out her mandate to reform girls' education, Plummer had first to assess the state of domestic science training in the schools. After several months of grueling touring, she concluded that domestic science training rested on a solid foundation in the girls' boarding schools and marriage training homes run by the missions. The training in laundry and needlework in these institutions equaled the standard of instruction in Britain. The Roman Catholic convents received widespread acclaim for the quality of their needlework and embroidery. Queen's College operated a thriving domestic science center that served girls in the mixed schools of Lagos, a plan that Plummer later adopted in other towns. The work done in the marriage training homes impressed her so much that she incorporated some of their methods into her reformed curriculum.[8]

The majority of girls, however, did not attend boarding schools or training homes. Most of them went to mixed schools, where domestic science received very little attention. In 1933, only thirty-eight hundred girls went to boarding schools while thirty-four thousand were enrolled in mixed schools (Nigeria Department of Education, Annual Report 1933). Often the only domestic subject taught in the latter schools consisted of needlework, and that not done very well. These schools employed few trained female teachers. Those in charge of needlework classes lacked adequate supervision because inept male supervisors knew little about the subject. Although Plummer found that school managers and headmasters offered willing cooperation, few appreciated the requirements and demands of domestic courses or the best way of arranging a timetable.[9]

After concluding her investigation of the state of domestic science in southern Nigerian schools, Plummer turned to the task of raising the status of domestic subjects in the general school curriculum and improving instruction methods. To her mind "domestic subjects [were] real crafts, demanding knowledge on the part of the workers" (Plummer 1956, 4). She began her reforms by adapting the coursework to Nigerian materials and culture. Satisfied with the methods of teaching laundry and needlework, she concentrated on revising the syllabi for cookery and housewifery. Neither subject as then taught related very well to Nigerian realities; they focused too much on European techniques and consumption habits. Sharply criticizing the cookery syllabus, she observed:

> It [was] clear that while girls liked to learn European cookery—which was regarded as a superior subject—they certainly did not wish to consume the products. Our soups, meat dishes, and puddings were tasteless and unattractive to them. Breads and cakes, on the other hand, were extremely popular, especially for feasts and entertainments.[10]

Consequently, she removed European dishes and methods from the syllabus, except for baking and egg dishes.[11]

In addition, Plummer encouraged the staffs of mission schools to collect recipes in their locales and use them in teaching. The CMS Girls' School in Ibadan had already done this; by 1932 *The Kudeti Book of Yoruba Cookery* was in its third edition. Generations of Yoruba school girls used it. Teachers in Igbo, Efik, Urhobo, Sobo, and Cameroonian areas made similar collections. Although Plummer hoped to publish an all-purpose Nigerian cook book at this time, it was not until much later that Rhoda Williams (later Mrs. Johnston) published *Miss Williams' Cookery Book* in 1957, followed by Adebisi Vincent's *A Cookery Book for the Tropics* in 1962, both very popular and still in use.

Once Plummer had carried out the Nigerianization of the cookery syllabus to reflect local needs, she set out to do the same in housecraft. The syllabus covered sweeping, scrubbing, cleaning, polishing, and the making of soap, starch, gari, and various flours (yam, plantain, and cassava). Customarily the instructors used the houses of the European teachers for demonstration purposes, with its attendant advantage of a constant supply of unpaid domestic labor. However, Plummer believed that it was "far better for the girls to be trained under conditions which they recognize, than for them to spend long hours in cleaning a European house."[12] Some schools like Methodist Girls' School in Sagamu had built a model house in the indigenous architectural style for use in instruction. Such model houses met Plummer's approval in terms of utility, sound training, and low cost of construction. She encouraged their construction throughout southern Nigeria.

The financial crisis of the depression years militated against the rapid expansion of education, a situation compounded by the fact that the implementation of the new domestic science reforms suffered from a lack of qualified female teachers. Undeterred, Plummer stressed the need to start with low-cost reforms, adapting inexpensive local materials and technology wherever possible: laundry and cooking sheds could be built with beaten earthen floors, half-walls of mud, wooden poles, and thatched roofs; cookery classes could utilize earthenware and wooden utensils, mud ovens, open fires, or stoves made from kerosine tins; irrelevant schemes in needlework, such as sleevelets, pram covers, and sideboard cloths, could be eliminated altogether.[13]

In order to make maximum use of facilities and teaching staff, Plummer proposed to set up a series of domestic science centers based on the one run by Queen's College. Thus all the mixed schools in a large town could send their female pupils to a central place for a day's instruction each week according to an agreed schedule. A single teacher with one assistant could easily handle such an arrangement. In 1933 she put forward a plan to build this type of center in Ibadan, where her headquarters was located. At first the Resident of Oyo Province and the District Officer turned down the proposal on the grounds of impending draconian cuts in education that year. "The training [was] not one of urgency," minuted the District Officer.[14] Eventually Plummer gained approval for the center, which opened three years later (Nigeria, Department of Education, Annual Report, 1936). Although by 1943 three other government centers operated in Ijebu Ode, Oyo, and Warri, the administration offered only limited financial support for these centers and few new ones opened (Nigeria, Department of Education, Annual Report, 1944/45).

In order to raise the status and respectability of domestic science, Plummer instituted a specially designed girls' examination for standard VI after 1936. It consisted of two papers in domestic science, a practical domestic science test, a paper in English (the same as that required for boys), and a paper in arithmetic that was simpler than that taken by the boys. Further, new professional regulations made domestic science training compulsory in all training colleges for women. All candidates for the Teacher's Higher Elementary Examination and later the ordinary elementary certificate for women teachers had to qualify in these subjects. This requirement effectively limited the range of courses girls could elect to take, making it very difficult for them to develop skills in pure science and math or

Table 2   SPECIAL DOMESTIC SCIENCE CERTIFICATES, 1934–1945

Year	Certificate of Merit	Housecraft Certificate
1934	35	36
1935	28	26
1936	30	40
1937	41	58
1938	35	59
1939	50	52
1940	42	50
1941	27	65
1942	33	62
1943	37	56
1944	30	45
1945	34	45
Total	422	594

SOURCE: NAI, IBMINED 1/6 LEO 76, vols. 1 and 2; and NAI, IBMINED 1/6 LEO 61, vol. 1.

to learn skills needed for occupations outside the domestic sector. As a result certain areas of the girls' curriculum suffered: the standard of arithmetic declined and history was sometimes dropped.

Further, the Education Department decided to issue a Housecraft Certificate and a Certificate of Merit, both deliberately ornate to enhance their appeal, to girls who passed out of specially organized domestic science classes or marriage training homes, but could not complete their elementary school.[15] To qualify for the Housecraft Certificate the candidate, who knew she must leave school before standard VI, took a special year's domestic course before ending her education. The Certificate of Merit was awarded to girls who finished a special two-year course in the marriage training homes. For all the enthusiasm of the educational authorities, not many girls actually obtained these certificates in any given year, as we can see from table 2. While the Education Department sternly warned that neither certificate constituted a qualification for employment as teachers, some young women and their parents did not readily understand this. Those who tried to use them met with bitter disappointment.

The Transition from a Home Focus to an Employment Focus

Until the mid 1930s domestic subjects taught in the schools of Yorubaland oriented girls' education to training for marriage, the family, and the home. Neither parents nor students contested the overall orientation of girls' education, nor questioned the conviction that woman's true destiny remained bound up in the traditional domestic life. At the same time, the Yoruba, and indeed most southern Nigerian peoples, expected women to share in supporting the household. Although a tiny percentage of the top elite had adopted British Christian middle-class ideals (Mann 1985), the majority of Yoruba never accepted the idea that women should confine their work to the home. By the 1940s, British female administrators and foreign missionaries began to fully comprehend the weight of economic demands made on Nigerian women. As a result they shifted the orientation of domestic science to training for earning income.

Although small signs of the potential of domestic science for income generation had appeared early, the reorientation of training was accelerated during the 1930s. Early on young girls proficient in needlework became dressmakers, first in Lagos, where European dress styles became popular with the educated elite. The 1881 census recorded 583 laundresses and seamstresses in the settlement of Lagos and vicinity. By the 1920s and 1930s dressmaking had become a popular and lucrative occupation for young educated elite women (Denzer, 1991). Even though elite parents, missionaries, and colonial administrators frowned on sewing as a low-status occupation in comparison to teaching, women in fact earned more income as seamstresses than they could as teachers. While the monthly salaries of teachers in the late nineteenth and early twentieth centuries ranged from fifteen shillings to three pounds, a seamstress easily made two or three times that amount in the same amount of time. Two business women in Ibadan, Mrs. Comfort Modupe Ogunsanwo and Chief Abiola Wilson, who both began their careers as teachers in the 1940s and then had turned to dressmaking, recalled that the potential of higher profits had convinced them to change their occupation (Interviews in Ibadan with Mrs. Comfort Modupe, September 1987, and Chief Abiola Ogunsanwo Wilson, 28 March 1990). Recent interviews with thirty Yoruba seamstresses, ranging in age from thirty-four to ninety, confirm this.[16]

Very early in her career in Nigeria, Plummer had complained

about the serious lack of employment opportunities for young educated women. Few opportunities existed other than teaching, nursing, and dressmaking.[17] To remedy this she encouraged the development of vocational classes in schools and the Young Women's Christian Association (YWCA) designed to teach marketable skills. These skills translated traditional female domestic skills—cooking, baking, sewing, and embroidery—into commercial enterprises. One of the first experiments in this direction was the creation at the CMS Girls' School in Ibadan of a special class of school-leavers that offered advanced instruction in baking, curtain-making, upholstery, and dressmaking. The class opened a small shop to sell bakery products, jams, and sweets. Popular with both Europeans and Nigerians, the shop did a brisk trade in cakes—including specialty cakes for weddings and Christmas—and sold from thirty to forty loaves of bread a day.[18]

Other schools and the YWCA also set up similar classes with a view to helping their pupils earn a living from their newly acquired skills. Baking bread and cakes proved specially lucrative. Several schools and training homes, including the CMS Training Home in Akure, sold bakery goods in their communities. Numerous girls sold baked products in the markets throughout the provinces. Some schools gave contracts to their former pupils to make school uniforms for their pupils. Although the Ibadan scheme was abandoned when the school took on the elementary training course for teachers, some of the other vocational classes were successful, and new ones opened.[19]

Throughout the 1930s parental resistance to sending girls to school steadily declined. The mid 1930s represented the turning point in the acceptance of girls' education.[20] Thereafter the number of girls applying for entrance to schools of all kinds exceeded the available number of openings. Table 3 indicates the rise in the enrollment of girls in southern Nigeria during the colonial period. The Yoruba provinces led the others in the education of girls. In 1936, the ratio of girls to boys in school was one to two in Lagos Colony, one to three in Abeokuta, Ijebu, and Oyo Provinces; and one to four in Ondo Province—substantially more than that of one to five in Calabar and Onitsha Provinces, one to ten in Warri Province, or the lowest, one to eighteen in Ogoja (Nigeria, Department of Education, Annual Report 1938).

Simultaneously, many new opportunities opened for the employment of girls, increasing during World War II. By the 1940s it was

Table 3   ENROLLMENT OF GIRLS IN PRIMARY SCHOOLS IN
SOUTHERN NIGERIA, 1862–1960

Year	Government schools	Assisted schools	Nonassisted schools	Total
1862*	—	—	154	154
1882*	—	—	976	976
1906	128	1,869		1,997
1915	87	2,966	3,736	6,789
1920	273	6,891		7,164
1929	1,099	11,807	13,575	26,481
1934	1,192	14,374	18,649	34,215
1938	1,291	20,060	31,801	53,152
1946[†]	—	—	—	105,000
1955[†]	—	—	—	513,692
1960[†]	—	—	—	1,083,147

SOURCES: Blue Book, Lagos Colony, 1862, 1882; Blue Book, Lagos Colony and the
Protectorate of Southern Nigeria, 1906; Blue Book, Nigeria, 1915–1938; Annual
Report, Department of Education, 1906, 1945/46; Federal Education Department,
Nigeria. Digest of Statistics, 1956, Table 3; and Federal Ministry of Education, Nige-
ria. *Annual Digest of Educational Statistics,* 1961.
* For Lagos Colony only.
† No division by category of school.

clear that social attitudes toward women's employment had changed
dramatically, as could be seen from the exchange that took place in a
"brain's trust" in Lagos early in August 1944 (*West African Pilot,*
August 8, 1944). Among the participants were Mrs. H. Ekemode, a
Muslim teacher, and Mrs. (later Lady) Oyinkan Abayomi (Coker
1987), a teacher and the founder of the then newly formed Women's
Party, and three other women. Several complained that the educational system prevented the average girl from pursuing careers other
than nursing and teaching. Mrs. Ekemode insisted that women could
perform many of the same jobs as men such as painting, designing,
and engineering, pointing to the experience of British women during
the war. Sounding a radical new note, Abayomi and Ekemode de-
nounced the custom requiring women to resign when they married.
While the female participants did not deny the importance of marriage and the family, they felt that women had the right to combine
work with marriage.

Meanwhile female government officers had revised their ideas about women's roles and employment. In 1948, Plummer, now the Deputy Director of Education for Women, began to investigate the family responsibilities of married women. Uneasy that girls' education appeared not to fulfill the needs of many young women, she needed evidence to support a proposal for technical education similar to that spelled out in the ten-year development plan for men. Anticipating opposition from her male colleagues, she conducted her study in strict confidentiality. In her letter to Alison Izzett, the Women's Welfare Officer, and a number of influential principals of mission-operated girls' schools, she confided: "I am getting into deep water; one question which has already arisen is the extent to which women are responsible for financing the family by their own earnings."[21] Assuming that Nigerian husbands supported their wives, her male colleagues contended that women did not need vocational training.

Izzett responded to Plummer's request with a detailed memorandum examining the financial obligations of educated, semi-literate, and illiterate wives, based on two thousand case histories handled by her department.[22] These showed that a husband's primary financial obligations were to his parents and siblings, not to his wife or her children, except in paying the rent. Ideally he also paid part of his children's school fees and bought their uniforms, but often a mother assumed part or all of this expense too. No matter what level of education a wife possessed, Izzett claimed, she was responsible for the maintenance of her children, feeding her husband, and providing for her own needs. Educated women married to husbands in government service or business often received a small allowance, which normally covered only part of the family's food expenses. Based on her findings, Izzett supported Plummer's proposal to include women in vocational training programs so that they could achieve more economic independence and fulfill their domestic commitments.

As an initial step in carrying out this goal, Plummer proposed to augment the scheme, already approved under the new ten-year development plan, to establish a number of regional trades schools so that it included facilities for women as well as men (Plummer, n.d.). Her plan called for setting up one large center and three smaller centers in each of the western and eastern regions. They would offer post-primary training for girls meant to develop higher levels of proficiency in trade skills than that given in short-term vocational classes and domestic science centers. Such training retained an orientation to "female" trades. The prospectus included two-year courses in dressmaking and needlework (including machine embroidery) or business training, as well as one-year courses in baking or domestic administration for matrons. The inclusion of a course in business reveals how much attitudes had changed regarding female employment. Unlike Britain and the United States, where women had dominated the clerical and nursing occupations for decades, in Nigeria in the 1940s men still formed the majority of nurses, secretaries, and typists (Denzer 1989). Not until the 1950s did nursing become an increasingly female profession and women enter secretarial positions in any number (Akansanya 1987; Olarinde 1991). Unfortunately, the administration regarded women's vocational centers as low priority and thus delayed their construction. At Independence (1960) only 98 women occupied places in state-owned vocational and technical schools in the whole of Nigeria, 57 of them in the recently opened center at Abeokuta (Nigeria, Federal Ministry of Education, 1961).

By the time of decolonization in the 1950s, domestic science training with a vocational orientation was entrenched in Nigeria's education system. Adopting usage current in the United States and Britain, the term "home economics" replaced the outmoded term "domestic science." Nigerian female education officers took over the supervision of girls' education, including Mrs. P. E. Adewale and Mrs. Adebisi Vincent, author of *A Cookery Book for the Tropics.* At the time hardly any prominent female leader in education, voluntary organizations, or politics queried the content of education for girls. Their main concerns centered on the expansion of educational opportunity itself: how to get more girls into elementary schools, secondary schools, and universities, as well as more scholarships for study at home and abroad.

With few if any exceptions, women nationalists had a vested interest in domestic science, since they had received this type of schooling themselves. Although they fought for the right to vote and to contest elections, none questioned the assumption that a woman's primary duties were to her husband and family. The indomitable nationalist, Funmilayo Anikulapo-Kuti (formerly Ransome-Kuti), qualified as a domestic science teacher in Britain in 1922. Among the activities pursued by the first women's clubs that she set up in Ijebu Ode and Abeokuta were sewing and cooking (Odugbesan 1968; *Daily Times,* 31 January 1953). Tanimowo Ogunlesi, leader of the Women's Improvement Society and an influential Action Group politician in the early days, established a girls' hostel that gave vocational training in dressmaking, catering, and housecraft (*West Africa*, 15 August 1953, 701; Interview with Tani Mowo Ogunlesi, 1989). Wuraola Esan, the only senator in the First Republic (1960–1966), taught domestic science in the CMS training center at Akure from 1930 to 1934 (Denzer, forthcoming), and domestic science formed a regular part of the instruction offered in the Ibadan People's Girls' School that she founded in 1945. She succinctly expressed the views of many of her contemporaries when, shortly before Independence, she urged her fellow senators to award more girls scholarships abroad:

> There are girls and women who would be very useful in the future development of Nigeria if given the opportunity to learn more about some simple things. Courses like Nursery, Nursing, Pottery, Dairy Farming and Canteen Management, Housekeeping and so on, I dare say, will be very useful in the development of Nigeria in future. We do need expert technicians—Engineers and such like, but we do need good housekeepers too. You are each of you here because there is some one to see that you do have your meals in time and that you are made comfortable after coming here to talk too much (Nigeria, Senate Debates, 2 April 1960, 197).

The Impact of Domestic Training on Women's Opportunities in Colonial Yorubaland

Although both the colonial administration and Yoruba parents believed that domestic training was a desirable component in the education system, their reasons for thinking so differed. The government wanted to propagate new values concerning domesticity. Parents wanted their daughters to obtain an education that related to their culture and reinforced Yoruba traditions concerning the roles and status of women. The British emphasis on training girls to be good wives and mothers reassured many Christian Yoruba of the basic similarity of goals in the two cultures.

The aims of the state in providing domestic training, however, went much further. The state utilized the reformed domestic curriculum to inculcate and popularize new habits of orderliness, cleanliness, hygiene, first aid, and sanitation in order to improve health conditions and lessen maternal and infant mortality. The adoption of many of these new practices did in fact promote better health and safer living conditions. Instruction in the domestic arts also taught girls the skills they needed to cater for new tastes for such items as bread, cakes, embroidered cloths, and European fashions. It also imparted new information about how to maintain in good condition imported consumer goods from Europe: furniture, footwear, clothes, metal utensils, china, and sewing machines.

Easily translated into commercial enterprise, dressmaking and needlework constituted the most popular of the domestic subjects (Denzer 1991). From the 1940s to the 1960s the number of seamstresses grew rapidly, for two main reasons. First, sophisticated elite women preferred Western fashions to the traditional style of *buba* (blouse) and *iro* (wrapper) for everyday wear. But even *buba* styles became increasingly intricate in the hands of better trained seamstresses (*Woman's World,* August 1967:13–15). Second, the greater availability of advanced training improved levels of local craftsmanship, especially in handling delicate fabrics, cutting patterns, and finishing garments. In response to the demand for training, many women entrepreneurs, often former teachers who had resigned their posts upon marriage, established private sewing institutes.[23] Many girls received their training in such institutions; for example, Mrs. C. O. Cole in Ibadan estimated that she turned out six hundred seamstresses in twenty years, as well as many bakers and caterers (*Nigerian Tribune,* 19 August 1950).

Not all the domestic subjects provided such economic benefits for girls; cooking and housecraft were less readily transformed into marketable skills. When Plummer first took up her post as education officer, she discussed the need for cookery lessons with a number of prominent African women, who told her that many girls did not know how to cook when they married.[24] She reformed the cookery syllabus on the basis both of their advice and of the assumptions inherent in her British training. It is doubtful, however, whether the majority of Yoruba girls needed or benefited from these classes, with the exception of baking, which became an important source of self-employment. Perhaps elite daughters in Lagos did not learn to cook, but they constituted a small minority of the schoolgirl population. The life histories of forty-five Yoruba women ranging in age from forty-five to one hundred in Ota (Ogun State) and Ibadan (Oyo State), give an understanding of the nature of Yoruba childhood training. Most informants state that their household duties as children included helping their mothers in cooking from a very early age.[25] They also listed their other duties as sweeping their compounds and houses, scrubbing, washing plates, and doing laundry.

Undergraduate studies of the informal education and socialization of female children in Nigeria show that these tasks were considered a normal part of their upbringing in many places (Erumere 1979, ch. 1; Mekwuye 1985, ch. 1; Oghale 1983, ch. 1). Thus much of the content of housewifery and laundry courses was also redundant. The time that girls spent in these classes would have been better spent learning arithmetic, science, and history.

The most important result of the expansion of domestic science training was that it facilitated women's entry into modern occupations in the colonial economy. Domestic science training in itself expanded opportunities for more employment for women, since it created many new openings for qualified female teachers. Plummer insisted that schools employ trained, preferably certified, women teachers to take charge of the domestic subjects. By 1936 a hundred mixed and government schools employed at least one woman on their teaching staff. Her insistence on professional qualifications in domestic science training raised the status of women teachers. The dramatic expansion of girls' education after the 1940s, combined with the Nigerianization of the civil service, created numerous openings for women as teachers and education officers. For the rest of the colonial period the demand for female teachers far exceeded the supply of potential recruits graduating from teacher training colleges.

Futhermore, domestic science training promoted many opportunities in self-employment. Many young educated women established small-scale businesses as dressmakers, bakers, and caterers. Others opened restaurants, cafes, and hotels. While these occupations often did not provide as high an income as men made at their jobs, nevertheless women gained considerable financial independence and a source of capital. They invested their profits in expanding their businesses and in education for their children, making sure that their daughters as well as their sons got as much schooling as they could afford. Many of their daughters became the influential professionals, business women, and politicians who paved the way for women's entry into fields of employment dominated by men after the 1950s and Independence.

Notes

Versions of this chapter were presented in the seminar series of the Women's Research and Documentation Centre, Institute of African Studies,

University of Ibadan, September 21, 1990; to a seminar jointly organized by the African Studies Program and the the Women and Development Program at the University of Iowa, November 11, 1990; and to a seminar jointly organized by the Women's Studies Program and the African Studies Program at Rutgers University, New Brunswick, November 6, 1990. I wish to thank the participants of those seminars for their stimulating questions and suggestions, many of which have been incorporated in this chapter. Further, I am grateful to my colleagues at the University of Ibadan—G. A. Akinola, Glenn Webb, Nkoli Ezumah, the late Joanne Uzoigwe, Jonathan Sadusky, and Elisha Renne—for their comments.

1. NAI, CMS (Y) 3/1/13: Executive Council Minutes, July 1906. Among the invited women were Mrs. Charlotte Obasa (later the leader of the Lagos Women's League), Mrs. Henry Carr (the wife of a prominent civil servant in the Department of Education), Mrs. Robbin, Mrs. C. Johnson, and Mrs. N. Johnson.

2. NAI, COM COL 1/498: CS to C. Obasa, 20 December 1923.

3. NAI, IBMINED 1/6 LEO 62, vol. 1.

4. NAI, IBMINED 1/6 LEO 61, vol. 1, 1–3: G. Plummer, report on marriage training homes for girls, 3 November 1933.

5. NAI, IBMINED 1/2 CIW 1190:58, 64–65: memo, G. Plummer to Chief Inspector of Education (SPs), October 24, 1932; memo, G. Plummer to ADE (Sps), 17 January 1933; and Bishop to ADE (SPs), January 1933. IBMINED 1/9 LEO 8, vol. 1, 41: memo, S. M. Grier (DE) to ADE (Ibadan), 9 November 1928.

6. NAI, IBMINED 1/1 DDW 610, vol. 1.

7. Faith Wordsworth came from a distinguished literary and ecclesiastical family: William Wordsworth, the poet, was her uncle; her father had served as the Bishop of Salisbury.

8. NAI, IBMINED 1/6 LEO 53, vol. 1, 176–182: G. Plummer, Report on the Progress of Domestic Subjects Teaching in Southern Nigeria, n.d.

9. Ibid. NAI, IBMINED 1/6 LEO 53, vol. 1, 10c: G. Plummer, memo, "The organisation of domestic science and needlework in mixed schools," 19 October 1933.

10. NAI, IBMINED 1/6 LEO 37, vol. 1: Annual Report on Girls' Education, 1932.

11. The health authorities combated many taboos against eating eggs. They used the schools to popularize the incorporation of eggs in local diets in order to raise the level of protein.

12. NAI, IBMINED 1/6 LEO 37, vol. 1: Annual Report on Girls' Education 1932.

13. Ibid.

14. NAI, OYO Prof 1/1129:5–6: Resident (Oyo Province) to DO (Ibadan), 30 August 1933; and memo, DO (Ibadan) to Resident (Oyo Province), 23 September 1933.

15. NAI, IBMINED 1/6 LEO 61, vol. 1, 7: Memo, LEO to ADE, SPs, 7 February 1934.

16. This fieldwork was carried out in 1990 and 1991 in Ibadan, Ilorin,

Ilesha, and other places with the assistance of final year students at the University of Ibadan.

17. NAI, IBMINED 1/6 LEO 37, vol. 1: Annual report on the Education of Girls in the Southern Provinces, 1934.

18. Ibid.

19. NAI, IBMINED 1/6 LEO 37, vol. 1: Annual Reports on Girls' Education in the Southern Provinces, 1932–1937; and NAI, IBMINED 1/2 CIW 2829.

20. NAI, IBMINED 1/6 LEO 37, vol. 1: Annual Report on the Education of Girls in the Southern Provinces, 1936.

21. NAI, MED (FED) 1/10 CADW47:6: Plummer to Sister Mary Aloysius (Holy Rosary Convent, Onitsha); to Miss J. Mars, CMS Training Class, Akure; and to Reverend Mother Mary Osmund, Convent of the Holy Child, Ifuho, Ikot Ekpene.

22. MED (FED) 1/10 CADW 47.

23. Particularly famous institutes were run by Mrs. C. O. Cole in Ibadan, Mrs. (later Lady) Olamide Bank-Anthony and Mrs. Cecelia Victoria Duncan in Lagos, *Nigerian Tribune,* 19 August 1950; 23 February 1952 and 30 April 1953; *Daily Times,* 2 April 1953 and 30 May 1953.

24. NAI, IBMINED 1/6 LEO 37, vol. 1: Annual Report on Girls' Education in the Southern Provinces, 1932.

25. These life histories were collected in 1989 and 1990 with the help of research assistants Ayodeji Ismail Oduwaye and Solomon Ayoade, then final-year students at the University of Ibandan.

Abbreviations Used in Notes

ADE	Assistant Director of Education
LEO	(Assistant) Lady Education Officer
COM COL	Commissioner for the Colony of Lagos
CS	Chief Secretary of the Government
DE	Director of Education
DO	District Officer
IBMINED	Ibadan, Ministry of Education
MED (FED)	Federal Ministry of Education
NAI	National Archives, Ibadan
SPs	Southern Provinces
SSP	Secretary of the Southern Provinces

Bibliography

Adepegba, Adeyeye Olawale Bidemi. 1989. Aspects of Brazilian-Nigerian Connections: Nineteenth Century to Inter-War Years., B. A. Honors Essay, Department of History, University of Ibadan.

Agiri, Babatunde. 1979. Methodist Girls' High School, Yaba, Lagos,

1879–1979: A Centenary History. In *A Hundred Years of Methodist Girls' High School, Yaba, Lagos, 1879–1979*, 7–37. Lagos: Centenary souvenir pamphlet.

Ajayi, J.F.A. 1965. *Christian missions in Nigeria, 1841–1891*. London: Longman.

Awe, Bolanle. 1969. A Brief History. In *100 Years of Anglican Girls' High School*, 5–20. Lagos: Centenary souvenir pamphlet.

———. 1977. The Iyalode in the Traditional Yoruba System. In *Sexual Stratification: A Cross-Cultural View*, ed. A. Schlegel, 144–160. New York: Columbia University Press.

Ayandele, E. A. 1966. *The Missionary Impact on Modern Nigeria, 1842–19114: A Political and Social Analysis*. London: Longman.

Census of the Settlement of Lagos and Its Dependencies. 30 June 1881. *Government Gazette, Settlement of Lagos*, 38.

Coker, F. 1987. *A Lady: A Biography of Lady Oyinkan Abayomi*. Ibadan: Evans Brothers.

Denzer, LaRay. 1989. *Women's Employment in Government Service in Colonial Nigeria, 1863–1945*. Working Papers in African Studies, #136. Boston: African Studies Center, Boston University.

———. 1991. The Seamstress in the Evolution of a Popular Woman's Occupation from Colonial Times. Paper presented at a seminar on Women and the Peaceful Transition Programme. 19–21 March, jointly organized by Kwara State Polytechnic and the Department of Women's Affairs, Office of the Kwara State Military Governor, Ilorin.

———. Forthcoming. Gender and Decolonization: A Study of Three Women Leaders in West African Public Life. In *Peoples and Empires in Africa: Essays in Memory Michael Crowder*, ed. J. F. A. Ajayi and J. D. Y. Peel. London: Longman.

Erumere, Mabel Oghenekevwe. 1979. Female Education in Ughelli Local Government Area. B. A. Honors Essay, Department of History, University of Ibadan.

Esemuze, Doris. 1988. The Role of Women in the Socio-Political Life of Iuleha, 1900–1960. B. A. Honors Essay, University of Ibadan.

Fadipe, N. A. 1970. *The Sociology of the Yoruba*. Ibadan: Ibadan University Press.

Hall, Catherine. 1979. The Early Formation of Victorian Ideology. In *Fit Work for Women*, ed. S. Burman. 15–32. London: Croom Helm.

Hinderer, Anna. 1872. *Seventeen Years in the Yoruba Country: Memorials of Anna Hinderer*. London: Seeley, Jackson and Halliday.

Johnson [Johnson-Odim], Cheryl P. Charlotte Obasa. 1978. In Nigerian Women and British Colonialism: The Yoruba Example with Selected Biographies, 97–131. Ph.D. diss., Northwestern University.

Mann, Kristin. 1985. *Marrying Well: Marriage, Status and Social Change among the Educated Elite in Colonial Lagos*. Cambridge, England: Cambridge University Press.

Mba, Nina Emma. 1982. *Nigerian Women Mobilized: Women's Political Ac-*

tivity in Southern Nigeria, 1900–1960. Berkeley: Institute of International Relations, University of California Press.

Medwuye, Edith, 1985. The Development of Female Education in Ika Local Government Area of Bendel State, 1900–1976. B. A. Honors Essay, Department of History, University of Ibadan.

Murray, A. Victor. 1933. The Education of African Girls. *Nigerian Pioneer,* 11 March.

Nigeria, Department of Education. 1923–1950. *Annual Report.*

Nigeria, Federal Education Department. 1957. *Digest of Statistics.*

Nigeria, Federal Ministry of Education. 1961. *Annual Digest of Statistics,* vol. 1.

Odugbesan, Clara. n.d. Bere: The Achievement and Contribution of a Brave Nigerian Woman Leader. Unpublished paper in the Funmilayo Ransome-Kuti papers, Biography Box, Manuscript Collection, Kenneth Dike Memorial Library, University of Ibadan.

Oghale, Regina Aghagba. 1983. The Development of Female Education in Isoko Local Government Area of Bendel State, 1925–1979. B. A. Honors Essay, Department of History, University of Ibadan.

Plummer, G. n.d. Memo on technical education for girls.

———. [1940] 1956. *The Teaching of Domestic Subjects in Africa,* 2nd ed. London: Longmans, Green & Co.

———. 1960. *Ibo Cookery Book.* London: Longmans.

Vincent, Adebisi. 1962. *A Cookery Book for the Tropics.* London: Allen & Unwin.

West Africa. 1953. The Lady Adviser from the West, 15 August, 701.

Williams, Rhoda O. 1957. *Miss Williams' Cookery Book.* London: Allen & Unwin.

Woman's World. 1967. Buba's for You, August, 13–15.

Part 2

Domestic Encounters

5 Colonial Fairy Tales and the Knife and Fork Doctrine in the Heart of Africa

Nancy Rose Hunt

Christmas of 1915 seemed "different from all the rest" for a group of British Baptists who sat down to dinner together in a home on a mission station in the Belgian Congo. "Instead of monkey stew for Christmas dinner, we had roast beef for the first time" ("Christmas" 1915, 11). For these nonconformist missionaries working in the equatorial forest on the Congo River, roast beef for Christmas dinner represented a significant breakthrough in domesticating their imagined surroundings. They were making Yakusu, their station in the equatorial forest, homelike. "The rose trees from England were flowering in our garden and the tables were gaily decorated" (Ibid., 11). Some Protestant missionaries called such efforts to recreate England in the Congo "a policy of make-believe . . . a loving fraud, but a hollow one" (Crawford 1912, 416). When Leopold II's son, Prince Albert, toured the colony in 1909, he stopped at Yakusu and entered inside a missionary home, he witnessed the make-believe, but not as hollow: "One would truly think one was in England."[1]

Scenes of "the white people . . . at table" did not often warrant mention in the *Yakusu Quarterly Notes* ("Jottings," *YQN*, 1935, 12; see also Mill 1956). It was when Christian Africans were participating in mission dining rituals, when the "policy of make-believe" coincided with the "knife and fork doctrine" (Congo Missionary Conference 1904, 47) that the monkey stew to roast beef theme made good copy for this mission station newsletter. In 1922, for instance, the recently arrived doctor's wife, Mrs. Chesterman, described going to "a unique dinner party" on Mr. and Mrs. Millman's veranda. Mrs. Millman's "house girls" served the invited men, who were African evangelist-teachers serving in villages in the mission district. The guests' faces "literally shone with recent contact with soap and water" as they sat down for the three-course, British-inspired menu. They ate roast meat with mint sauce, potatoes, peas and rice. "Of course it *was* a little difficult to convey peas safely to their destination by means of a fork, when you have never done it before," the doctor's wife teased, "but with the assistance of a dessert spoon all went well" (Chesterman 1922, 6). Mrs. Chesterman had only recently come to Yakusu. She remarked that the dinner party must have been "an inspiration to our host and hostess," who had been at Yakusu since its founding days in the late nineteenth century. They "knew these men as they *used* to be—all ignorant savages, and some of them actually cannibals" (Ibid., 7). The first time the choir "boys" and "girls" had a tea party in 1931, they joined the missionaries for biscuits and sardines over tea served in cups and saucers, another social event celebrating domesticity as lesson and reward for mission Africans. The lady missionaries doubled as guests like their husbands, though they also used the occasion to teach their African girls about etiquette and catering to company. Mrs. Millman described the tea party by distinguishing it from a savage past. Symbols of home, order, and authority seemed to come to life with approval: "The cane chairs and the wooden tables quietly creaked 'Things are different.' The photographs of the King and Queen of Belgium smiled to each other from their high places on the wall and seemed to say 'Delightful' " (Millman 1931, 4–5).

Yakusu is located in what has long been imagined by Europeans as the "heart of Africa" (Smith, n.d.). This mission station of the London-based Baptist Missionary Society, was founded in the mid 1890s when "Congoland," as anglophone missionaries called Belgian Africa, was still King Leopold II's private colony, the Congo Independent State. When the king's son came to the newly annexed Belgian Congo in 1909, the missionaries showed the prince the Millmans' home. Price Albert recalled the consequences of their pride in their work: "they made us see everything." The future king's tour of the church, school, hospital, and printing press became ritual as Yakusu became a regular visiting place for members of the Belgian royalty touring their colony. Prince Leopold III came in 1926; Albert returned as King accompanied by Queen Elizabeth in 1928; Princess Astrid came alone in 1933; and Prince Charles in 1947.[2] Mission preparations would begin weeks in advance in order to choreograph the pageant effectively. Mrs. Ennals recalled the anticipation and preparations as a godsend from "the realm of fairy tales and story books" (Ennals 1928, 15) that animated mission life. As these "middling class" British missionaries described the visits for their imagined observers, they inscribed their lives as colonial fairy tales, where kings and queens moored at the Yakusu beach, and mounted the steps of Yakusu's "Dover Cliff" ("Yakusu" 1912, 5) to drink a cup of tea and tour the mission and its rose gardens.[3] Rehearsals gave new meaning to the "policy of make-believe," and it was not a hollow fraud: "The day of the rehearsal was a great day, when Mokili and Mama [Mr. and Mrs. Millman] came round and 'pretended' to be the King and Queen, but after all that was only make believe and not the real thing. At last the great day came" (Ennals 1928, 16).

Missionary ladies devoted special care to enacting the entry into a missionary home for hospitality and refreshment. In 1928, Queen Elizabeth was "most interested in our domestic arrangements," asking to see the inside of the Millmans' " 'delightful little English cottage' " (Millman 1928, 8). An African girl would be told to make special cakes "for the moment when we shall say, 'Will Monseigneur honour us by taking a cup of tea and a cake made by this girl?' " (Millman 1926, 10). When Princess Astrid came in 1933, and they reached the Millman's house, Brown Mary was waiting, teapot in hand. The princess said, yes, she would like a cup of English tea:

> The Princess has been asked to sit in the chair occupied by the King when he came and she smilingly does so. "I want to ask you," she said, "Do you have girls to keep the house so beautiful or must you do it yourself?" I replied: "I have always had girls and even the flowers are arranged by them." "Today?" "Yes, Princess." "And the girl prepared this tea?" "Yes, Princess," "I am very interested. It seems wonderful. Why is it not done everywhere?" (Millman 1933, ii)

Girls as Boys, and Boy Elves as Narrative Habit

These incidents serve to introduce my subject, the representation of domesticity on a Protestant mission station located in Belgian Africa. Colonial domesticity has generally been examined as a process of limiting, confining, and domesticating African women through cultural imposition, and of inventing domestic institutions and traditions for them (Morrow 1986; Gaitskell 1983; Hunt 1990a). These episodes show that colonial domesticity was not confined to women, nor to the colonized, nor to the construction of gender roles in a colonial situation. Evangelical colonial domesticity was simultaneously about mentalities and about practices. This chapter examines how this simultaneity is revealed through narrative. The incidents above show that a variety of images were assembled to signify colonial domesticity: Victorian-influenced missionary domesticity and dining at Christmas within the equatorial forest; the desired "not quite/not white" (Bhabha 1984, 132; Hunt 1990a, 470) qualities of a domesticated savage as objectified in soaped faces, peas eaten with spoons, a sardine tea party; African girls holding tea pots, ready to serve cake and tea; and the observing Belgian king and queen, the state conveniently domesticated as approving father and mother, virtually as the senior missionary couple themselves. Yet whatever the domestic image used by the Yakusu missionaries to represent the progress of missionary evangelism to themselves and others, each rephrases, however differently, an evolutionary theme: darkness to lightness, savagery to civilization, heathens to Christians, monkey stew to roast beef.

The Victorian preoccupation with domesticity and "rituals of order and cleanliness" was one aspect of a new world view born of the industrial revolution (Davidoff 1974, 413). Leonore Davidoff has brilliantly analyzed how at the same time that this world view was dividing English society according to a new set of class divisions, it was associating and combining the polarity of working class versus middle (or upper) class with a series of others—masculine/feminine, urban/rural, public/private, white/black, home/empire, lady/woman, clean/dirty. These semantic polarities were formed in and through bodies, "were, partially at least, created in the nursery" (1983, 23). The dual vision of women, a legacy from classical culture and Christian theology, found new meaning in Victorian society, and this polarity (woman/lady) also had "much to do with new divisions of labor in the middle-class home" (Ibid., 23). The analytical problem of the transposition of the Victorian cult of domesticity and the Victorian "double exposure" of women (Ibid., 21) onto colonial terrain, then, is not only about the "policy of make-believe," the effort to recreate a piece of England with rose gardens and mint sauce in the middle of this heart of darkness. It is also about how these "middling class" British ladies were organizing households and dividing labor within them in the middle of the equatorial forest (Williams 1980). Missionary narrative, how missionaries assembled and (re)wrote Victorian polarities into evangelical parables, points the way.

As in much of colonial Africa (Levare 1928; Hansen 1989), in the Belgian Congo domestic servants were men, diminutively called "boys" (Comeliau 1945; *Femme* 1956). We have seen that Princess Astrid was surprised to see Brown Mary, an African girl, serve her a cup of tea. The princess basically asked: at Yakusu, are "boys" girls? The princess might have used the term "boyesse" to refer to a female "boy," though such experiments were still more at the level of discourse than practice in the Belgian colony.[4] Yet even if she had said "boyesse," Mrs. Millman would have laughed at such a term. Her "girls" were not mere colonial servants; they were her "house girls." She was God's servant, and they were like her children. Nevertheless, Yakusu Africans knew what Princess Astrid meant by a "boy." They would write in student compositions:

> White people are people who sit at a table to eat food. . . . They do not eat with their fingers, but with forks and spoons, and they are constantly saying to their boy "Never bring us dirty plates and spoons." (Chesterman 1929, 8)

When the king and queen had come in 1928, one girl turned to her teacher after the royal party had passed: " 'Mademoiselle, are the white men who are with the King his boys?' " This question became an anecdote in the quarterly news where Miss Wilkinson explained her joke to readers: "('Boy' being the name given to a white man's helper in the house)" (Wilkinson 1928, 18). The princess marvelled to see that a "boy" could be a girl. The "Mademoiselle" was entertained by the African supposition of white kings having white "boys." What made "boys" able to be girls but not whites? What were "boys" and "house girls" and "white helpers" and "Mesdemoiselles" anyway at this mission station in the "heart of Africa"? Education for girls at Yakusu generally followed African colonial patterns, emphasizing housekeeping and maternal training.[5] If having girls serve in your home was a form of educating them to be wives and mothers, why have "house boys" too?

In 1904, Mr. Stapleton reported on how the demand for mission-trained teachers was growing.

> Four times during the past month we have had a deputation of nearly forty young men and women, who paddled twenty miles on each occasion, to beg for a teacher. We got them away three times

with a few alphabet cards, though the third time we would have
been glad of a place to hide from their importunity. The fourth time
they won and went off proudly, having secured the personal boy of
one of the missionaries (1915, 4).

How are we to understand this story, where "boy" becomes teacher?
Certainly we are in a different colonial world than that where domestic servants were anonymous entities, "part of an inventory, distant
companions" (Hansen 1989, 42).

I began with royal visits, teas, and dinners, mission social events
that used domestic symbols—tea cups, forks, roast beef, rose trees
and soaped faces—to evoke the themes of rendering as home, domesticating the savage, making history. These domestic rituals were first
representations for those who enacted them, and then they were re-
represented as progress when inscribed as narrative in the quarterly
sent to mission supporters at home, in Britain.[6] Another kind of feature recurs in the pages of *Yakusu Quarterly Notes,* another way of
inscribing success in text. Rather than representations based on individual events, these are biographical tales about mission Africans.
They have simple plots—the story of a life and how it is marked with
progress. For girls, they tend to culminate in marriage: "weed
becomes flower" or "orphan/slave becomes Christian wife" are the motifs. Marriages between former "house girls" and "house boys," approved, if not in fact arranged, by missionaries, were the crowning
aspiration of mission endeavor (see also Morrow 1986), and the *Quarterly Notes* contains many of them. Stapleton's anecdote above cap-
tures a typical male trajectory: "boy" becomes teacher.[7] Another
common male variant was "boy" becomes nurse. Boy Sunday (Chesterman 1924) made it to the *Reader's Digest* with this kind of story.
The title was "My Man Sunday, How a Congo houseboy became a
conqueror of the dread diseases that ravaged his people" (Chesterman
1947). Dr. Chesterman described how when he arrived at Yakusu for
the first time, six boys who were to help "run our house" as cooks,
wash-jacks, and gardeners in return for their schooling, were lined up
on the veranda of the mission bungalow. "Our personal boy," a ten-
year-old named Sunday was among them. He subsequently dug a
chigger out of the doctor's foot and refused to join the local male
initiation ceremonies. These were crucial steps—intimate nursing
service and rejection of savage ways—in proving himself worthy of
training as a nurse in the hospital's school. He became a prized nurse-
evangelist at a village dispensary sixty miles away (Ibid.).

Drawing attention to "narrative habit" does not reveal humanitarian narratives like those from the eighteenth century analyzed by Thomas Laqueur, where detailing the suffering body was a literary strategy designed to engender moral compassion (1989, 200).[8] The literary strategy had more to do with engendering amused admiration and money. We find humorous career paths, Protestant social advancement in a pre-World War II colonial situation. The message was: we "can take savages and make them saints" ("Other Side" 1942, 14). The narratives were not limited to boy-becomes-teacher and boy-becomes-nurse. A serial story that ran for several issues in the *Notes* shows one life in caricatured, whimsical form. Each installment would begin with an abridgement of the preceding episodes in "Elf's Progress":

> A dainty little black face and sharp ears and an erect little figure is dubbed "the Congo Elf" by the Missionary. He is too young to work but is the Cinderella of his brother in the kitchen. The Missionary releases him to go to school. . . . His eagerness to learn how to read leads him to seek short cuts, but he has to realize that only steady work brings success. The first 'reading book' he bought was a hymn book! He is promoted to the kitchen as cook's helper. (1942, 13)

> The Elf fell into temptation and stole some cassava-mash cakes. He promised not to do it again and 'swallowed his punishment.' . . . Through a cycle accident Mrs Mill had to lie on her back for six weeks. . . . When I returned from the journey . . . [she] said that he had taken her orders daily at the bedside and managed the kitchen and cooked the food and brought a cup of tea early in the morning all by himself. (1943a, 18)

> He can add up figures in two columns but he does not just see what the 10s column means . . . he joins with the bigger boys in the French class. . . . Mrs. Mill has promoted him to under-boy in the house cleaning and she says that she sees he is trying to do his best, which is better perhaps than scholastic ability. She finds he is very clever with his hands, can undo seams, and opens tins very well. He is still the tease he was, and teases the solemn boy about twice his size who helps in the house. (1943b, 14)

This story represents the schoolboy and young convert as occasional "shirker" though faithful domestic helper. Despite his weaknesses, the missionaries held an affectionate feeling for this "boy," tellingly called an elf. The fellow's spiritual and moral progress are represented in a series of domestic service promotions within a missionary household. We don't see the elf become nurse or teacher:

progress is marked by a series of movements inside the domestic center of mission life. The boys we know about at Yakusu were not "part of white colonial households in the manner of pots and pans" (Hansen 1989, 72).[9] Those we know about had names, and we know about them because they made stories. They were the narrative material, the transforming/transformed jester figures of whimsical evangelical parables, like Bongamba, who began by impressing as "a likely boy," and was soon to be seen clothed and in a kitchen. Their careers usually included a period "clean[ing] knives and forks for an occupation" ("Children" 1911, 6–7). Boy elves were liminal characters, who moved from kitchens to bedrooms on the path from cannibalism to churches, schools, and hospitals.

Beidelman has argued that the coming of missionary wives and families to mission stations in colonial Tanganyika often "created a new and less flexible *domestic colonialism* exhibiting overconcern with the sexual accessibility or vulnerability of wives, with corresponding notions about the need for spatial and social segregation" (1982, 13; emphasis added). The development of such a "domestic enclave" (Ibid.), he said, "embodied a separation from and autonomy within the community that perhaps discouraged *intimate evangelism*. Such households also led to the use of servants, a situation which added to feelings of inequality" (Ibid., 70; emphasis added). Yakusu shows a pattern that refutes this notion of service "discourag[ing] intimate evangelism." For years, domestic colonialism did make for a form of intimate evangelism as "house boys" and "house girls" served in missionary households. The mission home was symbolic of mission domesticity, but it was also a concrete world where through their contact with missionaries they were to witness the domestic ideal, a companionate Christian marriage at work:

> [T]he greatest influence in building up the Christian home in Congo . . . [is] the missionary home planted in their midst. These people live in the concrete and their eyes are wonderfully quick. . . . [T]here is hardly a detail of our every-day life that is unnoticed by them. And to be taught at a mission station—to see the husband treat his wife with affection; see them sit down together to their meals; read the Book and pray together. (*Congo* 1918, 70)

The intimate evangelical approach often began with orphans who were raised, and bottle-fed, in missionary homes from infants: "if you had peeped in on us at dinner last night, you would have seen Ainaosongo on the Doctor's knee learning to whistle, and Batilangandi on my lap enjoying a banana. *They* were very happy, and *we* were 'at home' " ("Infant" 1922, 6). The evangelical idiom at play was servant: these missionaries saw themselves as God's Servants, and a willing African servant was to be a junior partner in this work. "House boys" were the privileged of the domesticated, the trusted Africans, the servants of God's Servants, almost members of the family. African idioms were also at play: "Adopting one of us as a 'Fafa,' the happy missionary so favoured has found himself shadowed by a willing servant" (Smith n.d., 80).[10]

Missionary homes were emblems of evangelical domesticity, but they were also pulpits and training sites:

> The home of the missionary is his best pulpit. . . . The home is the laboratory where he probes the secrets of the psychology of native boys who come to serve him as pupils in the kitchen, bedroom or garden and whom he admits to the circle of his family prayers and his daily school. . . . [N]ative races . . . call for a home, a missionary's home . . . which points to the Home above. (Mill 1935, 13–14)

Domestic service at Yakusu was organized as a component of "industrial education," a fundamental concept among Protestant missionaries who believed that "practical godliness" would erode natural African laziness and strengthen Christian character (*Congo* 1904, 45; see also Slade 1959, 206; Yates 1976; Curtin 1964, 62): "If we simply train their minds we will have on our hands a grand company of 'big heads' " (*Congo* 1918, 71). Mission days at Yakusu were divided between time in the classroom and time in "industrial" training: "Some start in the printing shop, some do chair-making and cane work, others work for the white man in his house as his cook or his washjack or his personal boy, or in his garden" (Parkinson 1929, 11).

At Yakusu the missionary homes were located along the main artery of the station along the riverfront. By the mid 1930s, the church enclosed them at one end, the hospital at the other, representing the two evangelical career openings for "house boys" successfully trained in scripture and hygiene in their masters' homes. As important as home was as symbol and training site, it would be wrong to imagine a missionary bungalow as having open doors and open spaces.[11] Space was compartmentalized and there was a hierarchy of domestic service jobs. Good performance on the job, in the classroom, in moral behavior was rewarded by greater responsibility in a missionary household and greater access to its interior rooms. One had to be trusted to move inside. Such was the elf's progress.

Moving up meant moving in: thus does student become "under-boy" in housecleaning. And moving in permitted moving out, thus "boy" becomes teacher or nurse. Domestic service became a method of training male workers and their female wives, ideally former "house girls," for mission outposts—schools and dispensaries—and thereby expanding the borders of the domesticated, evangelized domain.

Boys as Nurses, Domesticity as Hygiene

The distinction between colonial domesticity and colonial hygiene was fragile and blurred. Mr. and Mrs. Millman were among the first in the colony to write hygiene manuals for colonial schools (Millman 1921; Millman 1929). Hygiene manuals became a standard feature of school instruction from the early 1920s, and it was here that (male) Africans were told how to create a home, how to eat, and how to tell their wives to prepare their food (see Congo Belge 1926). They are texts about remaking and sanitizing African space and daily life, written for Africans, and they usually contain a section on hygiene and the importance of eating at a table with cutlery.[12] Hygiene became a colony-wide project to restructure, sanitize, legislate, and regulate African space, homes, gender relations, and eating and eliminating practices in the Belgian Congo.[13] What the Yakusu evidence reveals is not the "eugenics of empire" (Stoler 1989, 643–645), not the racial discourse of degeneracy and eliminating the unfit that was first articulated in the 1880s and gained legitimacy in the years preceding World War I (Mort 1987; see also Dubow 1987). One finds instead something much closer to colonial "sanitation and seeing," the cultural privileging of "openness, visibility, ventilation, boundaries, and a particular spatial differentiation of activities" (Thomas 1990, 160). Either finding would reflect parallels with metropolitan hygienic movements and the construction of "dangerous sexualities," but from different time periods. What is interesting is the time lag: these nonconformists were drawing on the pre-Darwinian language and social management visions of moral environmentalism, the early social medicine and associated female philanthropy of the mid nineteenth century (Mort 1987).[14] Procreation was less the obsession than was personal cleanliness and moral habits—in a word, soap. The very word "hygiene" came into use in the early nineteenth century as the distinction clean/dirty was redefined by the novelty of bathing with soap (Vigarello 1985, 183). Among Protestants working in the Congo a century later, soap was a "moral enterprise," imagined even as a worthy "commercial enterprise" (*Congo* 1918, 70).

Soap was not only for bodies, however. As we have seen, Bongamba was soon cleaning knives and forks for an occupation. Africans' "dirty" color of skin was less what inspired these missionaries in their sanitary rituals than how Africans were presumed to eat. As Norbert Elias has argued (1973, 121–183, esp. 144, 179–183), nothing is more constitutive of European hygienic sensibilities and the civilized/noncivilized polarity itself than the way the invention and use of forks stands conceptually opposed to cannibalism. (He quotes a 1859 English text to make this point; Ibid., 144.) The missionaries' conviction that they were working among former cannibals authorized the organization of domestic service at Yakusu as an appropriate form of industrial education. It was an extension of what in Protestant missionary circles was called the "knife and fork doctrine" (*Congo* 1904, 47). Not all missionaries agreed that Africans should stop eating with their hands from collective dishes: " 'Ah, Europeanized!' say some" (Ibid.). Indeed, in some Catholic (White Father) mission stations, plates and European food (and presumably knives and forks) were explicitly discouraged early in the century "to counter the tendency toward pride or aping European manners" (Yates 1967, 239). Yet, in general, however contested the issue was of how to avoid fostering "European caricatures" and "puffed up" Africans, insistence on cleanliness and industry were of capital importance to Protestants. Eating with knives and forks and cleaning them with soap as an occupation need not lead to "imitation whitemen" (quoted in Ibid., 228, 233, 238). Sanitizing and individualizing eating was in keeping with "self-reliance and individual responsibility . . . the keys to Protestant conceptions of the Christian society and the New African Man" (Ibid., 112). Learning the "rudiments of 'kitchen cleanliness,' " meant learning "orderliness, attention to detail, honesty in little things."[15] The missionaries' belief that they were working among former cannibals would have reinforced their zeal for the "knife and fork doctrine," and its elaboration in the training of nurses and the teaching of colonial hygiene (Millman 1930; Chesterman 1931–1932).

Stapleton's anecdote exposed an obvious trajectory. The pattern boy-becomes-teacher would have developed in a situation where the first converts played multiple roles as missionaries' personal servants (Slade 1959, 182). The more salient variant was boy-becomes-nurse:

"In the house he was my head boy, in the dispensary my head assistant," commented Sutton Smith early in the century (Smith n.d., 81). It began as an elaboration, as did all missionary (and for that matter all colonial) medicine, of the domestic needs of missionaries (Europeans) for nursing care when sick (Walls 1982). We saw above how Boy Elf tended to the missionary lady when she was sick. The boy-becomes-nurse trajectory resembled, even drew on the mid nineteenth-century demand for "closeness between good housekeeping and medical science" (Summers 1988, 47), when prior to the professionalization of nursing, the line between domestic service and nursing was slight. Others have shown how this closeness fostered the defining of nursing in Britain (and France) as a women's profession (Summers 1988; Poovey 1989; Gamarnikow 1978; see also Guiral and Thuiller 1978). This gender definition was "topsy-turvy" (Crawford 1912, 371) in much of colonial Africa.[16] Personal "boys" of turn-of-the-century European travellers in the Congo served as their personal quinine injectionists (Lloyd 1899, 208). A post-war popular account set in the Congo portrays observers surprised to discover that males served nuns their meals and rolled bandages in colonial hospitals, taking the domestic roles that in Europe were by then clearly defined as women's work (Hulme 1956).[17] Whatever the European colonial community seeking domestic service—private tourists (largely male), Catholic nuns (unmarried women), married Protestant missionary couples—the apparent inversion of roles as gender imaging moved between metropole and colony has to have been, on one level, a simple matter of who African societies released to work for Europeans, and this was largely men and boys, not women and girls. Nevertheless, identifying the parallel in career trajectory (domestic service to nursing) and the gender inversion on colonial terrain suggests that we will not understand why the category of domestic servant was constructed as male in much of sub-Saharan colonial Africa, if we do not understand the colonial gender construction of nurse.[18]

The focus of this essay is in how the boy-becomes-nurse pattern was elaborated into mission narrative, and how this elaboration provides insight into mentalities and into the organization and division of domestic labor within these missionary households. The attention to narrative indicates, again returning to Davidoff's analysis, how intricate the "rituals of deference" must have been in Mrs. Millman-type missionary households. These missionaries were not just evoking missionary homes as emblems of the cult of domesticity transposed onto colonial terrain. In Victorian England, the cult of domesticity and the glorification of Lady Bountifuls as supremely moral, philanthropic figures of salvation went with housewives playing multiple roles—"at once employer, tutor and surrogate mother" (Summers 1988, 3)—in complex households with large specialized staffs (Davidoff 1974, 412). The social origins of the Baptist Missionary Society missionaries in the Congo have not been studied, but until they are, it is fair to speculate that these missionary housewives would not have administered "elaborated upper-class households" with intricate "rituals of deference" back in Britain (Ibid.). Yet these wives of "not quite gentlemen" of "middling class" background would have known, even envied this upper-class world (Williams 1980), and colonial life would have nourished the "policy of make-believe." Someone like Mrs. Millman would have been dealing with daily problems of how to have hygienic meals served at her table, train a future nursing staff, and prepare girls as wives for this staff. She was simultaneously carrying around a set of fairy tales about bourgeois domesticity in her head, which were reaffirmed by some Belgian queens and princesses who would show up to observe English domesticity in the colony from time to time.

The cultural category that was being constructed at Yakusu was a domesticated savage, a new Christian African, and this category encompassed men and women, husbands and wives, teachers, nurses, and midwives. When royal visitors came, the missionaries not only showed an African nurse administering an injection in the hospital, African teachers teaching, and school girls ironing and sewing. Visiting queens and kings also needed to follow the Elf's Progress and go inside the "English cottage." Yet when they arrived the elf would not be an elf, but a girl, serving them a cup of tea. The girl was less a jester figure than a flower ("Girls" 1917, 12).[19] Girls and women were never spoken of as former cannibals, only as former slaves (see Hunt 1991), less carnal, disorderly women, if you will, and almost ladies.

Girls could be "boys" at Yakusu: their careers also circulated through missionary dining rooms and bedrooms for training in domesticity. Although both males and females were "servants," a gender-neutral term, there were gender assymetries in the "fork and knife doctrine." Men were becoming nurses and teachers, and women were supposed to be becoming their wives, at best African Lady Bountifuls, social mothers, extending evangelism and hygiene as teachers and midwives. If a missionary spoke of the advantages of giving a schoolboy domestic work in the home, he would say that he would benefit from being "initiated into the white-man's ways, and . . . the white-man's faith, through close association with him in the home" (Ennals 1950, 18). Yet if a woman missionary spoke about the benefits for girls, she would say they were learning to become better, cleaner mothers and wives. In either case, the knowledge being transferred, the meaning of the "white man's ways," was associated with colonial hygiene. Yet there were gender differences in how this knowledge was constituted and transferred. We saw how Boy Sunday made it to the *Reader's Digest* as a former domestic servant who became a nurse-evangelist. The boy-becomes-nurse trajectory was especially elaborated with the professionalization of medical missionary work and the founding of a nurse training school at Yakusu. Girls were instead learning mothercraft and midwifery (Millman and Millman 1929).

Not only the "social maps" but also the "ground rules" for girls and boys diverged (Ardener 1981). Little attention is devoted in the mission newsletter to explaining where and how schoolboys lived. When housing for nursing students opened in 1925, it was called a "little 'town,' " where they lived "two by two," with "one boy detailed for orderly duty" each week, "to be known as Le Garcon" (Chesterman 1925, 5–7). There was room for "colonial mimicry" (Bhaba 1984; Hunt 1990a) among these male nursing students, who proudly decorated their homes with flowers from the beds out front and rotated as the "boy" among themselves. Unlike the freedom of boys' space, girls' space was culturally elaborated as a home, with older girls acting as mothers to younger girls. Over time, more and more attention was devoted to elaborating this model as a structure of enclosure, imagined as traditional and reified in space. Girls cultivated their own food rather than flowers, mothered (served) their juniors, and were mothered in domestic training by serving lady missionaries in their homes.

Being a "houseboy" carried enormous prestige early in the century, "the pleasure of the feeling of pride in being able to say, 'I am Mokili's boy,' or 'I work the paka-paka (typewriter) of Kienge,' or 'I cook the food for Mama Ebongo' " (Smith n.d., 80). Yet "a mission station has a developmental pattern," and with growth in numbers, "important internal distinctions in prestige and lifestyle" develop among its converts (Beidelman 1982, 23–24). The boy-becomes-teacher and boy-becomes-nurse scenarios proved effective, and the Yakusu missionaries grew to depend on them. A high percentage of nursing students at the hospital school were previously "boys" in missionary homes, especially in the 1930s and 1940s.[20] By 1950, being a "house boy" was no longer prestigious; it was even "unpopular" (Ennals 1950).[21] New state educational regulations, which established an upper age limit for students, contributed to the worrisome "problem of domestic service in the missionary household in the Congo":

> The system of part-time service on the part of school-boys, and in some cases of school girls too, is an old-established one, and has very much to its credit. . . . From the earliest days of the Congo Mission those who were nearest to the missionaries, serving them in hundreds of small ways, are the ones who, in course of time, proved themselves to be those on whom ultimately responsibility rested as builders, carpenters, teachers, pastors, medical workers, and the like. . . . The day of a full school programme makes the part-time employment of school-boys not only unpopular, but more difficult to justify. . . . We look for relief in . . . the offering for domestic and other service of those who were so trained long ago. Though, of course, this service must be adequately paid for. (Ibid., 17–19)

Domestic service arrangements at Yakusu had always had an economic component to them.[22] Hiring students was cheaper than hiring full-time servants.[23] The medical missionaries especially regretted the changes affecting domestic labor. They could no longer screen future nurses through domestic service in the home. The medical director felt that nursing students were less desirable students than before:[24] "Now knowledgeable lads are not even 'kitchen-clean' when they come to the wards and operating theatre, and have to be 'house-trained' at great cost of time and patience and energy.[25]

Mesdemoiselles as Mamas, and Marriage and Excrement

"Go softly, Be mothers to them," had been the words of Mrs. Millman at a 1921 conference of Protestant missionaries working in the Congo when girls' boarding schools had been discussed (*Congo* 1921, 175). She feared crowded schedules and rigid institutional structures. Her career had been largely dedicated to adopting young girls, many orphans, but some placed by willing Christian parents, who lived in a special house in the back of her house.[26] She, Mama Mokili, the senior White Mama, and the wife of the senior *fafa*, guided them towards marriage and motherhood. "Our Girls," she called the articles introducing different ones, describing how they had come to live in the "girls' house," their progress in school and within her home, and the happy feeling she had the day each married. In 1911, Protestant missionary women discussed how best to organize domestic arrangements for girls separated from their village environments for training on the stations in the Congo.

> Is it best to keep all the girls boarding on the station in one compound, under the supervision of one lady missionary, who will take as far as possible, the entire charge of the girls; or is it best for the girls to be attached to the different homes and under the direction of the different ladies who may be on the station, each lady taking as many girls under charge as funds and time will permit? (*Congo* 1911, 66)

The latter method seemed to permit greater personal contact and affection, and the Conference recommended that "every lady missionary . . . take as many girls as possible into her home, with a view to winning them for Christ, and training them for future service in the salvation of their sisters" (Ibid., 68). This is what Mrs. Millman did, apparently following a general pattern of having a girls' house and a boys' house in separate enclosures within the compounds of married missionaries (*Congo* 1921, 180).[27]

Yet this system "require[d] very close supervision." Fears grew that having girls work and live side by side with boys was endangering their honor. Missionaries began to agree "that if a married lady has boys she should not have girls as well" (Ibid.). By 1921, boarding schools were felt to be the most effective method of training girls as a means of "elevat[ing] the home life of these people." It would provide a " 'home life' " that would not "take them too far out of their native environment . . . or unfit them for village life after they are trained" (Ibid., 169–70). The model proposed was a series of houses with seven or eight girls each of various ages, with the older girls as house mothers, and a fence around the whole compound to guard the girls. The house of the "native superintendant" would be located "in front to close up the rectangle" (Ibid., 170). Daily household tasks would be assigned to the members of the different "homes." It was advised, however, that the boarding school girls not lose touch with married missionary couples due to "the great value of the contact of these girls with the[m] . . . in their own homes" (Ibid., 172).

The Yakusu boarding school was founded in 1928, basically following this "home life" model except that the superintendent's house up front was occupied by two European single lady missionaries, two "Mesdemoiselles," as they are still called today at Yakusu. It was there—within the boundaries of the "fence"—that senior boarding girls went for contact with missionaries in their homes, cooking their food, serving them dinner, cleaning their bedrooms. The institution was called the "fence," a term suggesting boundary, enclosure. African women recall it as an enclosed, barricaded space with one door, and one had to be inside this door by 6 p.m. each day or meet with punishment.[28] Missionaries said that the term fence was a euphemism, and they were also fond of calling the institution the "girls' village." They called the nearby village of Yakoso[29] not a village, but a town, and this negative connotation (a rural/urban polarity) carried into the way they actively distinguished their fence girls from town girls—in potential, in dress, in hours of daily schooling. The "fence" placed girls in a bounded space safe from what might contaminate them: males, town girls, "raw natives."

The inclusion of single woman missionaries on Protestant mission stations in the Congo had long been a contested issue. Their incorporation caused disquiet about their sexual and psychological vulnerabilities, and seemed to threaten the value of married missionary women's work. There were worries that Africans would misunderstand, and it was difficult to develop surrogate families for these unmarried women. Issues of sexual asceticism and territoriality were involved. Guidelines were drawn as early as 1907 concerning the activities, living arrangements, and companionship of single woman missionaries. Their work was to be confined to working with children and women, and they were to live together in pairs. Some suggested that they not have male domestic workers. This obligatory companionship of another single lady missionary would ensure distance from European and African men *and* married missionary women (Hunt 1990b). The evidence indicates that the founding of the boarding school involved an institutionalization of girls' work at Yakusu under single woman missionaries and the creation of stricter "ground rules" for unmarried girls and women. Mrs. Millman's attachment to her work with girls helps explain why she resisted so strongly the coming of single lady missionaries to Yakusu (Ibid.): "Several single ladies located at a station may engage themselves in good works but someone's wife, through their presence, becomes a household drudge" (*Congo* 1902, 78–79). The "advent of our single ladies" made the development of boarding schools practical (*Congo* 1921, 179), and "the oversight of girls" was to be "one of the most important branches of single ladies' work" (Ibid., 180). Mrs. Millman's objections to the coming of single women would have been a way of resisting the eventual channeling of her "White Mama" energies from girls' and women's work to women's work alone (Wilkinson 1955).

The "fence" resolved not only the sexual and territorial tensions of protecting unmarried African girls living on a mission station, but those surrounding the incorporation of single woman missionaries as well. It gave these missionaries a territory and a surrogate family. We saw above the narrative trajectory through domestic space of Boy Elf. At the boarding school this trajectory was institutionalized, while being couched in a maternal idiom. As girls moved up and within in a hierarchy of age and domestic service jobs, they became the Mamas of the younger girls in the individual houses. In local African terms, this was not so unusual; they were becoming *cose,* the youthful maternal guardians of yet younger children. But the White Mamas at the head of the household were not Mamas at all; they were Mesdemoiselles, and this, I speculate, had enormous implications for intimate evangelism. It implied the reorganization of domestic labor (and domestic service career trajectories and idioms) within the household. Firstly, tasks could no longer be divided between boys and girls. Secondly, the ideology of intimate evangelism, which had justified the use of school children as domestic servants, had been cast either in terms of a maternal idiom with the supervising Lady Bountiful playing mother, or in terms of providing exposure to an ideal companionate husband and wife team. Either alternative would have been strained by the "fence."

African women's memories are extremely illuminating about the rigidities of hierarchy and control in the "fence." When you became a "Mama," you effectively became a "boy," because it was then and only then that you entered into the big White Mamas household and served at their table. The pinnacle to these movements, as Machuli Bolendela recalled, was to be in charge of the Mesdemoiselles' bedrooms. This meant you were ready for marriage. Machuli associated this rite of passage with two new tasks. One was folding the missionaries' large sheets, the other removing the missionaries' sanitary buckets.[30] The ironies in representation are palpable. The first task Machuli associated with age and physical capacity; a younger girl could not fold those sheets, she explained. She spoke of the second task in terms of the impact of memory on routine, recalling it as a revolting, degrading task that has meant that even today she cannot drink water fetched in a similar bucket.

Let us return to Davidoff's argument about the Victorian polarities that were "created in the nursery" and expressed in domestic service "deference rituals" (1974; 1983). Davidoff argues that a dualistic view of women, a legacy from classical culture and Christian theology, found new meaning in Victorian society, and that these new meanings had "much to do with new divisions of labor in the middle-class home" (1983, 23).

> In viewing Victorian women it is as if we are looking at a picture through a double exposure.
>
> Indeed, the dual vision of women, as woman and lady, becomes mixed with other polarities such as those between white and black, familiar and foreign, home and empire. (Ibid., 21)

Who was woman and who was lady in a situation where boys were "boys" and future nurses, and girls were "boys" and future wives and mothers? How did the polarity woman/lady get mixed up and played out in a concrete situation where the colonial household was indeed being used as training ground, as the apparently constitutive site of desired gender roles? As in middle- and upper-class English households, there was a complex organization of tasks that were themselves semantically organized according to the polarities clean/dirty, public/private. Yet in the colonial context of Yakusu, these polarities, as we have seen, were time and time again turned into Boy Elf-type evangelical parables, converted into career narratives. If making successful African evangelists was the goal, who would have performed those tasks "closest to defiling and arduous activities [that] were, whenever possible, to be kept out of sight"? Who would have dealt with the "recurring by-products of daily life"—rubbish, fecal matter, urine, blood—that in English households almost always fell to female servants, and in the absence of servants, to wives (Davidoff 1974, 413, 425)?

The available evidence makes it very difficult to reconstruct the concrete differences in the divisions, hierarchies, and trajectories of domestic labor between Mama Mokili's household of house girls and house boys and this new fence of girls led by Mesdemoiselles. Yet my sense of it is that boys and girls in Mama Mokili's household were on completely different tracks. Boys moved from knives and forks (kitchens) to delivering bedside tea (bedrooms), and then they were ready for the "work of the knife" (surgery) in hospitals. Girls were trained with needles, irons, and tea pots, in sewing, ironing, and entertaining, effectively moving from the less polluting, the less degrading end of the scale of domestic jobs to the most prestigious (serving the queen a cup of tea). African agendas may well have been critical here as well; one African father, for instance, turned over his daughter to the Millmans so she would learn to iron and sew.[31]

Domestic tasks and trajectories that formerly could be separated by sex in Mama Mokili's household became conflated in the Mesde-moiselles' "fence." The trajectories of "as-you-move-up-you-move-in" and "as-you-move-in-you-move-out" were relocated to this artificial institution where the "policy of make-belive" was pushed so far that everything operated by a maternal idiom, but no one was mother, and no one was wife. Someone had to play "boy" and someone had to play "master," and this was enacted around these asexual, barren Mamiwata[32] figures who were supposed to somehow be mothers but never were, and whose primary role was to guard the sexuality of their African counterparts every night by locking the one and only door to the compound as the sun set at 6 p.m. We do not know who disposed of fecal matter in Mrs. Millman's home, though I would doubt it was her "house girls," nor a privilege that came as one moved up and in. Her Brown Marys were already positioned too far along the continuum between dirt and cleanliness, good and evil, here cast in woman/lady, slave/Christian wife terms. Propriety may have been differently constructed for single woman missionaries, and only those who were most senior and most trusted were trusted with their excrement. The evidence is simply not in.[33] Regardless, the bounding of "house girls" within the confines of a boarding "home" and the intended extension of a maternal idiom to single woman missionaries meant that these "Mesdemoiselles" were less Mamas than husbands (male arbitrers), and their African servants less children than "boys."

We have seen that at Yakusu colonial domestic arrangements and colonial domesticating projects were linked, on the one hand, to the tropes of low-church equatorial evangelism (the ubiquitous we "can take savages and make them saints" expressions ["The Other Side" 1942, 14]), and, on the other, to the constitution of colonial boundaries and social markers as the concrete social realities of who ate and slept where and who served whom when were worked out. The domestic as a place (home, mission station, hospital, girl's boarding home) and the domestic as a process (making home, clearing the forest, soaping faces, rendering feminine and submissive) were implicated in signifying relationships of colonial power in gender and racial terms (Scott 1986). Domesticity at Yakusu encompassed more than housekeeping and mothercraft, and more than training girls to be mothers and wives. It embraced girls and boys, men and women. It concerned "intimate evangelism," creating a "home within the wilderness" (Mill 1935), and a missionary lady "training rough forest lads in her house" (Browne 1956, 14). It was an all-encompassing mentality in a colonial situation, with home as the leading metaphor representing the constructed boundaries, hierarchies, and intimacies of mission life. Practically, it was about organizing and dividing household labor, transferring knowledge about hygiene, and finding workers and converts in a context where girls were much less likely to be released from production and reproduction in African households.

There was always an interaction between the construction of colonial domesticity for the colonized and colonial domestic needs. Although "boys" were often men, domestic service should not be assumed to have signified male. To domesticate a savage was to engender racial difference, to signify relationships of power based on racial difference—the colonizer and the colonized, the missionary and the convert—in gender terms (Scott 1986). There was an element of feminine meaning to making men domestics and calling them "boys"—tamed sexuality—and this gender meaning was useful.

How the domestic is constructed in a particular cultural context is related to the inscription of boundaries in space—between colonizer and colonized, and among colonizers and colonized. At Yakusu, missionary homes were the emblems of colonial domesticity and the training ground for African mission workers. They were the spatial center, the pivot that allowed expanding the mission district's borders as domestic knowledge (hygiene) learned in a master's home was applied outside. By the late 1920s, as we have seen, a female enclave developed on the station, a female emblem for unmarried ladies and girls. This girls' boarding house provided a home for single European woman missionaries as much as it did for African girls, and female domestic service for these lady missionaries.

The boarding school resolved perceptions of purity and danger in a colonial situation by bounding unmarried women—European and African—into one closed space. In the process, intimate evangelism gave way to an enclave of domestic colonialism of and for women.

Notes

I am grateful for the Fulbright/Hays, Social Science Research Council, Belgian American Educational Foundation, and American Association of University Women fellowships for research and writing support. I would also like to thank Jan Vansina for critical comments on an earlier version of this chapter.

1. "Ils nous menènt d'abord dans leur home comfortable, on se croirait vraiment en Angleterre, quand on entre dans ces demeures où tout rappelle ces cottages anglais si propres, aux chambres claires et sympas, mais ornées de tous les bibelots, objets ou portraits qui attachent/ramenent les occupants à leur interieur par les souvenirs qui s'y rattachent par un morceau de la mère patrie qui y revit" (*Journal du prince Albert*, 1909, Archives des Palais Royaux, Brussels, dossier 75, 94). I am indebted to Jean-Luc Vellut for this source. Crawford spoke from the savanna regarding garden growing, so the "policy of make-believe" would have been more hollow than in the forest.

2. Prince Albert visited on 10 June 1909, and Baby Millman was born on 18 March, which may explain the more subdued reception of this first visit. The royal visits are documented in the following issues of the *Yakusu Quarterly Notes:* no. 6 (December 1909); no. 65 (January 1926); no. 75 (October 1928); no. 93 (April 1933); and no. 141 (September 1947). Relations between Protestant missionaries on the Congo and the pro-Catholic state, before and after Belgian annexation in 1908, are reputed to have been tense (Slade 1959; Reardon 1968); a close study of how these festive Protestant mission-colonial state pageants countered this reputation is outside my scope here.

3. These were especially Mrs. Millman's fairy tales; she wrote of the anticipation in 1933:

> At this moment, a quarter to eight o'clock on Tuesday morning the steamer Luxembourg is still moored at our beach near the steps which have been trodden by the feet of a King and Queen, of Princes and Dukes and a host of Lords and Ladies of high degree. The station is quiet. Not a drum is heard. A Princess is sleeping. The steamer clock which keeps the coast time points to seven. (Millman 1933,i)

4. The fact that "boys" were men seemed a pitiful loss of valuable male labor as early as 1924. "Notre Colonie, 1er juillet 1924. La Question des Métis au Congo Belge. Causerie faite au Cercle Africaine à Bruxelles, par le Dr Dreypondt," AI 14 (4674), "Mulatres Avant 1940," Archives Afri-

caines, Brussels. Yet, despite occasional discussion (Phillipe 1927), it continued to be assumed that domestic servants would be male, as numerous manuals for colonial women suggest (Comeliau 1945; *La Femme* 1956). The term "boyesse" was common colonial vocabulary in Katanga by the 1950s (Van der Vorst and Pohl 1961), by which time there were more general calls for introducing female domestic servants. Such experiments were often made with daughters of "boys" and women who had received domestic training in *foyers sociaux* (Duttileux 1950); see also, Rapport d'activité, Foyer Social Agrée, Coquilhatville, 1953, H H 20, 3–1, Centre d'Aequatoria, Bamanya, Zaire.

5. On Belgian African trends, see Hunt (1990a). On Protestant and Catholic differences in education in the Congo Independent State, see Yates (1967).

6. The *Yakusu Quarterly Notes* was first published in 1908 on the station press. By 1915, with its pink cover decorated with a floral design of domesticated banana vines, and its anecdotal, whimsical vignettes of mission life, it seems to have been under the editorial control of the mission matriarch herself. Mrs. Millman's own writing best typifies this style.

7. See Ennals (1928) for another example where domestic servants were left in a village to preach and teach.

8. On Victorian domestic narratives, see Poovey (1989).

9. Hansen explicitly excluded domestic service on mission stations from her study of domestic service in colonial Zambia, though she remarks that many servants first worked for missions, and that Europeans ascribed a "civilizing, educational function to domestic service in the early years" (1989,78).

10. Acquiring orphans and redeemed slaves was a classic way of locating a first generation of converts in Belgian Africa. According to Jan Vansina:

> These children become "clients," "dependents" and like those in African societies are masked by the use of near kinship terms but revealed by the terms "boy." To outsiders it looked as if all the African personnel was part of a mission "household"—like that of a leader—including the *lupanqu* (fence), a colonial institution here that rapidly spread from elsewhere, but visualizes . . . what exactly is the mission establishment and what not. . . . "[I]nterchangeable skills" . . . is precisely what sorted them out as "clients" or "dependents" of a patron called *fafa:* there is no labor contract here, no "private space," etc.

The history of orphans in the Congo, who in the early years were children raided by the state and slave traders and dumped in mission stations, "gives sinister meaning to the *fafa* syndrome," which became a common Protestant and Catholic strategy for locating committed converts (Jan Vansina, personal communication, May 1990; see also on orphans Delathuy 1986). On the history of orphans and missions, see also Slade (1959) and Yates (1967). On the "*fafa* syndrome" in a Belgian colonial memoir ("faisant de moi son bwana adoptif"), see Mamba (1934,89).

11. The boundaries public and private virtually collapsed as the home

became pulpit, laboratory, chapel, and school; for comparative evidence, see Hansen (1989,69).

12. The tradition continues. Such manuals are disseminated by Zaire's Catholic press and sold in Catholic bookshops today. They cover table manners and how to eat at tables with cutlery; see *Kujua Kuishi katika Watu Wengine* (1989,33–37).

13. Lyons (1988) has shown how African space was restructured as villages were relocated for public health reasons. Thomas (1990) on colonial Fiji is suggestive for what I assert here.

14. I am tracing influences from the metropole to the colony here, though in reading a mission newsletter like the *YQN* one must remain alert to how colonial practice is being represented and translated for metropolitan mission supporters. These missionaries seem to have been drawing on the culture of the new evangelism of the early nineteenth century and its emphasis on moral regeneration "through the purity of domestic manners and an ethic of practical Christianity" (Mort 1987,54) as they enacted the knife and fork doctrine on colonial terrain; more research on their social origins and theological inclinations is needed. The time lag in this transposition from metropole to colony does not preclude the possibility that in writing vignettes for the *YQN* the missionaries found (and knew they would find) an avid readership. A British audience of mission supporters, prone to contemporary eugenicist ideas and active in metropolitan social hygiene movements directed at the urban poor, may have found inspiration in these quaint accounts of reformed cannibals.

15. Baptist Missionary Society (B.M.S) Yakusu Annual Medical Report, 1954, Hôpital de Yakusu, Yakusu, Zaire.

16. Austen and Headrick (1983,69) note the boy-to-nurse trajectory for colonial Cameroun. de Craemer and Fox (1968) do not comment on the fact that nurses were male, but do explore it as a prestigious, if strained, position in the colonial period. Shula Mark's forthcoming book will illuminate the major exception, South Africa.

17. On the history of male aversion to domestic labor in Britain, see Davidoff (1974; 1983).

18. The history of colonial hospitals and nursing care must also attend to the inverted parallel.

19. Flowers and gardens were salient metaphors at Yakusu, and the place was reknowned in Belgian circles for its roses (Detry 1912,99). "Children *as* gardens was a favourite metaphor for writers on domesticity" in Victorian England; see Davidoff and Hall (1987,373). One missionary to the Congo commented, "We must teach these people to appreciate beauty. They call roses weeds" (*Congo* 1918,72).

20. Student records show that of male students admitted for nursing training, 4 out of 5 had previously worked as "boys" in 1935, 6 of 10 in 1936, 7 of 13 in 1937, 5 of 10 in 1938, 6 of 7 in 1939, 9 of 17 in 1940, 3 of 7 in 1941, 7 of 12 in 1942, 2 of 12 in 1943, 7 of 12 in 1944, 1 of 13 in 1945, 5 of 16 in 1946, 7 of 23 in 1947, 2 of 26 in 1948, 5 of 21 in 1949, 1 of 16 in 1950, 1 of 4 in 1951, 5 of 21 in 1952, 3 of 29 in 1953, 2 of 14 in 1954, 6 of 15 in 1955, 0 of 16 in

1956, and 2 of 22 in 1957 (Student Record Cards, 1935–1957, Hôpital de Yakusu, Zaire).

21. This change was evident in my discussions with local pastors and other mission folk in and near Yakusu in 1989–1990. Men in their sixties and seventies spoke gratefully of their acquaintances with missionaries that began as servant relationships. One pastor of about fifty was proud never to have been a "boy," intimating that the punishments were too severe. Nora Carrington, a missionary in the Yakusu region from 1940 until after the rebellion in the mid 1960s recalled that attitudes especially changed during the rebellion. She and her husband were accused of having "slaves" at this time, and let their servants go (interview, July 1990).

22. Yet dividing mission labor among numerous mission students, who received their schooling in turn for labor in missionaries' homes, also created a certain flexibility. One senses a hardening of master-servant relations in the 1950s as full-time servants slowly replaced the earlier schoolboy system. Christmas gifts and other benefits were specified according to each category of worker (Staff Meeting Minutes, 3 August 1949, 27 December 1949, 3 July 1950, 3 December 1953, District Pastor's Office, Yakusu, Zaire). Intimate evangelism became carefully regulated.

23. Since 1896, missionaries serving in the Congo were expected to pay out of their own pockets the rations and wages of "all boys used as personal boys, house-boys, cooks, wash-boys, or garden-boys" (Western Sub-Committee Minutes, 14 January 1896, Book no. 10, p. 88, Baptist Missionary Archives, Regent's Park College, Oxford).

24. B.M.S. Yakusu Annual Medical Report, 1954.

25. Ibid.

26. Unlike in other mission contexts (Grimshaw 1983), BMS missionaries working in the Congo were not able to raise their children in the mission field. The maternal idiom had an emotional depth; see *Congo* (1918,109–115).

27. It is unclear whether she also had a boys' house, though the houses that remain are constructed with "boyeries" out back.

28. Mama Yaluani, 1 October 1989, Yainyongo-Romée, Zaire; Mama Bokenge Limengo and Mama Tula, 30 November 1989, Yakoso; Machuli Georgine, 2 December 1989, Kisangani; Asha Marguerite, 3 December 1989, Kisangani; Machuli Bolendela, 3 December 1989, Kisangani; meeting with former Yakusu boarding school students, organized by Damali Basuli, 25 January 1990, Kisangani.

29. Yakoso is the local Lokele place name that was mispronounced by the first British missionaries as Yakusu. Today local folk can show exactly where Yakusu ends and Yakoso begins.

30. Machuli Bolendela, 3 December 1989.

31. There was a corresponding division of labor in hospital domesticity, of course; this is beyond my scope here.

32. The literature on Mamiwata figures is growing; see Ogrizek (1981–1982).

33. The history of colonial toilets has yet to be written. Who disposed of the colonizers' excrement is an important historical question, and the key to mapping the rituals of deference and gender imaging that I adumbrate here. On Africa, Africans, and excrement, see Mbembe (1990) and Epelboin (1981–1982).

Bibliography

Austen, Ralph A., and Rita Headrick. 1983. Equatorial Africa under colonial rule. In *History of Central Africa, Volume Two,* ed. David Birmingham and Phyllis M. Martin, 27–94. London and New York: Longman.

Ardener, Shirley, 1981. Ground Rules and Social Maps for Women: An Introduction, In *Women and Space,* ed. Shirley Ardener, 11–34. New York: St. Martin's Press.

Bean, A. 1956. The Fence *YQN* 154 (January): 5–8.

Beidelman, T. O. 1982. *Colonial Evangelism.* Bloomington: Indiana University Press.

Bhabha, Homi, 1984. Of Mimicry and Man: The Ambivalence of Colonial Discourse. *October* 28 (Spring): 125–133.

Browne, S. G. 1956. Mrs. Ethel C. Mill. *YQN* 156 (January): 14–15.

Chesterman, C. C. 1925. The Ba-infirmier. *YQN* 61 (January): 5–9.

———. 1931–1932. The Training and Employment of African Natives as Medical Assistants. *Proceedings of the Royal Society of Medicine* 25, pt. 3: 1067–1076.

———. 1947. My Man Sunday; How a Congo Houseboy Became a Conqueror of the Dread Diseases that Ravaged His People. *Reader's Digest* 51 (September): 95–100.

Chesterman, W. L. 1922. A Unique Dinner Party. *YQN* 52 (October): 6–7.

———. 1924. Yenga. Sunday Boy. *YQN* 59 (July): 8b–c.

———. 1929. A Few Quotations from Our Composition Class on the Subject of White People. *YQN* 78 (July): 8–8a.

Children Specially Supported. 1911. *YQN* 11 (March): 6–7.

Christmas at Yakusu. 1915. *YQN* 26 (March): 11–12.

Comeliau, Marie-Louise. 1945. *Demain, Coloniale!.* Anvers: Editions Zaire.

Congo Belge, Service de l'Hygiène. 1926. *Conseils d'Hygiène aux Indigènes.* Brussels: Imprimerie Industrielle & Financière.

Congo Missionary Conference. 1902–1921. Reports of the General Conference of Missionaries of the Protestant Societies working in Congoland. Bolobo: Baptist Mission Press and "Hannah Wade" Printing Press.

Crawford, Dan. 1912. *Thinking Black: Twenty-Two Years without a Break in the Long Grass of Central Africa.* London: Morgan and Scott.

Curtin, Philip D. 1964. *The Image of Africa: British Ideas and Action, 1780–1850.* Madison: University of Wisconsin Press.

Davidoff, Leonore. 1974. Mastered for Life: Servant and Wife in Victorian and Edwardian England. *Journal of Social History* 7: 406–428.

———. 1983. Class and Gender in Victorian England. In *Sex and Class in*

Women's History, ed. Judith L. Newton, Mary P. Ryan, and Judith R. Walkowitz, 17–64. London: Routledge & Kegan Paul.

Davidoff, Leonore, and Catherine Hall. 1987. *Family Fortunes: Men and Women of the English Middle Class, 1780–1850.* Chicago: University of Chicago Press.

de Craemer, Willy, and Renée C. Fox. 1968. *The Emerging Physician: A Sociological Approach to the Development of a Congolese Medical Profession.* Stanford, Calif: Hoover Institution on War, Revolution and Peace.

Delathuy, A.M. 1986. *Jezuiten in Kongo met zwaard en kruis.* Berchem: EPO.

Detry, A. 1912. *A Stanleyville.* Liège: Imprimerie La Meuse.

Dubow, Saul. 1987. Race, Civilisation and Culture: The Elaboration of Segregationist Discourse in the Inter-War Years. In *The Politics of Race, Class and Nationalism in Twentieth-Century South Africa,* ed. Shula Marks and Stanley Trapido, 71–94. London and New York: Longman.

Dutilleux, G. 1950. La femme détribalisée du centre extracoutumier. *Bulletin du CEPSI,* no. 14:106–114.

The Elf's Progress. 1942. *YQN* 128 (April): 13–14.

———. 1943a. *YQN* 133 (April): 17–18.

———. 1943b. *YQN* 134 (October): 14.

Elias, Norbert. [1939] 1973. *La civilisation des moeurs,* trans. Pierre Kamnitzer. Paris: Calmann-Levy.

Ennals, G. C. 1928. With the Little Ones. *YQN* 75 (October): 15–18.

———. 1943. Glimpses of Work among the Women. *YQN* 133 (April): 13–15.

Ennals, W. H. 1950. Help in the Missionary Household. *YQN* 145 (February): 17–19.

Epelboin, Alain. 1981–1982. Selles et urines chez les Fulbe bande du Sénégal Oriental. *Cahiers ORSTOM, Série Sciences Humaines* 18:515–530.

La Femme au Congo: Conseils aux partantes. 1956. Brussels: Union des femmes coloniales du Congo Belge et du Ruanda-Urundi.

Gaitskell, Deborah. 1983. Housewives, Maids or Mothers: Some Contradictions of Domesticity for Christian Women in Johannesburg, 1903–39. *Journal of African History* 24:241–256.

Gamarnikow, Eva. 1978. Sexual Division of Labour: The Case of Nursing. In *Feminism and Materialism,* ed. Annette Kuhn and AnnMarie Wolpe, 96–213. London. Routledge and Kegan Paul.

The Girls' School. 1917. *YQN* 34 (March): 11–12.

Grimshaw, Patricia. 1983. "Christian Woman, Pious Wife, Faithful Mother, Devoted Missionary": Conflicts in Roles of American Missionary Women in Nineteenth-Century Hawaii. *Feminist Studies* 9:489–521.

Guiral, Pierre, and Guy Thuiller. 1978. *La vie quotidienne des domestiques en France au XIXe siècle.* Paris: Hachette.

Hansen, Karen Tranberg. 1989. *Distant Companions: Servants and Employers in Zambia. 1900–1985.* Ithaca and London: Cornell University Press.

Hulme, Kathryn. 1956. *The Nun's Story.* London: Pan Books.

Hunt, Nancy Rose. 1990a. Domesticity and Colonialism in Belgian Africa: Usumbura's *Foyer Social,* 1946–1960. *Signs* 15:447–774.

———. 1990b. "Single Ladies on the Congo": Protestant Missionary Tensions and Voices. *International Women's Studies Forum,* 13:395–403.

———. 1991. Noise over Camouflaged Polygamy, Colonial Morality Taxation, and a Woman-naming Crisis in Belgian Africa. *Journal of African History,* 32:471–494.

Infant Welfare, Yakusu. 1922. *YQN* 50 (March): 4–6.

Jottings of the Junior. 1935. *YQN* 101 (April): 11–14.

Laqueur, Thomas W. 1989. Bodies, Details, and the Humanitarian Narrative. In *The New Cultural History,* ed. Lynn Hunt, 176–204. Berkeley and Los Angeles: University of California Press.

Levare, A. 1928. *Le confort aux colonies.* Paris: Editions Larose.

Lloyd, A. B. 1899. *In Dwarf Land and Cannibal Country.* London: T. Fisher Unwin.

Lyons, Maryinez. 1988. Sleeping Sickness Epidemics and Public Health in the Belgian Congo. In *Imperial Medicine and Indigenous Societies,* ed. David Arnold, 105–124. Manchester: Manchester University Press.

Mamba. 1934. *Les Derniers Crocos.* Brussels: Editions de l'Expansion Coloniale.

Mbembe, Achille. 1990. Notes (provisoires) sur la postcolonie. Unpublished manuscript.

Mill, A. G. 1935. The Home within the Wilderness. *YQN* 103 (October): 13–14.

———. 1956. Memories of Mokili's Life and Work. *YQN* 154 (January): 12–14.

Millman, E. R. 1926. Getting Ready. *YQN* 65 (January): 10.

———. 1928. The News. *YQN* 75 (October): 2–8.

———. 1931. Their First Tea Party. *YQN* 86 (July): 2–5.

———. 1933. The Royal Visit to Yakusu. *YQN* 93 (April): i–iv.

Millman, E. R., and W. Millman. 1929. *A Mothercraft Manual for Senior Girls and Newly Married Women in Africa.* London: Christian Literature Society, Carey Press.

Millman, W. 1921. *Hygiène tropicale pour les écoles, Njaso ya Bosasu.* London: Bible Translation and Literature Auxiliary.

———. 1930. Health Instruction in African Schools, Suggestions for a Curriculum. *Africa* 3:484–500.

Morrow, Sean. 1986. "No girl leaves the school unmarried": Mabel Shaw and the Education of Girls at Mbereshi, Northern Rhodesia, 1915–1940. *International Journal of African Historical Studies* 19:601–635.

Mort, Frank. 1987. *Dangerous Sexualities: Medico-Moral Politics in England since 1830.* London: Routledge & Kegan Paul.

Nelly. 1911. *YQN* 11 (June): 2–3.

Ogrizek, Michel. 1981–1982. Mami Wata, Les envoutées de la sirène. Psychothérapie collective de l'hystérie en pays Batsangui au Congo, suivie d'un voyage mythologique en Centrafrique. *Cahiers ORSTROM, Serie Sciences Humaines* 18:433–43.

The Other Side of the Screen. 1942. *YQN* 129 (July): 13–14.

Ouvroir et école ménagère, pour femmes et filles de boys de maison. 1956. *La Femme et le Congo* 155 (October): 9.

Parkinson, K. C. 1929. A Visitor and the School, *YQN* 78 (July): 10–12.

Phillipe, R. 1927. La femme noire peut-elle faire une auxiliare utile dans le ménage euroṕeen? *Bulletin de l'Union des Femmes Coloniales* 4 (March–April): 4.

Poovey, Mary. 1989. *Uneven Developments: The Ideological Work of Gender in Mid-Victorian England*. London: Virago Press.

Pour femmes et filles de boys de maison. 1956. *La femme et le Congo* 155 (October): 9.

Reardon, Ruth Slade. 1968. Catholics and Protestants in the Congo. In *Christianity in Tropical Africa*, ed. C. G. Baeta, 83–100. London: Oxford University Press.

Rogers, T. 1959. Impressive Impressions. *YQN* 148 (July): 13–15.

Scott, Joan Wallach. 1986. Gender: A Useful Category of Historical Analysis. *American Historical Review* 42:1053–1075.

Slade, Ruth M. 1959. *English-Speaking Missions in the Congo Independent State (1878–1908)*. Brussels: Académie Royale des Sciences Coloniales.

Smith, H. Sutton. n.d. *Yakusu, the Very Heart of Africa*. London: Carey Press.

Stapleton, W. H. 1915. Quarterly Notes No. 1, B.M.S. Yakusu July 1904. *YQN* 28 (September): 3–4.

Stoler, Ann L. 1989. Making Empire Respectable: The Politics of Race and Sexual Morality in 20th-Century Colonial Cultures. *American Ethnologist* 16:634–659.

Summers, Anne. 1988. *Angels and Citizens: British Women as Military Nurses, 1854–1914*. London and New York: Routledge and Kegan Paul.

Thomas, Nicholas. 1990. Sanitation and Seeing: The Creation of State Power in Early Colonial Fiji. *Comparative Studies in Society and History* 32: 149–170.

Van der Vorst, G., and J. Pohl. 1961. Le Francais tel qu'on le parle à Elisabethville. *Vie et Langage* 107: 87–94.

Vigarello, Georges. 1985. *Le propre et le sale, L'hygiène du corps depuis le Moyen Age*. Paris: Seuil.

Walls, A. F. 1982. "The Heavy Artillery of the Missionary Army": The Domestic Importance of the Nineteenth-Century Medical Missionary. In *The Church and Healing*, ed. W. J. Sheils, 287–297. Oxford: Oxford University Press.

We View the Landscape O'er. 1924. *YQN* 57 (January): 4–6.

Wilkinson, A. 1928. What the School Girls Think of the Visit. *YQN* 75 (October): 18–20.

Wilkinson, A. 1955. Dispelling the Mists. *YQN* 152 (October): 13–16.

Williams, C. P. 1980. Not Quite Gentlemen": An Examination of "Middling Class" Protestant Missionaries from Britain, c. 1850–1900. *Journal of Ecclesiastical History* 31:301–315.

Yates, Barbara Ann. 1967. The Missions and Educational Development in Belgian Africa, 1876–1908. Ph.D. diss., Columbia University, New York.

———. 1976. The Triumph and Failure of Mission Vocational Education in Zaire, 1879–1908. *Comparative Education Review* 20: 193–208.

6 Colonial and Missionary Education: Women and Domesticity in Uganda, 1900–1945

Nakanyike B. Musisi

Our aim is not so much to fill the girls' heads with knowledge, as to develop their character and make them good sensible women who are not afraid to work.[1]

Lord Landsdowne voiced British colonial policy with regard to education in Uganda as early as 1902 : "Education is certainly our business, but if the missions will do it for us, it may be better to give them the opportunity."[2] Education was thus left entirely in the hands of the missionaries until 1918.[3] Although the colonial government took this stand for practical reasons, the motive driving the Anglican and Catholic missions was that of using education to establish a Christian nation at the source of the Nile.

Educating mothers of Ugandan homes in the ways of "civilization" and Christianizing those homes to "save" the nation became important themes of missionary agenda, as expressed by Rev. T. B. Fletcher: "The making of a nation is in the hands of the mother. A nation cannot advance beyond the status and character of the mother."[4]

This chapter uses archival data to document the philosophy and events associated with the development of educational institutions for women in Uganda in the period between 1900 and 1945. In addition, it assesses the content of that education and how women responded to and were affected by it.

Prelude to a Domestic Education

Missionaries sincerely attempted to raise the status of women through education. The education they offered, however, first single-handedly and later in conjunction with the colonial government did not go beyond preparing women for the domestic life, nor did it differ significantly from precolonial education for women. The methods and philosophy of the missionaries were greatly influenced by the ideologies of domesticity prevalent at the turn of the century in both Uganda and Britain.[5]

In the period before colonization, boys' and girls' education differed notably. Boys were often sent to prominent chief's courts (*ebisaakate*) for political education as prestigious students in waiting (*abagalagala*).[6] The courtly school (*kigalagala*) prepared boys for their future roles in the public sphere. On the other hand, in the *bisaakate* girls were trained for their future roles in the nation as wives and mothers of the elite (Watson 1968). Girls were called "*bakembuga* in keeping," that is, wives-to-be of the aristocrats; they could not be referred to as *abagalagala*.[7]

The main differences between missionary education and traditional education was the fact that missionary education was taught by foreigners (or people who had been in contact with foreigners), with foreign tools of instruction, including the technology of writing, and in a classroom environment.

In the process of founding Gayaza Girls' Boarding School, missionaries worked closely with the chiefs. In their desire to maintain distinctive status as an elite, the chiefs held that if boys' boarding schools could replace the *ebigalagala* as schools for their sons, boarding schools must similarly be established for their daughters. Hence, a proposal to establish a girls' boarding school was tabled at a Women Missionaries' Conference in 1904. This proposal emphasized that the school's main purpose was to train daughters of chiefs and clergy as future wives of the same strata of society.[8] Stated Archdeacon Walker:

> If the boys and men are being so much better educated, the girls must be looked after too. I feel this is most important as so much depends on the mothers who have the early training of the children. . . . They [women] have no idea of the duties and responsibilities of life.[9]

The chiefs who insisted that cultivation and home management be central to the school's curriculum agreed to girls' education only after they were assured it would not take girls away from their domestic roles. Nevertheless, certain chiefs and indeed their wives remained skeptical about the effects of education for girls and opposed Gayaza.[10] One important wife replied when asked whether chiefs should pay for their daughters' education, "Oh dear, No, the

Europeans always spoil their girls."[11] For its special role, Gayaza started with a grant of only Sh41; additional financial support was to come from the chiefs and foreign subscriptions.[12]

Gayaza Girls' Boarding School: The Epitome of Domesticity

To ensure its success, education in domesticity had to be provided in a special environment. Gayaza Girls' was to be a boarding school, away from the city, from the boys' high schools, and from what the missionaries considered the "degenerating influence of pagan environment."[13] Indeed, the school, a fenced-in acropolis with its only entrance through a porter's lodge, was built eleven miles from Kampala. Girls were permitted to pass through its entrance only if accompanied by a matron.[14] Miss Allen, the headmistress, regarded the cane as "a wonder worker, to correct dull and lazy brains"[15], and did not hesitate to use corporal punishment when the need arose.

For Miss Allen, the school was not only to train "good housewives" but also "keen cultivators."[16] The girls woke every morning to dig in the plantation for almost two and a half hours as "was the custom of women in Uganda."[17] Practical domestic work combined with religious education to build character heavily outweighed the time given to academic studies. The daily timetable required the girls to wake up at 5:30 A.M. for cultivation and prepare themselves for school at 8:00 A.M. School started at 8:30 A.M. with prayers and Bible reading, followed by writing at 9:15 A.M.; 10:00 A.M. was for peeling plantain for midday meal. Morning classes, which resumed at 11:00 A.M. with a Bible lesson (two days a week), geography, or English, ended at 11:45 A.M. The afternoon classes started at 2:00 P.M., with Bible study followed by Arithmetic at 3:00 P.M. After school the girls fetched water and engaged in other extracurricular activities.

To justify the school's bias towards domestic training, Miss Allen wrote, "an industrious Muganda woman is . . . a great prize and by her exertion keeps the family table well supplied."[18] She reasoned that an excessive literary curriculum was not necessary, since

> when we simply fill them with knowledge, be it the Bible or Geography or Arithmetic, they do not know what to do with it. They can go and glibly tell tales to someone else, but are they educated by it? Have we given them power to cope with this and other secular matters? Are we not rather teaching them to follow a given line blindly than opening their minds to reason for themselves?[19]

The Gayaza curriculum, which reinforced the stereotype that an accomplished woman is a "successful manager of a plantation grove and an expert cook,"[20] contradicted a progressive perception within the Church Missionary Society (CMS) that such a role weighed heavily on women's lives.[21]

As expressed by Miss Allen, a basic philosophy of the Gayaza curriculum was "hand to mind"; that is, one was to move from manual work to the alphabet and other rudiments of learning—from the practical to the abstract:

> We find it well to begin with their capable hands, teaching them handcrafts, and after a time they like them, and are industrious over them. To sewing they take at once, but we do not teach them first to make an entire garment. Then we teach them the alphabet and other rudiments of learning and encourage them at the same time to bring their newly awakened thoughts to bear upon their manual work, the garments they want to make etc. The common sense and even initiative that they will develop over needle work is surprising. We find their minds and their bodies must be educated pari passim.[22]

This philosophy contrasts greatly with that underlying the curriculum of the Boys' High School at Mengo, which emphasized literary achievements and centered upon learning the Scriptures and English. The Budo philosophy was "hand and eye."[23]

Initial Manifestations of Rejection

Several aristocratic young women enrolled at Gayaza were not as enchanted by this domestically oriented curriculum as were certain chiefs and the missionaries. Traditionally, daughters of the aristocrats, especially the princesses, had been to some extent exempt from the harder routine domestic work. Such young women desired "to obtain clothes, to recline, to sleep"; preferring, in Miss Allen's estimation, "a life of useless indolence and selfish sloth"[24] rather than education in domesticity. Although not all girls reacted in this way, some vehemently rejected this domestic education, giving Miss Allen and her staff a hard time wherever possible.[25]

Some mothers (the *bakembuga*) objected on behalf of their daughters to the domesticity-oriented ideology of the school curriculum. CMS documents cite these women as asserting, "My daughters are daughters of a chief, why should they work. They must sit still and look after their hands and complexions."[26] Some chiefs argued that there was an overemphasis on practical domestic training and demanded that English be taught to all their daughters, adding, "[D]ull and lazy ones must be caned until they do learn." This surprised the missionaries, who wished to exempt the weak students.[27] One chief not only advocated instruction in English and harmonics, but made the remarkable suggestion that schoolgirls not cultivate. His suggestion provoked uproar and disagreement among other chiefs, one of whom exclaimed, "[W]hy, what use is a girl if she does not know how to cultivate."[28]

An unsigned article in the *Uganda Notes* indicates that some chiefs supported women's education because of its economic potential rather than its emphasis on domesticity.[29] To this perception the missionaries commented, "They cannot understand that it is fitting her for her work for life."[30] Such progressive chiefs advocated that less emphasis be put on practical domestic education.

Early Results of Gayaza

Gayaza High School succeeded in educating the daughters of chiefs and priests to be future wives of the elite, as witnessed by the marriages of Susana, daughter of Apolo Kagwa, to Yosiya Nadiope, a Musoga chief, and Airini Drusila Namaganda, daughter of Rev. Kaizi, to the young Kabaka Daudi Chwa. Gayaza also succeeded in instilling the ideology of domesticity firmly into this particular generation of aristocratic women, whose mothers knew little of such training. The school's success in this regard was quickly acknowledged and appreciated by the male elite. In the presence of about fifty chiefs, Apolo Kagwa, Buganda's Prime Minister and advocate of women's education, congratulated the missionaries on their success, and contrasted the former idle existence of aristocratic girls, concerned mainly with "dressing their finger nails and letting them grow long"[31] with "really useful things learned at the school."[32]

The lives and homes of past students such as Sara Mukasa exemplified the best of the school's curriculum. A daughter of one of the "finest chiefs in Uganda,"[33] Sara attended Gayaza between 1910 and 1917, and taught at Iganga Boarding School and Gayaza before being married to the newly widowed grand chief of Kyagwe, Ham Mukasa. Her marriage was arranged by Miss Allen.[34] Sara, who had eight children, made their clothes and yet "still found some time for outside interests like the Mothers' Union and involvement in the Girls' Day school."[35] Mrs. E. S. Daniell, who visited Sara's home frequently, found it "spotless as regards morals, a place where one always expects and finds progress and leadership in all that is for the uplift of the country."[36]

Mrs. Daniell praised Sara and Ham Mukasa's marital relationship: "[S]eldom do we see yet in Uganda such chums as this husband and wife." To Mrs. Daniell, the cups of tea and the bread and butter Sara served at meetings held in her home with its English furniture were all outward "expressions of our English life found in plenty of houses in Uganda today; but in this home we feel the presence of Christ himself, and we thank God and take courage."[37] Mrs. Daniell added,

> [A]lthough [Sara] wears English dresses and lives in an up to date Bungalow, she is keenly jealous of guarding the best of the native customs. For example, she goes out at sunrise every morning to dig and plant the household's food supply, helps in cooking native meals and by her example shows other wives who may not have had the advantage of Gayaza School training, the great truth of dignity of labour.[38]

Mrs. Daniell's views were reiterated in the *Uganda Church Review:* "We know of several of the wives of chiefs and others whose homes are examples of what a Christian home should be. Their homes are kept clean and comfortable, and the children are clean and tidy and are taught at home by their mothers before they are old enough to go to school."[39] By 1915, Gayaza Girls' School was the most prestigious of the four girls' boarding schools in Uganda run by CMS. The Roman Catholics and the Muslims had nothing equivalent to Gayaza, although the Franciscan Sisters, led by Rev. Mother Kevin, had created girls' schools at Nsambya, Nagalama, and Nsube as early as 1903. The curriculum of these schools also emphasized domesticity (needlework, mat-making, basket-weaving, cooking, washing, and general house work) as well as Christian doctrine.

Equally anxious to provide what it termed "environmental education to girls," the White Fathers' mission aim was "to popularise as widely as possible more elementary instruction." They did not consider it "prudent or advisable to attempt to give [women] an education unsuitable for this condition of life."[40]

Should Women's Education Be Tampered With?

The period between the two world wars was characterized by a number of changes in the education of indigenous Ugandans. The governors became more interested in "native" education than had been the case earlier, more funds were available to facilitate government expansion of social services, and external criticism of education in British colonies had developed. Moreover, within Uganda the missions and some Baganda men became critical of the kind of education offered.

One of the groups that took special interest in the education of the deprived (i.e., Muslims and women) was the Young Baganda Association (YBA). They appreciated the CMS boarding schools at Gayaza and Kabarole in Toro, but criticized the Roman Catholics for their lack of such facilities for women. Although they called upon the government to investigate this issue, the type of education they advocated for girls differed from that they envisioned for boys.[41] Their concern for women's education was revolutionary only in demand, not in content.

As part of the post-war educational expansion program in 1921, and before the government could respond to the YBA demands, the Mill Hill Mission opened a girls' boarding school at Nkokonjeru where girls trained for four years to become intermediate school teachers. In 1923 the same mission embarked on a similar educational project "with careful domestic instruction" at Nsambya.[42] The subjects taught at Nsambya and the number of hours devoted to each subject did not differ greatly from those at Gayaza.[43] In addition to their already established central schools, the White Sisters opened a High School at Villa Maria under European Sisters "to train character on practical lines."[44] The girls at Nsambya and Nkokonjeru were unusual because they "did not want to get married." They told Mother Kevin that they "did not want to spend their lives as other girls they knew, hoeing, cooking or resting without a thought outside the native hut and green bananas in which they lived."[45]

The government had been reluctant to involve itself in educational matters up to this time. Apart from praising "the practical down-to-earth curriculum at Gayaza," the 1920 government-sponsored Uganda Development Commission had little to say about women's education.[46] The government did not reply to the YBA letter of 12 March 1921 concerning the education of the deprived until 1922, reiterating its earlier position that "the education of women can be so much better carried out by missions than by the government."[47] However, the government acknowledged the necessity of its financial assistance to the missions, especially those running boarding schools, on the condition that "they . . . extend their women's educational work."[48]

An important issue for the government during the interwar period concerned the vexing question of whether "native girls should be educated after 14." Represented by Bishop Willis and educationist H.T.C Weatherhead, the CMS presented a memorandum on education in Uganda to the government that stressed the need to train women "in the care of children, cleanliness and the simple essentials of the home."[49] Because of the CMS's utilitarian belief in women's education, they strongly criticized the government's plan to spend only Sh2,000 on girls' education as compared to Sh22,500 on boys'. Nor was the government's lean budget on women's education supported by all those in the Uganda colonial government. Governor Archer was in fact defensive on the issue, and the Acting Provincial Commissioner of Buganda pleaded, "We cannot hope to raise the intellectual level of the race by concentrating upon one sex."[50] But despite criticism, the colonial government continued to spend little on women's education.

In the same year, however, Governor Archer invited M.E.R.J Hussey, Inspector of Schools in the Sudan, to visit Uganda to report on its educational needs. Among Hussey's most revolutionary recommendations was his request to involve government more in the education of Ugandans, rather than merely supporting missionary efforts. Recommending that a system of mass general education be established, Hussey emphasized the view that "changes in the education system be based on the customary life of the ordinary peasants and further training be geared to the needs of the colonial and native adminstration." Indirectly supporting the continuation of the prevailing domesticity-oriented ideology, the report proposed that the girls' education be left in the hands of the missionary societies.[51]

On the other hand, international discontent with colonial education lead to the creation of the Phelps-Stokes Commission between 1922 and 1924. The work of this Commission is often cited as having made a progressive contribution to African education in the British colonies. With regard to women's education, however, it represented a concerted effort to maintain the ideology of domesticity. Although critical of the narrow evangelistic education, the Commission's recommendations were not very different from those of Hussey, embodying unequal class, gender, and race relationships.[52] It praised the Gayaza and Ndejje curricula, where "educational work was well adapted to the life of women in Africa."[53] Moreover, it encouraged the formation of boarding schools, stating that they should be concerned, first of all, with food preparation, second, with household comforts, and third, with the care and feeding of children and the occupations that are suited to the interests and ability of women.[54] For women's special role, it advocated a different curriculum for boys and girls.[55]

Although the Commission made reference to the need for rudimentary professional training in teaching and nursing for women,[56] it strongly believed that domesticity symbolized the true roles of the African women. It noted, "the first responsibility of the women is for the supply and preparation of food. Primitive society imposes this upon the native women to an extent that can hardly be appreciated by members of the civilised communities."[57]

The Commission's report and recommendations led to the creation in 1925 of the London-based Advisory Committee on Native Education in British Tropical Africa Dependencies by the Secretary of State. The Advisory Committee acknowledged that more should be done with regard to the education of girls and women, especially in domestic hygiene.[58] It advocated improvements in women's education for two main reasons: to ensure that clever boys, for whom higher education was expedient, be able to look forward to educated mates; and to combat the high rates of infant mortality and unhygienic living conditions.[59] In this case, education for domesticity was not only desirable; it was necessary.

When appointed Director of Education in 1925, Hussey incorporated his recommendations and those of the Phelps-Stokes Commission into a five-year plan that included a building program, the revision of syllabi at all levels, and a regrading of the schools. Five grades of schools were created: sub-grade village schools, elementary vernacular schools, intermediate schools, central schools, and Makerere College. The first two grades of schools, which remained entirely under mission responsibility, had very low standards, offering religious instruction, language skills, and arithmetic primarily for baptismal purposes. The teachers were usually unqualified and underpaid or not paid; both teachers' and students' attendance was alarmingly irregular. The contact that the vast majority of women had with education for several years was at these schools.[60] In 1933, for example, there were 127 graded schools in the Protectorate, besides a very large number of subgrade schools for girls.[61] In 1936, 81,265 girls were enrolled in these schools and only 4,121 were in graded schools.[62]

The Universalization of a Domesticity-oriented Education

In 1926, the government declared its commitment to leaving girls' education in missionary hands, as long as the curriculum emphasized domesticity.[63] Nonetheless, Hussey recommended that a women's college be built at Gayaza and put under the direction of an experienced teacher from England. The college was to have a practical curriculum leading to household management, and as advocated by parents and prospective husbands, girls in a few schools were to receive intruction in English. Moreover, Hussey advocated a careful extension of the Gayaza paradigm throughout the country.

In that same year, in an effort to improve the very low educational standard of girls entering Normal Schools, the CMS proposed that all girls be brought together in one college where "they could be trained according to one standard."[64] This scheme led to even greater differences between men's and women's education.

As a consequence, women's colleges were founded in 1930 as finishing schools at Buloba (CMS supported) and Nkokonjeru (Mill Hill-supported). The main aim of these schools was, in Hussey's words, "to further the practical education of girls in the country, and so generally to raise the domestic and social side of the native life."[65] These schools were not intended to be very large, but it was hoped that their graduates would "take their place side by side with men, who up to this time had so many more advantages than women."[66]

Buloba catered to women leaving schools as well as young married women. Under Miss A. L. Allen's direction as headmistress, the education for domesticity initiated at Gayaza was incorporated into the Buloba curriculum, which provided courses in domestic science, child welfare, English, music, and other accomplishments.[67] According to Miss Allen, it was the request of the Baganda that "young ladies be taught to keep their houses like Europeans and manage their meals and cooking as educated people should." She added that her staff would "do their best to teach Domestic Science, House-wifery and Hygiene as it is taught in England to the older girls."[68] Registering a change in her perception of the aims of women's educa-tion, Miss Allen added, "it would be splendid for girls to choose vocations for themselves so that they could earn their own living by learning to type and secretarial work."[69]

Agreeing with the CMS about the need to improve and expand education for women, the Catholics founded a finishing school at Nsube in 1930. Just like Gayaza, Nsube was to teach craft and management, mother care, diet and preparation of meals, needle-work, and knitting was intended to give "a certain finesse to ladies of distinction and high birth."[70]

Successful in involving the government in these boarding school schemes, the CMS began to press for education for those whom it considered "so unfortunate as not to be educated in any of the schools." Thus it organized day school classes with needlework as a specialty.[71]

So far women's education had enabled them to enter only a lim-ited number of professions—primary school teaching, nursing, and home making—which were deemed suitable to European gender role definitions, and which accentuated and encoded maternal do-mestic instincts and roles.[72]

More Voices to Enforce Training in Domesticity

As evidenced by the amount of correspondence, the colonial govern-ment began to be more serious about women's education after 1935.[73] Yet at the same time, demand for both the theory and the practice of the domestic training that had been incorporated into the girls' school constitutions from the very beginning became more vigorous after 1930.

By the 1930s and 1940s, material progress had led to a cutural crisis in Uganda. At this critical moment, women began to be per-ceived as pivotal to saving the nation and its culture from imminent decay. In response to the perceived crisis, many Ugandan men joined the campaign to promote and further inforce domesticity in women's education.[74] It was emphasized that girls' education in the new age of materialism ought to serve two basic purposes. First, it should provide "new men" with "real companions and help-mates in life," and second, it should create "a place on earth where the child can have not only happiness but also a permanent home life, requisites such as guidance, helpfulness, encouragement, peace and the like."[75]

In the mid 1930s the Legislative Council joined the debate on domesticity. It voted to finance a preliminary investigation into the teaching of allied subjects to women.[76] In a move advocating separate education for boys and girls, the Council recommended that domestic science be taught in all schools and that an African Demonstrator in Domestic Science be appointed to act as a forerunner of future domestic science demonstrators. At about the same time, Kathreen Hudson, a "child hygiene and handcraft" specialist was appointed Woman Inspector of Schools.[77]

In 1936, in response to social dislocations associated with the economic crisis that clearly threatened the smooth running of the colonial state in many parts of Africa, the Foreign Office reproduced a study carried out by Mary G. Blacklock on how to improve women's and children's welfare in the colonies. While arguing that the welfare of children and women cannot be considered separately from that of men, Blacklock advocated the continuing difference in education for boys and girls. Blacklock stressed:

> In order to keep a home and to care for a family in a healthy manner, women require a special type of education. . . . (W)ere the women given the knowledge and opportunity to keep a healthy home and family, the good effects would naturally be felt also by the men and so by the whole community.[78]

The consequence of these conservative policies was that changes in secondary school education for girls, which might have enabled them to go beyond domestic skills, nursing, and teaching, occurred very slowly. Nevertheless, in 1938, in a move that provoked public distaste, the established gender segregation and unequal education system was challenged by King's College Budo by admitting four girls on an experimental basis.[79] In support of the venture, the Governor recommended that academic courses for girls be based on the provision of adequate buildings and staff, and that scholarships be offered to women.[80] This venture was an important step towards liberating women's education in Uganda.

During this same period, a committee headed by the Protectorate's Deputy Director of Education encouraged the establishment at Gayaza of a self-contained secondary section embracing two courses— one "with a domestic science and practical basis, the other being of a more academic type." Both courses were to lead to preparation for entrance at Makerere College.[81]

By 1938, only 28 girls were receiving secondary education in the whole of Uganda.[82] Budo had the disadvantage of charging high fees, which in itself dissuaded parents who were not in principle opposed to coeducation.[83] This disadvantage enabled advocates for separate schools to argue for the construction of separate, and cheaper, schools for women.[84] Because hundreds of girls were refused entrance to cheaper boarding schools, the government was forced to build more schools on the Buloba model, charging Sh5 for a hostel.[85] The Governor also recommended that a women's hostel be built at Makerere College to facilitate women's admission.[86] By December 1938, the government and the three missions had negotiated the terms under which additional secondary schools were to be established.[87]

These policy changes required that the women's curriculum be broadened to include the purely academic qualifications required for college entrance. Although teacher training, medical training, the arts, domestic science and agriculture were all mentioned as offering opportunities to girls to qualify at a higher standard,[88] the Director of Education was not in touch with the reality of events he helped to initiate. He strongly believed that girls' admission into the higher college "did not represent for girls the most urgent need of the time."[89] In fact, his fears were deep-rooted. He did not want to finance women's higher education and thus education beyond domesticity.[90]

By December 1938 the subcommittee of the advisory committee on education in the colonies nevertheless endorsed the need to arrange for the entry of women students to Makerere.[91] The first women students were admitted to Makerere College in 1945 with very limited opportunities.[92] "A girl who felt there was a real need for a woman lawyer to help with the improvement of conditions for women found there was no chance of a scholarship for her, though she could study sociology or home economics if she wished."[93]

Women Rock the Boat

Irrespective of such obstacles, the foresight of educated women went beyond that of the missionaries and the colonial state. They envisioned professional roles beyond the home in the Legislative Council and other areas of the civil service. A survey of the career goals of Ugandan women students carried out in 1967 indicates that their daughters and sisters were even more ambitious.[94] Such career goals informed educated women's response to important issues regarding their gender. For example, after women started earning their own living in the 1950s and early 1960s, some of them spearheaded a campaign to be taxed like men in order to dispel the low esteem that several years of patriarchal authority and education for domesticity had imposed on them.[95]

The life and political career of Florence Lubega, née Wamala, who was sent to Britain for training illustrates the values of this new generation of educated women. In England, Florence was to take a short course in journalism and mothercraft abroad, visit all branches of women's work and social centers, as well as experiencing English home life in order to come back and set an example to the women of the colony.[96] But Florence's ambitions extended further, beyond the confines of the home into the political arena.[97] She became the first Ugandan woman to sit in the Legislative Council and after independence became a member of Parliament.[98]

By 1945, education beyond domesticity had begun to challenge men in a very sensitive area: their right as husbands to control their wives. Although Florence and many of the educated women of her generation became wives, an article in a Luganda newspaper commented on the new trend: "educated girls are in the habit of rejecting potential husbands, preferring casual liaisons . . . they are using education as an excuse to delay their age of marriage because they wished to finish their studies and get a certificate." Seeing marriage as the women's highest achievement the author commented sarcastically: "[W]ill the certificate benefit you if you do not have a husband?"[99] Educated girls were not only delaying marriage, some were rejecting it altogether. They were also taking control of their reproductive rights. The author of a 1946 article in the same newspaper decried the educated woman's rejection of motherhood, and her preference for few children and even abortion at times, as well as the desire to leave her children with her parents to pursue a career.[100] Women had begun to set different priorities, opting for an agenda beyond domesticity.

The ideology and practice of domesticity pervaded the history of missionary and colonial education in Uganda in the forty-five years examined here. Run by men and women nurtured in patriarchal societies and sex-segregated school systems, the missions and the colonial state were male-dominated organizations blind to the short-comings of the education they offered.[101] The sexist view point of these institutions dictated the use of gender as the basis of the formal institutionalization of different education and treatment of girls and boys. Women's education was constructed in order that they might become better wives, mothers, and guardians of the family and household, essential to a stable society. Such a system could hardly promote equality between the sexes or competition with men; rather, it aimed at forming women efficient in their domestic role, subordinate to and separate from men.

Underlying the emphasis on domesticity was the well-articulated notion that maternal influence was of social value, to the colonial state and the Ugandans themselves, as well as to the kingdom of God. With "well"-educated mothers, it was argued, there would be less infant mortality, less social dislocation, warm, well-run homes for husbands (servants of the colonial system), and a Christian nation. It is noteworthy that this maternal influence did not necessarily require marriage. Religious Sisters (nuns) could equally act as a stabilizing force, benefiting society by teaching in schools and working in hospitals.

In retrospect it is clear that missionary education functioned in a complex and contradictory manner; it liberated women from the particular subordination inherent in their roles in traditional society by introducing them to new careers and earning power, yet it limited them to subordinate roles in the newly emerged social structure.

Despite considerable odds, even the first women educated in this system developed a consciousness of themselves that went far beyond the expectations of the education they were offered.[102]

Postscript

Uganda attained its independence on 9 October 1962, committed to improving the education of its citizens. In January 1963, a commission was appointed to "examine, in light of the approved recommendations of the International Bank survey Mission Report and Uganda's financial position and future manpower requirements, the content and structure of education in Uganda."[103]

The commission noted that although figures were not exact, most girls received only the first three years of formal education. For example, although 28,080 girls registered in 1957 for Primary I, only 11,678 were registered in Primary VI. As might be expected, the disproportion between the enrollment of boys and girls in 1963 increased with the level of student: girls made up 39.4 percent of the Primary I enrollment, but only 24.1 percent of the Primary VI enrollment. Several explanations were given as contributing factors to this discrepancy, including early marriage, home duties, parental dislike of mixed (coeducational) schools, fear of unsupervized journeys to school and the low status of women inherent in Ugandan society.

This commission gave several recommendations: (1) increased provision for girls' high schools for each province; (2) financial assistance to relieve the heavy cost to parents of girls who had to travel long distances to boarding schools; (3) appointment of a senior female officer in the Ministry of Education to oversee the special needs for girls' education; (4) instituting that girls should be allowed to choose subjects of special interest to women—such as home economics, art, and agriculture—for the School Certificate Examination; and (5) and that all primary schools be mixed but that post-primary education be either mixed (coeducational) or single-sex schools.

However, Article 203 of the commission noted, "In a developing society boys' education and girls' education will usually demand different treatment, for it is generally true to say that while boys prepare for one career, girls prepare for two. . . . This implies that girls' secondary education should be both general to satisfy the criteria for any educated person; and vocational to lay the foundation of a useful career in the world and in the home."[104] It emphatically stated,

> [T]his will involve careful scrutiny of the curriculum, for while we deprecate too much differentiation of curriculum between boys and girls, definite recognition of their different objectives should be made. As most girls will eventually become wives and mothers in a largely rural community, that would be a futile education that failed to prepare them for the duties of home making.

This commission's report, which was to guide Uganda's women's education policy for so many years to come, was thus not fully prepared to alter the fundamental direction of women's education. Implications of such attitudes continue even today to have a negative effect on women's education and career opportunities. Even though Ugandan women are making headway in other areas, the majority of those who manage to get post secondary education are still enrolled in what has traditionally been defined as "women's areas of specialization"— that is, nursing, teaching, and secretarial studies.

Abbreviations

CMG   Church Missionary Gleaner
CMI   Church Missionary Intelligencer
CMO   Church Missionary Outlet
CMS   Church Missionary Society
CMSA Church Missionary Society Archives
CMR   Church Missionary Review
CO   Colonial Office
ESA   Entebbe Secretariat Archives
FO   Foreign Office (London)
MUL   Makerere University Library
PRO   Public Records Office (London)
RA   Rubaga Archives
SMP   Secretariat Minute Paper (Entebbe)
YBA   Young Baganda Association
UCR   Uganda Church Review

Acknowledgments

I am grateful to Jane Turrittin for reading through the first draft of this essay.

Notes

1. Allen, Uganda Notes May 1909,87.

2. FO 2/600.

3. Both Muslim men and women lagged behind in formal education, since both were confined to irregular instruction in the Koranic schools. Fear of conversion to Christianity kept many away from formal missionary education; hence much of the data represented here excludes the Muslim women.

4. Uganda Notes 1920,23.

5. See Watson 1968,148; Alexander 1976,61; Delamont and Duffin 1978,164; Hall 1979.

6. The Chiefs' enclosures with such boys hence later came to be referred to as *Bigalagala.*

7. Because of the tradition of the *bisakate,* the willingness of Baganda chiefs to support boarding school education for girls was thus not as revolutionary as it has sometimes been claimed (T. Watson 1968).

8. CMSA:28 June 1904, G3 A7/04.

9. CMSA:8 August 1904, G3 A7/04.

10. Hattersley 1968,197.

11. Uganda Notes, November 1905.

12. CMSA: 8 August 1904 G3 A7/04.

13. CMSA: 3 and 5 October 1896; 27 October 1899; 6 November 1900; Allen 1910, G3 A7/05.

14. Uganda Notes, November 1905,172

15. CMSA: 24 October 1911, G3 A7/08.

16. CMR: July 1912, 433.

17. Allen, Uganda Notes, 1909,87.

18. CMSA:8 July 1908, G3 A7/06.

19. CMSA:8 July 1908, G3 A7/06.

20. Roscoe 1911,79.

21. Hattersley 1968,196.

22. CMI: July 1912,431.

23. For a full discussion of Budo see McGregor 1976.

24. CMI: July 1912,431.

25. Ibid.

26. Ibid.

27. CMSA:24 October 1911, G3 A7/09.

28. Ibid.

29. They thought that education meant teaching a girl to become a clerk or a dressmaker, or teaching her a trade in order that she might earn her living.

30. Uganda Notes, December 1913,285; the article was probably written by Miss Smyth or Miss Allen.

31. In Uganda this is synonymous with doing no menial work.

32. CMSA: 28 November 1910, G3 A7/05.

33. MUL CMO: February 1927,25.

34. Personal communication 1986.

35. MUL Uganda V 1918–1928,16.

36. Ibid.

37. MUL CMO: February 1927,25.

38. Ibid.

39. UCR 1930,134.

40. Quoted in Furley & Watson 1978.

41. ESA: 12 March 1921, SMP 6538.

42. ESA: 12 October 1923, SMP 7914.

43. For details see ESA 29 July 1925.

44. ESA Robillard SMP 7914.

45. RA October 1933,14; see also Louis 1964.

46. ESA 1920,25.

47. ESA 12 March 1921, SMP 6538.

48. ESA 28 Jan 1922, SMP 6358.

49. PRO CO 536/130.

50. ESA SMP 7215.

51. PRO CO 536/130.

52. Berman 1971; see also Cock 1980, ch. 8.

53. P. S. Report 157–158.

54. Scanlon 1964,67.

55. Ibid.,65.

56. Jones 1926,342

57. Ibid.,340.

58. Advisory Committee 1925,100.

59. Ibid.

60. Furley & Watson 1978,191.

61. ESA: 2 May 1933, SMP No. S 17/2 Ref C22. The graded schools comprised of the following: three Middle boarding schools, twenty-five Central schools, six Grade "A" Normal schools, seven Grade "C" Normal schools, seven Special schools and seventy-nine Elementary schools.

62. Kitchen 1962,172.

63. MUL UCR: July 1926,81.

64. ESA 1926, SMP A 32 pt. 1.

65. MUL UCR: November 1930,132.

66. Ibid.,113.

67. Ibid.,131.

68. MUL UCR: 1930,115.

69. Ibid.,115.

70. RA Souvenir n.d., 15.

71. MUL UCR 1930,113.

72. Cock 1980,294.

73. See letters in file ESA SMP S 17/2.

74. See, for example, a letter from an unidentified person, possibly a pastor; MUL UCR 1930,52.

75. Ibid.

76. ESA Legislative Council, 9 November 1938.

77. ESA S 1/9: 31 August 1933; SMP S17/2: 2 Sept 1933; see also SMP S 17/2: 15,16,24,25 August, 13 Sept 1933.

78. Blacklock, 19 June 1936,223–224, ESA 1936 SMP S 89.

79. ESA: 30 August 1938, SMP S 17/2 11 (124).

80. MUL 1938, file 5/1.

81. ESA SMP S 17/2 11ll (124).

82. Furley & Watson 1978,208.

83. SMP S17/2 (124).

84. Ibid.

85. MUL file No. 5/1.

86. MUL file No. 5/1.

87. ESA: 10 Dec 1939, S 17/2/163; SMP S 17/2 11 (124).

88. SMP S 17/2 11 (124).

89. ESA S 17/2/167.

90. ESA S 17/2 11 195.

91. ESA: 6 Dec 1938, S 17/2/178.

92. The first girls to be admitted to Makerere were Yemima Ntugwerisho, Marjorie Kamuhangi, Mary and Catherine Senkatuka, Margaret Mulyanti and Florence Lubega, née Wamala.

93. Macpherson 1964,161.
94. Evans 1972,23.
95. *Uganda Argus* 2 (1961):3; 1 January 1963,47.
96. ESA: 1 July 1939, S 17/2.
97. Interview September 1986 at Kampala.
98. In 1956 she went to Oxford to study constitutional reforms, a course she remembers being called "Colonial Studies." In 1957, she joined the Legco, replacing her husband, who joined the Buganda Lukiiko. Between 1962 and 1966 she served as an advisor to three Ministers, Kalule Setala of Community Development, Neko Nekyon of Planning and Community Development, and Alex Ojera of Community Development and Labour. From 1967 to 1971 she was a Member of Parliament. She is a founding member and former President of the Uganda Council Of Women.
99. MUL *Munno:* December 1945,332–333.
100. MUL *Munno:* June 1946,152.
101. Hammond and Jablow 1970,191; Cock 1980,281.
102. CMSA CMG: November 1919,153–154.
103. Uganda Government 1963.
104. Uganda Government 1963,67.

Bibliography

Archival Sources

CHURCH MISSIONARY SOCIETY ARCHIVES (CMSA)

Allen, A. L. and C. J. Smyth. 23 October 1911, CMSA G3 A7/09.
Allen, A. L. n.d. G3 A7/ 05.
Allen, A. L. Women's Conference. 8 July 1908, CMSA G3 A7/06.
Bird, G. E. 27 October 1899, G3 A7/ 05.
Chadwick, J. E. 6 November 1900, G3 A7/ 05.
Church Missionary Gleaner (CMG). November 1919,153–154.
Church Missionary Intelligencia (CMI). July 1912,431.
Church Missionary Review (CMR). July 1912,433.
Conference Minutes. 28 June 1904, G3 A7/04.
Daniell, E. S. 1931. The Home's Share. Mukono, Uganda.
Pilgrim, E. L. 5 October 1896, G3 A7/ 05.
C. J. Smyth and A. L. Allen. 28 November 1910, G3 A7/05.
Thomsett, M. T. 3 October 1896 G3 A7/ 05.
Uganda Church Review (UCR). D. I. Allan. 1930,134.
Uganda Notes (UN). 1905, 1909, 1913, 1920.
Uganda Notes, May 1909,87: A. L. Allen, Report on the Uganda High School for Girls.
Walker to Baylis 8 August 1904 G3 A7/04.

ENTEBBE GOVERNMENT ARCHIVES (formerly Entebbe Secretariat Archives [ESA])

Acting P.C. Buganda. Memorandum SMP 7215.

Bierman to Chief Secretary. 12 October 1923, SMP 7914.

Certain Aspects of the Welfare of Women and Children in the colonies 1936 SMP S 89.

To C.S. from Director of Education S 17/2/167.

Chief Secretary, 10 December 1939, S 17/2/163.

Excerpts from the Proceedings of the Legislative Council 9 November 1938.

Girls Education Correspondence 1926 SMP A 32 pt 1.

Honorable Chief Secretary, from the Director of Education 2 May 1933. SMP S 17/2 C 22.

Hon W. H Kaintze from S.C., 6 Dec 1938 S 17/2/178.

His Excellency from G. Fisher 1 July 1939 S 17/2.

Memorandum of Discussion between members of CMS (Namirembe Diocese) and the Deputy Director of Education. 18 July 1938 SMP S 17/2 11.

Memorandum of Discussion between members of Church Missionary Society (Namirembe Diocese) and the Deputy Director of Education, regarding Girls' Sec Education. 30 Aug 1938 SMP S 17/2 II (124).

J.E.S Merrick to C.S. 21 Jan 1939 S 17/2 11 195.

Minutes of the first meeting of the subcommittee . . . held at Nsambya 29 July 1925.

Robillard to C.S. n. d. SMP 7914.

Report of the Uganda Development Commission. Entebbe 1920,25.

H. O. Savile, Superintendent, Technical School, 28 January 1922, SMP 6358.

The Young Baganda Association to the Chief Secretary c.c. to Lukiiko Mengo and P. C. Buganda, 12 March 1921 SMP 6538.

MAKERERE UNIVERSITY ARCHIVES (MUL)

Mrs. E. S. Daniell. 1927. Sara: A Christian Mother in her Home. *Church Missionary Outlet.*

Mrs. E. S. Daniell. 1918–1928 The Home's Share. *Uganda* Vol. V.

Record of the Conversation with his Excellence the Governor of Uganda. 14–15 Feb 1938, file 5/1.

Munno. 1945. Abana Abalenzi Nabawala Okuyigira awamu Mumasomero (Co-education for Boys and Girls).

Munno. 1945. Okuyigirizibwa kwabakazi kigambo kikulu (Women's Education is Very Important), 332–333.

Munno. 1946. Okuyigirizibwa kwabakazi, Okuzala kwekweyongera kwegwanga (Women's Education, to Give Birth is to Increase the Nation's Population). 152

Record of the conversation with His Excellency the Governor of Uganda. 14–15 February 1938, file 5/1.

Uganda Argus. 1 January 1963,47; 2 February 1962,3.

The New Phase. Uganda Church Review July 1926,81.

PUBLIC RECORD OFFICE (PRO /FO /CO)

Landsdowne to Sadler, 7 August 1902, FO 2/600.
Notes read to the Committee assembled at Kampala on 18 January 1924 to consider future Educational Policy in Uganda Protectorate CO 536/130.

RUBAGA ARCHIVES (RA)

Souvenir of the Golden Jubilee 1923–1973. Little Sisters of St. Francis. n.d., 15.
The Little Sisters of St. Francis Nkokonjeru, Uganda Overseas Education. Vol. 1, October 1933,14.

ORAL SOURCES

Lubega Florence née Wamala. Interviews, September 1986. Kampala, Uganda.
Mukasa Mukasa. Interviews, August–December 1986. Mukono, Uganda.

Books and Articles

Alexander, S. 1976. Women's Work in Nineteenth-Century London: A Study of the years 1820–1850. *The Rights and Wrongs of Women,* ed. J. Mitchell A. Oakely, 59–138. Harmondsworth, New York: Penguin.

Berman, E. H. 1971. American Influence on African Education: The Role of the Phelps-Stokes Fund Education Commissions. *Comparative Education Review* 15 (2 June).

Blacklock, Mary G. 1936. Certain Aspects of the Welfare of Women and Children in the Colonies. The Liverpool School of Tropical Medicine. 19 June. Reproduced for the Use of the Colonial Office from the *Annals of Tropical Medicine and Parasitology.* [copy used ESA SMP S 89].

Cock, J. 1980. *Maids and Madams: A Study of the Politics of Exploitation.* Johannesburg: Ravan Press

Delamont, S., and L. Duffin eds. 1978. *The Nineteenth-Century Woman. Her Cultural and Physical World.* London: Croom Helm.

Evans, David R. 1972. Image and Reality: Career Goals of Educated Uganda Women. *Canadian Journal of African Studies* 6, no. 2:213–233.

Furley, O. W., and T. Watson. 1978. *A History of Education in East Africa.* New York: NOK Publishers.

Great Britain, Colonial Office, Advisory Committee on Education in the Colonies. 1925. The Native Education in British Tropical Africa, ed. Scanlon David. London; HMSO.

Great Britain, Colonial Office, Higher Education in East Africa. 1937. Report of the Commission, September 1937. [The da la Warr Report]. Col. No. 142. HMSO, London 1937.

Hall, C. 1979. The Early Formation of Victorian Domestic Ideology. In *Fit Work for Women,* ed. S. Burman, 15–31. London: Croom Helm/Oxford University Women's Studies Committee.

Hammond, D., and A. Jablow 1970. *The Africa that Never Was: Four Centuries of British Writing about Africa*. New York: Twayne Publishers.

Hattersley, C.W. 1968. *The Baganda at Home*. London: Frank Cass & Co.

Jones, H. G. 1926. *Uganau in Transformation, 1876–1926*. London: Church Missionary Society.

Jones, T. J. (ed.) 1925. Education in East Africa. A Study in East, Central and South Africa by the 2nd African Education Committee under the auspices of the Phelps-Stokes Fund. London: Edinburgh House Press.

Kitchen, Helen. 1962. *The Educated African*. New York: Praegar.

Louis, Sister M. 1964. *Love Is the Answer. The Story of Mother Kevin*. Dublin: Fallon's Educational Supply Company.

McGregor, G. P. 1976. *King's College Budo: The First Sixty Years*. Nairobi: Oxford University Press.

Macpherson, M. 1964. *They Built for the Future: A Chronicle of Makerere University College, 1922–1962*. Cambridge: University Press.

Roscoe, John. 1911. *The Baganda: An Account of Their Native Customs and Beliefs*. London: Macmillan & Co.

Scanlon, David, ed. 1964. *Traditions of African Education*. New York: Columbia University Press.

Uganda Government. 1963. *Education in Uganda: The Report of the Uganda Education Commission*. Entebbe: Uganda Government.

Watson, Tom. 1968. A History of C.M.S. High Schools in Uganda, 1900–1924: The Education of a Protestant elite. Ph.D. diss., University of East Africa.

7 "Educating Eve": The Women's Club Movement and Political Consciousness among Rural African Women in Southern Rhodesia, 1950–1980

Sita Ranchod-Nilsson

[T]he pace of social advancement of many Africans will not be set by themselves but by their wives. It may not be as fast as many would like to see it, since Eve is essentially a traditionalist.

J. Holleman (National Archives of Zimbabwe, 1958)

[W]ithout the women's clubs, we wouldn't have been able to do what we did during the war.

Interview with an African woman in Wedza, January 23, 1989

Scholarly investigations rarely address African women's experiences with colonial notions of domesticity in relation to the political upheaval of nationalist movements or liberation struggles. Yet, the two quotations above suggest that ideas about domesticity had very political purposes for colonial settlers and governments on the one hand, and for African women on the other.

After World War II homecraft clubs for African women flourished throughout colonial Africa.[1] Southern Rhodesia was no exception to this colonial trend of promoting Western ideals of domesticity among African women. The clubs began meeting in the 1940s and shortly after formed several national organizations. The Federation of African Women's Clubs (FAWC) was the largest of these homecraft organizations with a membership of 23,000 at the height of its popularity in 1975 (*Rhodesia Herald* 21 June 78). Like homecraft clubs throughout

Africa the FAWC was organized primarily by European women who were the wives of civil servants. They began by teaching African women "domestic skills" such as cooking, baking, sewing, home decorating, basic hygiene, and nutrition. But unlike homecraft clubs in most other African colonies the FAWC focused its efforts almost exclusively on rural African women.[2]

African women responded enthusiastically to the homecraft club movement. By the mid 1970s the Ministry of Internal Affairs estimated that 10 percent of the total adult female population belonged to homecraft clubs (NAZ/FH/63 n.d.). African and European women alike were thrilled with the success of the clubs and the changes they began to see in African households and communities. European women described the success of the clubs in terms of African women becoming liberated and entering the modern world. One supporter described the impact of the homecraft clubs as nothing less than a "silent revolution" in African communities (Wynne, NAZ/3078/659, 1970).

But colonial notions of domesticity were of limited value to rural African women. By the mid 1960s the initial enthusiasm was beginning to wane in response to rapidly growing membership and demands from club members for additional training in skills that were not part of the original emphasis on homecraft. The focus of the clubs shifted from teaching homecraft skills to providing adult education for African women, including training in agricultural methods, leadership, club management, adult literacy, and communications. By the mid 1970s it was apparent that no amount of homecraft training or adult education could surmount the growing nationalist commitment to the liberation war, and as a result the club movement nearly ceased functioning until the end of the war.

The story of the FAWC in Southern Rhodesia challenges ideas about the ways in which notions of domesticity are manipulated to maintain colonial class relations. Homecraft clubs in other African colonies[3] and earlier efforts at teaching housewifery skills at mission schools in Southern Rhodesia were primarily concerned with training African women to be "proper" wives for the emerging African male elite (Gaitskell 1983; Geiger 1987; Hansen 1992; Hunt 1990; Schmidt 1987). In other words, homecraft clubs helped to maintain colonialism by incorporating the wives of African elites into a gender ideology of the elite class that focused on domesticity. The European organizers of the FAWC may have shared the goal of maintaining colonialism, but their approach was very different. The bonds that the European organizers sought to build with African women were based on the notion that all women shared an interest in domesticity. The FAWC focused their efforts on rural women in an effort to address the conditions of poverty and "backwardness" that were, in fact, symptoms of the fundamental structural flaws of the Rhodesian political economy. The Rhodesian government's continued support for women's clubs in rural areas was part of a larger policy effort, known as community development, to promote "self-help" and limited democratization among rural Africans in order to stem the mounting support for African nationalist movements. In the case that I examine in this chapter I argue that these efforts were not only unsuccessful but that the homecraft clubs led to the development of a gender consciousness that rural women eventually expressed during the liberation war.

The story of the FAWC also challenges the idea that African women can be easily manipulated for political purposes. As members of the FAWC African women made sure that the clubs met their needs, which ultimately challenged the European organizer's assumption that all women shared a concern with domesticity. In a primarily exogamous society the homecraft clubs provided a forum in which the women marrying into communities could get together and discuss their problems. In many communities this led to the development of a gender consciousness among African women, as they realized that their household problems were common to other African women and existed in the context of a racist colonial economy. During the liberation war many of the rural women's clubs ceased their formal meetings but informally maintained contact for the purpose of aiding the guerrilla forces. Under these circumstances the cooperation between African women and European women virtually collapsed.

This chapter focuses on the FAWC as a national organization and highlights the case of the FAWC in Wedza district. I place the cooperation of European and African women in the context of the changing racial political economy of Southern Rhodesia during a thirty-year period from 1950 to 1980, a period that saw the growth of African nationalism, a protracted guerrilla war, and independence for the new country of Zimbabwe. The study is based on archival sources and interviews with former club members collected in Zimbabwe and Great Britain in 1988 and 1989. After briefly outlining the political and economic situation through the 1950s I discuss the origins of the FAWC as a formally constituted organization. I then explore the ways in which the FAWC as a voluntary organization working with rural African women cooperated with the settler government in their community development programs. The experiences of women in Wedza district illustrate how African women used the organization to meet their immediate needs and how the women's clubs provided the structure in which African women developed a gendered political consciousness that was eventually part of the rural mobilization during the guerrilla war. Finally, I conclude by suggesting that the case of the FAWC in Wedza provides support for the argument that household concerns must be considered within a broader framework of social, political, and economic processes.

The Colonial Background

Since the early decades of this century the European settler government in Southern Rhodesia promulgated policies of African land alienation in order to control agricultural markets and ensure adequate supplies of cheap African labor. A great deal has been written about the settler's early attempts to alienate African land and labor and the African peasant responses (Phimister 1977; Phimister 1988; Ranger 1985; Schmidt 1987). While this vast literature highlights African resistance to the undermining of agriculture, particularly the resistance of peasant households to men leaving to work for wages in mines and on farms, it has only in exceptional cases raised questions about the role gender played in this process (Ranger 1981; Kriger 1985; Schmidt 1987). I suggest that women, as the primary agricultural producers, were key to the emergence of an African peasantry and the subsequent resistance to the disintegrating effects of male labor migration. Women were forced to shoulder a heavier agricultural burden and take on additional tasks such as plowing, during a period in which agricultural returns fell sharply (Phimister 1988, 205). In response, women from poor peasant households fled to towns and missions to escape the harsh conditions.

African male authorities, who needed the labor of African women for agriculture, and colonial officials, who saw an opportunity to placate African men, were concerned about maintaining control over African women. In Chapter 8 in this volume, Schmidt argues that the colonial government bolstered the patriarchal control of

African male authorities over their wives and daughters in an effort to maintain a form of indirect rule that relied on "traditional" household authority structures. At the same time, the few positions of authority that did exist for women in rural communities in midwifery, traditional healing, and artistry were undercut by the imposition of Western medicine and manufactured goods.

The control of women remained a central issue for both the state and African male authorities until 1930 when the government enacted the Land Apportionment Act (LAA), which established the basis for the racially segregated, unequal distribution of land rights that remained basically unaltered until independence. Although Europeans made up only approximately 3 percent of the population, the LAA gave them control over more than half the land in Southern Rhodesia, almost all of it located in the most fertile areas. Thus, after 1930 access to land was greatly restricted for Africans and control of women's labor did not guarantee sufficient levels of production. In short, the reproduction of poor peasant households could no longer rely on female agricultural labor but depended also on cash remittances from male migrants (Phimister 1988). The main issues of contention between colonial officials and Africans thus shifted from the control of African women to the control of land (Ranger 1981).

The new focus on land did not mean that domestic turmoil within African households dissipated. On the contrary, the limited access to land meant that day-to-day survival became increasingly difficult and that the household negotiations over resources and labor intensified. Indeed an examination of civil cases concerning domestic matters such as divorce, child custody, return of *lobola* (bridewealth) or household goods, and seduction indicates that during the 1930s the "increased economic difficulties . . . seem to have greatly intensified domestic struggle" (Barnes 1987, 39). In these cases gender struggles can be seen as indicating the extent to which men and women grappled with issues concerning control and autonomy within a broader context of colonialism that rendered them increasingly powerless and interdependent (Lovett 1989, 36–37).

Following World War II Southern Rhodesia experienced a period of rapid economic growth in commercial agriculture and manufacturing. At the same time, record levels of European immigration, returning exservicemen, and population growth in the reserves combined to create pressures for land reorganization. The Native Land

Husbandry Act of 1951 (NLHA) was meant to address land and labor concerns by creating a system of individualized land tenure in the reserves and forcing landless African men into a stable urban labor pool. African opposition to the Act was fierce since the NLHA completely disregarded customary claims to communal land and created a large landless population. In addition, forced resettlement, cultivation, and destocking led to increased support for African nationalists who politicized the issue of African land rights. Household negotiations between men and women were again strained under the burden of declining living standards as rural personal incomes fell by approximately 13 percent (Bratton 1978, 15).

African women bore the greatest cost of the settler government's rural policies as they struggled to maintain households in the face of diminishing resources, male labor migration, and increasing oppression by government policies and African men. The high costs of implementing the NHLA, African opposition to the individualized land tenure, forced methods of cultivation, and forced resettlement caused the government to abandon it in the early 1960s, but the basic principles of unequal land distribution set out by the LAA remained unchanged throughout this period. Concurrently, the government abandoned its highly centralized structure in favor of a more decentralized administrative approach known as community development, under which African women were recognized as central to economic and political development.

The Federation of African Women's Clubs

The proposition that European and African women shared much in common is farfetched in the context of Southern Rhodesian political economy. The term "household" had very different meanings for European women from the industrialized economies of Great Britain or even Southern Africa, and African women from subsistence or peasant economies. In Chapter 8 Schmidt describes how the early efforts to teach domestic skills to African girls and women were organized by missionaries for the purpose of training proper wives for African evangelists and elites. After World War II, the task of teaching African women housewifery skills was undertaken by the wives of civil servants with the support of the colonial government for the purpose of improving conditions in the Native Reserves. In the context of the Rhodesian political economy during that period, the focus on teaching Western domesticity to rural African women can be seen as one of a number of last-ditch efforts to make the racially biased system work.

According to Miriam Staunton, national chairman[4] of the FAWC from 1965 to 1971, the early organizers of the clubs were those women "who, by the circumstances of their lives, were in close contact with the majority race in Rhodesia, . . . missionaries, African teachers' wives, demonstrators' wives, farmers' wives, nurses or doctors" (NAZ/FH/63 1970a). Accounts of the experiences of early European settlers describe the women as "high spirited" and "adventurous" (MacDonald 1926; MacLean 1974). They were also steeped in Victorian notions of domesticity and wifely propriety. This is particularly true in the case of wives of Native Department officials, who consistently voice their pride at being able to create "civilized" homes in the harsh conditions of the bush. Thus, in her anecdotal history of the Native Affairs Department, Joy MacLean describes the reaction of Mrs. A. A. Campbell, wife of the native commissioner at Insiza district when she saw her home for the first time in 1897:

> Like many another [sic] Native Department bride, Mrs. Campbell had to show admiration for the mud huts built by her husband and which were to be her future home, and to try to forget the luxuries of her girlhood. Native Department wives became adept at turning these huts into attractive homes, making furniture out of packing cases. They also quickly learnt to make appetising meals from the few provisions available, and, to concoct a variety of recipes from the eternal venison. (MacLean 1974, 102)

Aside from trying to maintain Victorian notions of domesticity, settlers' wives, particularly the wives of civil servants, were *incorporated wives*. According to Hilary Callan, incorporation in this sense refers to, "the condition of *wifehood* in a range of settings where the social character ascribed to a woman is an intimate function of her husband's occupational identity and culture" (Callan 1981, 1). Settler wives saw themselves as helpmates to their husbands: a wife's ability to create a "civilized" home in the territory reflected positively on her husband. Wives set up clinics, schools, and trading posts where they, through contact with Africans, could help husbands maintain good relations with African workers (Kirkwood 1984b).[5] The availability of domestic servants allowed European women to maintain the tradition of voluntary service and "do-gooding" characteristic of British middle-class society (Ibid., 159).

All of these characteristics were part of the Rhodesian ethos or gender ideology of the European women who began organizing the homecraft clubs in the 1940s.

The early organizational efforts that preceded the FAWC's formation were the result of individual efforts, mainly by European women and one African woman. Some rural administrators' wives in the 1940s and 1950s were shocked at the conditions of poverty, particularly the infant mortality rate that existed in the reserves. They often blamed these conditions on the "backwardness" of the African women. Ina Beck, wife of the assistant native commissioner in Mrewa district, started a class for the African messenger's wives because she was "shocked by the appalling death rate amongst the African children, due so often to ignorance on the part of the mothers" (NAZ/FH/63 1970a). She told a friend, "I simply could not take babies dying ad lib" (Ibid., 2). Other Native Department wives were perhaps more sympathetic. Miriam Staunton recalled her first meeting with a group of African women in 1948. To demonstrate how she washed her baby, she used her daughter's doll:

> [H]ow humbled I felt. I could explain how I washed my baby each day in her own bath using germ-free water from a tap in my bungalow. These women in front of me probably had to walk several miles to a local river, or pond, where the water could be infected with bilharzia or some pollution and a crocodile could be lurking! How could I expect washing of babies to be carried on each day in these circumstances? (NAZ/ORAL/256 1986)

The FAWC's own literature attributes much of the early organizing effort to Helen Mangwende, the educated daughter of an African British South Africa Police officer who was described as a "keen Church worker." In 1941 she married Chief Mangwende of Mrewa district. Mrs. Mangwende lived in a European-style house and often acted as an interpreter for Ina Beck. Like the European women who organized the early clubs, Mrs. Mangwende was also concerned about the impoverished conditions in the reserves from the vantage point of a civil servant's wife.[6] She single-handedly organized groups of African women to teach about clean water, proper sanitation facilities, nutrition, and hygiene. Later, from 1942 to 1950 she worked with groups of women and solicited the help of local Women's Institute members,[7] the district commissioner's wife, and the land development officer's wife. By 1952 Mrewa district had between 17 and 20 clubs. Largely due to Helen Mangwendi's efforts, the Federation of

African Women's Clubs was formed and an executive committee was appointed in 1953. With the exception of Helen Mangwendi, this committee was made up of European women from similar class positions: the civil servants' wives and a missionary. Many of the FAWC's volunteers in the rural areas were also wives of civil servants living in the reserves, such as agricultural officers, district commissioners, and teachers (NAZ/FH/63 1970a).

From the very outset the FAWC was unique because it emphasized teaching housewifery and mothercraft skills to *rural women*. Club meetings provided demonstrations in areas of domestic skills such as cookery, sewing, knitting, crocheting, hygiene, child care, and nutrition. Many African women described themselves as having "no knowledge" before attending women's clubs, perhaps referring to the fact that few rural women completed even a primary school education during that period. Or, as one woman from Wedza suggested, women did not know about nutrition in the new commercial environment; they thought it was all right to feed their children on "cokes and buns" (Interview with Lillian Kamanga, 11 May 1989). But at the women's clubs they received an education in Western notions of domesticity. In a 1963 report to the national secretary the Tuli Farmers' Women's Club described their activities:

> We have done the following lessons: (a) Cookery: Yellow-cake, Baking powder Bread, Meal Bread, Scones and Tomatoe [sic] jam, (b) Sewing: Men's shirts and ties, children's frocks, boys sunsuits, pillowcases and tablecloths, etc., (c) Knitting: men's pullover's, jerseys and scarves, (d) A Hygiene lesson which was given by Demonstrator Hazekiel on taking care of home, kitchen and milk. (Olipah N. Moyo, Personal Papers of Stella Tyndal-Biscoe, 1963)

The club organizers emphasized what they thought to be the similar concerns of women across class and race lines. The idea that all women could help one another was further emphasized with slogans like, "each one, teach one." But the club organizers also made it clear that they were addressing the "backwardness" of African women. According to an FAWC pamphlet for African women, the clubs were set up as "an opportunity, not only for social contact and recreation outside the home, but for advancement in the knowledge and skills which will enable [the African woman] to create better living conditions for her family" (FAWC pamphlet, Personal papers of Stella Tyndal-Biscoe, 1963).

During the 1950s government attempts to alleviate rural poverty were mainly confined to implementation of the NLHA. However, they did provide the FAWC with some minimal financial assistance to pay the salary of an organizing secretary, to buy a motor car, and to support a small amount of vocational training. It was not until the end of the decade that the government began to recognize the potential of the homecraft clubs. In 1959 the Secretary for Internal Affairs praised the club's efforts to raise money to support community projects and help members in times of family tragedy (NAZ/FH/63 1970a). These remarks perhaps foreshadowed the increase in government support that would come under community development.

Community Development

Throughout the so-called Third World, community development policies were implemented by the United Nations and the British Colonial Office with the assistance of the United States Agency for International Development (USAID) (Mutizwa-Mangiza 1985). In 1962 the Rhodesian government officially adopted a version of community development approach that was appropriate to the racially biased political economy of Southern Rhodesia. With community development the government was abandoning its emphasis on forced cultivation methods and resettlement in favor of a more integrated approach to development that included all facets of community life such as education, health care, and public works, in addition to agricultural methods. Communities participated in development by determining their own "felt needs" and implementing and financing projects that would fulfill those needs. The government maintained control of community development efforts through the newly created Ministry of Internal Affairs that coordinated a number of services, including agricultural extension, community extension, education health services, and mass media.

In addition to defining development more broadly, community development also transferred powers of local government to so-called local authorities. In an effort to balance "traditional" and modern political authority, chiefs and headmen sat alongside popularly elected representatives on African Councils. Much of the community development literature in Southern Rhodesia refers to the need to make Africans into good, responsible citizens through this very limited attempt at democratization at the local level. As it was originally conceived community development was meant to appease

African nationalists' demands for national political participation. But, in 1962, the same year that the shift to community development was announced, the Rhodesian Front (RF) was elected. The RF ensured that despite the change in the administrative structure no government power was transferred from European hands and the basic orientation of the Rhodesian political economy remained the same (Bratton 1978).

The government and the club leadership saw African women as central actors in determining the "felt needs" of local communities and influencing responsible African citizens. Through homecraft clubs African women's efforts could be channeled to meet community development goals. In a 1974 study of rural development in Southern Rhodesia A.J.H. Hughes supports the government's approach to African women by arguing, "[O]ne of the main roles of representatives of any development agency is to act as 'merchants of discontent,' in order to encourage a desire for change among members of the population they are seeking to influence. Homecraft training could do just this" (Hughes 1974,115). In other words, through homecraft clubs, the government could create the changes it desired. Women at a home economics training course in Gwanda were told:

> [Women's] clubs could play an important role in the development of their communities by assisting or doing projects. The trainees were reminded that as mothers of families they were the first teachers of all generations. . . . Trainees were told that the whole outlook of a home, family or community reflected the type of women within that area. (NAZ/3078/659 1975)

The government recognized women's clubs, including the FAWC, as voluntary organizations that were making efforts to stimulate development in the Tribal Trust Lands (TTL)[8] and increased assistance with contributions from the Beit Trustees, the TTL board, and the state lotteries, as well as from individual firms and private donors (NAZ/FH/63 1970a). In 1963 the TTL board and the state lotteries donated the first two Landrovers, affectionately named "Trustie and Lottie," to serve as mobile demonstration units. These units were staffed by European demonstrators and their African assistants, who traveled throughout the country providing a variety of homecraft demonstrations on nutrition, baby care, and domestic skills. By the end of the decade, the FAWC had four mobile units that were fully staffed by Africans. The ministry of internal affairs also provided training and demonstration assistance to promote community development. The ministry created the Women's Group Liaison (WGL) to coordinate the activities of all the organizations working toward the advancement of African women. Through its membership in the WGL the FAWC was able to send women to training courses at government training centers such as Dombashowa, and make use of various departments at the ministry such as Agritex for club demonstrations. In addition, all the clubs worked closely with government-employed Community Advisors and Women's Advisors who worked at the district level to ensure that the goals of community development were met.

The FAWC in Wedza District

Wedza district is located approximately 170 kilometers southeast of Harare just off the highveld.[9] This central location, with its relatively fertile soil and good seasonal rainfall, meant that the Wedza reserve was generally suitable for agricultural production. Its close proximity to the capital city also meant that it was easily accessible and thus after 1951 had a relatively high rate of male labor migration. Unlike many other districts Wedza remained relatively underpopulated by the standards of the native department until the 1950s. In the 1920s and 1930s African producers often cooperated with agricultural demonstrators and grew "some of the best crops in Rhodesia" (Ranger in Phimister 1988, 186). Centralization came to the district in 1947, and even though land was still comparatively plentiful, local farmers were generally uncooperative. "Drastic penalties had to be imposed on all those who declined to follow 'good farming practices' " (Phimister 1988, 276). By the early 1950s people from the overpopulated Soswe Reserve in neighboring Makoni district were resettled into Wedza reserve. The subsequent overcrowding caused increased resistance to forced cultivation practices and an increase in male labor migration.[10]

In the 1950s the burden of the overcrowding and the lack of resources in the reserves fell on women who had difficulty raising crops for sale on small pieces of land, limited access to extension services, and no guaranteed access to the cash incomes from their migrant husbands, fathers, or sons. As conditions grew worse more men went to work in towns. Mr. Matatu, an agricultural extension worker in Wedza district during the 1960s, told me, "[W]hen I came here I found that many men were employed in towns. Only women were left on the land to supervise agricultural production" (Interview in Wedza, 13 February 1989). Although many women were in charge of household agriculture, most often they had no control over the income it brought in. Even in cases where women had access to cash from selling crops, vegetables, or craft items, they often were not entitled to keep the money or make decisions about how to spend it. One woman described her situation in this way:

> [W]e were afraid because if the husbands found out that you had some money you would be in trouble because after the sale of crops he took all the money and so where would you say you got the other money from? The husbands did all the buying and women could not go to a shop to buy anything they liked. (Interview in Wedza [a], 31 January 1989)[11]

The club movement in Wedza reserve got off to a shaky start in the 1950s, but quickly rebounded after the implementation of the NLHA in 1959. The FAWC was the most popular group in the reserve and they often met together with the Catholic Women's Clubs (CWC), another group active in parts of the district. African women were enthusiastic about the clubs, where they could learn sewing, cookery, crafts, and agricultural methods and participate in shows and competitions with other clubs from the area. Women came to the clubs despite the initial objections of many husbands. Men were suspicious of their wives attending club meetings and reluctant to give them money to buy materials for sewing and needlecraft work. But women, alone or in groups, tried to persuade their husbands that the clubs would, in fact, benefit men. One woman described how she used to go about this:

> Sometimes if my husband refused me to go to the club I would maybe say something like this, "I have something that I have to give the chairwoman at the club." After telling my husband that, he would allow me for only that once. Then at the club I would tell the others that my husband is not interested in me coming to the club and would get some advice from other women. Sometimes the chairwoman arranged to pay a visit to my home and talk to the man, explaining to him whatever things they did and learned at the clubs. In turn, I would also try my best to do what pleased him like keeping a home clean, washing his clothes, preparing him good and clean food. In this way I might win his approval to go and attend the club. (Interview in Wedza [a], 31 January 1989)

But other accounts of male resistance to women attending the clubs reveal the ideology of male control over women's mobility and sexuality. Many women gave accounts similar to this one:

> These husbands refused us from going to clubs because they were ignorant. They did not know that if a wife went to the club she got knowledge. They wanted wives to stay home and do housework only. They said that if you wanted to go somewhere, it was laziness, or maybe you wanted to chat unproductively with other women or maybe you were going for prostitution. This, then, caused misunderstanding in the home. If you insisted that he should allow you sometimes, he wanted to beat you. (Interview in Wedza, 31 January 1989).

Eventually women overcame the resistance of African men to the clubs. Often the first articles of clothing clubs worked on were pieces to give to men, such as shirts or sweaters. At their first competition one women's club ceremoniously presented men with ties (Tuli Club Report, Personal papers of Stella Tyndal-Biscoe, 1963). The European organizers were also aware of the resistance African women were getting from their husbands. Stella Tyndal-Biscoe, former FAWC secretary, said she always spoke with the appropriate African chief to win his approval before allowing a local women's club to join the FAWC because "this made things easier for the women at home" (Interview with Stella Tyndal-Biscoe, 11 May 1989).

Perhaps women in Wedza were so determined to attend the FAWC meetings because they fulfilled a number of needs. In Shona society's primarily exogamous communities opportunities to know other women through work parties or rituals had become less frequent in the difficult circumstances created by land shortages and resettlement. The clubs gave women an opportunity to get together, share common problems, and develop strategies to cope with a variety of household problems. In one village in Wedza the FAWC met together with the CWC and in addition to learning cooking, sewing, and child care skills women often discussed family problems at their meetings. This club organized cooperative child care so that women could spend time on their income-generating projects, which at that time were crucial to family survival. A member of the club described their situation in 1965:

> [T]here wasn't enough food because people weren't using manure and the land was poor. Some people were starving and had to work in other people's fields for food. Through the club women organized

groups to brew beer for sale. Each member of the group would donate fifty cents to the designated brewer on a weekly basis to brew beer and sell "sadza [the staple porridge made with maize meal] and meat. With the money they earned, women were able to pay their contributions to the clubs and begin a savings club. (Interview in Wedza, 15 February 1989)

Women in each village echoed the sentiment that prior to the war for independence their overriding concern was the need for a steady cash income, which they could not depend on their husbands providing.

African women found that the clubs could fulfill their needs as they turned their training in homecraft skills into income generating activities. These activities included selling needlecraft items and cultivating club gardens where vegetables were grown for sale in African villages and on local European markets. The club women used what money they earned from these activities to pay their children's school fees and purchase household goods and food.

At the clubs women also developed strategies to keep some of the cash they were earning from their husbands. One woman told me:

women complained that their husbands didn't give them money. In the clubs they were taught how to sew clothes and sell them for pocket money. They would show the husband a quarter of the money and hide the rest. (Interview in Wedza, 1 February 1989).

When women saw that through the clubs they could learn skills which would help them alleviate some of their problems, the FAWC began a period of dramatic growth. Table 4 demonstrates the rapid growth of the FAWC; between 1961 and 1970 club membership more than quadrupled.

By 1964 the need to provide their members with more advanced and varied skills, plus the need for additional materials, equipment, and staffing was straining the financial and administrative capacities of the national organization (NAZ/FH/63 n.d.). The FAWC was not attracting enough educated African women to volunteer as club leaders for all the new clubs. In a 1967 letter to her mother in England, Miriam Staunton lamented the fact that educated African women did not seem to share the settler's affinity for community service: "Our failure in our Club movement is that we have not yet attracted enough educated African women to help us, but we must be patient. One does not learn the spirit of service in a day" (NAZ/HS/3085 1967). Although these educated African women may in fact have been disinterested in community service, available evidence

Table 4   FAWC MEMBERSHIP AND NUMBER OF CLUBS, 1956–1978

Year	Number of Clubs	Number of Members
1956	121	—
1959	200	—
1961	184	2,800
1965	450	6,800
1968	760	14,800
1970	1,100	16,500
1973	1,100	21,000
1975	—	23,000
1976	—	19,000
1978	—	7,000

Sources: NAZ/FH/63, "An Outline of the History of the Federation of African Women's Clubs, 1970. NAZ/3078/659 "Chairman's Report" 1968; Hughes 1974:172; *Rhodesia Herald* June 21, 1978.

suggests that they may have been more concerned with the growing African nationalist movements that addressed their immediate concerns of access to land, economic opportunity, and education (Ranger 1985). In the wake of the shortage of educated African women volunteers, uneducated women with "natural leadership abilities" were stepping forward to fill the demand for club leaders.

With this tremendous growth in the number of clubs the basic aims of the FAWC began to be questioned and doubts expressed about the gender assumptions that bound European and African women in their mutual concern with domesticity. The focus on homecraft skills was not meeting the needs of African women, who were no longer satisfied with the limited emphasis on homecraft; they now demanded that the club provide a broader scope of adult education, including agricultural methods, literacy, club management, leadership training, and communications. The revised constitution of 1968 characterized the FAWC as an organization that provided adult education rather than homecraft training. In a further effort to meet the needs of the clubs, the FAWC organizational structure decentralized, delegating to the regional councils the responsibility to provide programs of adult education to meet the needs of their own regions. While the national executive committee of the FAWC strained under the administrative burden of the changing organization, they were also proud of what was often referred to as the "liberation" of African women from what where considered backward tribal ways. Ultimately, they retained faith in their original assumptions about gender that bound European and African women together. In an article ironically titled, "African Women are Winning Their Silent Revolution," Helen Wynne wrote, "People of differing clans and tribes have met together and found themselves, not strangers one to another, but sisters sharing common problems, common needs, common aspirations" (NAZ/3078/659 1970a).

While the European club members discussed the liberation of African women, the African nationalist movements were preparing to launch a guerrilla war for independence that would last nearly a decade. As rural dwellers, African women club members were keenly aware of the issues raised by members of the liberation forces during rural mobilization: lack of land, economic opportunity, and education. When women discussed their difficult household relations, their comments also reveal an understanding of the problems caused by government policies:

> The husbands were sometimes called to attend meetings by the headman, or any leaders, where they were told to pay taxes, to cut their number of cattle, or whatever. They [then] told the women what the talks were about and did whatever they were told to do. Therefore, we could not do anything. We also had to do as they said. (Interview in Wedza, 31 January 1989)

Ultimately neither the FAWC nor the community development program could adequately address the symptoms brought on by the fundamental deformities of the Rhodesian political economy. Educating African women in order to promote good citizenship meant very little in a society where democratic participation was denied to the African majority. Similarly, promoting community "self-help" projects could not address the conditions brought about by a racially biased system of land distribution. What women's club activities did, however, through their emphasis on group participation, was to raise African women's consciousness about injustices they all suffered.

Women in a few of the villages in Wedza district said that prior to the war they occasionally expressed their dissatisfaction with a particular government policy, such as forced destocking or the prohibition from planting rice in marshy areas. In another village one woman told me that during the 1970s they discussed the African

nationlists' view of history, which their children told them when
they came home on school breaks. But prior to the war there was no
evidence of African nationalists organizing in the FAWC.

As the liberation war began in the northeast in 1972 and spread
throughout the country, European and African women were forced
to take sides and assumptions about common gender bonds between
European and African women fell away. Rhodesian propaganda emphasized images of European women defending their homes while
liberation forces mobilized rural women to support the fight for African land (Frederikse 1984). As early as 1974 Ethy Pearce, the national chairman of the FAWC, exhorted club members not to discuss
politics at club meetings:

> Our aim is to teach women to become good home-makers, to care
> properly for their families, and to take a useful part in the life of
> the community. Political matters must NOT be discussed at club
> meetings, as this is not part of our work, and if members start to
> talk about politics at Club gatherings it is the duty of the Chair-
> man to stop them. (NAZ/3078/658, 1974)

As the war spread through the rural areas, particularly after 1975,
the FAWC found it increasingly difficult to sustain the idea that
European and African women were cooperating in areas they had in
common. In Manicaland, an eastern province, demonstrators could
no longer travel and club members could not attend meetings in the
midst of the war. By 1978, membership had fallen to less than one
third of what it had been at its peak in 1975 (see Table I) and the
organization was in a financial crisis (*Rhodesia Herald,* 21 June
1978). That same year the FAWC national newsletter contained the
following exhortation: "Let us all do all we can towards bringing
peace to our land, and continue to pray for Rhodesia" (NAZ/3078/659
1978).

But African women were no longer praying for Rhodesia; they
were supporting the liberation movements fighting for what was to
become Zimbabwe. During the war most clubs stopped meeting, although club members retained their networks for the purposes of
supporting the liberation forces. Former club members put their new
organizational skills to work for independence. Village donation
committees were responsible for collecting donations of food, clothing, blankets and cash for "the comrades." In the villages that I
visited where women were in charge of the donation committees, all
were former club leaders. They said that they were good leaders

because of the management and communication skills they learned at the women's clubs. Other women supported the liberation efforts by cooking and providing other domestic services and carrying out intelligence work, while those young women with no children traveled with the guerrillas as *chimbwidos* or left the country to undergo military training.

The African women who remained in the rural areas, the wives and mothers, also brought many of the domestic concerns raised in the women's clubs to the rural mobilization efforts during the war. In Wedza, women asked the guerrillas to intervene in domestic disputes such as, among other things, lack of financial support or physical violence from their husbands, jealousy over girlfriends, and unwanted divorces. Women were in key positions in villages in Wedza because of the generally high rates of labor migration. The guerrillas responded to their problems in a way that was most often sympathetic to women. The women in turn actively supported the guerrillas.

"The history of the FAWC over the past twenty years," notes Geraty, "is a proud record of race relations, of women working together, not as white women to black woman, but as one woman to another, to help the African woman to build up her family life and living conditions, which in turn has helped to build up the community" (Geraty, (NAZ/FH/63 1970). Yet from the African perspective, women's clubs, including innovations introduced with the community development approach, were primarily changes in form and not substance (Bratton 1978). The opportunities offered to African women by the FAWC, or any of the other homecraft organizations, did not alter the fundamental racially based inequality of the Rhodesian political economy that was at the root of the conditions in the Tribal Trust Lands.

Yet, in another sense, the women's club movement marked a real turning point for women in Wedza. Women's clubs represented the gender ideal the settler government held of African women that sought to make them into better housewives and mothers. The development literature has long been critical of programs that stress housewifery skills, or even small income-generating projects, because they marginalize women (Rogers 1983). My observations of the women's clubs in Wedza lead me to a different conclusion. African women saw the clubs as an educational resource and used them toward their own ends: first, to increase their independence and autonomy by gaining resources through income-generating projects;

second, to take certain types of collective action within households to wrest some autonomy from husbands; and finally, to gain the organizational and leadership skills that would be put to use in the village committees during the liberation war. In this light, the case of the FAWC clubs provides evidence to challenge the idea that European women and the colonial government easily manipulated African women by using ideals of domesticity in order to sustain colonialism.

The clubs also provided a forum in which women developed a gendered political consciousness; they began to see their similar situations in the context of colonial oppression and male dominance. Later, during the rural mobilization sessions many women raised these issues with members of the liberation forces who had established themselves as the new legitimate authorities in many rural areas, including Wedza. And while it is difficult to substantiate the causal links that would connect this consciousness directly to the FAWC in Wedza, the evidence does suggest that former FAWC members were often very active in the liberation war.

Notes

1. The role of homecraft clubs in other African colonies is taken up by Deborah Gaitskell (1983), Susan Geiger (1987), Karen Tranberg Hansen (1992), Nancy Rose Hunt (1990), and Audrey Wipper (1976a and 1976b).

2. The obvious exception to this would be the formation of Mandaeleo ya Wanawake in Kenya during the 1950s. Mandaeleo also focused its efforts on rural women. See Wipper 1975–1976a, 1975–1976b.

3. The Maendeleo ya Wanawaka organization in Kenya also geared its activities toward rural women (Wipper 1975–1976a and 1975–1976b).

4. All FAWC documents refer to "chairman" of the organization and although this gender-biased terminology is no longer commonly accepted I use it when referring to the head of the national executive committee.

5. In another piece, Kirkwood discusses Victorian gender ideology at finishing schools in London. There women were taught to act as mediators in situations where tensions are potentially threatening and dangerous to a man (Kirkwood 1984a, 109). This notion is also appropriate to the case of the wives of European civil servants in Southern Rhodesia.

6. Chiefs in Southern Rhodesia were members of the civil service in the sense that they were paid by the government. Native Commissioners, later District Administrators in the 1960s, had broad powers to dismiss and replace uncooperative chiefs.

7. The National Federation of Women's Institutes of Rhodesia was initially interested in the situation of European women in Rhodesia. However, in the 1950s it too began to sponsor African women's clubs, some of which

were raised to the status of women's institutes when the members demonstrated that they were capable of managing their own affairs.

8. After 1962 the Native Reserves were referred to as Tribal Trust Lands (TTL).

9. Wedza was originally a subdistrict of Marandellas. During land reorganization in 1964, it became a district.

10. Figures on labor migration were not kept by district authorities during this time period. Several studies of African households conducted after independence yield differing figures. In a 1982 study Diane Callear found that 41 percent of the households surveyed had the male head of household working away and remitting income. In a 1985 study for Agritex Kate Truscott found that just over half the men in reporting households considered themselves migrating workers. However, she points out that a random sample carried out in 1984 showed a rate of 28 percent. In my own sample 63 percent of the women who were married prior to 1976 had husbands working away from home (1985).

11. Interviews were conducted with small groups of 3 to 10 women in 15 villages in Wedza district. Since respondents were promised anonymity because of the sensitive nature of the research topic, they are referred to here by date only. In cases where more than one interview took place in one day separate interviews are designated with lower case letters.

Bibliography

Archival Sources

NATIONAL ARCHIVES OF ZIMBABWE (NAZ),

NAZ, FH/63 1970a. An Outline of the History of the Federation of African Women's Clubs. Miriam Staunton.

NAZ, 1970b, "A Study of the 'Federation of African Women's Clubs' as an Agency Involved in Adult Education in Rhodesia." Anne Geraty. June 5, 1970.

NAZ, n.d. The Development and Coordination of the Women's Club Movement in Rhodesia—Its Influence in Bridging the Gap Between Rural and Urban.

NAZ, 3078/659, 1970a FAWC. Helen Wynne, "African Women are Winning Their Silent Revolution"

NAZ, FAWC. 1968–1978. National Newsletters.

NAZ, 1975. FAWC. Home Economics Course, 20th May–13th June.

NAZ, 1968. FAWC. Chairman's Report.

NAZ, HS/3085. Correspondence. Miriam Staunton.

NAZ, 163/44/32, 1959. Place of Women in African Nationalism. J. Holleman.

NAZ, ORAL/256. Interview with Francis and Miriam Staunton, November 1986.

Oral Sources

Lilliam Kamanga, former FAWC member, Harare, 11 May 1989.
Mr. Matatu, Agricultural Extension Officer, Wedza, 13 February 1989.
Woman in Wedza, 23 January 1989
Woman in Wedza (a), 31 January 1989.
Woman in Wedza (b) 31 January 1989.
Woman in Wedza, 1 February 1989.
Woman in Wedza, 15 February 1989.

Books and Articles

Barnes, Teresa, 1987. African Female Labour and the Urban Economy of Colonial Zimbabwe with Special Reference to Harare, 1920–1939. MA Thesis, University of Zimbabwe.
Bratton, Michael. 1978. *Beyond Community Development: the Political Economy of Rural Administration in Zimbabwe.* London: Catholic Institute for International Relations.
Callan, Hilary. 1984. Introduction. In *The Incorporated Wife,* ed. Hilary Callan, 1–26. London: Croom Helm.
Farquhar, June 1974. *The Mukamba Tree.* Bulawayo: Books of Rhodesia.
Frederikse, Julie. 1984. *None But Ourselves: Masses vs. Media in the Making of Zimbabwe.* New York: Penguin.
Gaitskell, Deborah. 1983. Housewives, Maids or Mothers: Some Contradictions of Domesticity for Christian Women in Johannesburg, 1903–1939. *Journal of African History* 24:241–256.
Gaitskell, Deborah, and Elaine Unterhalter. 1989. Mothers of the Nation: a Comparative Analysis of Nation, Race and Motherhood in Afrikaner Nationalism and the African National Congress." In *Women-Nation-State,* ed. Nira Yuval-Davis and Floya Anthias, 58–78. London: Macmillan.
Geiger, Susan. 1987. Women in Nationalist Struggle: TANU Activists in Dar es Salaam. *International Journal of African Historical Studies* 20:1–26.
Hansen, Karen Tranberg. 1992. White Women in a Changing World: Employment, Voluntary Work, and Sex in Post–World War II Northern Rhodesia. In *Western Women and Imperialism,* ed. Nupur Chauduri and Margaret Strobel, 247–269. Bloomington: Indiana University Press.
Hughes, A.J.B. 1974. *Development in Rhodesia Tribal Areas.* Salisbury: Tribal Areas of Rhodesia Research Foundation.
Hunt, Nancy Rose. 1990. Domesticity and Colonialism in Belgian Africa: Usumbura's *Foyer Social, 1946–1960. Signs* 15:447–474.
Kirkwood, Deborah. 1984a The Suitable Wife: Preparation for Marriage in London and Rhodesia/Zimbabwe. In ed., *The Incorporated Wife,* ed. Hillary Callan, 106–119. London: Croom Helm.
———. 1984b. Settler Wives in Southern Rhodesia: A A Case Study. In *The Incorporated Wife,* ed. Hillary Callan, 143–164. London: Croom Helm.
Kriger, Norma. 1985. Struggles for Independence: Rural Conflicts in Zimbabwe's War of Liberation. Ph.D. diss. Massachusetts Institute of Technology.
Lovett, Margot. 1989. Gender Relations, Class Formation and the Colonial

State in Africa. In *Women and the State in Africa,* ed. Jane Parpart and Kathleen Staudt, 23–46. Boulder: Lynne Rienner.

MacLean, Joy. 1974. *The Guardians.* Bulawayo: Books of Rhodesia.

MacDonald, Sheila. 1926. *Sally in Rhodesia.* Sydney: Cornstalk Publishing Co.

May, Joan. 1983. *Zimbabwean Women in Customary and Colonial Law.* Harare: Mambo Press.

Mutizwa-Mangiza, N. D. 1985. Community Development in Pre-Independence Zimbabwe. Supplement to *Zambezia.*

Needham, Winifred Jane. 1959. A History of the Federation of Women's Institutes of Southern Rhodesia. Private publication.

Phimister, Ian. 1977. Peasant Production and Underdevelopment in Southern Rhodesia 1890–1914, with Particular Reference to Victoria District. In *The Roots of Rural Poverty in Central and Southern Africa,* ed. Robin Palmer and Neil Parsons, 225–267. Berkeley: University of California Press.

———. 1988. *An Economic and Social History of Zimbabwe, 1890–1948.* London: Longman.

Preston, H. 1961. The African Woman and the Changing Pattern of Africa. Native Affairs Department Information Sheet No. 22, Southern Rhodesia Information Service, March.

Ranger, Terence. 1981. Women in the Politics of Makoni District, Zimbabwe, 1890–1980. Unpublished paper.

———. 1985. *Peasant Consciousness and Guerrilla War in Zimbabwe.* Berkeley: University of California Press.

Rhodesia Herald, 21 June 1978.

Rogers, Barbara. 1983. *The Domestication of Women: Discrimination in Developing Societies.* New York: Tavistock.

Schmidt, Elizabeth. 1987. Ideology, economics, and the role of Shona women in Southern Rhodesia, 1859–1939. Ph.D. diss. University of Wisconsin, Madison.

Truscott, Kate. 1985. Socio-Economic Factors Related to Food Production and Consumption: A Case Study of Twelve Households in Wedza Communal Land, Zimbabwe. Paper produced for the FAO Expert Consultation on Broadening the Food Base with Traditional Food Plants. Harare, Zimbabwe, 18–23 November 1985.

Tyndal-Biscoe, Stella. Personal Papers, 1961–1971.

Weinrich, A. K. H. 1971. *Chiefs and Councils in Rhodesia.* Columbia: University of South Carolina Press.

Wipper, Audrey. 1975–1976a. The Maendeleo ya Wanawake Organization: the Co-optation of Leadership. *African Studies Review* 18:99–119.

———. 1975–1976b. The Maendeleo ya Wanawake Movement in the Colonial Period: the Canadian Connection, Mau Mau, Embriodery and Agriculture. *Rural Africana* 29:195–214.

Part 3

Race, Class, Gender, and Domestic Work

8 Race, Sex, and Domestic Labor: The Question of African Female Servants in Southern Rhodesia, 1900–1939

Elizabeth Schmidt

From the onset of European occupation of Southern Rhodesia in the 1890s and up until the 1930s, settlers, missionaries, and government officials debated the pros and cons of African female domestic service.[1] This highly emotional debate involved the defense of economic and political interests, as well as ideological constructions of race and gender. Within the European community, men and women were frequently at odds over the issue, while the various interest groups—missionaries, settlers, and industrialists—also found it difficult to agree. The colonial state favored one faction or another, depending upon the circumstances, but always putting long-term political objectives above immediate economic concerns. Within the African population, there was general opposition to the employment of African women and girls in domestic service. Although men and women, young and old, voiced their disapproval, their reasons were varied and often contradictory. This chapter examines the forces working both for and against the employment of African women and girls in European households and explores the complex struggles that ensued during the period 1900 to 1939.

Before the colonization of Southern Rhodesia, the distinction between the domestic and the social in African society was more political than economic. While African men were generally responsible for public governance and lineage and community matters, women had primary responsibility for food preparation and child rearing. However, both women and men were actively engaged in productive activities outside the household that were crucial to its survival. The European ideology of "domesticity," which implied that men were breadwinners and women reproducers of the labor force, had no place in precolonial African cultures. The ideal of women remaining at home, cooking, keeping house, and raising children while men earned wages in the wider society was an imported ideology rather than an indigenous cultural concept.

The transplanting of the European ideology to African culture was largely the work of European missionaries and the wives of colonial civil servants. (See Chapter 7 on European-initiated home-craft clubs for African women.) At mission schools and in after-school clubs, boys learned skills that prepared them for employment in the European dominated economy, while girls were transformed into model Christian housewives. They were taught to keep house and to raise healthy, disciplined children in modified European fashion. Women's unremunerated work in the home maintained and reproduced the male wage labor force. Thus, the domestication of African women was central to the development of colonial capitalism in Southern Rhodesia.

In colonial Africa the exact configuration of domesticity was necessarily shaped by race and class position. The European women who taught African women to cook, clean, and sew did not perform these tasks in their own homes. As employers of African servants, they were able to devote time to volunteer work and social welfare activities—precisely because they were freed from domestic work (see ch. 7). Nurturers, rather than breadwinners, teaching African women much as they taught their own children—such women conformed to a different version of the domestic ideal.

The upper middle-class domesticity of European women was predicated upon the availability of African servants. According to European domestic ideology, cooking, cleaning, housekeeping, and caring for children were quintessential "women's tasks." However, the employment of African women as live-in servants in European households—and the consequent neglect of their own families—conflicted with European attempts to domesticate them. Ultimately, the European ideal of women at home and men engaged in wage work in the wider society, buttressed by European women's fear of African women's sexuality, took precedence over the gender-specific nature of the tasks. African women would remain in their own domestic domain, while African men would enter that of Europeans to work for wages. The European domestic domain thus became the African wider social sphere.

This outcome, however, was not predetermined. Within the European population, mine owners and commercial farmers commonly advocated the employment of young unmarried African girls in domestic service. Upon marriage, they were expected to quit their jobs and assume their "natural" caretaking role as wives and mothers. Missionaries generally held a contrary view, opposing the employment of African women at any stage in their life cycles. While missionaries trained African girls to sew, cook, and launder, they claimed that their primary purpose was not to prepare the girls to work for Europeans, but to create proper Christian wives for African teachers, evangelists, and other members of the emerging African elite. Although some mission-trained girls subsequently entered domestic service, they were not, as a rule, encouraged to do so.

State officials vacillated from one side of the debate to the other. Owners of capital and state officials considered female servants to be cheap substitutes for African men. The employment of women and girls would free men for "productive work" on European farms, mines, and in other primary industries. However, colonial officials, unlike owners of capital, had to consider long-term political objectives. However desirable female domestic service might be from an economic standpoint, the practice of "emancipating" African women threatened to undermine African male power, and consequently the entire system of chiefly authority.

Numerous other factors worked against the employment of African women in European homes. African women themselves resisted pressures to work for Europeans. Despite the assumption that female servants would be young and unmarried, European mistresses were reluctant to train girls who were bound to leave a short time later. Thus, they pressed their servants to remain for longer periods. Given the high priorities of marriage and motherhood, it is not surprising that few African women were willing to give up their future prospects in order to care for the children of someone else. Furthermore, domestic labor was among the most poorly paid, intensely supervised, and isolating forms of work. If African women were in need of a cash income, they usually chose to work independently, brewing and selling beer or hawking grain and vegetables, activities that could accommodate their child-care and housekeeping responsibilities and that were much more lucrative than domestic service (cf. Hansen 1990, 126–127; 1986b, 21).

Approaching the matter from a different perspective, African men objected to the departure of their daughters from the rural areas, where they were so crucial to agricultural production and lineage reproduction. Male elders feared losing control over young women, their marriages, their bridewealth, and their labor (Schmidt 1990; 1991). It was assumed that any African female in the urban areas would be "ruined" by some man—whether black or white. Hence, bridewealth, if it could be obtained at all, would be reduced in value. Similarly, older women opposed the departure of younger women and girls, who bore the brunt of household and agricultural production.

The decades-long debate concerning African female domestic service was sprinkled with references to the "black peril"—sexual offenses allegedly committed against European women by African men. The "black peril" hysteria in Southern Rhodesia, incipient in the early years of the twentieth century and continuing through the 1930s, was an important catalyst for public and private investigations into the feasibility of replacing male with female domestic labor. A powerful undercurrent was the fear of "yellow peril"—miscegenation as a result of sexual relations between European men and African women. In a settler society dominated by Victorian sexual mores, the "virginal" European woman was glued firmly on her pedestal, while the supposedly "animal-like" and "wild" African woman was the secret object of white men's sexual desires. While European men were intent upon protecting "white womanhood," their wives were frequently more concerned about the proximity of African women to their husbands' bedrooms. The concern of African women for their own safety and that of African men for the honor of their daughters and wives—the "white peril"—received little attention in the intra-European debate.

Given their hostile predisposition toward African women, it is not surprising that many European women resisted the substitution of African female for African male labor. As the custodians of European civilization and white skin privilege, European women assumed primary responsibility for upholding the "dignity" and "prestige" of the Empire by maintaining social distance between the ruler and the ruled. Far greater than their fear for their own safety was their concern that their husbands and sons show proper respect for the British crown and European womanhood by keeping their hands off African women. Castigated as failures if their husbands sought the companionship of African women, European women struggled with their men over the domestic servant issue.

The solution that was optimal for capital did not prevail. The victors, for various and contradictory reasons, were African women and men, European women, missionaries, and state officials who championed political over economic objectives. While African women entered domestic service in increasing numbers, especially in the post-World War II period, African men continued to dominate the domestic labor force in Southern Rhodesia, not only through the 1930s, but in Zimbabwe up to the present day (Clarke 1974, 14, 62; Weinrich 1976, 227, 230–231; Zimbabwe Women's Bureau 1980, 45–46; Stoneman 1981, 100–101; England 1982, 76–80).[2]

The Quest for Cheap Labor in the Domestic Arena

From the first years of the twentieth century, the colonial state took great interest in the question of African female domestic service, encouraging unmarried African women and girls to work in European households. Upon marriage they were expected to return to the rural areas to grow food and care for their families. Their places would be taken by another crew of industrious unmarried girls. According to the state, the employment of African women and girls in domestic labor would free African men for more productive work on European farms, in the mines, and in other primary industries of the territory. "Much work is at present performed by males which could, and ought to be, placed in the hands of females," commented the Native Affairs Committee of Enquiry in 1911 (SR: 39; see also FWIa:9, 21, 39, 45, 54; FWIb, Appendix:1, DCb: 84).

Native commissioners, the officials in charge of African administration at the district level, made regular inquiries into the female employment situation. Year after year, their annual reports showed that progress in this area had been nonexistent. African women were refusing to work for Europeans, instead earning money on their own terms, often by illegal means. Some were even abandoning back-breaking agricultural labor in order to invest their energies in more lucrative pursuits. In the Salisbury District on the eastern edge of the capital, for instance, the native commissioner reported in 1909 that there were "extremely few" African girls in domestic service (AR 1909, 22). "The women are yearly becoming more lazy and indolent," he lamented, adding,

> I do not know of a single case of a girl or woman entering service. The young women living in the vicinity of the mines spend their

lives making and selling beer and in general immorality. Where in previous years the women had to do their share of tilling the lands, this work in many cases is now done by natives from other Districts employed by the fathers or husbands of the women who become richer by the earnings of the latter. (AR 1909, 55)

The situation did not vary greatly for the next two decades. In 1932, the native commissioner noted once again, "[T]here is no sign of native girls of this district wishing to enter domestic service" (AR 1932, 8).[3]

Those groups in the European community that complained about the shortage of African female servants seemed to have little understanding of the critical role played by young girls in the household labor force. Pre-teen and teenaged African girls assisted their mothers with agricultural production, food preparation, laundry, and other household chores. They fetched water and firewood and cared for younger siblings. If their brothers were at school or in paid employment, young girls contributed an even greater share of the household labor. In place of their brothers they might herd and milk the cattle, drive a team of oxen, or steer the plow. Given the diversity of tasks assigned to young girls, their labor was even less dispensable to the household than that of their brothers (Holleman 1952, 60, 73; Schmidt 1988, 50–56, 69).

Undercutting Male Wages

Despite their preoccupation with the female servant problem, state officials considered the shortage of female labor to be a sudsidiary concern. They were disturbed by it only insofar as it contributed to the scarcity of male labor in other economic sectors. Testifying in 1930 to a commission of inquiry established by the all-European Federation of Women's Institutes of Southern Rhodesia, W. R. Benzies charged that while local African men refused to work for European farmers, the towns were "overrun" with men seeking employment in domestic service. "If females only were employed in this branch of labor," Benzies maintained, "a larger proportion of males would be available for employment in the country" (FWIa:32). A similar opinion was voiced by Ethel Tawse Jollie, a prominent settler and the first woman elected to the Southern Rhodesian Legislative Assembly. "Already the rate of pay demanded by trained cooks and house-boys in town is higher than many people who employ them can really afford," she noted. "At the same time there is often a shortage of farm labor, which is less well paid" (FWIa:63).

The relative attractiveness of servants' wages was evident in 1932, when male servants in Bulawayo were paid an average of thirty to thirty-five shillings per month (DCb:67). In contrast, male agricultural workers throughout the territory earned an average of twelve shillings and three pence a month plus food, while mine workers earned twenty-five shillings and ten pence plus rations (Mosley 1983, 158–159). The employment of female servants would not only release men for other work, it would drive down domestic wages. Female servants in Umtali earned an average of twelve shillings and six pence to fifteen shillings per month in 1932, approximately half the average male earnings (DCa:4).

While European women attempted to depress their servants' wages, African women and girls deemed their earnings inadequate and struggled to increase their pay packets. In 1932, Mrs. Russell complained to a government commission that "native girls . . . demand as high wages as native boys and they do not give the same service" (DCb:80–82). European women consistently misunderstood the dynamics of resource control in African households. Regarding the girls' income as pocket money, rather than resources crucial to household subsistence, they typically complained that a servant's "father seemed to get hold of all her money." Others assumed that girls wanted money only for luxury items, such as "pretty clothes," and "attractive things" (DCa:29, 37; DCb:87, 93).

Indicating that African households counted on the contributions of female members, a delegation of African men strenuously objected to the low pay received by female domestic workers. Seven members of the Native Association of Umtali protested the fact that "their daughters get only sufficient money for themselves and not enough to send home to their parents." In contrast to their rural counterparts, these new, western-educated elites did not oppose the employment of their daughters in European households. They simply demanded a just wage. With remarkable candor the delegation stated,

> We have heard that the Missions have advised people not to give the girls a lot of money. These girls ought to be able to give their parents something in return for the money spent on their education. We object to the advice given by the Missions. (DCa:35)

Domestic Labor Versus Domesticated Wives

It was around the issue of African female domestic labor that European missionaries and the colonial state experienced one of their many squabbles over "native policy." Although some missionaries trained African girls in domestic skills, Reverend Mussell of Epworth Mission insisted that "the primary aim of missions is to train native women not for domestic service but to improve them for their own homes by making them into better mothers," as well as proper wives for African teachers and evangelists (DCa:160; also see DCa:2, 19, 40–41; NFDL: 7; AR Mrewa 1918,88). In some instances missionaries objected less to the idea of African women working for wages than they did to the possibility that the women, lacking moral supervision, would "go wrong." Deemed inherently immoral in sexual matters, African women and girls exposed to the "temptations" of city life would invariably become prostitutes, the missionaries claimed (AR Mrewa 1918, 88).

African fathers and male guardians, as well as younger men, shared some of the missionaries' concerns. What the elders dreaded most was not that their dependent daughters earn money per se, as their households would also benefit from such earnings. Their deepest concern was loss of control, the threat posed by female employment to their authority as patriarchs, since even a small degree of economic independence would remove young girls from their fathers' sphere of authority. The fathers stood to lose control not only over their daughters' labor power—particularly critical as male migration increased—but also over their sexual behavior, choice of marital partners, and the bridewealth that normally accompanied arranged marriages. A man whose daughter went to the urban areas might never receive bridewealth for her, as she would likely enter into an informal union with a man or series of men. If bridewealth was, in fact, transferred, chances were that it would be a small amount. The marital value of such a girl would be diminished as her husband would assume that she had been "spoiled" in the town locations (FWIa:32–33, 36, 41, 43, 44, 46, 56; DCa:35, 156; AR Goromonzi 1911, 46–47; AR Salisbury 1919, 10; AR Mrewa 1918, 88). An African woman who was not "properly" married through a transferral of bridewealth, or at least her husband's labor service, was looked upon with contempt. She had not fulfilled her most important social functions, that of producing children for her husband's lineage and providing bridewealth cattle for her brother so that he, in turn, could father children for their mutual patrilineage (Holleman 1952, 66, 169, 205–206; Bourdillon 1982, 28, 47; May 1983, 22–23). Fathers were understandably worried that their daughters might become objects of scorn and ostracism.

Law, Order, and Male Authority: Controlling African Women

State officials had important political reasons for attempting to control African women's behavior. Having based their system of colonial administration on the manipulation of indigenous authority structures, coercing and cajoling local leaders into implementing state policies, colonial officials could not afford to let those structures be undermined. While European officials were expected to keep order at the level of the state, male heads of household, village elders, headmen, and chiefs were expected to maintain tight control in the villages and homesteads. Rather than destroying African male authority *in toto,* the colonial state attempted to harness it for its own ends.

The flight of women to missions, mines, farms, and urban areas posed a serious threat to the maintenance of law, order, and male authority—and consequently, to the entire system of indirect rule.[4] Given the widespread objection of rural patriarchs to their daughters' employment, those girls who presented themselves for domestic service were frequently regarded with suspicion by the European community. According to one missionary, "The best type of native parent is not anxious to let his daughters come into town owing to the [moral] dangers." Consequently, another missionary concluded, "[T]he only girls to be obtained for service are likely to be rebels against parental authority and not the best sort of girls" (DCb:65; FWIa:56).

A staunch supporter of the system of African chiefly authority, the Federation of Women's Institutes was concerned that domestic service not serve as an escape hatch for women and girls leaving their homes without the permission of their husbands or male guardians (FWIa:9–10). The European women's organization suggested an amendment to the pass law, Ordinance 16 of 1901, stipulating that African women and girls seeking domestic employment be required to obtain permits from senior administration officials. Such permits would be granted only "at the request of the guardian ... of the native female in question" (FWIa:9–10). Like their male counter-parts, European women were more concerned with the maintenance of African male authority and control over female mobility than with any grievances that might cause women and girls to flee their homes in the first place (DCa:112; also see DCa:22–23; DCb:2).

In 1932, following the advice of the Federation of Women's Insti-tutes and numerous witnesses of its own, the state-sponsored Depart-mental Committee on Native Female Domestic Service, proposed,

> Native girls entering towns should be required to present them-selves at the office of the local official of the Native Department for registration, and . . . should be required to bring with them evidence to show that their coming to town to seek work has the approval of their parents or guardians. (NFDL:10–11; also see DCc:12)

The recommendation became law in 1936, with the passage of the Natives Registration Act. Henceforth, the state had the legal means to control the flow of African women into the towns and, in the process, to bolster the domestic authority of rural elders.

The Resistance of Female Servants

While some Europeans clamored for more African female domestic workers, others complained that girls were vastly inferior servants compared to boys and men. In many instances, descriptions of the girls' "unsuitability" for domestic service brought to light vivid im-ages of female resistance. Contrary to the stereotype of the submis-sive female, African women and girls actively contested European authority by insisting upon better treatment, neglecting their duties, "dawdling," "forgetting," feigning illness or lack of comprehension, and finally, as a last resort, desertion.

In some instances, female servants raised the ire of their employ-ers by demanding more varied rations of higher nutritional content. That such girls did not know their "place" and aspired to European standards was more than some European women could bear. Mrs. W. Russell of Bulawayo voiced the concern of many employers when she complained that female servants were completely spoiled:

> The girls do not want mealie meal for breakfast. They demand oatmeal porridge. They demand food other than the natives ordi-narily get. It should be sufficient if a girl get mealie meal, sugar and milk. Wherever they are trained their tastes should be kept

simple. I have no reason to think that the Missions put these ideas into their heads, but they might help to combat things like this. (DCa:126, 137; DCb:80)

Then striking difference between African and European diets constituted an import social and cultural boundary that, according to European stipulations, was not to be transgressed. Some settlers went so far as to claim "that the African constitution thrived on the [maize] porridge alone." The motivation for this assertion was not purely economic. By showing Africans to be "different," European settlers reinforced the cultural constructs that maintained social distance and hierarchy (Kennedy 1987, 164). In challenging these norms, female servants threatened to upset a delicately balanced social order.

Other Europeans contended that African girls were simply more "backward" than their brothers and thus could provide little satisfaction as domestic servants. In 1902, the Jesuit father, Richard Sykes, maintained that the girls taught by the Dominican Sisters at Chishawasha Mission were "so feather-headed and incapable of understanding anything serious connected with life, that it is impossible to engage their attention for more than a few moments at a time or to get them to do any work, even such as sewing or washing." If such girls are to be made to work at all, the priest maintained, "eternal patience is needed. . . . The implanting in them of habits of industry will be most painfully slow" (Sykes 1903, 181; also see FWIa:18, 35).

Throughout the colony, "raw native females straight from their kraals" were held in particular contempt. They were considered to be obstinate, disobedient, and disrespectful to their mistresses. A "raw" African girl, contended H. Franklin, "is devoid of personal cleanliness, hygiene, and takes a half-hearted interest in her work; worse still, her morals are negligible. She detests being continually reminded to perform some neglected duty" (FWIa:40). Miss Sturgeon, a matron at Umtali High School's Junior Hostel, held that the girls employed by the hostel were "generally slow and useless," and charged that "they go sick for very little reason." Taking exception to Mr. Franklin's generalization, she claimed that the worst offenders were not the new arrivals from rural homesteads, but those who were "just from school" and apt to put on airs. Although they had come from various mission schools, they were unable—or unwilling—to do any of the tasks assigned to them. "I have tried to train them but find it impossible," Miss Sturgeon complained (DCa:10).

The possibility that African servants were intentionally "not learning" as a form of resistance merits consideration (Kirkwood 1984, 157; Phimister 1988, 83, 86; Beinart and Bundy 1980, 272). In February 1898, for instance, Mary Lewis, a settler wife, wrote about her difficulties with her male domestic help, "In teaching them a duty such as turning out a room, no detail must be overlooked the first time, or the same omission will be repeated *ad infintum* until it gets so on his mind that dismissal is the only cure." Mrs. Lewis claimed that many European women who had "been reared in homes refined or luxurious" were forced to learn the arts of housekeeping— cooking, laundry, gardening—before they could teach and supervise their servants. She had one male servant who was so "scornful of [her] attempts" that she could not control him. To salvage her dignity, she fired him (Lewis 1960, 36). Whether male or female, servants who were privy to their mistress's ignorance and insecurity were likely to manipulate the situation to their own advantage.

Other purported weaknesses of African females were considered even more serious. African girls were more "prone to desertion" than boys, charged the native commissioner of Umtali. "On the slightest disagreement with their mistresses or even without any apparent reason, [girls] will suddenly disappear," he complained. It was not, he stressed, a purely biological phenomenon. "Until the pass ordinance was introduced," he noted, desertion "was a common fault with [adult] male natives." Similarly, the desertion of African boys was "only now being checked by the operation of the Juvenile Employment Act," which rendered desertion from service a criminal offense. A number of Europeans urged that the Juvenile Employment Act be amended to include African girls (FWIa:23; also see DCa:16, 22–23).

Mrs. Bell, wife of the superintendent of the Junior School Hostel at Umtali, complained that because so few girls were available for service, those who were employed had an unfair edge over their employers. "If ever we have any reason to scold a girl or reprimand her in any way she knows she cannot be replaced easily and this places us in an awkward position," Mrs. Bell protested. Once a girl knew she would not be fired, she was likely to become indisciplined and gain the upper hand. Conversely, if the girls decided to leave, nothing could stop them. Out of a total of eleven female servants at the hostel, five were planning to return home at the end of the term, Mrs. Bell testified (DCa:30, 34).

The Black Peril

The decades-long debate concerning African female domestic services was sprinkled with references to the black peril—sexual offenses allegedly committed against European women by African men. Taken in by the stereotype that African men were harder and more efficient workers than women and girls, many Europeans both desired male labor and feared it. The need for African male labor was counterbalanced by the conviction that white women in close contact with black men were in certain danger of being raped or otherwise molested.

The basis of the black peril hysteria was the European presumption that white women were objects of black men's uncontrollable sexual desires. Tony Marston, the young English observer in Doris Lessing's novel, *The Grass Is Singing,* concluded that one of the foundations of the color bar in Southern Rhodesia was "the jealousy of the white man for the superior sexual potency of the native" (Lessing 1961:197). While proclaiming that black men were like animals, unable to contain their sexual passions, white men discreetly covered their own deep feelings of sexual inferiority. For the sake of "white civilization" and the survival of the colony, it was essential that European men maintain their dominance and authority in all spheres—political, economic, social, and sexual. If black men could be cast as lecherous villains, rather than victims forced by settler law to live apart from their wives and families, European society could absolve itself of responsibility for the damaging effects of male labor migration on African family life.

The wave of black peril accusations that swept through Southern Rhodesia between 1890 and 1939 mimicked those in South Africa, where large numbers of white women claimed they had been sexually assaulted by black men. Van Onselen notes that in South Africa, "the majority of such attacks of public hysteria coincided with periods of stress or acute tension within the political economy" of the territory (van Onselen 1982, 47, 50–51). In the case of Southern Rhodesia, major black peril scares took place in 1902, 1905 to 1906, 1908, 1910 to 1911, 1924, 1929, and 1932 (Kennedy 1987, 235 n. 62; Phimister 1988, 195). The outbreaks of 1902 and 1932 occurred during periods of severe economic depression, when wages fell and Africans and Europeans competed for scarce jobs and agricultural markets. Those of 1908 and 1910 to 1911 coincided with a dramatic increase in

European immigration. According to Dane Kennedy, such strains on the social fabric "set white settlers at odds among themselves." Ultimately, when these pressures had "frayed the racial threads that bound them into a cohesive community, the specter of black peril arose to instruct and remind white settlers of their common needs and their common fears" (Kennedy 1987, 145–146). In other words, black peril accusations—the vast majority based on unfounded claims—seem to have been intentionally fomented in order to forge racial unity in the white community during periods of social and economic duress (Kennedy 1987, 129; Stoler 1989a, 137–138).

Yellow and White Perils

While black peril was on everyone's lips, some Europeans were more apprehensive about the less publicized yellow peril—miscegenation as a result of sexual relations between European men and African women. Representations to the Native Affairs Committee of Enquiry in 1910 and 1911 alleged that "irregular sexual relations" frequently existed between white men and black women, with concubinage being "infinitely more frequent" than marriage (SR:par. 6.43; also see Kennedy 1987, 175–178). As Tony Marston, the young Englishman in Lessing's novel, observed, such "white ruling-class hypocrisy" was the first thing to strike a new arrival in Southern Rhodesia. For it was a country in which "coloured children appear plentifully among the natives wherever a lonely white man is stationed" (Lessing 1961, 197; also see Mason 1958, 241–243).[5]

Such relations were not simply the result of an imbalance in the ratio of European women to men during the early colonial period. Victorian racial and gender ideology placed European women on a pedestal and held them up as the epitome of purity and chastity. At the other extreme, African women represented to the European mind all that was carnal—the embodiment of lust and animal sexuality. Writing to the *Rhodesia Herald* in 1926, N. H. Wilson related his view of African female sexual behavior. "Their passions are stronger," he wrote. "They have more of the animal about them in sex matters and they have not the restraint and control that white women have." As such, these women were alluring to European men, who would find the same uninhibited behavior totally objectionable in their wives (Steele 1972, 125).

Whether many African women consented to such relationships of their own free will is highly questionable. As in the United States antebellum South, many European masters exercised seignorial rights over the bodies of black women employed in their homes, hence the term "white peril."[6] Lawrence Vambe, who was born near Salisbury in 1918, notes that toward the end of the 1930s, an increasing number of African women were employed as nannies for European children. He claimed that sometimes these women were "expected to sleep with their white masters while the "missus" was away" (Vambe 1976, 190–191; also see Kennedy 1987, 140, 175–176). While black women may have subtly resisted the mistress in the kitchen, to resist the master in the bedroom was a different matter. A black woman's "ignorance" of proper procedures or "misunderstanding" of her mistress's command was rationalized by the prevailing racial and gender hierarchies. However, to resist the master's sexual advances, when his meaning was unequivocally clear, was to show blatant insubordination. A woman who engaged in such actions was "asking" to be fired—or worse.

During the first two decades of colonization, when settler society was composed primarily of hunters, adventurers, and mining prospectors, transgressions of the sexual color bar were generally tolerated. Disproportionately single and male, European settlers were less concerned with "keeping up standards" and "protecting white womanhood" than with meeting their own sexual, emotional, and housekeeping needs. While buttressed by social mores, the color bar was not enshrined in law. After the first decade of the twentieth century, the proportion of females in the European population increased dramatically, expanding from 34 percent in 1911 to 44 percent in 1921. Within the course of a single generation, immigration and high marriage and birth rates resulted in the establishment of a permanent, family-oriented European community (Phimister 1988, 100). Violations of the sexual color bar were no longer so readily endured.

As guardians of western civilization and its moral code, European women had a political as well as a personal stake in discouraging sexual relationships between European men and African women. Carnal relations between the white master and the "subject races" reduced European dignity, threatening the ideological underpinnings of the colonial order (Gartrell 1984, 168–169, 171; also see Kennedy 1987, 141, 143, 153–154, 176; Stoler 1989b, 651–652). Acting as a vice squad policing "the sexual boundaries between the races," white women were crucial to the maintenance of the relations of domination upon which the colonial order was based (Gartrell 1984, 169, 182; also see Kennedy 1987, 167, 174, 176–177, 179; Strobel 1987, 378, 380, 383; Stoler 1989b, 648–649). If the perpetuation of colonial rule was based upon the assumption of white supremacy and contingent upon the maintenance of European prestige, privilege, and power, then it was incumbent upon European women to enforce social distance between the dominators and the dominated (Brownfoot 1984, 190; Hansen 1989, 98–106; Stoler 1989a, 147–149). True to this function, the majority of European women in Southern Rhodesia opposed the employment of African women in their households—where they would be constant temptations to the master and his sons.

European Alternatives to African Labor

The choice between black and yellow peril could be avoided altogether only if alternatives to African labor were provided. Hence, a broad range of proposals were considered, including the employment of European girls of Rhodesian birth, the importation of female servants from "home," increased utilization of labor-saving devices, and a move to reinvolve European wives and daughters in housework. The Federation of Women's Institutes heard many of these suggestions in 1930, including the recommendation that the availability of "cheap electric power" be expanded in the urban areas "to enable European women to do more of their own domestic work" (FWIa:5, 8, 34,48; DCa:115).

There were two major barriers to the employment of European girls in domestic service. The first was the negative view of domestic work. Few white women would willingly accept the demotion from mistress to maid, as they generally considered household chores to be fit only for blacks. If European women were seen doing such work, especially by Africans, they would lose their dignity and prestige (Kennedy 1987, 153; Strobel 1987, 384). The second constraint was economic. Bishop Chichester contended that "it would be economically impossible to employ European girls in domestic service," as the wages they would demand would be far too high. Moreover, he asserted, "I do not think they would do anything like the amount of work native boys do" (DCa:118).

While the government's Native Female Domestic Labor Committee stated that the employment of European girls, rather than African men or women, "in all forms of domestics work" was the ideal course, it was not the most practical one. The local supply of available European girls was extremely limited. Importation from abroad was not feasible on a large scale. Finally, the Committee concluded, "there are financial and social reasons which prevent the substitution of white servants for natives from forming a solution of the problem of domestic labor" (NFDL:16).

The unwritten implication was that European women could not be seen performing the same menial tasks as their social inferiors. Perhaps the Committee recalled what Lessing later described as the most important ground rule of Southern Rhodesian society: "Thou shalt not let your fellow whites sink lower than a certain point; because if you do, the nigger will see he is as good as you are" (Lessing 1961, 189). For the sake of preserving European law, order, and political domination, there was a need to preserve appearances. Perhaps it was for this reason that the Committee predicted that the majority of European households would continue to employ African servants, be they male or female (NFDL:16). African women and men, European women, missionaries, and the colonial state saw to it that those employees would be predominantly African males.

Notes

1. When discussing the colonial period, Zimbabwe will be referred to by its colonial name, "Southern Rhodesia." Unless otherwise indicated, documents cited in the footnotes are housed at the National Archives of Zimbabwe in Harare, Zimbabwe.

2. The same pattern held true in colonial Northern Rhodesia and continues in present day Zambia. On the Witwatersrand of South Africa, it was not until World War II that African women began to outnumber men in the domestic service sector. For an extensive analysis of the question of female domestic labor in Northern Rhodesia/Zambia, see Hansen 1984,219–238; 1986a,57–81; 1986b,18–23; 1989; 1990. For the South African case, see Cock 1980; Gaitskell 1979,44–69; 1983,241–256; Gaitskell et al. 1983,86–108; van Onselen 1982,1–73.

3. The refusal of local women to enter domestic service was not unique to the Salisbury District. Throughout the entire territory there were 590 African women and 17,239 African men engaged in domestic service in 1921. By 1926, the numbers had increased to 910 and 24,007 respectively (FWIa:18).

4. Colonial officials in Northern Rhodesia and Tanganyika expressed a similar understanding of the relationship between patriarchal control over female mobility and sexuality and the survival of the system of indirect

rule. See Chauncey 1981,136, 153; Parpart 1986,143; 1988,115, 119–120; Chanock 1985,111–124, 207–208; Mbilinyi 1988,3, 11–12, 25.

5. For a discussion of a similar situation in Northern Rhodesia, see Hansen 1989,87–98. For the Uganda Protectorate and colonial Nigeria see Gartrell 1984,168; Callaway 1987,48–51.

6. For a discussion of white men's rape of black slave women in the American South, see Lerner 1973,149–163, 210; Jones 1986,20, 27. For the South African case, see Gaitskell 1979,49–50; van Onselen 1982,17, 64 n. 67.

Bibliography

Archival Sources

NATIONAL ARCHIVES OF ZIMBABWE

(AR) N9/1/1–26: Annual Reports for administrative districts, 1898–1923; CNC S235/501–518: Annual Reports for administrative districts, 1924–1940.

(DCa) CNC S235/475, *Departmental Committee on Native Female Domestic Service.* Evidence taken at Umtali, 15–17 August 1932. Evidence taken at Salisbury, 13–16 September 1932.

(DCb) S1561/48, *Departmental Committee on Native Female Domestic Service.* Evidence taken at Bulawayo, 29–31 August 1932.

(DCc) CNC S235/475, *Report of the Departmental Committe on Native Female Domestic Labour.* 27 October 1932.

(FWIa) CNC S235/475, Federation of Women's Institutes of Southern Rhodesia. *Report of the Standing Committee on Domestic Service.* July 1930.

(FWIb) S1561/48, Federation of Women's Institutes of Southern Rhodesia. "Memorandum: Suggested Terms of Reference for a Commission of Domestic Service." May 1930.

(NFDL) S1561, Correspondence: Native Female Domestic Labour Committee, Salisbury, to Colonial Secretary, October 1932.

JESUIT ARCHIVES, HARARE

(SR) Box 317. Southern Rhodesia. 1911. *Report of the Native Affairs Committee of Enquiry, 1910–11.* Salisbury: Government Printer.

Books and Articles

Beinart, William, and Colin Bundy. 1980. State Intervention and Rural Resistance: The Transkei, 1900–1965. In *Peasants in Africa; Historical and Contemporary Perspectives,* ed. Martin A. Klein, 271–315. Beverly Hills: Sage Publications.

Bourdillon, Michael. 1982. *The Shona Peoples; An Ethnography of the Contemporary Shona, with Special Reference to their Religion.* Gweru: Mambo Press.

Brownfoot, Janice N. 1984. Memsahibs in Colonial Malaya: A Study of European Wives in a British Colony and Protectorate, 1900–1940. In *The Incorporated Wife*, ed. Hilary Callan and Shirley Ardener, 186–210. London: Croom Helm.

Callaway, Helen. 1987. *Gender, Culture and Empire; European Women in Colonial Nigeria.* Chicago: University of Illinois Press.

Chanock, Martin. 1985. *Law, Custom and Social Order; The Colonial Experience in Malawi and Zambia.* New York: Cambridge University Press.

Chauncey, George, Jr. 1981. The Locus of Reproduction: Women's Labour in the Zambian Copperbelt, 1927–1953. *Journal of Southern African Studies* 7:135–164.

Clarke, Duncan G. 1974. *Domestic Workers in Rhodesia; The Economics of Masters and Servants.* Mambo Occasional Papers, Socio-Economic Series No. 1. Gwelo: Mambo Press.

Cock, Jacklyn. 1980. *Maids and Madams; A Study in the Politics of Exploitation.* Johannesburg: Ravan Press.

England, Kersten. 1982. A Political Economy of Black Female Labour in Zimbabwe 1900–1980. B.A. thesis, University of Manchester.

Gaitskell, Deborah. 1979. "Christian Compounds for Girls": Church Hostels for African Women in Johannesburg, 1907–1970. *Journal of Southern African Studies* 6:44–69.

———. 1983. Housewives, Maids or Mothers: Some Contradictions of Domesticity for Christian Women in Johannesburg, 1903–39. *Journal of African History* 24:241–256.

Gaitskell, Deborah, Judy Kimble, Moira Maconachie, and Elaine Unterhalter. 1983. Class, Rase and Gender: Domestic Workers in South Africa. *Review of African Political Economy* 27/28:86–108.

Gartrell, Beverley. 1984. Colonial Wives: Villains or Victims? In *The Incorporated Wife*, ed. Hilary Callan and Shirley Ardener, 165–185. London: Croom Helm.

Hansen, Karen Tranberg. 1984. Negotiating Sex and Gender in Urban Zambia. *Journal of Southern African Studies* 10:219–238.

———. 1986a. Domestic Service in Zambia. *Journal of Southern African Studies* 13:57–81.

———. 1986b. Household Work as a Man's Job; Sex and Gender in Domestic Service in Zambia. *Anthropology Today* 2:18–23.

———. 1989. *Distant Companions: Servants and Employers in Zambia, 1900–1985.* Ithaca: Cornell University Press.

———. 1990. Body Politics: Sexuality, Gender, and Domestic Service in Zambia. *Journal of Women's History* 2:120–142.

Holleman, J.F. 1952. *Shona Customary Law, with Reference to Kinship, Marriage, the Family and the Estate.* London: Oxford University Press.

Jones, Jacqueline. 1986. *Labor of Love, Labour of Sorrow; Black Women, Work and the Family, From Slavery to the Present.* New York: Vintage Books.

Kennedy, Dane. 1987. *Islands of White; Settler Society and Culture in Kenya and Southern Rhodesia, 1890–1939.* Durham: Duke University Press.

Kirkwood, Deborah. 1984. Settler Wives in Southern Rhodesia: A Case Study. In *The Incorporated Wife,* ed. Hilary Callan and Shirley Ardener, 143–164. London: Croom Helm.

Lerner, Gerda, ed. 1973. *Black Women in White Ameria; A Documentary History.* New York: Vintage Books.

Lessing. Doris. 1961. *The Grass is Singing.* Harmondsworth: Penguin Books.

Lewis, Mary Blackwood. 1960. Mrs. Mary Blackwood Lewis's Letters About Mashonaland, 1897–1901. *Rhodesiana* 5:14–53.

Mason, Philip. 1958. *The Birth of a Dilemma; The Conquest and Settlement of Rhodesia.* London: Oxford University Press.

May, Joan. 1983. *Zimbabwean Women in Colonial and Customary Law.* Gwero: Mambo Press.

Mbilinyi, Marjorie. 1988. Runaway Wives in Colonial Tanganyika: Forced Labour and Forced Marriage in Rungwe District, 1919–1961. *International Journal of the Sociology of Law* 16:1–29.

Mosley, Paul. 1983. *The Settler Economies; Studies in the Economic History of Kenya and Southern Rhodesia, 1900–1963.* Cambridge: Cambridge University Press.

Parpart, Jane L. 1986. Class and Gender on the Copperbelt; Women in Northern Rhodesian Copper Mining Communitites, 1926–1964. In *Women and Class in Africa,* ed. Claire Robertson and Iris Berger, 141–160. New York: Africana Publishing Co.

———. 1988. Sexuality and Power on the Zambian Copperbelt: 1926–1964. In *Patriarchy and Class; African Women in the Home and the Workforce,* ed. Sharon B. Stichter and Jane L. Parpart, 115–138. Boulder: Westview.

Phimister, Ian. 1988. *An Economic and Social History of Zimbabwe, 1890–1948; Capital Accumulation and Class Struggle.* New York: Longman.

Schmidt, Elizabeth. 1988. Farmers, Hunters, and Gold-Washers: A Reevaluation of Women's Roles in Precolonial and Colonial Zimbabwe. *African Economic History* 17:45–80.

———. 1990. Negotiated Spaces and Contested Terrain: Men, Women, and the Law in Colonial Zimbabwe, 1890–1939. *Journal of Southern African Studies* 16:622–648.

———. 1991. Patriarchy, Capitalism, and the Colonial State in Zimbabwe. *Signs* 16:732–756.

Steele, Murray Cairns. 1972. The Foundations of a "Native" Policy; Southern Rhodesia, 1923–1933. Ph.D. diss., Simon Fraser University.

Stoler, Ann L. 1989a. Rethinking Colonial Categories: European Communities and the Boundaries of Rule. *Comparative Studies in Society and History* 31:134–161.

———. 1989b. Making Empire Respectable: The Politics of Race and Sexual Morality in 20th-Century Colonial Cultures. *American Ethnologist* 16:634–660.

Stoneman, Colin, and Rob Davies. 1981. The Economy: An Overview. In *Zimbabwe's Inheritance,* ed. Colin Stoneman, 95–126. London: Macmillan.

Strobel, Margaret. 1987. Gender and Race in the Nineteenth- and Twentieth-Century British Empire. In *Becoming Visible: Women in European History,* ed. Renate Bridenthal, Claudia Koonz, and Susan Stuard, 375–396. Boston: Houghton Mifflin.

Sykes, Richard, S.J. 1903. Chishawasha in 1902. *Zambesi Mission Record* 2 (January).

Vambe, Lawrence. 1976. *From Rhodesia to Zimbabwe*. London: Heinemann.

van Onselen, Charles. 1982. The Witches of Suburbia: Domestic Service on the Witwatersrand, 1890–1914. In *Studies in the Social and Economic History of the Witwatersrand, 1886–1914*. Vol. 2, *New Nineveh*, 1–73. London: Longman.

Weinrich, A.K.H. 1976. *Mucheke: Race, Status and Politics in a Rhodesian Community*. New York: Holmes and Meier.

Zimbabwe Women's Bureau. 1980. *Black Women in Zimbabwe*. Salisbury: Zimbabwe Women's Bureau.

9   Men at Work in the Tanzanian Home: How Did They Ever Learn?

Janet M. Bujra

> *I didn't know how to wash up or clean floors—at home our sisters do that.*
>
> *Male house servant*

> *It's just natural for them [men]. They* know.
>
> *Female employer*

Ideology, as Edmund Leach once remarked in relation to myth, is "a language of argument, not a chorus of harmony" (1954, 279). Ideologies of domesticity are no exception, though feminists have sometimes argued otherwise. In this case study of male domestic servants in Tanzania, I show that not only do workers hold inconsistent or situational ideologies regarding gender and work—housework being unmanly at home, but manly if it generates a wage packet—but employers too hold contradictory views, their view of men as the best and most suitable domestic workers conflicting with their own domestic arrangements in which women take the major responsibility.

The historical predominance of men in domestic service in this example offers a mirror image to more familiar patterns of domestic work as a female ghetto, often explained as the transfer from the home to the work place of domestic skills, the lowly status that devalues those skills and the demeanor of subordinates. This too I want to question, by looking critically at struggles over the way in which skills appropriate to this occupation are defined, acquired, and evaluated. By considering a case where men rather than women have always been the dominant labor force in domestic service, I argue that an apprenticeship in gender subordination is not essential even to acquiring domestic skills for wage work: class subordination is sufficient in itself to produce this effect, while class differences render the ideological link between gender and domesticity a contradictory one.

Recognizing that ideological discourse is often a babel of competing voices also throws into question the thesis that gendered forms of occupational segregation in the Third World are simply imposed from outside.

This study is based on field work carried out in 1986 in Tanga, an industrial town of over 100,000 people in northern Tanzania,[1] and on historical research both in Tanzania (National Archives and personal interviews) and in Britain by way of tracing European excolonial residents of what was then the territory of Tanganyika. The account encompasses events that happened "within living memory," with the earliest reminiscences relating to the 1920s. Within this period much has changed in Tanzania: especially consequential was the end of colonial rule in 1961, which gave way to an independent African government, and Tanzania has since attempted an exercise in "socialist" policies and practice (see Coulson 1982). Domestic service, however, persists, not as an unchanging institution, but as one that has not been dramatically transformed.[2]

My account concerns domestic workers of a particular kind: those whose employment is of a relatively formalized contractual nature, and who work for employers at the highest class level. In Tanzania domestic help is taken on by families at all levels of society, but in many cases this involves taking in adolescents (usually girls or young women, and often, but not always, poorer relatives) who help out in return for their keep, assistance with school fees, or clothes (Mascarenhas and Mbilinyi 1983:19; Koda et al. 1987:5). Sometimes it involves the payment of pocket money, or of cash to parents. At best this relationship can be one of mutuality, at worst one of exploitative degradation.[3] At the higher levels of society such informal arrangements are increasingly supplanted or supplemented by domestic service based on the impersonal cash nexus, performed by strangers for a wage.

During the colonial period the employers of such servants in Tanganyika were mainly Asians and Arabs (mostly engaged in commercial ventures), and Europeans (colonial officials, settler farmers and estate managers, missionaries, commercial agents, etc.) In the post-colonial period, the proportion of European and Asian employers has declined, and the employing class now includes an expanding category of Africans, most of whom are officials in state and parastatal companies (enterprises set up by the state but with organizational authority from government).

The majority of formally employed servants have always been male,[4] and men continue to be the *preferred* workforce by most employers, even though women are now beginning to move into the occupation in increasing numbers, and are often paid less than men. Domestic skills, when performed as wage labor, are regarded in Tanzania as male skills. That this has long been so, and in the least likely areas, is evidenced by this comment from the Women's Service League for Tanganyika (WSLT) in 1948: "Boys have usually proved more satisfactory as nurses to children than have women." In 1986 I still found a few examples of young men being employed by African women as baby minders, even one for a female child, and all of these were highly spoken of by their employers.[5] Men are also employed to clean and cook, to wash and iron, to garden and to guard houses. As I show here, most of these tasks, with the major exception of the last, were sex-stereotyped amongst Africans themselves as "women's work," and commonsense might have led us to expect a predominantly female work force in this occupation, or at least a preference for those assumed by both Europeans and Africans "naturally" to have these skills—that is, women. I explain why this is only now beginning to happen, and how, in this particular case, men have ended up doing "women's work" better than women.

Socialization and the Segregated Labor Force: The Debate

The skills mobilized in domestic wage work are of two kinds, the first commonly denoted "performance skills" (technical aptitude in the performance of tasks), the second "ideological skills" (the successful adoption of appropriate demeanor—in this case servility, humility, deference, etc). Feminists and others have often assumed that there is a transfer of technical skills and appropriately deferential attitudes from the domestic arena or school to the workplace, and that it is the "fit" between the two that makes domestic service a "woman's job."

This thesis was originally formulated in feminist writings on the developed capitalist world: women's work in general, and the lowly status accorded to it, was argued to be an extension of women's domestic role. Western feminist scholarship defined socialization of women as an apprenticeship in acquiring the relevant skills, and the relative cheapness of women's labor as the appropriation by employers of women's domestic skills, ideologically and materially devalued (Comer 1974; Oakley 1976; Taylor 1979; Phillips and Taylor 1980). Such theses were then reworked to explain gender segregation in wage work in Third World countries, most notably in the case of factory work by Elson and Pearson (1981a, 1981b), but also in the case of domestic service (Cock 1980; critique by Gaitskell 1986).

There is another strand in feminist thinking that draws on and develops the work of Braverman (1974) on skill as it has been transformed by the emergence of industrial capitalism. This position recognizes that notions of skill are socially and ideologically constructed, not as a simple reflection of the gender hierarchy, but as an outcome of political struggle, especially over the length and form of training. Gaskell (1986) argues that male workers have always had the political muscle to force employers to subsidize lengthy periods of apprenticeship, thereby controlling and restricting the numbers in the particular field. This is "a process of managing the image of skill as much as it is learning to do a job" (379). Conversely, Gaskell argues, "Women's unskilled status is produced at least in part by training that is widely accessible and formally short" (378), nor do women have the power to make it otherwise. While this argument retains the assumption that there is a clear contrast between male and female workers,[6] it at least has the merit of founding their distinctive treatment in struggles in the workplace rather than reducing it to a mere "reflection" of structures elsewhere.

Gaskell's point about the accessibility of training for women, however, returns us to the family and the school—for the home is where, she claims, girls learn domestic skills (369), while typing is now available for girls within the school curriculum as preparation for life as a clerical worker. Although the general accessibility of this training means that it is almost impossible to create monopolies in what are considered to be women's skills, the assumption that these are the finally appropriate and ready-made skills for wage labor is not proven. In trying to apply it to the case of domestic servants one would have to question the presumption in Gaskell's thesis that domestic skills are common to all households and hence readily transferable from one to the other. Since skills can in fact be shown to vary by class, what is learnt at home in one class is not always the most useful knowledge for the workplace. This is compounded when ethnic/cultural differences are added to differences of class.

Male Servants in Tanzania

In this attempt to understand how men in Tanzania come to be doing a job that is usually taken to be women's work, I argue that it is necessary to unravel assumptions about gender from attempts both to explain the process of skill acquisition and the political struggle over the social construction of skills. Men, whether in Africa or elsewhere, are not usually, I would argue, technically and ideologically prepared for domestic service in the normal course of their upbringing. Since the majority of domestic servants here are men, this then raises the question of where and how they acquire the skills and appropriate attitudes to perform this job successfully.

That they did perform it successfully in Tanganyika during the colonial period is confirmed by those who employed them:

> The men were more efficient with normal housework—and more in tune with the ways of Europeans. . . . I taught M new dishes but the standard of housework and laundry work was high. S, my last house-boy, did my husband's uniform and evening kit very well indeed. Also as a waiter he was superb and laid a dinner table perfectly. (Personal communications from European excolonial employers.)

That men perform this job successfully today is attested to by the continuing practice in Tanzania of employing them in preference to women, even where there is a choice, and even amongst the more recent employing class. Glowing testimonials to their aptitude, skill, and utility are frequently offered, as in the following:

> Boys[7] are more useful because they will work both inside and outside . . . Girls can't do heavy work. They are slower than boys and they like to chatter. Boys are industrious and speedy.

Only two employers out of the sixty I interviewed claimed that women were (as one of them put it) "more attuned to the idea of housework" than men. This is to be contrasted with the opposing view that Tanzanian men do not even have to learn how to cook, wash, and iron: "It's just natural for them. They *know*."

If we listen to what working men and women have to say about domestic skills in Tanzania we would hear a different point of view. Almost without exception, servants are migrant laborers from rural areas. Men amongst them say, "At first I found all this [washing, helping to cook, cleaning the house] very difficult. At home all that is done by our mothers"; "I wasn't used to doing those kind of jobs.

Mama does that work at home—our job is to herd the cattle and goats." Men also deny that they help their wives in such tasks at home. A cook tells you that at home his wife cooks all the food, and most men are offended at the suggestion that they might assist with housework: "I never sweep at home." The response to whether help would be offered when needed tended to be, "Maybe, but I would have to know what the problem was first," or as another put it, "I might, if she were ill."

Such responses are, so far, familiar. Conversely, many men in Tanzania expect to wash their own personal clothes, especially best clothes, and if the clothes are to be ironed they will do this too. Women are far less likely to know how to iron than men.[8] This at least then might be considered a male skill that could be transferred to the work place, though the irons with which such men would be familiar are heavy charcoal irons, whereas those in use in the homes of employers are now almost universally electric.

Women also have expectations regarding the aptitudes and domestic behavior of men: "A man can't rear a child"; "A husband expects his meals to be ready for him, at his convenience"; "At home, girls are taught housework and to cultivate—their value as future wives depends on it." Observing the sexual division of labor in the homes of ordinary Tanzanians one sees that it is women's responsibility to prepare food, to clean, and to care for small children, and that husbands are either absent from the domestic scene, or if present they do little more than dandle babies, sleep, eat, or sit around with friends. Young children's play is also clearly gender-differentiated: small boys make ingenious lorries and cars out of tins, sticks and bits of rubber, while girls are to be seen "cooking" sand and mud in coconut halves. Confirmation of this domestic division of labor can be found in other accounts that touch on gender and household work in Tanzania (Koda et al. 1987, 30, 50, 66; Mbilinyi 1987, 116).

In Tanzania then, men do not enter employment as servants with ready-made domestic skills, rather the opposite: they have to overcome an aversion to performing what is seen as women's work. We should not, however, jump to the conclusion that what a girl learns at home in this particular case is necessarily "appropriate" or even marketable knowledge for securing domestic work at a higher class level. The home conditions of poor peasants do not prepare them for the kinds of work they are expected to perform in the houses of the well-off. Peasant houses are built of mud and wattle, with thatched roofs and beaten mud floors. Furniture is minimal—beds and stools, occasionally a table. The source of fuel for cooking is firewood, the pots resting on three stones above the fire, the kitchen being in the main room of the house or a separate hut. The home of employers are not only much bigger ("a separate room for everything" as one exservant put it), they are typically built of stone, brick, or concrete, with glass windows, expensive and varied items of furniture, kitchens with piped water, electric stoves and generally refrigerators, occasionally even washing machines. The work demanded and the standards set by the employer bear little relation to what a girl might learn at home.

Thus one African employer who had two teenage girls from the countryside working for her explained that when there was washing to do she called in the young man who was her cowherd. She explained that the girls were still learning—their mothers had taught them cooking, but washing bedsheets (by hand) was heavy work and they couldn't yet do it well. Another complained that her female servant, "still forgets to dust and to clean the cooker—they don't have those kinds of things in their own houses." In even more detail, as one servant, Selia, explained to me:

> We don't know how. . . . Our ways of doing things are not the same as those of Europeans or Indians. For example, in my house I have no bottle brush—if we want to clean a bottle, we put sand in it and shake until it is scoured clean. So if I come to work and see a bottle brush, will I know how to use it? Or the lavatory—at home, we have a hole over a pit which we swill down with water occasionally; or in the countryside, people are used to just digging a hole, doing what they have to do, and then covering it up. Eh Mama! if you come and see a shining lavatory, a flushing one, would you know how to clean it? And cooking—we don't grind spices, for example. Every tribe has its own way of cooking which you have to learn.

Even the agenda for child care amongst the well-off is at odds with what a peasant girl would already know. A Goan woman who employed the woman I have just quoted saw no contradiction in saying, "[N]either of us knew how to look after a baby when P was born," even though Selia had already had three children, one of whom was now grown up. One could indeed argue then, that women, far from having an advantage over men in the knowledge of appropriate domestic skills, would in fact have to unlearn familiar domestic habits, whereas men have no such conflicting socialization to break with.

There is a further instance where domestic service does not build automatically on preexisting gender-related socialization. In Tanzania, as in most of Africa, it is women who do the bulk of the agricultural work for subsistence needs (Mascarenhas and Mbilinyi 1983, 94–95). When it comes to hiring a "garden boy" however, no employer thinks of taking on a woman—this job, like that of watchman, is unquestioningly sex-stereotyped in Tanzania.

Not only is there a lack of coincidence between the home and the work place as far as skills are concerned, there are also some significant gender crossovers of skill taking place. Clearly the transfer of skills is not an adequate explanation of sex-stereotyping in this occupation. If men do not enter domestic employment with skills learnt at their mothers' knees, then this cannot be used as an explanation of their predominance in that occupation, or their status as a preferred workforce. Men must acquire the appropriate skills in some other way, generally on the job. And if men can learn such skills in the course of their job, then so too can women.

Employers' Views of Domestic Skills

Employers expect to have to train servants to fulfill their own requirements, assuming no prior skills in either women or men. "Individual employers liked their individual ways," was how one excolonial put it, whereas an Asian family in Tanga today described how their servant had "worked for Indians before, but we still had to train him, especially in how to wash clothes. He insisted on rubbing them with his hands, but we do it differently— we lay the clothes on the floor and scrub them with a brush." An African employer explained how she had to train the young woman who worked for her: "She didn't know how to iron or cook or dust. I had to show her how to wash my *khangas* [wrappers], how to hang them to dry in the shade, and not to iron them but to fold them in a special way."

Men were and are seen to be quicker to learn domestic skills than women, although employers give varying accounts of how long this takes: from two to three days up to several months. No matter what sex the servant, the period of training was recognized to be a testing one for both sides, entailing assertions of power on the part of the employer and bids for autonomy on the side of the servant. Employers did not always win the battle; servants were able to exert some

independence in defining standards of work. From the colonial period comes descriptions like the following:

> Cook No 1 cooked quite well . . . but his kitchen was very dirty and
> untidy. He had previously worked for a single man who had never
> entered the kitchen. My incursions were regarded with disfavour . .
> in his opinion "everyone has their own job." . . . She refuses to learn
> to iron, she says it "burns her blood." We are still not satisfied—he
> is dirty . . . always forgetting to sweep the cobwebs away. We have
> to stand over him all the time.

A European employer said of her male servant:

> My boy was already trained. At first I tried to insist on him doing
> things my way, but it became boring, every day reminding him. For
> example, dusting—he does it merely as a favour, not because he
> thinks it is important—they think it is a European thing—they
> don't do it at home. You have to live with patterns of work they
> have learnt from other employers.

The interest of employers in the performance skills of their servants would seem to be a twofold and contradictory one. On the one
hand, servants can be paid low wages precisely because they are
defined as "unskilled." In the late 1940s there was pressure from the
British Parliament on the Tanganyikan colonial administration to
set a minimum level to servants' wages. Locally this was resented, it
being said that "incompetent unqualified servants [may be] demanding wages far in excess of their capabilities" (Labour Commissioner,
Archives, File V14/32824, 1 Sept 1948). Incoming colonial officials
were warned in advance of the going rates of pay for various kinds of
servants (see, e.g., WSLT 1948). One way that wages could be kept
down was to employ those who could claim no prior training: "If a
housewife is capable of training a cook, a young boy would be worth
teaching, and could be employed for a considerably lower wage than
one with experience" (WSLT, 5). A modern twist to this same employer self-interest is evidenced in the comment of an African
woman on the practice of bringing young girls from the rural areas
to be servants in the town: "[T]hey are so ignorant they are grateful
for anything . . . they have not yet learnt to be greedy."

Conversely, a trained servant contributed much to the comfort and
well-being of the employer: "Servants trained by German residents
knew how to do housework well," said one excolonial. "[I] usually
found trained servants," said another, "though not always to our
own standards. [The] English tended to employ those employed origi-

nally by English, Germans by Germans, Asians by Asians etc. Greeks—well they did not bother much" (personal communications, 1987). It was generally necessary to pay higher wages for more specialized servants. In 1948 a cook could earn over Sh100 a month, although the average was nearer Sh65 or Sh70. "Houseboys" earned around Sh60 a month, female ayahs (nursemaids) around Sh50, while garden boys only earned Sh35 (see WSLT 1948, 2; National Archives V14/32824).

Present-day employers also recognize the benefits they can derive from skilled servants: "I expected to have to train her, but she already knew the work" explained an African employer. "She told me she had previously worked for an Asian family. Her standards were higher than mine! When you got up in the morning she'd already have swept and washed the floors." An African employer compared her male servant with the young woman she also had working for her:

> I taught both of them, but the girl didn't learn properly—she can't wash the nappies or clean and she is a poor cook. But the boy learnt fast and now he is incredibly good—cooks beautifully, cleans and polishes assiduously, is always eager to help and never seems to be tired.

As this last quotation suggests, employers were concerned about more than performance skills. Less tangible features of the relationship such as willingness to work, loyalty, honesty, and reliability were characteristics they appreciated almost more than technical skills in servants. In the old days this could take a decidedly feudal form, as described by one elderly European woman: "When I ran a temperature or did not feel well, O slept before my bedroom door (without my knowing it). When I found out he excused himself that he could not sleep at home thinking that I might need him. . . . [T]he old boys addressed me as Bibi Mkubwa (Grand madam)." Or as one European man put it: "All our servants were very loyal and excellent workers and maintained the high standards of my own senior appointment" (personal communication, 1987). One old servant's testimonial summed it all up: "He is a very faithful boy. He has never missed a day's work and is completely honest."

Things have not changed so very much in Tanzania today. The kind of servant who is appreciated is one who "does what he is told to do, doesn't answer back and is polite." An Asian woman praised her two servants (a man and a woman): "They work willingly, without making faces—that is most important." Dishonesty in servants is a frequent cause of complaint, and both male and female servants are blamed for this. But it is female servants who are more often felt to lack the respect necessary for the servant role: they are frequently said to be too familiar and too inquisitive about their employer's affairs. They are also said to be unreliable: "[G]irls are always sneaking off to neighbours' houses or to town, and leaving the house unprotected."

Training in Domesticity: The Servants' Perspective

From the point of view of domestic servants, the acquisition of skills has a different significance. If employers can be persuaded to recognize particular skills, then this may be utilized as a lever in bargaining for higher wages, especially if specialization restricts the supply of labor in these fields, thus leading to a better price for a particular job. It is only when workers are organized that these mechanisms can work effectively; otherwise they may have an adverse effect, leading individual workers to invest in the acquisition of special skills that are neither adequately rewarded nor appreciated.

During the colonial period it was common for wealthy European and Asian employers to have a complement of five or six servants, each one a specialist: a cook, a cook's assistant, a headboy, a houseboy, a washerman, a nurseboy or nursemaid, a garden boy, and so on. But by 1948, the WSLT was insisting that the "present cost of living" made the specialized servant prohibitive: "It should be the policy, whenever possible, to try and reduce the number of servants by encouraging them to undertake more than one kind of work" (6). Nowadays few employers have more than one or two servants, and general ability is more in demand than specialized skills.

While a Union of African Cooks and Houseservants existed in the colonial period, it was never strong enough to restrict the numbers entering domestic work, and in spite of calling at least one strike it was unable to force employers into paying better wages (Illiffe 1979; Shivji 1983). But in the early colonial days, the supply of houseservants in Tanganyika did not match demand and wages were relatively high compared to other types of work. Mlagala recounts the history of Lulapangilo Zakaria Mhemedzi, who began work as a servant for a European in the mid 1930s: "[H]e earned twelve shillings a month at first, raised to fifteen shillings in the second month because of his ability to wash and iron" (1973, 121). This was on the Lupa gold fields where Mhemedzi *chose* to be a servant rather than endure the harsh conditions suffered by miners. During this same period of economic depression, miners earned on average Sh10 per month, plantation laborers in Tanga received Sh12 to 15, general laborers in Tanga only Sh10 (Shivji 1986,48). Five years later Mzee Mhemedzi abandoned training as veterinary guard when he discovered he could earn as much by continuing in domestic service (Ibid., 125). Even in the early 1950s the average male wage was only around Sh40 per month (Ibid., 65), whereas, as we have seen above, domestic servants were mostly paid Sh50 and above, and some specialized servants were able to earn double this amount.

Since Independence, the pool of migrant labor in urban areas has expanded, without much corresponding expansion of industry. In this situation, which threatens the existing workforce of domestic servants, it is impossible for workers collectively to impose controls over the entry of new recruits, or to put pressure on employers to recognize much in the way of skill differences. Individualistic competition is intensified, but this does not mean that workers no longer have an interest in acquiring skills. Servants themselves recognize that an aptitude for domestic work, or the capacity to learn quickly, is still a matter of economic survival.

Servants who have spent a lifetime in this occupation are conscious of the fact that technical abilities are not the only factor in securing their jobs. A studied deference is also required. One old man, in telling me of his experiences in the period just before the war for independence, imitated the high-flown and patronizing tones of his European employers: "Bring tea, boy!" "Boy! Fetch water for bath!" But he also remembered his responses: "Yes Memsa'ab, ready Memsa'ab." A woman in her fifties, who had learnt cleaning in a school run by Catholic Sisters was eager to tell me how the Sisters had taught her to wash floors and polish window panes, but also to display an honest attitude: "[I]f you found anything left by the children you went and put it in the office." This show of honesty was vital to both employers and employees. Many old servants were proud of the fact that they could be trusted with money to go to the market, be left in charge at home and so on.

Today, displays of humility are less required by employers, or at least have been effectively resisted by workers in the context of socialist Tanzania. "They used to call us 'Boy', but now they say 'worker.' " This man affirmed that his employers "call me by my [first] name"—although he, like almost all other servants, does not reciprocate, using instead a term of respect. They are conscious that they should not be too familiar with employers: "I don't know what my employer's work is. A servant can't ask too many questions." They may not even attempt to use their employers' toilet facilities "out of respect." And the proper demeanor of "willingness" was seen as necessary to getting and keeping work. One woman said that her daughter would have no chance of getting a domestic job: "You have to have a cheerful face, not let your face fall or look sulky if you are asked to do something. She couldn't keep that up!" Conversely, a servant has to put up with bad-tempered employers without answering back. Servants might be asked to do degrading or demeaning tasks such as washing underwear, to which they should not demur. A young man described another instance:

> They have a dog. And for a Muslim, if the dog sniffs at you, you are polluted. I have to . . . feed it and bath [sic] it with tick medicine. I can't refuse or they will say: "If you don't want the job, be on your way." So I keep quiet.

The capacity to endure insults, to put on an appearance of docility and eagerness to work, to feign respect even where you did not feel it—all this was recognized to be necessary if one were to keep one's place. The modes of servility had to be learnt on the job by hard experience.

Technical aptitudes seem to have been acquired more willingly. I discovered that there were three major ways in which either men or women learned how to become adept in cooking and cleaning. The first and most obvious was that they were taught by employers, usually the woman of the house. Men in particular boasted of their ability to learn quickly. One who had worked for Indians said his first employer had shown him what to do—"but me, I only have to be shown once and then I understand. I learn fast." They saw the workplace as one in which a set of conventions at variance with those of their upbringing applied, conventions to which they were prepared to adapt in order to survive: "At home all that is done by our mothers. But I didn't feel bad doing it—I wanted to learn so that I could earn some money". They described how they were taught to wash floors, to cook, to adjust the dial on an electric iron. And how some employers were kind and helpful while others were never satisfied, constantly found fault, and docked their pay if they broke or lost things. "She used to rub her finger along the top of the cupboard and say: 'You not dust here!' "

Some men denigrated the domestic skills they had learnt, such as the man who said he worked as a servant because "[i]f you haven't any other skills [*ujuzi*] you have no choice. It doesn't take much learning." But his comparative reference was telling: "I am ashamed when I see people with whom I went to school and they have big jobs like doctors and managers." Other men however, spoke with pride of their ability to "polish the floors until they shone," or of particular skills that they had struggled to acquire: "The hardest thing to learn was ironing—it really needs skill—you can easily burn the clothes."

Women learnt in precisely the same way. A woman of twenty who went to work for a European described her experience:

> I didn't know how to do the work, but the woman said she would teach me. She showed me how to wash windows, clean the floors and sweep, also to do all their washing. She taught me not to use so much soap. Our clothes are very dirty so we use a lot of soap but Europeans' clothes are cleaner.

Other women told of how they were introduced to "red floor polish," and told how to clean the floor not by "sloshing water all over it and spattering the walls." One woman explained how her Asian employer had taught her how to make *chapatis*, and to prepare many different kinds of vegetables with a variety of spices: "[T]hey don't just throw spinach in with some coconut milk like we do." Women recognize that the skills of the workplace were different to those of the homes from which they had come, and that this was partly to do with ethnic differences, but also to do with material class distinctions: "[T]heir house had painted walls and electric light everywhere, lots of furniture, clothes and radios. . . . [T]here was so much washing to do because they were always changing their clothes."

There were two other ways of learning marketable domestic skills. Men in particular talked of learning from fellow workers: "The other servants showed me what to do." In the colonial days this was more feasible because each household had several servants. A boy might come in as a "cook's *toto*" (assistant) or as a houseboy under a headboy and work his way up in the job. One old man described how he started work in the 1920s as a nurseboy, living in with his European employers. Gradually he was taught by other servants how to do housework, and more importantly, what Europeans expected of servants. In later life therefore, he knew what was expected of him, he "didn't have to be told anything." One of the excolonials provided an interesting twist to this: "we once found that our headboy was charging the cook's *toto* a small monthly amount for being trained in housework!" Whether or not this was a common practice I cannot say.

Although now learning from other servants is not so easy, as few households employ more than one, I still found several instances of it. A young man told me how other servants had explained to him how to clean and wash floors, though he also insisted that "it doesn't take much learning." Another said that the nursemaid in the first house he had worked showed him what to do, "what the mistress expected of you and what she didn't like." For employers this is a cost-free method of training—indeed the existing staff are expected to see it as evidence of the trust in which they are held. Several employers described older servants being left to train the younger ones.

A final mode in which skills are transmitted is outside work altogether. Although neither men nor women learn these marketable domestic skills in the *normal* course of socialization, the skills once learnt were sometimes passed on within families. This was especially true of Indian culinary arts. An African woman described to me how she hoped that her ability to cook would get her a domestic job—"I can cook egg *chapatis* and *pilau* and many different dishes like that." When asked how she learned, she explained, "My father worked as a cook for Asians, and he taught my mother, and she taught me. And now I have taught my son: when he cooks you would be astonished—he cooks like a woman." A man told me that before he got a job as a houseboy his father's brother, who had also worked as a servant for many years explained the work to him. Another man learnt by moving in with his brother who was a live-in servant. By watching and helping him he became adept in the job. Men also described how fathers or brothers had taught them to iron their school clothes, so that later all they had to learn was to use an electric iron. Occasionally it was male friends who passed on the skills. In all these ways, then, we can see men learning to handle domestic jobs, not as part of the usual pattern of male socialization, but as a specific apprenticeship for wage labour. Their mentors are as likely to have been men—whether family, friends, or other servants—as women.

Wage rates for domestic service are in theory governed by minimum wage legislation today, although this is widely ignored by employers. In 1986 the minimum monthly wage was Sh810, but the average wage uncovered in my survey of employers in Tanga was just below Sh800. The highest wage was a very exceptional Sh1800, the lowest Sh400. The calculations that determine wage levels are quite complex, but we can say that skills, whether of performance or demeanor, are only recognized reluctantly by employers. The only domestic workers who can claim a skill increment are cooks, but very few specialized cooks are hired today (I found three amongst ninety-six domestic workers). Long and loyal service may be acknowleged by occasional wage rises, though usually only after a period of grumbling on the part of the servant. The longest serving employee I discovered in my survey was still paid only Sh1000 a month, after forty years of service in the same household. Moreover, if employers move away and servants are forced to seek new work, they do not carry with them those increments accrued from lengthy and skilled service.

There are, however, two areas of specialization that can more readily be translated into market advantage: laundering and cooking. It was nearly always men who saw an opportunity in these areas. Thus one old man told me how, while working for Europeans, he had observed the washerman very carefully. "I wanted to know how to wash and iron so that I could use this knowledge for myself." Later he set up as an independent laundryman, a job he was still doing thirty years later. Self-employed laundrymen are a common sight in Tanga, and many acquired their skills through private employment. I have never seen a woman doing this job, either in a private house or as an independent artisan, even though women do washing at home.

However, a woman told me how she had learnt to make *sambusa* (a savory snack) in the course of her work as a servant, and how she later established a business with her children and a neighbor, cooking and selling *sambusa*. Knowledge of the arts of cooking are more especially prized by male servants, however, and they feel aggrieved if employers do not pass on these skills to them. Although few cooks are now employed in private houses, they are better paid; more importantly, these skills can be transferred to a considerably more lucrative occupation—that of hotel work, where good cooks are regularly poached by competing entrepreneurs. Both in private houses and in hotels, cooks are almost always male. Given this situation, male servants may be prepared to endure low wages if they are learning skills that can be advantageous to them later.

Gender, Skills, and Class

Accounting for the lack of men amongst the workers in "world market factories" in South East Asia, Elson and Pearson reach the following conclusion: "If men are to compete successfully, they also need to acquire the 'nimble fingers' and 'docile dispositions' for which women workers are prized. But for this they would require to undergo the same social experience as women . . . to experience gender subordination." (1981b:155). As this case study shows however, men, like women, can learn nimble fingers and servile dispositions *on the job;* they need bear no relation to processes of gender subordination, because class domination is sufficient in itself.

I am not arguing here that women's or men's premarket skills (and the ideologies of gender inequality by which they are evaluated) are irrelevant to gender segregation in the work force, only that these skills and ideologies are not a sufficient explanation (and in some cases no explanation at all) for this phenomenon. Premarket skills and ideologies are not transferred unproblematically to the wage sector, though fortuitously they may sometimes be appropriate. In the case of domestic service, what women do at work is not simply an extension of their domestic role, because domestic labor is transformed by the terms on which it is carried out. The skills and attitudes appropriate to the wage sector are a product of the structure of relationships (power, hierarchy, solidarity) in the workplace itself, rather than an outcome of processes of gender socialization, especially when the material base of such socialization is marked by class (and often ethnic) distinctions.

In an attempt to explain the limited patterns of incorporation of women into the Ghanaian wage economy Scott eventually concludes, "This situation is the outcome of exclusionary mechanisms introduced by a foreign state and based on alien ideology" (1986, 179). Clearly such a solution would not work here, because not all the employers of servants—even in the colonial period—were foreigners. Even if they had been, it would be difficult to see the employment of male servants as a manifestation of an "alien ideology," for if Europeans brought any assumptions with them about an appropriate work force for domestic service it would have been that it be composed of women.

Hansen adds a provocative twist to the "employer preference" thesis, by reminding us that employers too are gendered, and that in the case of domestic service women employers often have a greater role in recruitment than do men. This important insight is then marshalled to back an explanation of why men predominate amongst domestic servants in Zambia:

> To account for the numerical dominance of men in service . . . a manufactured gender role which depicted African women as sexually loose and tempting to male employers must be reckoned with. Neither white women during the colonial era, nor Zambian women today wanted to employ African women as domestic servants, for fear of their [perceived] sexuality. (1986a, 22; 1989)

She adds, however, that African women did not particularly wish to be domestic servants either.

There is no doubt that the home as workplace is a profoundly contradictory context, where the intimacy between family members is brought into uncomfortable liaison with the distance required between class unequals. In the day to day close encounters of domestic life there is always the potential for sexual interest to overstep the social boundaries of class—though what is at issue in this case is not "simply" sex, but power, or a complex and contradictory mix of gender power and class power. Whereas this is usually power exerted by male employers over female servants, it can also be that of males (even servants) over female employers. For example, female employers' (manufactured?) fears of the sexual advances of *male* servants in South Africa combined with racist sentiment to generate a so-called black peril in the early years of this century (van Onselen 1982:45–54; see also ch. 8). My own study uncovered fears of both kinds, though they were not as frequently expressed as I had anticipated. Only one female employer (an African) preferred male servants because, as she said, "[G]irls steal everything, even our husbands." Female servants themselves occasionally spoke of sexual harassment by male employers, though here again it is necessary to state that some liaisons of this kind were considered advantageous by women: "You remember X? She was fortunate—she got taken up by her European [employer] and he built her a house". Conversely there were a few employers—all Asians—who expressed fears of violence, or even rape, from male servants, though in one case this was a fear expressed by a man about the safety of his womenfolk.

A complex of anxieties, whether expressed openly or not, surrounds the relationship of domestic service—fears of sexual or physical intimidation, of insubordination, of the alienation of familial affections. The important question here, however, is how the intimacy that is *beneficial to employers* is demarcated from that which is held to be dangerous to the essentially class basis of the relationship. The anxieties themselves are often contradictory in their effect on recruitment practices, cancelling out employer preferences as a simple explanation of gender divisions within the work force. If we are to find a more convincing explanation for the continuing predominance of men in this occupation we need to look not just at the demands of employers, but also at the terms on which they are satisfied. This is essentially a question about the supply of labor, and about the reproduction of labor power.

Men predominate in domestic work for the same reason that they predominate in all other forms of wage labor in Tanzania today. The coercive process whereby a wage labor force was constituted in colonial Tanganyika was not gender-neutral. It entailed forced labor, zealous recruitment, and male taxation (Shivji 1986), but it was also built on the dual need to maintain the rural productive basis for social order while at the same time drawing off exploitable labor. Gender enters the picture here by way of the sexual division of labor in agriculture, perhaps one of complementarity in the precolonial period, but increasingly one in which women's labor became central to the production of family food, while men's input decreased and became more seasonal. It was accordingly male rather than female labor power that was surplus to subsistence requirements. Consequently, when wage workers were required to work as agricultural laborers, office messengers, dockworkers, miners, or domestic servants, it was men who offered themselves for employment, leaving women in the rural areas with an intensified burden of cultivation and care of dependent family members. When women followed the men into towns it was seen as disturbing evidence of "detribalization," of a threat to the social order (Molohan 1957). Mbilinyi insists that "state intervention was used to keep women in rural areas and block their labour migration" (1988, 563).

Thus the stereotype of domestic servant was molded in male form as an outcome of processes of male labor migration. Once this act of ideological rethinking had been forced on employers and workers alike, its persistence was remarkable. As Scott remarks, "[O]nce gender segregation has crystallised in an occupation . . . it exerts a strong normative pressure on the market: there is resistance to substitution even when supply and price conditions change" (1986, 160).

In Tanzania such conditions are now changing. In the early colonial period men were able to demand wages comparable or superior to those of workers in other occupations. Growing pressure on rural households in an increasingly commoditized economy has now led to a rise in the number of women migrating to towns, where they have begun to compete with men for jobs at the bottom of the occupational hierarchy, as well as searching out niches in the urban economy where the production or petty trade of goods or services allows for a marginal existence (Sabot 1979; Mbilinyi 1985; Burja 1987). Women are now actively seeking jobs as maids of all work in private households, but they must offer their labor cheap if they are to compete with men already established in this field. The average wage for women servants in Tanga in 1986 was only Sh670, compared with Sh956 for men (employer survey).[9] Women also come up against resistance from employers who have been accustomed to think of men as having more to offer.

Men do not automatically move up into higher-grade occupations when a new wave of "green" labor begins to move in. They will only do so if more attractive opportunities present themselves. A feminization of domestic service is said to have occured in South Africa in the 1940s "as manufacturing industry expanded sharply . . . opening up better paid jobs for African men" (Gaitskell 1986:7). But Tanzania's industrial sector has been stagnant for several years, and unemployment has been a continuing problem (Coulson 1982, 196).[10] Men who do not have many other choices hold on to their servant jobs where they can.

If there is beginning to be a transformation in the gender and skill makeup of this occupation, it is due both to the changing composition of the labor supply and to the changing character of the employing class. A stratified labor market has emerged here, reflecting distinctions of class, but locally perceived in ethnic terms. European employers take on the greatest number of staff and pay wages at levels above the minimum wage. They also employ the greatest proportion of male servants, as well as those with the most specialized skills such as cooks or gardeners. African employers take on fewer domestic workers and expect them to be general workers rather than specialists. They employ the lowest proportion of men and pay wages on average below the legal minimum wage. On all these counts Asians fall somewhere in the middle. The new ruling class is remunerated on a lesser scale than its colonial predecessors; it is more concerned with petty capital accumulation than with excessively conspicuous consumption. On this account, the sheer cheapness of domestic labor can weigh more heavily than questions of "quality" or skill. African employers are also in a better position to mobilize networks of kin and clients to bring in young female servants from the countryside. Although they express a preference for male domestic workers, they are increasingly employing women for inside work. And whereas the African employing class is expanding, fewer and fewer Europeans are permanent residents.

Although women are now more available as domestic workers, and more in demand in some quarters, men have continued to hold their own overall because they are still regarded as the "best men for the job" and are motivated to sustain this view amongst employers.

Acknowledgments

I would like to thank Marjorie Mbilinyi and Caroline Ramazanoglu for their constant encouragement in the writing of this chapter; the Economic and Social Research Council of Britain for funding my research; and the many people in Tanzania and Britain whose interest and support were vital to the success of my work.

Notes

1. The data used here are based on participant observation, the collection of life histories of male and female servants, and a survey of (mainly female) employers. Forty-four life histories of women servants and ex-servants were collected; thirty-four of men. Sixty employers were surveyed, of whom 40 percent were African, 45 percent Asian, 11 percent European, and 5 percent respectively Arabs and Goans. Nearly all my work was carried out in Swahili, although English was used with Europeans, and assistance from a Gujerati interpreter helped me to interview some Asians whose English was limited or whose Asian Swahili I could not follow. Quotations from my life history work and survey are supplemented by other quotations culled from everyday life.

2. There has even been confirmation of the institution in which the wage for at least one domestic servant is built into the salary of high officials (Peter and Mvungi 1985,191).

3. Mgaya insists that "[t]he present practice amongst the working class to employ ayahs is exploitative and incompatible with the socialist aspirations of our country" (1976,145).

4. No accurate statistics exist on the number of domestic servants either in Tanzania today, or during the colonial period. Colonial Government statistics occasionally included an "estimate" of numbers in this occupation, but without breakdown in terms of gender. Literary and archival sources, however, speak almost without exception of servants as male. In the postcolonial period a random sample of over 5500 adult residents (52 percent male, 48 percent female) in seven of Tanzania's largest towns uncovered 144 domestic servants amongst "wage earners" (Bienefield and Sabot 1972). Who was counted as a domestic servant is unclear, and women's work is nearly always underestimated in survey data, but the findings provide some confirmation for my contention that domestic service at the higher class levels is still a predominantly male occupation: 86 percent were men. My own count of the ninety-six servants employed by a sample of sixty high income families in Tanga in 1986 showed that almost three quarters were male. Similarities in their terms and conditions of employment led me to count as servants both "inside" and "outside" domestic workers: gardeners and watchmen as well as cooks, cleaners, and washermen. The outside workers were all male, while amongst the inside workers, men were still in the majority (56 percent).

5. This is not unusual in Africa: see Hansen on Zambia, 1986a,22; van Onselen on South Africa, 1982,27–29.

6. This is overstated, in so far as even in Europe many men work in industries (the building trade, shop work) that are poorly unionized or where union power is insufficient to impose recognition of skill differentials or lengthy apprenticeship schemes on employers.

7. She used the Swahili word *wavulana* meaning teenage boy/young man. *Wasichana* is the female equivalent, also used for young servants. This nomenclature does not have the derogatory implications of the terms "boy" or "girl" used in English, although these English terms are also used by Africans on occasion.

8. This is almost certainly to be explained by the earlier entry of men into wage labor in the colonial period, as well as parental acceptance of formal education for boys compared to their resistance to girls' education. Both work and school were places where smart, clean, and pressed clothes were insisted upon.

9. However, it should be noted that 44 percent of the women here were living in as "part of the family," receiving payments in kind in the form of food and shelter as well as wages. Although this can be seen as a supplementary material advantage to such women, it also has to be interpreted as a sign of their lack of leverage in the employment relationship. Few servants cared to live in, as it allows them no free time and no end to their work. Only 19 percent of men lived in, and most of these lived in servants' quarters

where they enjoyed free shelter but provided their own food. Another factor in women's lower average wages is that few of them have long service in one family, most having been in post only for a few months.

10. Carter summarized the reasons for Tanzania's grave economic situation in 1986 as follows: "the toll on foreign exchange reserves exacted by the war in Uganda, the effects of the oil price shock of 1979–1980, the world recession, adverse terms of trade in Tanzania's exports, a series of drought years, and above all the decline in agricultural and industrial performance" (1986,3). More recently there has been a slight recovery, so that Carter writes of a "rehabilitation of industry" in 1988 following the Economic Recovery Programme and IMF intervention (1988,15).

Bibliography

Bienfeld, Manfred, and Richard H. Sabot. 1972. *The National Urban Mobility, Employment and Income Survey of Tanzania.* BRALUP report: University of Dar es Salaam.

Braverman, Harry. 1974. *Labour and Monopoly Capitalism.* New York: Monthly Review Press.

Bujra, Janet. 1987. Survival in a Stagnant Economy: The Struggles of (Some) Women in Tanzania. Paper presented to the Development Studies Association Annual conference, Manchester University.

Carter, Roger. 1986. Tanzania's Economic Recovery Programme. *The Bulletin of Tanzanian Affairs* 25:3–7.

———. 1988. The Economic Recovery Programme: Progress and Prospects. *The Bulleting of Tanzanian Affairs* 31:15–19.

Cock, Jacklyn. 1980. *Maids and Madams.* Johannesburg: Ravan Press.

Comer, Lee. 1974. *Wedlocked Women.* Leeds: Feminist Books.

Coulson, Andrew. 1982. *Tanzania: A Political Economy.* Oxford: Clarendon Press.

Elson, Diane, and Ruth Pearson. 1981a. "Nimble Fingers Make Cheap Workers": An Analysis of Women's Employment in Third World Export Manufacturing. *Feminist Review* 7:87–107.

———. 1981b. The Subordination of Women and the Internationalisation of Factory Production. In *Of Marriage and the Market,* ed. K. Young, et al., 144–166. London: CSE Books.

Gaitskell, Deborah. 1986. Girls' Education in South Africa: Domesticity or Domestic Service? Paper presented at the annual conference of the African Studies Association in the United Kingdom.

Gaskell, Jane. 1986. Conceptions of Skill and the Work of Women. In *The Politics of Diversity,* ed. Roberta Hamilton, and Michele Barrett, 361–380. London: Verso.

Hansen, Karen Tranberg. 1986a. Household Work as a Man's Job: Sex and Gender in Domestic Service in Zambia. *Anthropology Today* 2 (3): 18–23..

———. 1986b. Domestic Service in Zambia. *Journal of Southern African Studies* 13 (1): 57–81.

———. 1989. *Distant Companions: Servants and Employers in Zambia 1900–1985*. Ithaca: Cornell University Press.

Illiffe, John. 1979. Wage Labour and Urbanisation. In *Tanzania under Colonial Rule*, ed. Martin Kaniki, 276–306. London: Longman.

Koda, Bertha, et al. 1987. *Women's Initiatives in the United Republic of Tanzania*. Geneva: International Labour Organization.

Leach, Edmund. 1954. *Political Systems of Highland Burma*. London: Bell.

Mascarenhas, Ophelia, and Marjorie Mbilinyi. 1983. *Women in Tanzania: An Analytical Bibliography*. Uppsala: Scandinavian Institute of African Studies.

Mbilinyi, Marjorie. 1985. The Impact of the Economic Crisis on Women's Employment, Wages and Incomes in Tanzania. Paper presented at the Professorial Inaugural Lecture, University of Dar es Salaam, Tanzania.

———. 1987. "Women in Development,": Ideology and the Marketplace. In *Competition: A Feminist Taboo?* ed. Valerie Miner and Helen Longino, 106–120. New York: The Feminist Press.

———. 1988. Agribusiness and Women Peasants in Tanzania. *Development and Change* 19:549–583.

Mgaya, Martha. 1976. Study of Workers in a Factory in Tanzania. MA thesis, University of Dar es Salaam.

Mlagala, Martha. 1973. The Traveller: Lulapangilo Zakaria Mhemedzi, In *Modern Tanzanians*, ed. John Illiffe. East African Publishing House.

Molohan, M.J.B. 1957. *Detribalization*. Dar es Salaam: Government Printer.

National Archives of Tanzania.

Oakley, Anne. 1976. *Housewife*. Harmondsworth: Pelican Books.

Peter, Chris, and Sengodo Mvungi. 1985. The State and Student Struggles. In *The State and the Working People in Tanzania*, ed. Issa Shivji, 157–198. Dakar: Codesria.

Phillips, Anne, and Barbara Taylor. 1980. Sex and Skill: Notes Towards a Feminist Economics. *Feminist Review* 6:79–88.

Sabot, Richard H. 1979. *Economic Development and Urban Migration: Tanzania 1900–1971*. Oxford: Clarendon Press.

Scott, Alison. 1986. Industrialisation, Gender Segregation and Stratification Theory. In *Gender and Stratification*, ed. Rosemary Crompton and Michael Mann, 154–189. Cambridge: Polity Press.

Shivji, Issa. 1983. Working Class Struggles and Organisation in Tanzania, 1939–75. *Mawazo* 5 (2): 3–24.

———. 1986. *Law, State and the Working Class in Tanzania*. London: James Currey.

Taylor, Pam. 1979. Daughters and Mothers—Maids and Mistresses: Domestic Service between the Wars. In *Working Class Cluture*, ed. John Clarke et al., 121–139. London: Hutchinson.

van Onselen, Charles. 1982. *Studies in the Social and Economic History of the Witwatersrand, 1886–1914*. Vol. 2, *New Nineveh*. New York: Longman.

Women's Service League of Tanganyika. 1948. *Notes on African Domestic Labour in Dar es Salaam*. Dar es Salaam: Government Press.

10 Cookstoves and Charcoal Braziers: Culinary Practices, Gender, and Class in Zambia

Karen Tranberg Hansen

From the early colonial period in what then was Northern Rhodesia until today in the cities and towns of Zambia, domestic service has been a crucial wage occupation for a large proportion of men and, after independence in 1964, an increasing number of women. Their work experiences between then and now have changed and the consequences are vexing. This was the sentiment of BaNkuwa,[1] a man in his late sixties, whom I began interviewing in 1984 about his life and experience as a domestic servant to colonial white and expatriate employers after independence. "Domestic servants," he said, "lead miserable lives. In the past, they were smart. Today, cooks look like gardeners. If I had known this would become a woman's job, I would have sought work as a driver" (Hansen 1989, 215). Out of work, he complained that expatriate employers now leave the country too soon and that there are too few jobs available for skilled cooks such as he. When I asked if he would work as a servant in a Zambian household, he smiled, saying "I can't cook Zambian food." We laughed, both knowing that of course he was able to prepare Zambian food; his point was that he did not consider it to be proper work for an experienced cook.

Exploring the confrontation between ideas about work, gender, race, and class embodied in BaNkuwa's comments, this chapter considers the acquisition of skills and knowledge in colonial household employment. As such, it provides a commentary on my own analysis of continuities and changes in domestic service between the colonial period and the present in Zambia (Hansen 1989).[2] Since that study did not examine cooking practices per se, it is in the spirit of challenge that this chapter offers food for thought on cooking. In it, I raise questions about the transfer and/or transformation of skills acquired in domestic service to African households. I also examine some of the causes and consequences recent changes in the supply of foodstuffs are having on culinary practices in urban Zambian households. My specific interest is with the clash of notions concerning work, gender, and race that took place in the colonial kitchen and their refiguration in class terms in Zambian servant-employing households at the present. I am particularly concerned with the work of the cook, although I throughout, except where specified, make use of the term domestic service. And although kitchens mean very different things (Douglas 1984, 17; Lawrence 1982, 104), I occasionally use the term kitchen metaphorically for domestic service.

While acknowledging the important light that research in social history has thrown on work as a key concept in colonial ideology and the crucial role attributed to wage labor as a means for socializing Africans into new disciplines, I suggest that the importance of domestic service in this respect has largely eluded such scholarship (Cooper 1983; 1987; 1989). To be sure, the labor process throughout most of the colonial economy aimed at "breaking in" rural Africans as workers. It entailed everywhere a process of domestication. But private household services was a focal point in this process in settler colonies, for it pitched black servants and white employers in a close battle over the civilizing meaning of domestic skills. During most of the colonial period in Northern Rhodesia, servants were second to miners in terms of numbers of wage-employed Africans, and most of them were men. Their mere numbers prompt questions about their experience of work, and the fact that they almost overwhelmingly were men raises questions about gender relations, as does the gradual entry of women into service after independence.

British ideas of the proper social order in the colony hinged on maintaining African village life fairly unchanged so as not unduly to upset rural self-sufficiency and prompt urban proletarianization.[3] Late Victorian wisdom in this contrived village idea—in notions about family structures (assuming male authority), work (assuming man as breadwinners and women as housewives), and gender relations (assuming women's subordination to men)—was sufficiently ambiguous to permit interpretations that were at a variance with the bourgeois household ideal. The British in Northern Rhodesia never sought to make Africans over entirely in their own image. In the mind of contemporary whites, race made too much of a difference and so did gender. Race placed all Africans at a different level of opportunity (i.e., "civilization") than whites. But the ideology of white over black rested on gender assumptions that did not consistently oppose notions of male and female, skills and emotions, economic and domestic. The difference that gender made had the effect of construing African women and men unlike one another, and African women as even more different from white women and certainly not suitable for work in white households. So in colonial domestic service, notions of African capability and gender clashed dramatically. African women's important role as wife, mother, and farm worker was in discord with ideas concerning skills, endurance, and work capacity attributed to men servants. Because of these ambiguities and inconsistencies, domestic service is a particularly challenging arena for an examination of how Zambian men servants worked over the skills they acquired in white colonial households in the cultural ordering of their own relationships.

After a brief discussion of cooking, I first explore the kitchen as a battlefront between tools, people, and ideas that produces not only meals but particular social relations to do with gender and class. I then enter some colonial servant employing households, examining the servants' acquisition of skills. I next describe the extent of transfer/transformation of cooking skills to African households, raising questions about gender and the civilizing function of domesticity. And lastly I turn to the work of postcolonial servants to explain BaNkuwa's self-proclaimed incapacity to cook Zambian food.

Cooking and the Civilizing Encounter

For an analysis of cooking, Jack Goody takes us to the door of the household in his study of the difference between the cuisines of West Africa and those of Europe and Asia. Criticizing Claude Levi-Strauss's binary abstraction of culinary systems into so many recipes (1970; 1973; 1978) and Mary Douglas's cultural grammar of meals (1971; Douglas and Nicod 1974), Goody proposes a comparative explanation in terms of local economic production and social differentiation (1982, 17–39). Cooking, he argues, needs to be analyzed in the context of the total process of production, preparation, and consumption of food. He suggests that we find a "high" cuisine where people have differentiated access to resources. The extreme form of this differentiation is the allocation of special foods to specific roles, offices, or classes, and a gulf between them not only of quantity, but of quality, of complexity, and of ingredients (1982, 99). He also notes that the "high" and the "low" cuisines are divided sexually, and that hierarchy, specialization, and elaborate cooking are associated with men as cooks. Only in societies such as Africa did women cook at the courts of kings, but, Goody qualifies, not as household servants but as wives. What is also different in Africa, he says, is the virtual absence of alternatives or differentiated recipes either for feast or for class.

Having explained why most precolonial African societies lack a differentiated cuisine, Goody discusses the impact of industrial cooking on food and consumption style, and the creation of a new mix of diets everywhere. He observes a "tendency towards homogenisation of taste that accompanies the industrial processes of the world system," closing consumption gaps in the more advanced countries and opening them in the more peripheral (1982, 189). He is careful to note that "the direction of these changes is not determined by the world system alone. The nature of the indigenous societies is of prime importance; so too is the nature of the particular colonial encounter" (1982, 183).

Goody's acknowledgement that styles of cooking are shaped also by the particularities of the encounter between colonial culture and indigenous practices leaves open the possibility for different interpretations. In his study of the rise of sugar consumption in the West, Sidney Mintz recognizes the complicated and many-sided forces involved in changing consumption patterns. He argues, "[P]atterns will not yield unless the conditions under which consumption occurs are changed—not just what is worn, but where and when, and with whom; not just what is eaten, but where and when, and with whom" (1986, 194). The state and the market are not the only forces that provoke shift in consumption styles. An account of such changes needs to take us *inside* the household and reckon with the ideological in a wide sense of that term. As my discussion of cooking in domestic service will illustrate, this aspect certainly ties in with the socioeconomic pattern, but does not reflect it in any straightforward way.

When colonial officials in Northern Rhodesia attributed a "distinct educational value" to domestic service, they thought of their African menservants, whom they believed they might "make over" and civilize, instilling new skills, notions of individual responsibility and morality, and values of work, time, order, and cleanliness that servants would apply to improve their own household organization (Hansen 1989, 27). Many colonists thought that there was "hope" for the domestic worker. When, for example, the new capital of Lusaka was planned in the early 1930s, a personal servants' compound was laid out, separate from the general African compound, with the belief that "the boy through association with European family life, has reached a higher standard of domestic culture and civic behavior than the more unsophisticated labourer" (Bradley 1981, 13).

But the meanings of these new skills were not self-evident. They were refracted through notions of class condescension and racism that were central to the molding of domestic service conventions in Northern Rhodesia. The difference between European and African diets constituted an important social and cultural barrier that was not erased by the African cook's work in colonial households. Thus cooking has ambiguous meanings caused by the different experiences people have of it, or, in Pierre Bourdieu's words, the dispositions "they derive from their position in economic space" (1984, 101). Cooking meant different things, depending on place in a race-divided and class-structured society, and, as I discuss shortly, on gender. While that oppressive opportunity structure scarcely allowed the transformation of Africans in the mirror image of Europeans, it did not preclude them from reworking these notions on their own terms. In short, domestic work, the colonial kitchen, and styles of cooking are influenced by more than household management with tools and resoures, the distribution of power in the economic sphere, and lifestyles and tastes (Davidoff 1976; Douglas 1971). It is also affected by people's experiences in cooking, ideas about who does it and where, and thus is it about the construction and possible transformation of particular social relationships.

Cooking, Race, and Class

Colonial whites considered Africans to be members of societies so totally different from their own in social, cultural, and moral outlook that they had to be "broken in," worked, and handled, in short to become domesticated. In private household service white women faced the task of turning African men, whom they considered as "raw natives," into domestic workers, skilled at "keeping house like in London" under circumstances where many amenities were lacking. Most colonial households employed a fair number, because servants' wages were low and because it was assumed that Africans were incapable of doing more than a simple job. So there were separate cook, house, laundry, scullery, wood, water, garden boys, and so on. From the point of view of the employer, these male servants formed a hierarchy of domains between kitchen, home, and grounds in a strict division of labor, with the kitchen at the top. The number of servants depended on locality, whether rural or urban, on the amenities present, as well as on the composition of the employing household, that is, whether or not there were children. The servants ranged from six to twelve in the early days and from three to five from the World War II years and onwards (Hansen 1989, 30–83).

Domestic work was hard work. It was labor intensive and largely done without the use of labor saving appliances even when vacuum cleaners, floor polishers, washing machines, and a variety of kitchen gadgets became more readily available. Employers considered their servants to be clumsy and butter fingered and/or unable to understand how household applicances worked. So, houseservants polished floors by hand, brushed and aired the rugs and did hand laundry. In the kitchen, the cook chopped, beat, ground, and kneaded by hand.

The colonial servant's job was specialized. He was cook, tableboy, houseboy, or worked on the grounds, and he could look forward to advancement through the ranks. Like many others, BaNkuwa had begun as a garden boy. This was around 1938, when at the age of 17 he left his Ngoni grandparents near Chipata to seek work on the Copperbelt, where his parents already were. He was soon moved into the kitchen as a *piccanin*, that is, the cook's helper. He later migrated to Southern Rhodesia, advancing through the ranks to cook in white households employing specialized servant staffs. He returned to Zambia in 1963 on the eve of independence, holding a series of jobs as skilled cook for expatriates of many different nationalities till the early 1980s.

Because employers considered them to be simple, they also thought that their servants were impressionable. Just what skills did men like BaNkuwa acquire during their life-long work in domestic service? His statement contains references to three types of skills, which I discuss in turn: cooking, etiquette, and fashion.

Men, as Janet Bujra explains in Chapter 9 for the case of Tanzania, did not enter domestic service with ready-made skills. They were trained. As a cook, Nkuwa was taught and expected to prepare a differentiated cuisine. Using a variety of locally available and imported foodstuffs, African cooks in colonial households were crucial to their employers' efforts at reproducing a familiar life-style. Some cooks could read recipes, others committed them to memory. They were taught and coached by their madams, who expected them to be able to prepare coffee and tea, and breakfasts; to make bread, cake and pastry; soup stock and sauces; to master the arts of boiling, frying, and roasting of meat, poultry, and fish; and to prepare a variety of desserts (Bradley 1939; 1948; 1950, 19–20). It is not surprising that BaNkuwa, who had worked for many different white employers, including Greeks and Jews, considered his specialized skills, which included the preparation of ovoglomo and gefillte fishe, with pride.

On my 1988 visit to his house in one of Lusaka's low-income townships, I found BaNkuwa sitting outside drinking tea with his wife. In fact, he was serving her. The serving of tea is one example of etiquette BaNkuwa learned as a worker in a labor process that was hierarchically structured in social and spatial terms. When on duty, servants wore uniforms, but rarely shoes; they were not supposed to talk unless they were spoken to; they were usually called by their first name and referred to as "boys"; they were not to use the facilities of the main house. There was subordination and discipline everywhere. Although many servants lived in small shacks at the end of their employers' gardens, this space was not theirs. They were called on at their employers' discretion and were considered always available. Their lives outside of work were not really private, for the employers decided whether spouses and dependents could live in, when and which visitors could call, and what sort of leisure-time activity might be undertaken.

Servants looked smart, said BaNkuwa. Working in white households, they certainly had a better chance than other workers to observe the rituals of dressing, the care for clothing, and the concern with fashion and style their employers pursued. They had better access to hand-me-downs. Servants were known as good ballroom dancers. Life-time servants told me how they would stand at the employer's verandah watching the whites dance and then go practice in their quarters. Many joined ballroom dancing clubs that had sprung up in most of the towns in the 1930s and 1940s. These clubs held practices several times a week and competition dances almost monthly at which whites would be invited to judge, selecting the best performers in a variety of dance styles (waltz, quick step, fox trot, and in the 1950s, tango and jive) and the best-dressed man and woman. An account of such an event in Livingstone in 1949 describes the standard of dancing as exceedingly high and the effect of the range of dress as startling: "[T]he men for the most part wore full evening dress, a lot of it many years out of date but very well taken care of." The women dressed in a variety of styles, "almost to a woman in hand-me-downs from the husband's or partner's bwana'a dona" (O'Shea, as quoted by Hansen 1989, 162–163).

Some employers and some Africans believed that the servants' privileged knowledge of the European way of life led to their easy way with African women. Chief among the activities white householders related about their men servants were drinking, gambling, and sex. They often attributed servants' tardiness on Mondays to weekend brawls, drinking, and cavorting with women in the compounds. The stereotype of the servant as womanizer struck a cord in a snappy song by popular musician Alick Nkatha in the 1950s. The song depicts the servant pursuing a beautiful woman with promises of morning coffee, toast and butter, and "so many dresses you'll be changing clothes all day" (Fraenkel 1959, 51–52). Whether or not this stereotype reflected reality, many employers preferred to hire married men as their servants, with the assumption that a married man takes his job seriously since he has wife and dependents to provide for.

My discussions with colonial menservants, their wives, and their employers converge on one issue: the disassociation of African men's paid domestic work from any female gender connotation. Domestic service, as I said before, was a "job of work" which men learned from their employers. It was wage labor. And men did wage labor; women stayed home. The work of African servants was skilled work, men's work.

Domestic Skills, Knowledge, and Culture

Did men like BaNkuwa apply these skills in their own context of living? An answer to this question is ambiguous, for it depends not only on cultural practices based on gender and age that informed interpersonal interaction in African households, but also on the restrictions colonial rules and regulations placed on the transfer of Western derived notions of domesticity to African homes. Gender relations in African households required women to feed the family. Zambian women's cooking consisted of a starchy staple and a relish of vegetables, meat or fish eaten with it, the difference between rich and poor being largely one of quantity eaten rather than of quality of ingredients and elaboration of preparation. To be sure, there were variations. For starches, there were sorghum, millet, cassava, and maize. The cultivation and consumption of maize increased during the colonial period when maizemeal became the staple for the rapidly growing urban populations. Different regions had their own specialties; some groups ate rodents, others fish. The relish might contain more or less meat, chicken, fish (dried or fresh; roasted or fried), and insects. It included many different vegetables (e.g., greens, beans, groundnuts, mushrooms). There are several ways of preparing the relish. The most common procedure makes use of cooking oil, onions, and tomatoes. Another method adds baking soda to okra, at time including onions and tomatoes. And grated groundnuts are sometimes used instead of cooking oil. Salt, if available, adds taste to the Zambian meal, which does not commonly include the red hot pepper that so spices the standard meal in much of West Africa. Oil seeds, onions, and tomatoes are not indigenous crops in Zambia. In so far as Zambians today consider them to be basic ingredients of a proper meal, they represent a recreated tradition that is a product of fairly recent history. But in the final analysis, these practices do not produce differentiation in Goody's sense, but constitute variations of exclusion or inclusion on the shared basics in the starch/relish theme.

From my own study, I know of no one single instance of African men servants exercising their skills in preparing, for example, Irish stews or roasts in their own households. There, cooking was a woman's task, and the work of a servant, a skilled cook, was a "job of work" that ceased on the threshold of his own household. European cuisine would under all circumstances have been too expensive for most servant households. The rapidly growing consumption of tea, refined sugar, white bread, cooking oil, and jams, reported in urban surveys from the late 1930s and on, was incorporated into African diets but did not transform them (Bettison 1959; Thomson 1954; Wilson 1942, 211–231; Woodruff 1955, 70). Even if African men had wanted to apply their acquired skills in cooking with their own kitchens, their wages were so low as not to allow the purchase of the requisite ingredients. This wage differential determined by the color bar was built into the organization of commerce and retail on the assumption that African diets, and consumption patterns in general, were different from those of Europeans. Separate butcheries and special sections for African customers in European shops sold lesser quality meat, known as "boys' meat." Had wages allowed the purchase of choice cuts, the kitchen technology in most urban African households would have complicated their preparation. Even if the employers' house had electricity and piped water, servants' quarters rarely included such amenities. Cooking was done by charcoal fuel, out of doors, and most households possessed but one charcoal brazier. If undertaken inside, cooking produced smoke and grime. This time-consuming process was best suited for the preparation of an inclusive relish, rather than for many individual dishes. Wages, finally, were too low to enable servants to create the kind of home envisioned in the European-derived domesticity ideal, organized around values of order, privacy, and domestic bliss. Servants' quarters were typically one- or two-room affairs, at times shared by several servant households. Such housing (not houses) affronted African notions of propriety between the sexes and the generations, forcing a man to sleep in the same room as his wife and children, and causing embarrassment about where to bathe and dress.

Perhaps it was in the matter of clothing and style that men servants most successfully transferred knowledge they acquired at work in colonial white households to their own and to those of their acquaintances. African workers from other walks of life sought servants' advice on how to dress. In their "Sunday best," servants were indistinguishable from clerks, at least until the post-World War II years, when some occupational specialization and limited advancement were granted to educated Africans whose conditions of life and purchasing power improved somewhat. Although whites during the opening of decades of colonial rule in Northern Rhodesia, as elsewhere, insisted on a clothed native being better than a naked one (Packard 1989), the servants' sporting the finery of their employers only prompted scorn. The well-dressed African's challenge to the boundary-marking functions of European clothing was now ridiculed as clear evidence of the absence of "taste."

If men servants were to set an example of domesticity, they would first have had to reorganize their own homes. But better housing, better wages, and training for African women were slow in coming. If everything was in order and everything had a place in the colonial white household, statutory rules and regulations curtailing African initiatives prevented the transfer of that kind of order to the African household. And had it not been for their need for creature comforts, most white employers cared little about how their household workers lived. This is demonstrated in a discussion during the 1940s about how many servants white employers in civil service were entitled to and how to house them. While everyone agreed that servant housing was deplorable and ought to be improved, the question of standards for servants' quarters proved problematic when compared to those of the emerging African elite, whose housing conditions also left much to be desired. But there was no agreement about whether servants should live in and be allowed to have wives and dependents with them. In the view of most whites, African women meant trouble. Having African wives and children on the premises would cause noise and uncleanliness, yet without some permanent female company, servants would probably solicit women's services when off work, and this would adversely affect their constancy in work (Hansen 1989, 172–173). Prevailing white notions about African maleness thus took for granted that wives or consorts supplied men servants with household work and sex. The fact that African women regularly provided African men with such domestic services did not cancel out the moralistic stance in the white evaluation of African women, whose alleged loose sexual morals were held to make them unsuitable servants in white households (Hansen 1990).

While colonial authorities attributed civilizing functions to domestic service in white households, that is to say, to African men's work, they blamed African women for the slow development of "proper homes." In the colonial white view, urban African women sat around and were lazy; or they solicited men while their partners were at work. They were slow to take to the domestic science and homecraft classes philanthropic groups, mainly churches, began to organize from the mid-1930s (Hope 1944; Powdermaker 1962, 109; Taylor and Lehmann 1961). The debate about recruiting African women into domestic service during the post-World War II years when the mining economy boomed and men's labor was needed elsewhere, attributed women's poor potential as servants to their alleged loose morals. Although overtly concerning skills, the debate conflated gender and sexuality (Hansen 1989, 120–138). Speaking in the language of skills (i.e., cooking), colonial employers agreed with their African men workers that African women could not cook, that is to say that they had not mastered the skills of a differentiated cuisine.

The few African women who did work in colonial households were hired as nannies. They did not relieve white women of the chief tasks of child care, but watched the children, pushed the pram, and washed the nappies—something which "nurse boys" also did, and in larger numbers than women. They may have worked as Betty Kaunda did in the early 1940s, long before she became the president's wife, looking after the district officer's baby for a couple of hours after school. She worked in this capacity in a succession of colonial households until she left home for boarding school (Mpashi 1969, 15–17). Thus, African women who acquired Western-derived domestic skills did not do so in white households. The chief outlet for the ideological aspect of domestic science was the homecraft courses organized by church and mission groups and the newly established (1952) welfare department (Mann 1959; NAZ/NR 2/512 1949–1959). Such courses were not organized for the purpose of enabling African women to replace the skilled male cooks in paid domestic service or to engage in other forms of wage labor. They aimed at instilling notions about proper homes and upgrading the home life of the emerging African elite by making women into suitable wives, skilled in nutrition, baby care, simple cooking, house cleaning, and handicrafts. Some husbands sent their wives to homecraft centers. Before Barnabas Mwamba in the late 1950s moved into a bigger house at his promotion as development councillor, he enrolled his wife at a homecraft center for a three-month course. She had already attended a homecraft course for two years after completing Standard IV (i.e., 6 years of education) before marrying. Yet, Mrs. Mwamba found such training useful, especially to relieve household squabbles "due to carelessness and negligence on the part of the wife to perform her household duties satisfactorily" (*Nshila* 1959, 26). The cultural arrogance, paternalism, and gender assumptions informing such teaching are exemplified in cookbooks for Africans (e.g., Kaye 1939, Cartwright and Robertson 1957), in recipes for European-type dishes like scotch eggs and chocolate cake (*African Listener* 1955, 7), and columns about how to dress well, with matching handbags, shoes, and hat (*African Listener* 1957a, 12; 1957b, 9) featured in magazines for elite Africans published by the colonial information service.

It is difficult to assess the impact of domestic science education on the many African women who were exposed to it, yet it is certain that the results occasionally were at variance with the white teaching staff's intentions.[4] When their husbands had been appointed ministers on the eve of independence, Betty Kaunda and Salmone Kapwepwe moved from tiny houses in the African township Chilenje into larger government houses. They enjoyed having more space, since their households, including extended family members, numbered eleven and eight respectively. To help them run their homes, they employed male domestic servants, Mrs. Kapwepwe three, and Mrs. Kaunda, who was looking for an expert cook, two. Cooking in such elite households was thus not done by women, but by male cooks. These households had not switched entirely to European-style food, for as Mrs. Kapwepwe explained, "[W]e usually receive many visitors from our home district in the Northern Province who are not used to the European-type food" (*Nshila* 1963, 40–41).

In short, those African households that opened up for a partial penetration of European notions of domesticity were mainly those that were better off, where men certainly did not make a living as domestic servants, and wives did not cook on a regular basis. Thus the transformative potential of colonial domestic service was limited. Rather than creating better homes and wives, this work reproduced distinctions between emerging Zambian classes and between women and men. For most of the colonial period in Northern Rhodesia, racial distinctions built into the material organization of daily life prevented African men servants from transferring the skills they acquired from domestic work for whites to their own households. Urban housing arrangements clashed with African notions of gender, age, and space, and normative assumptions about gender made men servants, then and now, resist the transfer of their cooking skills to their own households where food preparation remained African women's work.

Cooking, Gender, and Postcolonial Households

For a man like BaNkuwa, domestic service meant a specialized lifetime occupation during which he, with the help of benevolent employers, accumulated sufficient savings to build a small house—still unfinished during my last visit in 1988—in one of Lusaka's low-income areas, and managed to send his children to school. The children have left home, the wife trades in the market, and there are few external demands on household income. Perhaps for this reason, he was able to be choosy when looking around for a job as a cook. When overall employment shrank in the economic decline that set in during the mid 1970s due to the country's dependence on copper revenues from falling export sales, domestic service kept on growing. Yet, few men today are likely to repeat BaNkuwa's experiences, although they are crowding the domestic service market for want of occupational choice. So do youth and women, who are entering domestic service in larger numbers than ever before. An important attraction for an occupation that no one really wants because of its low wages and stringent labor demands is the house that often still comes with the job. Sizeable infusions of foreign aid and loans, including large amounts from the International Monetary Fund (IMF), have never aimed at relieving pressures on the urban job and housing markets, and they have had little success in making rural producers feed the nation. The rate of urbanization, already high by sub-Saharan African standards at independence, keeps increasing, attracting persons with few saleable skills to the domestic service sector.

The main change in this occupational domain in postcolonial Zambia has been among the employers, who today are predominantly black Zambians.[5] The nature of the work undertaken in private households has changed as well. The colonial staff of specialized men servants has been replaced—except among a tiny segment of the servant employing classes whose workers often are paid by means of company payroll—by one general servant: a man who works inside the house and on the grounds. In return for this work, he receives a wage that makes the viability of his own household precarious, thus threatening his ability to head a household and command the services of a woman, in short, to be a man in control. When asked to cook for his black Zambian employers, he complains of doing "women's work." This does not mean that domestic work has become a woman's job, for men servants outnumber women by far. While men still take servant jobs because they have few other choices, they bitterly resent the subordination they experience in the work relationship to their black Zambian employers, who demand that they do everything within the house and on the grounds, including the cooking of Zambian food, which is women's work. It was BaNkuwa's unwillingness rather than his inability to prepare Zambian food, that is, doing women's work, which made him reluctant to take a job in a Zambian household.

The gradual leveling out of distinct task specializations into the work of the male general servant is a product of an ongoing recomposition among the employing classes: from white colonial employers mainly of British background to black Zambian employers, and within the steadily declining number of whites, a shift from largely British colonists to expatriates from many different parts of the world. Only few of these expatriates have had any experience with live-in servants before coming to Zambia. Except in embassy circles, among high-ranking experts, and in the upper echelons of the Zambian civil service, few households today employ skilled cooks. Men of BaNkuwa's generation will tell you that today even *wazungus* (whites, expatriates in general) eat *nshima* (maize porridge). This does not mean that expatriates regularly eat the urban Zambian food staple of maize porridge, but that women expatriate householders do most of the cooking, which is less elaborate than the cuisine served up by the colonial cook.

The last but certainly not least noticeable change between the colonial period and the present is that larger numbers of women than ever before are employed in private households.[6] As I noted above, it was not the growing entry of women but the gendered meaning of cooking in Zambian households that BaNkuwa had in mind when he spoke of domestic service becoming a "woman's job." For women are not taking over men's jobs, but are hired chiefly as nannies. Because of their substandard wages and poor treatment, Zambian women consider domestic service as a job best to be avoided. When they do take a job as paid help in private households, it is as a last resort and mainly because of lack of household support. Assuming that their female workers have shelter elsewhere, Zambian householders rarely provide housing or the housing allowance to which low-income workers are entitled. Women's wages are lower than men's, since employers assume they are part of households to which male heads contribute. Yet, most women servants are single heads of households with dependents to support.[7] They quit their nanny jobs as soon as they find something better, either a man to take care of them, or some economic means with which to start an informal sector activity. Only because they need child care do Zambian women employers tolerate their nannies, of whom they see several come and go throughout their childbearing years.

When they have had it with their nannies and/or when they can afford it, Zambian women hire men servants whom they in any case consider to be better domestic workers and to be sure, better cooks. Yet cooking is a contested domain because of its implications about status/class and its sexual connotations. In my Lusaka survey, I came across Zambian civil servant households in which the male cook prepared "English" food (e.g., meat and boiled vegetables, served separately) for the household head, and the wife cooked Zambian food (*nshima* and relish) for herself and the children. In not-so-well-off households without cooks, I found the nanny making the children's food, while the wife took special care in the preparation and serving of her husband's Zambian meal. Many such husbands are still served separately and not simultaneously with the rest of the household. In such households, a satisfactory meal does not differ much from that Audrey Richards described for the rural Bemba in the 1930s. Such a meal "must be composed of two constituents: a thick porridge . . . and the relish . . . eaten with it" (1969, 46). Outside of the household, buns (and other bread products, if available), tea, soft drinks, and bottled beer, and a variety of prepared snacks (e.g., sausages, meat pies, samosas as well as *nshima* and relish) are consumed by urban wage workers on their lunch breaks. But neither during the colonial period nor at present has this consumption altered the basic procedures of Zambian cooking nor the composition of the standard Zambian meal: starch and relish.

When Zambian female householders claim that their women servants are poor cooks, they are not speaking of meals per se but of the sexual connotations of meal-related behavior and the possiblities entailed in the woman servant's making and serving of meals to the male household head. As in several other parts of Africa (see, e.g., Clark 1989), the wife's preparation of food for her husband is a central obligation of marriage in Zambia. Receiving cooked food thus becomes symbolic of the legal and economic relationship between husband and wife. "Hence," according to Audrey Richards' observations from the 1930s," it becomes a privilege and a matter of pride" for wives to attend to their husbands' food (1969, 129). The symbolic meanings and sexual connotations about preparing and receiving cooked food have not altogether disappeared from postcolonial urban Zambian households. The tensions they create between female householders and women servants give rise to many fears, among them allegations of women servants adding love potions to the relish.[8] Since the wife wishes to reduce the likelihood of compromising sexual encounters, she insists on being in charge of cooking her husband's meals herself.

While much of what goes on in Zambian kitchens today calls forth a sense of *deja vu*, the possibilities for cooking innovations remain potentially wide open. The food pages of a locally published women's magazine *Woman's Exclusive* do not differ much from those in the West. Its "cookery corner" features neither "traditional" foods, nor the colonial period's English-type cooking, but a blend of "foreign" dishes (1984a; 1984b; 1989). Its readers, who in all likelihood have little practical involvement in the kitchen and employ both cooks and nannies, comprise among others the tiny jet-set who go on shopping trips abroad and run Lusaka's small boutiques. They are among the television-viewing Zambian audience who watched Maggie Kaweche's cooking show "The Solution" in the mid 1980s. Ms. Kaweche, about whose marital status rather than her cooking newspaper readers and television viewers wrote many inquiring letters, never wore an apron, but sported the latest fashions and different hairstyles at each show while demonstrating how to prepare savory soups, pork chops, lemon meringue, and other delicacies on her electric stove, using beater, blender, and the newest in kitchen technology. She did at times, when sponsored, include recipies using Zambian products such as sorghum and groundnuts.

While entertaining, the impact of Maggie Kaweche's cooking lessons was limited.[9] Viewers were watching Maggie, not her cooking, and the greater part of the urban population does not have electricity, nor does the rest of the country. The proportion of households with electricity increased from only 11.9 to 17.9 percent between 1969 and 1980. In the most urbanized areas, that is the Copperbelt and Lusaka Provinces, electricity was available to between 30 and 40 percent of the households in 1980. Nearly eight out of ten households in the urban areas depended on wood fuel and/or charcoal for cooking in 1980. This means that electricity served mostly lighting purposes and that only a small proportion of electrified households used this source of power for cooking (Republic of Zambia 1985, 45). Many households do not possess an electric stove, and if they do they may not use it on a regular basis.

Special occasions include *kitchen parties,* the all-women's celebrations held before marriage when female relatives and friends get together, bringing presents "for the kitchen" and money, and in ribald performance style telling the prospective bride about her duties and responsibilities in marriage. There is much banter, talking, singing, dancing, and drinking of beer. Food is served in an assemblage that throws light on the nature of festive cooking in Zambia and its appropriation of items from elsewhere. Among the foods on the plastic wrapped plate each guest received at a Lusaka kitchen party in a middle-income household in July 1989 were the following: a piece of chicken; a boiled egg; a samosa; a sausage; cabbage, beans, and rice. I do not recall if there was a roll, for flour was a scarce item then, and bread was mainly available on the black market. The individual serving at the kitchen party provides a striking contrast to the usual meal served out of one pot and ritual occasions where food is served jointly. In more lavish, or scaled-down versions, such individually served meals are consumed at kitchen parties held at all class levels except the poorest in Zambia's towns. Such parties provide one of the few outlets for women to speak undisturbed among themselves about men—truly, a woman's exclusive.

Except among households of the class in power, the few really wealthy citizens (who have differential access to consumer goods and perhaps generators), and those in the direst of straits (who are reduced to eating *nshima* only), the cuisines in postcolonial urban Zambia have much in common. They are all affected by cuts in the supply of water and electricity, for example, and those who have cookstoves keep the brazier and a supply of charcoal ready. Thus, the consumption styles of servants and their black Zambian employers hardly differ, except in magnitude and diversity of relish and thus in protein content and source. This is largely due to the strained economy and the many temporary bottlenecks in the distribution system, forcing rich and poor, expatriates and Zambians, to shop in the same places. Recurrent scarcities of basic consumer goods (e.g., maizemeal, charcoal, cooking oil, sugar, salt, flour, rice, soap, and detergent)—spices and condiments notwithstanding—are in part to blame for the shift from a cuisine of luxury to cooking of necessity. In so far as these shortages are a product of the efforts toward economic restructuring imposed on the government by international loan and aid providers, they tell a revealing tale of how IMF priorities are hitting Zambian kitchens (cf. Bolles 1983). A recent Lusaka survey indicates that economic stringencies are forcing poor households to cut down on protein sources, reduce the number of meals per day, or even eat *nshima* without relish, with dire consequences for the nutritional status of those who have always eaten least and last: women and children (Muntemba 1987, 24–26). Finally, food access depends not only on the relationship between local production and imports, externally imposed demands, and gender and age distinctions in consumptions, but also on food aid, especially of maize, rice, and wheat, that give foreign governments and philanthropic groups a new role in shaping Zambian kitchens (cf. Khare 1986; Lindenbaum 1986).

In postcolonial Zambia, cooking clearly has lost much of its significance in setting boundaries between groups. The ability of persons of means to make claims for social recognition by appeals to style and taste carries little leverage in a society where the opportunity gap between rich and poor has widened, and the segment in the middle vastly outnumbers the rest. The great mass of the Zambian urban population is setting food consumption styles and in the process boiling down differences between cuisine and cooking in more ways than one: between classes, broadly speaking, and between local and external influences. But while food no longer serves as a powerful means for the marking of social boundaries, cooking and the question of who cooks, continue to do so. When reduced to their simplest ingredients, the processes that are shaping food behavior in Zambian kitchens reveal themselves: men work as professional cooks; wives prepare meals for husbands; and nannies feed children.

Boiling It Down

The confounding of several referents to cooking (i.e., work, skill, style and manners, and gender) in BaNkuwa's remarks at the outset of this chapter tells in plain style that the effects of the colonial encounter, and of recent changes in the production and marketing of foods on styles of cooking of all classes in Zambia, are more complex than the kind of homogenization process depicted by Goody. Ideas about cooking and domestic work in Zambia are certainly linked to the changing historical relationship between this part of southern Africa and of Africa quite generally to the West, to the process of decolonization, and to the internationalization of formerly distinct consumption styles. These ideas are also becoming affected by IMF priorities and foreign food aid (Friedmann 1990; Raikes 1988). This is not a story of straightforward cultural continuity or of wholesale Westernization, but of the making of an everyday world of cooking whose activities and meanings were intensely debated and contested by servants and employers, women and men, members of their households, persons from different walks of life, the colonial administration, and its postcolonial successor. The qualitative leap in cooking potential, brought about by Zambia's presence in an international world has thus not escaped from the ambivalence between gender and class in the work of the kitchen. The boiling down of which I have spoken is a different outcome from Goody's homogenized meal, which leaves out the spice, the ideological ingredients.

The adoption of styles of cooking and domestic arrangements in postcolonial Zambia has developed a momentum of its own, shaped by the slowdown of the economy and by local cultural practices. Except for variety and quantity of relish, cooking shares the same basic ingredients and is much alike across the urban Zambian class spectrum. Because of problems in the supply of power and commodities, the cookstove and the charcoal brazier coexist, as do their distinct social usages. While Zambian cooking has appropriated elements from other cuisines, it has worked them over on its own terms—those that make for the persistence of the male cook, the wife who prepares meals for her husband, and the nanny who feeds the children. Thus if domesticity in postcolonial Zambia entails a transformative potential, neither it nor its colonial variant had or have the capacity to resolve the struggle on the household front between women, men, and their employers over the different meanings of cooking. As we produce more and richer scholarship on the colonial encounter and its effects on different aspects of life in Africa, including domesticity, the task of exploring the impact that postcolonial encounters with the IMF and foreign food aid are having on the cultural recesses of kitchens and their meanings in the household political economy remains equally challenging.

Acknowledgments

This paper is based on research funded in 1982 by the McMillan Fund and the Office of International Programs at the University of Minnesota, from 1983–1985 by the U.S. National Science Foundation grant no. BNS 8303507, by a grant from the U.S. Social Science Research Council and the Africa Committee of the American Council of Learned Societies in 1988, and by faculty grants from Northwestern University in 1985, 1986, and 1989. A previous version was presented in the February 1, 1991, colloquium in the Department of Anthropology, University of Michigan, and I thank the audience for valuable comments. I am especially indebted to my younger Zambianist colleagues, Mark Auslander, Deborah Spitulnik, and Elizabeth Weinberger for their arguments about variations in Zambian cooking. While they may still not agree with my interpretation of Zambian cooking as undifferentiated, their challenge compelled me to contextualize the starch/ relish theme more emphatically. They offered several other insights for which I also thank them.

Notes

1. *Ba* is a Bantu prefix indicting seniority and respect.

2. My study draws on extensive archival research in Great Britain, Zambia, and Zimbabwe begun in 1982, and field research in Zambia 1983–1984, 1985, 1988, and 1989, including the collection of life history data from retired employers of colonial servants in Great Britain and Zambia, elderly servants, and a sample survey in 187 servant-employing households in middle-to upper-income residential areas in Lusaka, involving separate interviews with the chief domestic servant and the employer.

3. Because of the nature of my sources, most of my discussion of colonial European, or white, attitudes refers to the British. The fact that African, Asian ("Indian"), and Afrikaans-speaking households also employed servants does not mean that the master-servant relationship in British households was atypical or out of the ordinary. On the contrary, since the British were the dominant group in political terms, they set the norms and standards against which social interaction and practices were evaluated.

4. Neither the education nor the welfare departments had much success with their homecraft classes and clubs for women in the African townships. The white staff of the departments realized this, as indicated, for example in NAZ/NR 2/27 African Welfare, General Correspondence, 1944–54, and NAZ/NR 2/512 Native Education, Female, 1949–1959.

5. In my sample survey of 187 servant-employing households in Lusaka, 42 percent of the employers were Zambian, 33 percent whites, and 25 percent Asians.

6. These 187 households employed among them a total of 311 full-time servants, 232 of whom were men and 79 women. Focusing on the chief domestic worker in these households, we interviewed 131 men and 56 women. Most of these women were employed as nannies. I suggest that women comprise between one third and one fourth of this occupational group.

7. Thirty-five percent of the women servants in my sample survey were married and lived with their husbands (compared with 67 percent men), 13 percent had not married (compared with 20 percent men), and 52 percent (compared with 13 percent men) were either divorced, widowed, or living away from their spouses and supporting children without receiving financial assistance from a man on a regular basis.

8. Some Zambian women will go to great expense to buy love medicines to attract a man's love and ensure his financial attention. On this, see Keller (1978) and Jules-Rosette, especially her discussion about urban medicine (1981, 129–168).

9. According to Deborah Spitulnik, Radio 4, a new radio channel in Zambia launched in 1989, aired a call-in cooking program "In the Kitchen" some time during 1989. The listeners who called in comprised three broad categories: (1) male servants providing detailed explanations of recipies they

cooked for expatriate employers; (2) Zambian teenagers from urban elite households who seemed to be reading recipies from European cookbooks (e.g., for chocolate cake with icing, apparently making up a familiarity with fancy cooking they did not have, nor would the ingredients be readily available for purchase); and (3) persons cooking Zambian food like *nshima* and *kapenta* (dried fish) who had a hard time giving "recipies" for procedures of cooking that everyone is supposed to know. Like the television show "The Solution," the potential impact of the radio program was limited, in this case to those literate in English who happened to be "at home" at 10 a.m. in the morning when the program went on the air, and who had access to a telephone (Deborah Spitulnik, personal communication, 17 October 1990).

Bibliography

African Listener. 1955. Recipes. 41: 7.

———— 1957a. The Well-Dressed Woman. Part 1. 63:12.

———— 1957b. The Well-Dressed Woman. Part 2. 64:9.

Bettison, David S. 1959. Numerical Data on African Dwellers in Lusaka, Northern Rhodesia. *Rhodes-Livingstone Communication*, no. 16.

Bolles, A. Lynn. 1983. Kitchens Hit by Priorities: Employed Working-Class Jamaican Women Confront the IMF. In *Women, Men and the International Division of Labor*, ed. J. Nash and M. P. Fernandez Kelly, 138–159. Albany: State University of New York Press.

Bourdieu, Pierre. 1984. *Distinction: A Social Critique of the Judgement of Taste*. Cambridge, Mass.: Harvard University Press.

Bradley, Emily. 1939. *A Household Book for Africa*. London: Oxford University Press.

————. 1948. *A Household Book for Tropical Colonies*. London: Oxford University Press.

————. 1950. *Dearest Priscilla: Letters to the Wife of a Colonial Civil Servant*. London: Max Parrish.

Bradley, Kenneth. 1981. Lusaka: The New Capital of Northern Rhodesia. *In Situ: The Journal of the Zambia Institute of Architects*, October: 3–24. Reprinted from a limited ed., pub. Jonathan Cape, London, 1935.

Cartwright, D., and C. Robertson. 1957. *How to Cook for Your Family*. Published in association with the Northern Rhodesia and Nyasaland Publications Bureau. London: Longmans, Green and Co.

Clark, Garcia. 1989. Money, Sex and Cooking: Manipulation of the Paid/Unpaid Boundary by Asante Market Women. In *The Social Economy of Consumption*, ed. H. Rutz and B. Orlove, 323–348. Society for Economic Anthropology Monographs no. 6. Washington, DC: University Press of America.

Cooper, Frederick. 1983. Urban Space, Industrial Time and Wage Labor in Africa. In *The Struggle for the City: Migrant Labor, Capital, and the State in Urban Africa*, ed. F. Cooper, 7–50. Beverly Hills, Calif.: Sage Publications.

————. 1987. *On the African Waterfront: Urban Disorder and the Transformation of Work in Colonial Mombasa*. New Haven: Yale University Press.

————. 1989. From Free Labor to Family Allowances: Labor and African Society in Colonial Discourse. *American Ethnologist* 16 (4): 745–765.

Davidoff, Lenore. 1976. The Rationalization of Housework. In *Dependence and Exploitation in Work and Marriage*, ed. D. M. Barker and S. Allen, 121–151. London: Longman.

Douglas, Mary. 1971. Deciphering a Meal. In *Myth, Symbol and Culture*, ed. C. Geertz, 61–82. New York: W. W. Norton.

————, ed. 1984. Standard Social Usages of Food. In *Food and the Social Order: Studies of Food and Festivities in Three American Communities*, ed. M. Douglas. New York: Russel Sage Foundation.

Douglas, Mary, and M. Nicod. 1974. Taking the Biscuit: The Structure of British Meals. *New Society* 19 (December): 744–747.

Fraenkel, Peter. 1959. *Wayaleshi*. London: Weidenfeld and Nicolson.

Friedmann, Harriet. 1990. Family Wheat Farms and Third World Diets: A Paradoxical Relationship Between Unwaged and Waged Work. In *Work Without Wages: Domestic Labor and Self-Employment Within Capitalism*, ed. J.M. Collins and M. Gimenez, 193–213. Albany: State University of New York Press.

Goody, Jack. 1982. *Cooking, Cuisine and Class: A Study in Comparative Sociology*. Cambridge: Cambridge University Pres..

Hansen, Karen Tranberg. 1989. *Distant Companions: Servants and Employers in Zambia, 1900–1985*. Ithaca, NY: Cornell University Press.

————. 1990. Body Politics: Sexuality, Gender, and Domestic Service in Zambia. *Journal of Women's History* 2 (1): 745–765.

Hay, Hope. 1944. An African Women's Institute. *Oversea Education* 15(3): 104–107.

Jules-Rosette, Benetta. 1981. *Symbols of Change: Urban Transition in a Zambian Community*. Noorwood, N.J.: Ablex Publishing Corporation.

Kaye, Elsie A. 1939. *A Cookery Book for Use in African Schools*. Approved by the African Literature Committee of Northern Rhodesia, available through the International Committee on Christian Education for Africans. London: the Sheldon Press.

Keller, Bonnie B. 1978. Marriage and Medicine: Women's Search for Love and Luck. *African Social Research* 27:565–585.

Khare, R. S. 1986. Hospitality, Charity and Rationing: Three Channels of Food Distribution in India. In *Food, Society, and Culture: Aspects in South Asian Food Systems*, ed. R. S. Khare and M. S. A. Rao, 277–296. Durham, N.C.: Carolina Academic Press.

Lawrence, Roderick J. 1982. Domestic Space and Society: A Cross Cultural Study. *Comparative Studies in Society and History* 24 (1): 104–130.

Levi-Strauss, Claude. 1970. *The Raw and the Cooked*. London: Cape.

————. 1973. *From Honey to Ashes*. London: Cape.

————. 1978. *The Origin of Table Manners*. New York: Harper & Row.

Lindenbaum, Shirley. 1986. Rice and Wheat: The Meaning of Food in Bangladesh. In *Food, Society, and Culture: Aspects in South Asian Food Sys-

tems, ed. R. S. Khare and M.S.A. Rao, 253–275. Durham, N.C. Carolina Academic Press.

Mann, Mary. 1959. Women's Homecraft Classes in Northern Rhodesia. *Oversea Education* 31 (1): 12–16.

Mintz, Sidney W. 1986. *Sweetness and Power: The Place of Sugar in Modern History.* New York: Penguin Books.

Mpashi, Stephen A. 1969. *Betty Kaunda.* Lusaka: Longmans of Zambia.

Muntemba, Dorothy C. 1987. The Impact of the IMF/World Bank on the People of African with Special Reference to Zambia and Especially Women and Children. Paper presented at conference of the Institute for African Alternatives on the Impact of the IMF and World Bank on the People of Africa, held at City University, London, September 7–10.

NAZ (National Archives of Zambia) /NR 2/27. 1944–1954. African Welfare, General Correspondence.

NAZ (National Archives of Zambia) /NR 2/512. 1949–1959. Native Education, Female.

Nshila. 1959. One Recipe for a Happy Marriage. 48 (November 24): 22–23.

———— 1963. Ministers Wives Find Big Houses Cost Big Money—but Love Them. 132 (February 12): 40–41.

Packard, Randall M. 1989. The "Healthy Reserve" and the "Dressed Native": Discourses on Black Health and the Language of Legitimation in South Africa. *American Ethnologist* 16 (4): 686–703.

Powdermaker, Hortense. 1962. *Cooper Town: Changing Africa.* New York: Harper and Row.

Republic of Zambia. 1985. *1980 Population and Housing Census of Zambia.* Analytical Report Vol. 3. Lusaka: Central Statistical Office.

Raikes, Philip. 1988. *Modernising Hunger: Famine, Food Supplies & Farm Policy in the EEC and Africa.* London: James Currey.

Richards, Audrey I. 1969. *Land, Labour and Diet in Northern Rhodesia: An Economic Study of the Bemba Tribe.* London: Oxford University Press.

Taylor, John V., and Dorothea Lehmann. 1961. *Christians of the Copperbelt: The Growth of the Church in Northern Rhodesia.* London: SMC Press.

Thomson, Betty Preston. 1954. *Two Studies in African Nutrition: An Urban and a Rural Community in Northern Rhodesia.* Rhodes-Livingstone Papers, no. 24.

Wilson, Godfrey. 1942. *An Essay on the Economics of Detribalization in Northern Rhodesia,* pt. 2. Rhodes-Livingstone Papers, no. 6.

Woodruff, H. W. 1955. The African Native Market. In *The Federation of Rhodesia and Nyasaland: Economic and Commercial Conditions in the Federation of Rhodesia and Nyasaland,* 67–73. Overseas Economic Surveys. London: Her Majesty's Stationary Office.

Woman's Exclusive. 1984a. Cookery Corner. 3:22–23.

———— 1984b. Cookery Corner. 4:26–27.

———— 1989. Cookery Corner. 1:31.

11 *Creches, Titias,* and Mothers: Working Women and Child Care in Mozambique

Kathleen Sheldon

Access to reliable child care for working families has been a basic women's demand in all regions of the world. Mozambique, though extremely poor, has been a leader in the expansion of government-supported child-care centers, called *creches* in Portuguese. While many capitalist countries are not willing to take on the costs of motherhood despite defining women primarily as mothers, the social-ist government of Mozambique introduced a series of supports for working women, including child-care centers.

This chapter examines the options women had for child care while they performed agricultural labor or urban work under Portuguese colonialism, the introduction of child care during the armed struggle for liberation, the expansion of such programs following independence, the situation in the central port city of Beira in the 1980s, and current problems under chronic wartime conditions and new economic austerity measures.

One of the most important variables affecting women's ability to work for a wage is their access to child care, whether through relying on family members (especially other women) or through placing their children in a formal or informal day-care center. Brydon and Chant present evidence from a wide variety of industrial and nonindustrial societies indicating that women who have child care for their children are able to take advantage of work opportunities. The apparent increase in urban-based extended family formations in many areas of the world may be related to the increasing numbers of working women with small children. When there is no day-care offered, these women must live with other adults who can care for their children while they are at their jobs (Brydon and Chant 1989, 151–158; also see Joekes 1989).

Mozambique is an agricultural country; while there has been

some development of local industry, exports are dependent on products such as cashews, shrimp, tea, and cotton. The majority of men and women continue to work as farmers, producing food for their own families' consumption.

In Mozambique, women's options for caring for their own children have undergone important changes in this century. Rural women took their babies with them while performing agricultural labor, or were able to rely on relatives to watch over small children in the field or village. During the colonial era it was common for urban working women (who were very few in number) to leave their children with relatives in the rural areas, or to rely on family members to watch children in the cities.

When Mozambique ended Portuguese colonialism in 1975, Frelimo, the liberation front that had fought for independence, became the ruling socialist party. Women's liberation was an important component of the new government's policies. The government based its approach to women on a Marxist position that called for women to join the wage labor force. Policies geared to support the expected influx of women into the work force included legalizing paid maternity leave and allowing on-the-job nursing time for working mothers with new infants.

The development of a national network of creches was part of this program, developed under the auspices of the Social Action Department of the Ministry of Health. As a result of this policy, many urban and rural work places have or plan to have on-site child care for the children of workers. The targeted work places are those with a high percentage of women workers, including cashew processing and garment factories, and agricultural cooperatives.

It is clear that post-Independence child-care choices were expanded. It is also true that women remained the primary caregivers, both as creche workers and as the parents who had daily responsibility for the children. A contradictory situation developed in that women's needs were indeed being met, but gender inequality was not questioned.

Child care as an aspect of female domesticity was altered, as the state intervened to provide public creches. And yet domesticity associated with women was reinforced, as the child-care programs focused primarily on women entering the formal sector of the economy. This suggests a blurring of the old demarcation between domestic/private/female and political/public/male. Caring for children had been private and domestic, based in the family and relying on women's labor. The socialist state offered a public and political alternative, where women's labor remained central. The association of child care with women carried over into the new arena, and women were still defined as mothers or potential mothers while men were not comparably defined as fathers as their primary role. This chapter examines the specific attributes of this process in Mozambique.

Child Care under Colonialism (1920s to 1975)

Under the Portuguese colonial system women were subject to the convergence of two belief systems that agreed on the importance of women's role as mothers. Both Portuguese colonial and African social norms emphasized women's place in the home as care-givers to their children and as performers of other domestic or home-based chores. The overwhelming expectation and reality was that women would marry and have children once they reached puberty.

With respect to African norms, there were two primary systems of descent in Mozambique. In the south societies were generally patrilineal, while in the north matrilineal formations were more common. In addition, there was an Islamic patrilineal society along the northern coast. Two practices that occured with varying frequency in different parts of Mozambique were the payment of bridewealth (*lobolo*) upon marriage and polygamous marriages. Although the literature has emphasized child custody issues rather than daily tasks associated with caring for children, both of these descent systems had an impact on women's child-care responsibilities (Isaacman and Stephen 1980; Medeiros 1985; Urdang 1986; Welch and Sachs 1987).

In all regions, women were responsible for the day to day child care. In case of divorce custody was determined according to the child's lineage. In patrilineal societies the father through his lineage would have custody, while in matrilineal groups the mother's brother or other male kin would become the child's guardian. Women's responsibility for their children and the threat of losing them following the breakup of a relationship was a powerful reason for women to remain in unhappy marriages.

Most Mozambican women worked on the family plot performing subsistence agricultural labor. Commonly women carried their infants to the field with them, facilitating breast-feeding on demand

and thus integrating their productive work and child-care responsibilities (Junod [1926] 1962, 334 on southern Mozambique; Medeiros 1987, 19 on northern Mozambique). Women also often had kin close by who could help with child care, including the infant's older siblings and grandmothers (Earthy [1933] 1968, 22–23, 84–85). A new mother's youngest sister sometimes joined the household to care for the baby, particularly by carrying the infant on her back to stop excessive crying (Loforte and Medeiros 1987, 16).

The Portuguese colonial government was strongly informed by Catholic ideology. Beginning in the 1930s the Catholic church controlled African education and infused the courses with its expectations of proper behavior and occupations for men and women. One teacher training school offered advanced courses for girls in sewing, cooking, nursing, and child care in addition to academic courses in history, Portuguese, and mathematics ("As Alunas da Escola de Habilitação" 1962). Although the existence of academic courses might have offered new opportunities for African girls, very few benefited, as evidenced by a female literacy rate of under 5 percent at independence. The Portuguese/Catholic assignment of women to domestic work including child care did not question the assumptions of local African societies.

The colonial officials preferred that women remain in the rural areas under the guardianship of their husbands. The reality was that in southern Mozambique men were often absent, performing labor in South Africa's mines or engaged in other migrant work. Male out-migration was also common in central and northern Mozambique, as men escaped the brutality of Portuguese colonial labor systems. In addition, the Portuguese implemented forced cultivation schemes in some areas that increased women's agricultural work load. Many women moved to the cities as the quality of rural life deteriorated under the impact of colonial policies (Penvenne 1983, 1986).

The number of women working for a wage under colonialism was quite small and generally concentrated in the capital, Lourenço Marques (now Maputo). Yet the issue of child care was a central one. Women sometimes left children in the rural areas with relatives, but often they brought children with them to the urban areas in search of work. One of the reasons for women to seek waged work was to support themselves and their children following the dissolution of their marriages. A study in a cashew factory in the 1950s found that of

1,308 women working there, only 19 were legally married. The major-ity of the cashew workers (1,127) lived without a man, whether in a legally recognized marriage or a customary relationship. Yet 883 of the cashew workers had children (Silva 1960, 56).

The presence of single mothers in the cities in the mid twentieth century was a source of concern to Portuguese authorities, who called it "a serious, major social and moral problem" (Silva 1960, 56). Yet despite the overwhelming evidence that the majority of working women did not have a man as the primary breadwinner in their home, women's wages were legally set at about half of men's wages. One authority even suggested that the low wages forced women to turn to prostitution in order to earn enough money to survive, yet this insight did not lead to an increase in the minimum wage (Penvenne 1983:151).

In Mozambique the numbers of women working for a wage have always been much lower than those of men. Few industries were open to women, and some job categories associated with women in other world areas were mainly held by men. Even domestic service was predominantly male, though some women did seek such work (Penvenne 1983, 152). In Beira in 1940 only 225 African women were engaged in domestic service, in contrast to 8,572 men (Colónia de Moçambique 1940, 6–7).

Given the Portuguese assumption that women would not be work-ing for a wage and the expectation that they should be caring for their own children, it is not surprising that there were no day-care centers available for women working in the urban factories. While the Swiss Mission ran a boarding school in Lourenço Marques, this did not answer the need for infant and toddler care, nor did it meet the demand from families who lacked the financial resources neces-sary to pay the fees (Penvenne 1986, 13–15).

Women sometimes brought their infants to work on their backs wrapped in a *capulana*, a length of cotton cloth. At times the women were subjected to harsh treatment. As one cashew worker remem-bered, there were certain guards during the colonial era who would push women down to the ground during disputes; "[I]f you had a baby on your back, the child would go from your back and fall." One guard used a wooden paddle to beat the workers, and it didn't matter to him whether "you were pregnant, or had a baby, or were elderly" ("O Partido" 1978, 16). Older children were left alone or in the care of neighbors and relatives who often were young children themselves. Whatever the result, it was a matter of concern to women, who had few options.

Child Care During the Liberation Struggle

The role of women in the liberation struggle during the 1960s and early 1970s was a contested issue. Many women did participate by mobilizing rural women to join the independence efforts and by providing food and other supplies to Frelimo militants (Isaacman and Isaacman 1984), but they gained leadership roles only with difficulty. As Frelimo's first president, Eduardo Mondlane, comments in his history of the struggle for independence, "nobody [that is, no men] had thought of making women officers" until women themselves raised the issue (Mondlane 1969, 186).

Josina Machel, first wife of the late president Samora Machel, was one of the central leaders. She was instrumental in bringing women's contributions to the fore, and in expanding their acceptance as activists and militants. One of her projects was the establishment of an orphanage where children could be cared for if they had been orphaned as a result of their parents' anticolonial activity. The orphanage was under the direction of Frelimo's Section of Social Affairs, which she headed. Militants from the Women's Detachment cared for the children. They were not trained as child-care providers, though some had experience from the mothering of their own children. While the ratio of fifteen women for nearly forty war orphans appears to be more than adequate, these women were also responsible for cultivating all the food required by the institution and as a result described the center as being understaffed ("The Josina Machel Orphanage" 1973).

The expansion of formal public care for children was one of the first and most recognized contributions that Mozambican women made during the armed struggle. The existence of the orphanages and child-care centers increased women's ability to participate in other aspects of the struggle. Combining child-care responsibilities and armed struggle was even romanticized, as is demonstrated by a published photograph of Maria Njanje holding her rifle and her child ("Education in Free Mozambique" 1971, 6). But at the same time, the basic assumption that child care was women's responsibility was not questioned.

Frelimo described the family as the "basic cell of society," a common ideological stand for socialist nations (Urdang 1981; Molyneux 1984). The exaltation of women's mothering role did not end with the defeat of Portuguese colonialism in 1975, but was integrated into Frelimo's socialist policy as well.

Working Women and Child Care after Independence

Women gained important legal rights following independence, including constitutional equality and paid maternity leave of sixty days following the birth of a child (ninety days for twins). Many women combine this with their thirty vacation days in order to stay home with the new infant for three months. Additionally, in cases of illness during pregnancy they are granted medical leave with guaranteed job security. After the birth they are entitled to return to work with no employment problems.

In one case at Beira's Belita garment factory, a worker who had suffered a miscarriage was ordered by her physician to stay home and off her feet beginning in the fourth month of a subsequent pregnancy. Because it was medically required, she did not lose her job. Others continued working until the day of the birth, though they were permitted to shift to less strenuous work as the pregnancy progressed. A garment worker in her seventh month of pregnancy was not working at the sewing machine, but was performing other work such as folding sheets that had been hemmed by machine. One woman commented that she had worked during her pregnancy, but away from the sewing machine; she explained, "with my belly, it was not all right" to be at the machine.

Following delivery women have a legal right to time off to nurse the baby until the child is two years old, half an hour in the morning and half an hour in the afternoon. This can be taken at mid morning and mid afternoon if the baby is at a nearby day-care center. Many women opt to leave half an hour early at lunch time and at the end of the day so as to return home to nurse.

Women often cited these legal rights as evidence of advances for women under Frelimo. While Belita was exemplary, other work places did not always follow the law and it could be a source of struggle within the workplace. Even at Belita the issue of women being absent from the sewing machines for health reasons was a source of controversy that was only resolved with the intervention of the Ministries of Health and Labor as well as the women's organization (see Sheldon 1991). Such legal safeguards were certainly an advantage for women working in the formal sector. Those in the informal and agricultural sectors were not usually able to exercise these rights.

The provision of child care to working women throughout Mozambique has been a priority since independence. The role of the state in providing that care, through the Ministry of Health's Social Action Department, is unusual in Africa, where most child care is provided by private individuals and voluntary agencies (Ohuche and Otaala 1981, 23). A survey taken in Ghana, for example, revealed that only 8 percent of working women sent their child to a day-care center; about half of the women in the study relied on female relatives, and about one fourth hired nannies (Date-Bah 1986, 252). The lack of public day care is also a problem in Nigeria, where working mothers are forced to enter into competition for the services of individual domestic workers who generally are untrained girls or young women. Urban migration and other social changes mean that working women can no longer rely on the extended family to provide that care (Fapohunda 1982). And in South Africa, where some attention has been paid to African women caring for white children while their own children are left with relatives, there also appears to be an increase in the number of African women working independently as child-care providers for other African women (Cock, Emdon, and Klugman 1984; Cock and Emdon 1987).

Mozambique was not only concerned with providing child care to relieve women's burdens. Additional issues that increased the interest of the government in child care and child development were the introduction of proper socialist education for Mozambique's future citizens, and the provision of clothing and a midday meal to help the children in attendance achieve good health (Sitoe 1984a and 1984b).

The continuing problem of orphans and abandoned children, a tragic result of social dislocation and poverty, also brought about an emphasis on centers where such children could be placed. The support of the women's organization Organização da Mulher Moçambicana [OMM]) in developing such centers was outlined in the resolutions passed at OMM's Second Conference in 1976. The child-care centers were to incorporate political programs, cultural and sport activities, production, literacy, and schooling for older children ("II Conferência" 1976, 35). In the early years of independence, people were exhorted to build child-care centers as a contribution to national development and as a component of organizing national consciousness ("Os Infantários" 1976).

Samora Machel commented in a 1976 speech that OMM was formed partly in recognition of women's central role in educating future generations:

> We were conscious that woman is responsible for all generations. It is the woman who is in constant contact with children. It is the woman who imparts revolutionary concepts to children through her contact and particular responsibility. (Machel 1985, 170)

Such statements coupled with the role of OMM in organizing child-care centers indicate the central role of women rather than working parents in determining which segment of the population was being served by such centers.

Originally it was planned to introduce neighborhood-based creches, but the local political structures often did not have the resources to support the centers. While the Social Action department coordinated and encouraged child-care programs, they did not have the budget to fund them. Thus local businesses and work places have played a prominent role in developing child-care centers. Typically the company provided the space and material such as beds, bedding, and utensils, while a small sum was deducted from the wages of workers whose children attended the creche. Those companies with many female employees were most likely to provide day care. Of fifteen companies surveyed in 1979, the six with creches included three cashew factories and two garment factories, all with a majority of women in their work forces (Isaacman and Stephen 1980, 124).

Not only have women rather than men been seen as the main beneficiaries, but working-class and professional women rather than farming women have had an advantage in gaining access to child-care centers. Agricultural policies in the 1970s that emphasized state farms (where few women found year-round employment) rather than family subsistence farming also contributed to inadequate child care for rural women.

Despite a lack of statistics, it appeared that the provision of day-care centers was increasing in the organized centers of agricultural work during the late 1970s and early 1980s, especially in cooperatives and communal villages. Information on the success of this initiative is scarce; Urdang mentions a short-lived creche in one communal village, but does not explain what problems led to its demise (1986, 47). Creches in communal villages as well as cooperatives suffered from serious shortages of necessary supplies (Direcção Nacional de Acção Social 1987, 17–19; Urdang 1989, 146–149). More often women continued to work in the fields with their infants tied on their backs or relied on kin and neighbors to watch young children.

More recently in the Green Zones (agricultural belts around major cities), women in cooperatives have had access to formal day-care centers. In 1989 I visited the OMM cooperative "A Luta Continua" in suburban Maputo and observed their creche, newly rebuilt and supplied with toys and equipment through Swedish development aid. It will serve sixty children from the families of cooperative members and from those living in the neighborhood.

Other urban working women are less fortunate. Market vendors, for example, have little or no access to formal care. Infants and small children are frequently seen with their mothers in both the official permanent markets and in the informal sidewalk and roadside areas. In 1989 at the official Mercado Mazambane in Maputo's Aeroporto neighborhood, I spoke with one woman selling vegetables who had her seven-year-old son with her. Her other five children were at home with her mother-in-law.

Another limitation is the shortage of creches in smaller cities. They have not developed as extensive a program of creches as have the larger urban areas; for example, work places with female employees in the northern province of Cabo Delgado did not have a single creche in 1987 (Medeiros 1987, 35).

It is still assumed that women are the ones who have the responsibility for child care and who will thus benefit from the establishment of such centers. The convergence of "women" and "mothers" into a single concept was clearly indicated in a speech made by OMM's president Salomé Moiane to the Fifth Frelimo Party Congress in 1989. She used the term "The Mozambican Mother" interchangeably with "The Mozambican Woman" when conveying official greetings from the women's organization (Organização da Mulher Moçambicana, Secretariado Nacional da OMM [1989]; see also a cover of OMM's magazine, emblazoned "Children are our reason for being" [As crianças são a nossa razão de ser," *Mulher Moçambicana* 1987]).

What is the explanation for this seeming contradiction, where the state is providing important social supports for women yet continuing to maintain a gender-based division of labor? Maxine Molyneux's analysis of women's interests and the state in Nicaragua suggests a useful comparative framework for understanding this situation (1985; see also Moser 1989). Molyneux differentiates between specific government programs that support women and the larger assessment that incorporates gender analysis. A state will not generally be willing to introduce a gender-based analysis that will entail major structural transformations to bring women into an equal status with men. But some states, especially socialist governments working to develop nonhierarchical structures, may be answering specific gender demands, while avoiding or delaying action on broader gender issues. Programs such as the expansion of health services and education will benefit women indirectly, while other projects will target women in order to increase female participation in the larger goal of national development.

The introduction of child-care programs in Mozambique is directed at working mothers rather than at all parents needing such help. Thus, expectations about mothers being primary caretakers for children underlie the effort, and the broader strategic gender interests are not addressed at all within the child-care program. For instance, an article in the newspaper described the centers as educating the children of "working mothers." The opening paragraph said that this was a matter of particular concern to "young mothers actively participating in the construction of the country" (Lopes 1983).

It is useful to assess such programs by analyzing the extent to which they contribute to the empowerment of women. Child-care programs, by alleviating some of the daily tasks of women, allow them to contribute in other ways to their own economic and social betterment, as well as to national development (see Sheldon 1990).

Child-Care Centers in Beira

My research in Beira in the early 1980s illustrated the continuing role of women as mothers, and the growth of local creches. Of six creches studied or visited, the 1º de Junho center (for June 1st, International Children's Day) and 1º de Maio center (for May 1st, International Worker's Day) were neighborhood-based rather than workplace-based. Other creches I visited were directly tied to workplaces, especially those with many women workers such as Caju, the cashew factory; Belita garment factory; Mobeira, a factory that produced biscuits and other flour-based food; and the Central Hospital of Beira.

In all cases the creches were administered and partially funded by the Social Action department of the Ministry of Health. Financial support for child care also depended on creative arrangements with local businesses. For instance, Creche 1º de Junho benefited from the direct support of RENAB, Beira's ship repair yard, and children of RENAB workers had priority in enrolling ("Acordo de Cooperação na Area Social" [1983]). In contrast to most workplaces involved in providing child care, this was primarily a male workplace; its fiscal solvency was an important factor in its recruitment to work with the creche. Parental involvement was also encouraged (Direcção Provincial de Acção Social, n.d.).

It is significant that all three sectors of women workers in my study in the early 1980s had access to day-care centers affiliated with their workplaces. The state policy of developing child-care centers in various workplaces was proceeding despite a lack of trained personnel and supplies (Lopes 1983; Manuel 1984; "Creche e Parque Infantil" 1983). The cashew factory had a small center on the factory grounds to serve the two hundred and fifty female workers (about half of the total work force). Belita, the garment factory, served just over one hundred women workers, about one third of their total work force; they had organized a center in their neighborhood in the early 1980s, originally in conjunction with other nearby factories. And the day-care center on the hospital grounds opened with a great deal of fanfare in 1983 during my residence in the city.

On a tour of Belita's facility in late November 1983 it appeared bright and clean with twenty-four teachers to care for ninety-six children aged a few months to five years. Water had to be carried up to the creche on the second floor and food was sometimes in short supply, but it was well organized and full of lively, energetic children.

Four of the seven working mothers I interviewed at the garment factory used the creche. They had previously relied on paying a person for child care based in their homes or had found a family member willing to help. One worker's mother watched the children (her grandchildren) from time to time, particularly when they were ill. Another worker's sister cared for her children, though the Belita worker was unhappy with that situation because she believed her sister sometimes beat the children. One woman began work when her oldest child was eighteen, and so could count on her older children to watch the younger ones. While all of the women who had switched to the creche were content with their experience there, one new mother preferred to keep her first baby at home and had hired a young girl to care for the infant. With a creche available, however, this was her choice rather than a necessity.

The creche at the cashew factory provided a partial solution or the cashew workers with small children. It catered to preschool-aged children, leaving children in primary grades with no care when school was not in session. All elementary schools sponsored two or three sessions each day in order to accommodate the demand, so school-aged children were in school for only a fraction of the day.

The cashew factory creche itself was small, dark, and poorly supplied, making it a problematic remedy to the need for child care. I was told they were prepared to care for seventy-two children, though there were less than half that many there when I visited in July 1983. They had cribs for naps, and the factory paid for the children's food, which was cooked over a charcoal fire. The caretakers were older women who had worked in the factory and were thus known to the mothers, though their training was limited. Three of the twenty-seven cashew workers I interviewed said that they did bring their babies to the creche, and it was a relief to them to have it on the grounds. In all three cases, older children were cared for at home or were living with grandparents outside of Beira.

Despite the problems of supplies and funding, the Provincial Ministry of Health continued to develop child-care centers in response to the great need they saw. In 1983 there were eight day-care centers in Beira, and seven of them took children as young as two months of age. It was clear from my observations at several of these centers that there was more infant care available in Beira in the early 1980s than in, for example, Hartford, Connecticut (where there were only seventy-one spaces citywide for infants under three years of age) (Rodríguez 1983). The issue was obviously one of political will rather than finances and funding.

Child Care in a Time of Conflict

The situation in Mozambique in the late 1980s was very difficult. The country's economy had essentially collapsed as a result of the combined impact of colonialism, policy errors, and most importantly, the continuing war of destabilization waged by South Africa through its proxy, Renamo (the Portuguese acronym for Mozambique National Resistance). Just when the economy could least support the expansion of Mozambique's child-care system, the need increased dramatically.

In 1987 Mozambique adopted the economic restructuring program (PRE) proposed by the World Bank and the International Monetary Fund. The results after two years showed that although the economy appeared to be making the first slow steps to recovery, ordinary working people were living in even greater poverty. The World Bank/IMF programs commonly stress privatization, and some of the best social programs put forth by the Frelimo government, including child care, were under fiscal pressure primarily as a result of a lack of funds in a wartime austerity economy. This was recognized by the government, and the restructuring program was altered in 1989 to include analysis if not alleviation of the social impact of the new policies.

The numbers of Mozambicans fleeing to the cities to escape rural violence increased, and the presence of hundreds of abandoned children living on the city streets was regularly reported and readily observable (National Directorate of Social Action 1989; Tembe 1989b; Simbine 1990). One approach the government took through the Ministry of Health was to place children with kin or others willing to care for orphaned and abandoned children, and to avoid establishing an extensive population settled in orphanages.

As the economy fell into disarray, women had a greater need to earn a wage and support their families. Maputo and Beira counted thousands of women hoping to survive by selling meager quantities of goods on the street corners in the absence of steadier employment; women in such situations had little recourse for child care but to have their children accompany them if relatives and neighbors were unable to help.

I saw first hand the impact on child care in August 1989 when I visited Beira's peri-urban agricultural areas, the Green Zones. I was accompanied by a representative from OMM's Beira office and two staff members from the Green Zones Office Women's Program. The women's project within the municipal Green Zones office was funded by UNICEF. Mathematics, literacy classes, and agricultural improvement courses were offered to urban women farmers. In the neighborhood of Chota the women taking classes were supported by the presence of a creche called the Centro Infantil Josina Machel, which was administered by the Social Action Department of the Ministry of Health.

The creche consisted of two five-hundred-square-foot cement buildings with tin roofs and screen windows around the top of the wall. There were about twenty-five children in each age group, one of two- and three-year-olds and one of four- to six-year-olds. Each group had two teachers. The creche had a capacity for more children, but many families had dropped out due to food shortages and other difficulties of the creche. Dadolota Mondlane, the director of the creche, had training in child care as had the teachers (see also Direcção Nacional de Acção Social 1987:21–23). The teachers had received no salary for two months, and even when it was paid it was very small, 20,000 meticais a month (approximately U.S. $25.00 in 1989). When the teachers wanted tea for their break, they had to pay for it. Parents were supposed to pay 2000 meticais ($2.50) each month to the creche, but many could not afford it. The creche had only had maize porridge, called *massa,* and plain soup for the children to eat. The children sang a song, "Toda a dia, massa só, massa só" ("Every day, only porridge").

The situation in Maputo was also dramatic. The need was far larger than could be met. Out of an estimated 200,000 children under five in the capital, only about 2000 were enrolled in regular day-care centers (Tembe 1989a). Statistics from the Ministry of Health's Department of Social Action underlined the need. Of 300 centers listed, 245 were what were called *"escolinhas"* (little schools) or alternative creches. These were essentially neighborhood-based centers where some adult women watched over children in a yard or under a cashew tree with no supplies or even a permanent building. The women were paid, but at the minimum wage (3500 meticais in 1987); their salaries came in part from a fee of 150 meticais paid by participating parents. (The discrepancies between wages and fees in this center in 1987 and the Beira center in 1989 reflect the continual drastic revaluation of the local currency as part of the economic restructuring program.) In some neighborhoods the women's organization played an important role in the continuation of the escolinhas (Direcção Nacional de Acção Social 1987, 13–15).

One report mentioned that each teacher had responsibility for 70 children, making teaching, or any efforts beyond the most elementary watching, an impossibility (Direcção Nacional de Acção Social 1987, 13). Some escolinhas did not operate all day, but in two sections or rotations; thus they did not help women who required eight hours of care for their children. The alternative centers had 20,872 children registered as being in their care, out of a total of 27,114 children in centers. These escolinhas were one way that the government was trying to keep up with the need, though they were unable to fill the gap with better-established child-care centers (Direcção de Saúde de Cidade do Maputo 1989).

An article in the national news magazine stated that some creches have had to close temporarily as the Social Action Department is forced to make budgetary cutbacks. Centers affiliated with businesses and cooperatives were continuing to operate, but the economic constraints were affecting the program's outreach overall (Laissone 1990).

While the situation of rural creches was not discussed in that article, it was clear from earlier reports that they suffered greater shortages of educational supplies than urban centers. One creche at a communal village in Magude district operated for only half a day because they could not serve a lunch at midday (Direcção Nacional de Acção Social 1987, 17). Given the economic and security difficulties, it was unlikely that many rural centers functioned in the late 1980s and early 1990s.

Although the provision of child care was a central requirement for women's integration into the national economy, the austerity measures made expansion of that program impossible, and even continuation at existing levels was difficult. This again hurt those outside the formal economy more than those in factories or offices. Women working at regular waged jobs were more likely either to have access to on-site child care, or to have the family wage necessary to hire someone to watch the children in the home.

The provision of child care in organized centers to support working mothers has been a cornerstone of Mozambique's social programs. State support for women as mothers has been significant, particularly given Mozambique's extreme level of poverty. While day care has continued to receive recognition as an important social need, it has been impossible to meet the immense demand.

The efforts of the staff and workers in Mozambique's child-care programs have been heroic, though consistently undercut by poverty and war. The uncritical assumption that women should have exclusive care of children has influenced the decisions made about locating child-care centers and targeting certain population groups. Working mothers have been recognized and supported by the Mozambican government, yet the primary assumption of women as mothers has been reinforced by that same recognition and support. Despite the intervention of the state into a previously private and domestic sector of women's labor, the work of caring for children has not become work for both men and women. Women remain the primary caretakers, and continue to identify themselves and to be socially identified as mothers, reinforcing the connection between women's responsibilities and domesticity.

Acknowledgments

This paper is dedicated to the *titias* (literally "aunties," an affectionate term for preschool teachers) in the 1º de Junho and 1º de Maio child-care centers in Beira, Mozambique, who cared for my daughter Mercie; and to the wonderful infant care providers and preschool teachers who have made my own work possible by caring for Mercie and my son Ben.

My research on this topic included informal observation and participation as a parent at two centers, visits to several child-care centers on a more formal basis, and interviews with nearly sixty working women in Beira. The interviews questioned women about their work histories and family responsibilities, the intersection of these two areas of women's lives, and changes in women's situation from the period of Portuguese colonialism to the current government. Children and child-care issues made up a significant part of the interviews (Sheldon 1988).

I have benefited from comments on various drafts from Karen Tranberg Hansen, Jeanne Penvenne, and Steve Trazynski, and from my colleagues in the Affiliated Scholars Program at UCLA's Center for the Study of Women, especially Jaclyn Greenberg, Margaret Rose, and Kiren Ghei. An earlier version was presented at the Eighth Berkshire Conference on the History of Women, June 1990, Rutgers University, New Jersey.

Bibliography

Acordo de Cooperação na Area Social, RENAB, E.E. "Creche" 1 de Junho. 1983. Typescript, Beira.

As Alunas da Escola de Habilitação de Professoras. 1962. *Voz Africana* 29 (June 2): 8–9.

Brydon, Lynne, and Sylvia Chant, 1989. *Women in the Third World: Gender Issues in Rural and Urban Areas.* New Brunswick, N.J.: Rutgers University Press.

Cock, Jacklyn, and Erica Emdon. 1987. "Let Me Make History Please":

The Story of Johanna Masilela, Childminder. In *Class, Community and Conflict: South African Perspectives*, ed. Belinda Bozzoli, 457–477, Johannesburg: Ravan Press.

Cock, Jacklyn, Erica Emdon, and Barbara Klugman. 1984. Research Report: Child Care and the Working Mother. *South African Labour Bulletin* 9, 7:58–59.

Colónia de Moçambique. 1940. População Indígena por Concelhos e Circumscrições, Segundo o Sexo e a Ocupação." In *Censo da População em 1940, Vol. 4, Populaça Indígena*, 6–7. Lourenço Marques.

Creche e Parque Infantil Serão Abertos na Beira. 1983. *Diário de Moçambique* (8 April).

Date-Bah, Eugenia. 1986. Sex Segregation and Discrimination in Accra-Tema: Causes and Consequences. In *Sex Inequalities in Urban Employment in the Third World*, ed. Richard Anker and Catherine Hein, 235–276. New York: St. Martin's Press.

Direcção de Saúde da Cidade do Maputo, Ministério da Saúde. 1989. "Informação Estatística sobre Dados das Instituições de Infância e Número de Crianças na Cidade do Maputo—1989. Typescript, Maputo.

Direcção Nacional de Acção Social. 1987. *Boletim Informativo: Alternativas de Atendimento à Criança—1987*. Maputo: Ministry of Health.

Direcção Provincial de Acção Social. n.d. Indice do Regulamento da Comissão de Pais dos Centros Infantis. Typescript, Beira.

Earthy, E. Dora. [1933] 1968. *Valenge Women: The Social and Economic Life of the Valenge Women of Portuguese East Africa*. London: Frank Cass.

Education in Free Mozambique. 1971. *Mozambique Revolution* 46:4–7.

Fapohunda, Eleanor R. 1982. The Child-Care Dilemma of Working Mothers in African Cities: The Case of Lagos, Nigeria. In *Women and Work in Africa*, ed. Edna G. Bay, 277–288. Boulder, Colo.: Westview Press.

Os Infantários que o Povo Construiu. 1976. *Tempo* 289 (18 April): 22–28.

Isaacman, Allen, and Barbara Isaacman. 1984. The Role of Women in the Liberation of Mozambique. *Ufahamu* 13, 2–3: 128–185.

Isaacman, Barbara, and June Stephen. 1980. *Mozambique: Women, the Law and Agrarian Reform*. Addis Ababa: United Nations Economic Commission for Africa.

Joekes, Susan. 1989. Women's Work and Social Support for Child Care in the Third World. In *Women, Work, and Child Welfare in the Third World*, ed. Joanne Leslie and Michael Paolisso, 59–84. Boulder, Colo.: Westview Press.

The Josina Machel Orphanage. 1973. *Mozambique Revolution* 55:20–21.

Junod, Henri. [1926] 1962. *The Life of a South African Tribe*. Vol. 1, *Social Life*. New Hyde Park, N.Y.: University Books.

Laissone, Inácio. 1990. Que Futuro para Centenas de Crianças? *Tempo* 1013 (11 March): 16–18.

Loforte, Ana Maria, and Eduardo C. Medeiros. 1987. A Situação da Mulher: Normas, Práticas Respeitantes a Fecundidade, Gravidez, Parto e Primeira Infância (Cidade de Maputo). Typescript, Maputo: Universidade Eduardo Mondlane.

Lopes, Arlindo. 1983. A Batalha pelo Futuro. *Domingo* (23 January): 22–23.

Machel, Samora. 1985. Defining Woman's Enemy. In *Samora Machel: An African Revolutionary*, ed. Barry Munslow, trans. Michael Wolfers, 169–178. London: Zed Books.

Manuel, José. 1984. Criado Subsector de Defesa dos Direitos de Criança. *Diário de Moçambique* (11 April): 8–9.

Medeiros, Eduardo. 1985. *Moçambique: Evolução de Algumas Instituições Socio-Familiares.* Col. "Documentos de Trabalho" No. 4, Centro de Estudos sobre Africa, Instituto Superior de Economia. Lisbon: Universidade Técnica de Lisboa.

——. 1987. A Situação da Mulher: Normas, Práticas e Tabus Respeitante a Fecundidade, Gravidez, Parto e Primeira Infância: Cabo Delgado. Typescript, Maputo: Universidade Eduardo Mondlane.

Molyneux, Maxine. 1984. Women in Socialist Societies: Problems of Theory and Practice. In *Of Marriage and the Market*, ed. Kate Young, Carol Walkowitz, and Roslyn McCullagh, 2nd ed., 55–90. London: Routledge and Kegan Paul.

——. 1985. Mobilization without Emancipation? Women's Interests, the State, and Revolution in Nicaragua. *Feminist Studies* 11:227–254.

Mondlane, Eduardo. 1969. *The Struggle for Mozambique.* London: Penguin.

Moser, Carolyn O. N. 1989. Gender Planning in the Third World: Meeting Practical and Strategic Gender Needs. *World Development* 17:1799–1825.

National Directorate of Social Action. 1989. *Programme in Support of Children in Difficult Circumstances 1988/89.* Maputo: Ministry of Health.

Ohuche, R. Ogbonna, and Barnabas Otaala. 1981. *The African Child and His Environment.* New York: Pergamon Press for the United Nations Environment Programme.

Organização da Mulher Mozambicana, Secretariado Nacional da O.M.M. [1989]. Mensagem da Mulher Moçambicana em Saudação ao V Congresso do Partido Frelimo. Typescript.

O Partido e a Luta dos Trabalhadores na "Caju Industrial." 1978. *Tempo* 405:15–20.

Penvenne, Jeanne. 1983. Here Everyone Walked with Fear: The Mozambican Labor System and the Workers of Lourenço Marques. In *Struggle for the City: Migrant Labor, Capital, and the State in Urban Africa*, ed. Frederick Cooper: 131–166. Beverly Hills: Sage.

——. 1986. *Making Our Own Way: Women Working in Lourenço Marques, 1900–1933.* African Studies Center Working Papers No. 114. Boston: Boston University.

Rodríguez, Joseph. 1983. Day-Care Demand Outstrips Capacity. *Hartford Courant* (21 December).

II Conferência da O.M.M.: Engajar a Mulher na Tarefa Principal. 1976. *Tempo* 323 (12 December): 26–35.

Sheldon, Kathleen. 1988. Working Women in Beira, Mozambique. Ph.D. diss., University of California, Los Angeles.

——. 1990. *"To Guarantee the Implementation of Women's Emancipation as Defined by the Frelimo Party": The Mozambican Women's Organization.*

Office on Women in International Development, Working Paper No. 206. East Lansing: Michigan State University.

———. 1991. A Report on a "Delicate Problem" Concerning Female Garment Workers in Beira, Mozambique. *Signs: Journal of Women in Culture and Society* 16 (3): 575–586.

Silva, Maria da Conceição Tavares Lourenço da. 1960. *As Missões Católicas Femininas.* Estudos de Ciências Políticas e Sociais No. 37. Lisbon: Centro de Estudos Políticos e Sociais, Junta de Investigações do Ultramar.

Simbine, Gabriel. 1990. Crianças da Rua: Quantas São? *Tempo* 1004 (January 7): 22–27.

Sitoe, António. 1984a. Contribuição para uma Infância Saudável. *Domingo* (April 8): 9.

———. 1984b. Doze Horas por Dia Formando Homens de Amanha. *Notícias* (April 9): 2.

Tembe, Alfredo. 1989a. Creches: Ter Sorte ou Dinheiro. *Tempo* 967 (April 23): 14–17.

———. 1989b. Crianças de Rua: Algumas Mãos Remam Contra a Maré. *Tempo* 995 (November 5): 12–15.

Urdang, Stephanie. 1981. The First Cell of the Party: The Family in Mozambique. *Southern Africa* 14, 2:14–16.

———. 1986. *Rural Transformation and Peasant Women in Mozambique.* Rural Employment Policy Research Programme, World Employment Programme Research Working Paper. Geneva: International Labour Office.

———. 1989. *And Still They Dance: Women, War, and the Struggle for Change in Mozambique.* New York: Monthly Review.

Welch, Gita [H]onwana, and Albie Sachs. 1987. The Bride Price, Revolution, and the Liberation of Women. *International Journal of the Sociology of Law* 15:369–392.

Index

accumulation. *See* consumption; property

African elite, 51, 121, 128, 131, 134, 173, 176, 182, 186, 196, 223, 277, 278

African women: agricultural cooperatives, 291; and child care, 298–299, 305. *See also* gender division of labor; Green Zones; work

Allen, Miss A. L., 174, 175, 176, 177, 181, 182

American Colonization Society, 100, 114n1

architecture: domestic, 2, 26; European views, 43, 57; missionary views, 52–55, 151, 152, 159–160; Tswana, 52–55, 57, 58. *See also* home; space

Asma'u, Nana, 77, 78, 93n4

ballroom dancing, 272–273

Baptist Missionary Society (Belgian Congo), 143–171

beer brewing, 209, 223, 226. *See also* work

Beira, 290, 296, 300–302, 303, 304

Belgian royalty, 144–145, 147

bridewealth, 4, 43, 199, 228, 229, 292. *See* also marriage

cannibalism: European views, 144, 150, 153

child care, 24; in Beira, 300–302; under colonialism, 292–295; day care centers, 291–292, 297–306; help from kin, 291, 292, 294, 301; in Mozambique, 290–309; and women's work, 290–292, 303

child labor, 6, 7, 104, 105, 106, 107

Christianity, in Liberia, 100, 102, 108. *See also* missions and missionaries

Church Missionary Society (CMS): in Nigeria, 118, 120–122, 125, 129, 133; in Uganda, 175, 177, 178, 179, 181, 182

"civilization": European notions, 46, 51, 54, 56–57, 146–153, 172, 233, 267; Liberian notions, 99–101, 102, 103, 104, 105, 106, 108, 112; training for, 44–51, 98–115, 143–171, 269–270

class, 7, 8, 11, 12, 24, 26, 27, 242, 245, 255, 258, 259, 260, 262, 278, 283, 284, 285; bourgeois British, 4, 44, 60, 64, 161, 201; embodied, 112, 113; habitus, 99, 113; working-class British, 59–64, 65, 146, 161. *See also* African elite

cleanliness. *See* hygiene

clothing, 1, 2, 11–12, 21, 175–177; care of, 106, 247, 249, 255, 256, 272; "European" style, 49, 50, 54, 55, 56, 57, 58, 98, 102, 134, 227; Hausa, 84; "native," in Liberia, 108, 109, 111, 114n3; Tswana, 54, 60; Yoruba, 134. *See also* fashion

colonial civil service, 9; women, 123, 131. *See also* European women

colonial culture, studies of, 11–12

colonial nostalgia, 12

commodity production. *See* wage labor

community development, 197, 204–206, 211

consciousness: gender, 197–198, 211; political, 198, 214

consumption, 1, 10; change of patterns, 49, 51, 56, 269, 274, 282, 283, 284; effects of scarcities, 7, 80, 283, 285, 304

cookbooks, 125, 132, 201, 277

cooking, 1, 2, 7, 9, 24, 27; and class, 270, 283, 284; "English," 144, 153, 177, 181, 230–231, 268, 271–273, 274, 277, 281, 282; in expatriate households, 280; gendered meaning of, 266–289; Indian, 255, 256, 257; innovations in, 269, 281, 282, 284, 285; styles of, 266–289; Zambian, 266, 268–269, 272–273, 279, 281. *See also* meal etiquette

cooks: skilled male, 262, 266, 267, 271–272, 278, 280; training of, 254–257, 271–272; women, 248, 256, 257, 276, 281

cookstoves: charcoal burner, 248, 275, 282, 283, 285; electric stove, 248, 282, 285

curriculum: academic, 174, 176, 181, 182, 183, 184; domestic science, 156, 173, 174, 175, 179, 276, 277–278; in girls' schools, 118, 119, 120, 121, 124, 125, 126, 127, 129, 133, 134; industrial, 151, 153; parents' attitudes, 122,